D1074894

TURNING POINTS
IN MODERN TIMES

TURNING POINTS IN MODERN TIMES

Essays on German and European History

KARL DIETRICH BRACHER

Translated by Thomas Dunlap

With a Foreword by Abbott Gleason

HARVARD UNIVERSITY PRESS

Cambridge, Massachusetts, and London, England 1995

Copyright © 1995 by the President and Fellows of Harvard College
All rights reserved
Printed in the United States of America

Originally published as *Wendezeiten der Geschichte: Historisch-politische Essays 1987–1992,* © 1992 Deutsche Verlags-Anstalt GmbH, Stuttgart.

Publication of this work has been subsidized by Inter Nationes, Bonn.

Library of Congress Cataloging-in-Publication Data

Bracher, Karl Dietrich, 1922–
[Wendezeiten der Geschichte. English]
Turning points in modern times : essays on German and European history /
Karl Dietrich Bracher ; translated by Thomas Dunlap ;
with a foreword by Abbott Gleason.
    p. cm.
Includes bibliographical references and index.
ISBN 0-674-91353-1 (alk. paper). — ISBN 0-674-91354-X (pbk. : alk. paper)
1. Germany—History—20th century. 2. History, Modern—20th century.
I. Dunlap, Thomas. II. Title.
DD237.B6713 1995
943.08—dc20   94-34988
CIP

DD
237
.B6713
1995

051795-3045H6

Contents

Foreword

Abbott Gleason

Karl Dietrich Bracher is one of the most eminent living historians of Nazi Germany. His introduction of structural and functional analysis to the study of the Weimar Republic and the Third Reich was central to the profound reorientation of modern German historiography in the late 1950s and 1960s. For many years a professor of history at Bonn, he has been since 1978 editor (along with Hans-Peter Schwarz) of the influential *Vierteljahrshefte für Zeitgeschichte*. He is and has long been a well-respected speaker on contemporary political subjects in both Bonn and this country.

At the very center of Bracher's scholarly preoccupations since early in his career has been the belief that one cannot understand Germany's experience in the twentieth century without grasping the enormity of the challenge to European and American democracy posed by Nazi and Soviet totalitarianism. The concept of totalitarianism was *the* defining and mobilizing concept of the cold war.[1] It was used to describe the unparalleled threat facing European and American democracy from a new kind of insatiably aggressive and invasive state; it provided a typology of that state, based centrally on Nazi Germany and the Soviet Union, and it channelled the anti-Nazi energy generated by the Second World War into the postwar struggle with the Soviet Union. Above all, it provided a terrifying and plausible vision of a Manichaean, polarized world, in which the leaders of the Western side (the "free world") would have to struggle until victory was won, or perish.

Among Americans and Germans, the term "totalitarianism" was best known and most passionately fought over by political scientists and historians, who debated its merits and demerits for many years, beginning around 1960. In the United States the scholarly disputants argued mostly about Soviet Communism; in Germany they used the paradigm to focus debate about the nature of both the German and the Soviet dictatorships. In Italy the term was less central and the debate less strident, but the Italians also looked back on their Fascist past and tried to decide whether they had been long in the grip of a totalitarian state, or briefly, or not at all.

In both Germany and the United States, the apparently academic and scholarly debates were deeply entwined with the political issues of the cold war. How bad *was* Soviet Communism? As bad as Nazism in Germany? To many in the West it seemed so. But comparing Communism to German National Socialism had political consequences. If the successful statist extreme Left were admitted to be comparable to Nazism, what would be the fate of more moderate Socialist and Social Democratic regimes? Shouldn't *any* serious socialist oppose this term, therefore, as detrimental to the whole left side of the political spectrum? And again, ought not the blame for the cold war be much more evenly distributed than it had been by political elites in the West? Had not the "Soviet threat" been greatly exaggerated in the late 1940s—perhaps with an eye to reviving predatory capitalism, rather than to turning back predatory Communism?[2]

Truly radical theorists like Theodor Adorno and Herbert Marcuse thought that the most dangerous totalitarian threat was from consumer capitalism, which displaced and even "drugged" the critical impulses of ordinary men and women with consumption and technology, perpetuating the hegemony of a social order that prevented the promises of nineteenth-century socialism from being realized.

In Germany and the United States especially, the term also became entangled in the struggle, conducted mostly on university campuses, between the political elites of the late 1940s and 1950s and their radical challengers of the 1960s. The 1960s radicals generally eschewed the term, and most of them hated it. It was the ultimate intellectual underpinning of the "cold warriors" they opposed: whatever criticisms one might make of the free world, the cold warriors argued, the world of the Communists was as bad as that of the Nazis. In that situation, who could not understand the world of Western capitalism to be *incomparably* superior to the totalitarian world of the fanatics to the East? Such a view made radical social change vastly more difficult to achieve.

In France, the term did not become the focused subject of debate until the mid-1970s, because of the domination of a political Left more given to anti-Americanism than anticommunism. In 1977 Jean-François Revel published *The Totalitarian Temptation,* asking whether there "lurked within [the inhabitants of Western democracies] a wish for totalitarian rule." If so, he continued, it would explain why among left-wing people in noncommunist nations, "the faults of free societies are so magnified that freedom appears to mask an essentially totalitarian reality, while the faults of totalitarian societies are so minimized that those societies appear to be free, in essence, if not in appearance."[3] Revel's books testified to the dramatic waning of Sartrean intellectual hegemony over French intellectual life in the 1970s. In fact, much of the famous debate between Jean-Paul Sartre and Albert Camus almost thirty years earlier had centered on Camus's contention in *The Rebel* (1951) that European revolutions, from the Jacobins to the Bolsheviks, had betrayed the limited aims of "rebellion" for unrealizable, utopian goals that were bound to end in totalitarianism. But in those days, almost no respectable person on the French Left would admit to being actively anticommunist. Camus was almost without allies in France, although his admirers in the English-speaking world and later in Eastern Europe were legion.

In Eastern Europe, no one wrote (or even spoke) of totalitarianism publicly until the 1970s. Two things happened to make discussion possible. First, the heavy hand of the Soviet Union had by then entirely discredited the traditional Left and eliminated any vestige of sympathy for what the Soviet elite called "real socialism," meaning the system that they had imposed on the states of the region. Second, the Soviet Union and its satellite regimes had become sufficiently entangled in diplomatic and economic relations with the West by the end of the decade that they were most unwilling to risk drastic and major repression. The anti-Soviet opposition in Czechoslovakia centered in Charter 77 and the embryo of Polish Solidarity both mobilized their members with campaigns against Soviet totalitarianism.

Finally, the term played an important role in the efforts by American neoliberals and neoconservatives to generate support for a much harder line toward the Soviet Union in the late 1970s and especially during Ronald Reagan's first term as president. Led by Jeane Kirkpatrick, those intellectuals revived and highlighted an old distinction, made originally by the German and American political theorist Carl J. Friedrich. They argued that the divide between merely "authoritarian" governments and those that were "totalitarian" amounted to a kind of abyss. Authoritarian governments, identified by Kirkpatrick with "traditional" nondemocratic regimes, "do not," she wrote, "disturb the habitual rhythms of work and leisure, habitual places of residence, habitual patterns of family and personal relations. Because the miseries of traditional life are familiar, they are bearable to ordinary people who . . . learn to cope, as children born to untouchables in India acquire the skills and attitudes necessary for survival in the miserable roles they are destined to fulfill. Such societies create no refugees."[4]

Totalitarian regimes, by contrast, were radically utopian in their cease-less effort to make the world over in their own image. Authoritarian governments might be modified by quiet diplomacy or economic incentives. Communist totalitarianism was inevitably and unshakably opposed to American interests worldwide. It was principally the rise to power of Mikhail Gorbachev and the subsequent reform and collapse of the Soviet Union that led political neoconservatives to de-emphasize or quietly abandon their use of the term.

In almost every European nation in which the cold war was a domestic political issue, the paradigm of totalitarianism had its famous detractors and defenders—the latter almost always being those who championed anticommunism and who believed most passionately in the rightness of the cold war: Raymond Aron and Albert Camus in France; George Orwell in England; Vaclav Havel in Czechoslovakia; Jacek Kurón and Adam Michnik in Poland. No American exactly corresponded to such figures, but one might mention Zbigniew Brzezinski and, again, Kirkpatrick, two academics who played important political roles in the 1970s and 1980s, and Friedrich, the Harvard political theorist who was the term's first academic champion in the United States.

Karl Dietrich Bracher's is the principal German name on this list. He has been the most respected academic spokesman there for the term since the 1950s, and he became its political champion, too, in the ideological wars of the 1960s. He has never abandoned it to its enemies or critics and continues to defend it in this volume, contrasting it as starkly as ever with merely "authoritarian" regimes.[5]

Bracher's biography has been much bound up with the Second World War and with his experiences connected to the United States. He was drafted into the German army as a young man, and after being captured in North Africa, he spent time in the United States as a prisoner of war, in Kansas. After the war, while pursuing his studies at the University of Tübingen, he participated in the Salzburg Seminar for American Studies and studied at Harvard in 1949. The kind of political science in which he became interested in those years was also much associated with the United States. "My encounter with . . . a previously unknown, optimistic conception of history in America's democracy," he graciously writes, "formed a strong contrast to my experience of the German dictatorship and the European catastrophe, with its underlying sense of pessimism."

At the same time, one must not lose sight of other influences he speaks of, perhaps even more significant and certainly deeper: the "humanistic-liberal" world of home and school in Stuttgart; his pursuit of classical studies; the Schleicher family—his wife's—involvement in the resistance to Hitler.[6]

In the early 1950s, when Bracher was working on the history of the Weimar Republic, the eminent historian of political systems and structures, Ernst Fraenkel, returned from the United States to the Free University of Berlin; there he met the young Bracher, whose interests, like his own, combined political science and history. Fraenkel's prewar study, *The Dual State* (New York: Oxford University Press, 1941), had enjoyed some influence in the English-speaking world, and it is likely that contact with Fraenkel and other emigrant scholars, including Franz and Sigmund Neumann, pushed Bracher and his colleagues Gerhard Schulz and Wolfgang Sauer in the direction of the totalitarian paradigm in the major works that were subsequently published: *The Dissolution of the Weimar Republic* (1955), *The National Socialist Seizure of Power* (1960), and *The German Dictatorship* (1969).[7] They attempted to grasp the regime as a specific but historically derived totality, to integrate the best known version of a political science "syndrome" or "model" of totalitarianism with a deeply researched and grounded historical narrative.[8]

Over the course of the 1950s, Bracher came to understand the concept of totalitarianism as being ever more central. In *The Dissolution of the Weimar Republic,* it was applied explicitly only to the German Communist and Nazi parties (which grew out of the German revolution of 1918) and no very serious effort was made to define it. In *The National Socialist Seizure of Power,* however, Bracher reproduced Friedrich and Brzezinski's six-point syndrome in the introduction and combined it with a historical essay on how twentieth-century events made the rise of totalitarianism possible.[9] In so doing, he explicitly accepted J. L. Talmon's assertion that "the modern totalitarian dictatorship is a child of this democratic age."[10] Despite his respect for Friedrich's six-point model, he regarded Nazi totalitarianism as characterized by a revolutionary dynamism that found insufficient reflection in Friedrich's typology. His belief in the centrality of the radical utopianism that Talmon posited as the historical basis for totalitarian development has, if anything, become firmer over the years.[11]

Political criticism of the term "totalitarian" as applied to the Soviet Union and the Communist states of Eastern Europe grew toward the end of the 1960s and in the following decade, and mingled with the growing concern of the liberal (and conservative) professoriat about the New Left's Marxism, anti-Americanism, and hostility to traditional academic values. For many scholars of Bracher's generation, however, the concept of totalitarianism was fundamental to their deepest sense of what postwar Germany meant. "The Federal Republic of Germany," Bracher wrote in 1978, "continues to live under the impact of two experiences which were essential in giving it shape: the destruction of Weimar democracy by the National Socialists in 1932–33 and the establishment of a second dictatorship in Eastern Germany after 1945. In both cases one-party rule with totalitarian claims was implemented. Totalitarianism of the Right and of the Left were the fundamental experiences. The founders of the Second (West) German Republic, therefore, insisted on open democracy and a constitutional structure devised to protect the state from totalitarian tendencies."[12]

The debate over totalitarianism had become extremely politicized by this time. Bracher was now concerned less with the academic plausibility of the totalitarian model than with the leftward movement of German politics, which he feared was making totalitarian modes of thinking more acceptable in West Germany. The fundamental distinction between dictatorship and democracy, he felt, had been blurred by the New Left.

As with that of many scholars of his generation, Bracher's work exudes a sense of the fragility of German democracy, even though his stated outlook is confidence in Germany's and Europe's necessarily linked future: "If we look back over the varied history of the development of democratic ideas and constitutions," he writes in "The Ethos of Democracy," "we must keep in mind the constant possibility of a relapse into authoritarianism or a seduction into a totalitarian politics." For him, the "idea of democracy" has only deepened in interest over the years, being "the product of a highly complicated social, political and above all intellectual and moral effort."[13] He returns again and again, in the essays collected here, to comparisons between the Federal Republic and Weimar, and he retains his interest in and fervent support for the Basic Law of 1949, which established postwar Germany on a constitutional footing.

One gets the impression that Bracher, like many contemporaries, has had difficulty coming to grips with the fact that the cold war has really ended. His optimism is laced with a prudent skepticism about the future. *Can* Europe really deal with what Vaclav Havel and others call the "post-communist nightmare"? And is it not possible that "rising fundamentalist movements in many parts of the world" could bring back something like the mobilizing, totalitarian ideologies of the past?[14] Karl Dietrich Bracher leaves the next generation in no doubt as to where he has stood and still stands.

Preface

This book is the successor to my 1987 collection of essays entitled *Die totalitäre Erfahrung* (The Totalitarian Experience). The engagement with the theme of totalitarianism, as dominant in our century as it is controversial, has now been given added weight by the largely unexpected, though unequivocal, events of 1989 and their world historical consequences.

Indeed the collapse of Communism and its ideology, and even more so the shocking and frequently suppressed recognition of the totalitarian reality of its forms of rule, signal a new epoch in the history of the twentieth century. They bring full circle a development that led from World War I into the totalitarian revolutions of 1917, 1922, 1933, and 1948, ending finally, after World War II and the defeat of National Socialism, in more than forty years of confrontation between Communist dictatorship and Western democracy.

However, the failure of the two opposing and yet comparable dictatorial movements and systems, with their antagonistic and homophobic ideologies, this twofold refutation—first in the middle and now at the end of the century—of different and tangible forms of totalitarianism, does not mean that the problems that led to the rise of totalitarianism and made it possible have now also come to an end. On the contrary! Coping with this legacy has proved to be a task that labors under the full burden of seventy-five years of tyrannical history and its ideological justifications. This has cast a new and sharper light not only on the totalitarian experience itself, but also on the prehistory and consequences of the great epochal turning points that have swept over us largely unexpectedly (as was the case in 1989, as well). And because these turning points were so unexpected, the impact of change and responsibility following in their wake hit us with much greater force.

These essays on contemporary history, written during the transitional years of 1987 to 1992, are grouped under three historical-political themes. After three brief essays, one autobiographical in nature, one dealing with the philosophy of history, and one reflecting on recent events, the discussion turns to how we might deal with the experiences of historical crises. The second group of essays addresses the continuing legacy of National Socialism in Germany's "dual recent past." The final section looks at the perennially threatened chances for the realization of democracy in Germany and Europe. However, in the second attempt at democracy in this century, these chances look incomparably brighter in Germany—and, one hopes, in Eastern Europe as well. (I have dealt with this most recent history at length in the concluding chapter of the new edition of my book *Die Krise Europas 1917–1992*, Propyläen Geschichte Europas, vol. 6, Studienausgabe, 1993).

Historical and political reflection seeks to detach itself from the direct account of events in order to be able to explain and locate them, to interpret their interconnections, and to gain basic lessons and insights—and not just "for another time" (Jacob Burckhardt). To be sure, the extent to which history can convey lessons and yield something useful remains a matter of controversy. But to neglect history and the great confrontation between liberty and totalitarianism in the name of a new future would mean underestimating the continuing danger of a (nationalistic) relapse into the disastrous aberrations of the first half of the century and after. Transitional periods are always also periods that test us. A Europe that has escaped self-destruction and division should be able to make better use of them than it did after 1918 and 1945.

I am grateful to Professor Abbott Gleason for his valuable foreword dealing with the concept of totalitarianism, which is one of the themes of my book. In these essays, my main concern is with the analysis of revolutionary turning points in history, and especially the chances of democracy in our century of dictatorships.

As always, I am deeply grateful for the critical assistance of my wife, Dorothee, née Schleicher.

Karl Dietrich Bracher

HISTORICAL
CRISES
AND
LESSONS

The Weimar Experience

When I set to work on my study *Die Auflösung der Weimarer Republik* (The Dissolution of the Weimar Republic) in the early 1950s (I was born in 1922), many contemporaries were perplexed, because I came to my subject from a background in ancient history, literature, and philosophy. In my parents' humanistic-liberal home, and at the Stuttgart Gymnasium I attended, these interests had worked as an antidote to the totalitarian spirit of the time. They remained an intellectual reference point during my war service in northern Africa and after 1943, when I was held as a prisoner of war by the Americans. My encounter with and experience of a previously unknown, optimistic conception of history in America's democracy subsequently formed a strong contrast to my experience of the German dictatorship and the European catastrophe, with its underlying sense of pessimism.

Thus during my studies in a POW camp in Kansas, and even more so during my wider ranging studies at Tübingen after the war, my love for ancient history became a bridge across which my gaze fell upon history as a whole, before it came to rest on the deeply distressing and controversial recent past, which I knew from bitter personal experience. My dissertation in ancient history—which did not appear in print in the turbulent year 1948 due to a shortage of paper (though it was recently published by Böhlau, in 1987)—already took aim rather boldly at a fundamental problem in the history of political ideas in times of crisis: the question of decline and progress in the ideology of the early Roman Empire. By examining the classical discussion about the transformation of the Roman Empire, I was, at the same time, dealing with the then-topical theme of the crisis of progress, which is in many ways reminiscent of today's discussion about crisis and decline. To pursue this problem in a comparative and contrasting fashion for the modern period as well, I turned my attention more keenly to America, to contrast and compare its image of the "New World" since the seventeenth century with the recent history of Germany and Europe. The Salzburg Seminar for American Studies in 1948, and a year of research at Harvard, allowed me to link up with the political sciences. My wife, who comes from a family that had been involved in the German resistance to Nazism, also contributed her critical experiences to my efforts to frame the problem in a topical and concrete way.

Weimar was still close. Few wished a return to the agitated atmosphere of the First Republic, which I had experienced during its unhappy end. To be sure, during the early postwar years Germany's first democracy and its failure were a frequent topic of discussion. In particular, people were seeking an explanation for the incomprehensible, the onslaught of barbarism, the seductive power of totalitarian dictatorship. The discussion on Weimar became an important reference point in the process of building the Federal Republic. But the issue of concern to me in my study of ancient history, on the one hand, and in my encounters with the doyens of the political and social sciences (like James Bryce, Max Weber, Guglielmo Ferrero) and my conversations with Arnold Brecht, Sigmund Neumann, and Ernst Fraenkel, on the other, went well beyond Ranke's dictum of history "as it actually happened." It was later indicated in the subtitle of my 1955 book on the Weimar Republic: the problem of power and the disintegration of power in democracies.

This approach to a complex theme provided three focal points and directions for research. First, my studies had made one thing clear to me: in contrast to the prevailing notions of a more or less sudden process of the "destruction" or "failure" of the Weimar Republic, what we were actually dealing with was a multicausal and step-by-step process of dissolution, which I had sketched out in a preliminary study in 1952. Second, in contrast to mere description, but also to the terse explanatory models of Marxist or liberal, conservative or nationalist bent, all of which in some way contain apologetic elements, I was concerned with analyzing power structures. This meant that an accurate description of events had to be preceded by a systematic analysis, which I called the "problems of the structure of power." Third, based on this approach I also tried to structure the narrative of the process of dissolution itself. I did this by drawing a distinction between different phases in the process: the loss of power by the democratic forces, the power vacuum in the political sphere, and finally the gradual seizure of power by a dictatorial movement. That movement took decisive advantage of the paralysis, indeed partial self-paralysis, of parliamentary democracy—it assumed the reins of government in what appeared to be a democratic and legal way, but subsequently it became impossible to dislodge.

While the book was in preparation at the Berlin Institute for Political Science (founded in 1950), and after its publication, the structure I had devised for it met with criticism and objections. The combination of systematic and historical analyses aroused methodological and theoretical misgivings. Invoking the formula that the approaches of history and political science are fundamentally different, some critics considered me too historical, while others regarded me as being too much oriented toward the political sciences.

In fact, at the time not a few German historians viewed the book as odd, "unhistorical," even American. It also received an unfriendly and factually inaccurate review in the journal *Historische Zeitschrift,* to which I was denied the opportunity to respond. I may be permitted to point out, in all modesty, how different the situation was at the time of the "Fischer controversy" that flared up six years later; then it was not a young lecturer working on the boundary between history and politics, but an already well-established, tenured professor of history who caused a stir. But the sharp criticism was counterbalanced by encouraging voices at home and especially from abroad. What made the work controversial at the time was its broad historical sweep and its focus on the uncomfortable, pervasive question: Was the failure of the Republic preordained both by the burden of the German tradition of an authoritarian state and by considerable structural flaws in the Republic, owing to which the outbreak of the Great Depression, with its mass unemployment, would have especially serious consequences? Was the catastrophe preprogrammed from the very beginning and virtually unavoidable? This question had to be tested against an immense body of contemporary literature.

Most controversial of all were my structural analyses in the first, systematic part of the book. They dealt with the problematic German sense of being special *(Sonderbewußtsein),* which had grown since the early nineteenth century; with the unexpected military defeat and the unloved compromise-structure of the first democracy; with the early emerging tendency toward a dualism between a parliamentary and a presidential system with unclear political responsibilities. To this had to be added the widespread criticism of the party system and the party-state as such, along with militant movements and the rise of totalitarian parties on the Right and the Left; the existence of serious problems in the economic and social structures; a predemocratic mentality in the bureaucracy and the judiciary; and finally—as described by Wolfgang Sauer—the special status of the Reichswehr. All these structural aspects contained neuralgic points and traumatic elements for a possible dissolution of democracy. Whether these factors came into play depended, however, on the conduct of the affected persons and groups and those who had become the actors in the years of crisis from

1930 to 1933. I described this process in the second part of the book, under the title "Stages of Dissolution."

Let me mention a few points from the controversy. There was, to begin with, the general assertion that, given the special nature of its premises and the very conditions of the Versailles Treaty, it was ahistorical to measure the Weimar Republic by the standards of a parliamentary democracy. But was it not true that parliamentary democracy was the decisive constitutional and structural principle of this polity? There was also repeated criticism of my argument that the Weimar Republic was a "typical" model for studying the problem of how political power is attained and retained, of how it erodes and is lost. Juan Linz's *The Breakdown of Democratic Regimes* (1978) has shown the extent to which that approach has been vindicated today by international comparative studies. Finally, objections were raised time and again against the alleged determinism inherent in an approach that focused on the structure of power. Those critics failed to realize the importance I accorded to acting and thinking people.

That these arguments were more than anything else politically motivated, even if they were couched in the language of the historian, can be seen especially from the crucially important way in which scholars assessed the decision of March 1930 to transform the parliamentary government of the Great Coalition into the authoritarian presidential regime of the Republic's final phase. Contrary to the accusation that I was committed to the thesis of the inevitability of the development toward catastrophe, my analysis was at all times concerned to show that alternatives were very much in existence up to the last moment. Determinism tends to mark the arguments of those who simply rule out the possibility of a party-political solution to the crisis as early as 1930, and who regard the road to an authoritarian system as inevitable from that point on. Their arguments involve a highly questionable juxtaposition (questionable also in regard to terminology) of democracy and "state," of politics and "sober government by experts." This is then used to justify Brüning's abrupt formation of a government, which occurred without an attempt at parliamentary negotiation and solely through Hindenburg's presidential power; there followed the fateful dissolution of the Reichstag in July 1930, which destroyed the governing majority. Instead of lamenting in general terms the failure of "the" parties or of democracy as such, I was concerned, then and later, to bring out the intentions on the part of certain people to pursue an authoritarian and eventually totalitarian restructuring of the Republic. These intentions, along with the policy of presidential government by emergency decree according to Article 48 of the Weimar Constitution, also paved the way for a release (whether forced or tolerated) of the parties and parliament from political responsibility. The controversy surrounding this loss of power by parliamentary democracy, and the resulting power vacuum with the prospect of a nondemocratic seizure of power, placed questions about responsibility in sharper focus; of central importance was the issue of whether, even if the alternatives were dwindling, political action up until the very end could have avoided a dictatorship.

The concept and significance of a power vacuum also remained controversial. After Brüning's fall, with a minority government that lacked any parliamentary backing, the power vacuum sealed the paralysis of party democracy. Meanwhile the actions of a few string-pullers opened the way for the seizure of power by the National Socialists, whose leaders and supporters at first lacked a majority. My uncovering of these entirely rational connections in terms of their underlying structure and the people involved in them was intended to counter demonological, collectivist, or "tragic" interpretations, regardless of whether they invoked a capitalist or socialist conspiracy, the guilt of foreign countries, an undeserved German "fate," or even the alleged incompetence or impossibility of democratic government in times of crisis.

Today as I look back over the history of that book, I note its shortcomings as well as its unsolved problems. What I can say is that I worked empirically as best as I could, and at the time assigned great importance to electoral statistics (even if my calculations were done with pen and paper), though it is true that the areas of economic and foreign policy should have been treated more exhaustively. Today I would also devote even more attention to the importance and role of ideologies. *Die Auflösung der Weimarer Republik* and the subsequent volumes *The National Socialist Seizure of Power* (1960) and *The German Dictatorship* (1969) have outlived the controversies of the last decades, and not least the misleading inflation of theories of fascism and the temporary ostracism of the concept of totalitarianism. This survival is due not to the absolute correctness of all details and interpretations, which is unattainable, but more to their approach, grounded in my own life experiences and the history of scholarship, and especially to the continuing international importance of the topic, not least after the great upheavals of 1989.

Weimar remains an exemplary case. It allows us to study the fragility of a parliamentary democracy with a directly elected president under the pressure of socioeconomic crises and the assault of explosive political and ideological forces, as well as the temptation of and seduction by extreme right-wing and left-wing, antiliberal and totalitarian tendencies within a state and society. The paralysis and decay of the liberal state, reduced to helplessness against dictatorial movements in the power vacuum of 1932, was not least a result of confused norms, a weakened readiness to fight back, and misguided notions about tolerance toward the enemies of democracy.

There are two contradictory legends about the development and spirit of the 1950s. One claims that they failed in the task of historically coming to terms with the past. The other says that the intrusion of nonhistorical approaches and perspectives, especially of political science and sociology, prepared the way for a culturally revolutionary reinterpretation of the past long before the magical year 1968. Both versions are extreme; they fail to do justice to the situation at the time. The legend of the apolitical fifties misjudges their importance particularly in establishing a critical study of contemporary history—and this long before the proclamation of the so-called critical history.

The new direction in scholarly work—pursued at the time at the Munich Institute of Contemporary History and in the *Vierteljahrshefte für Zeitgeschichte,* and also at a number of institutes of political science in an effort to work through (with international cooperation) the most recent past—was, of course, not yet marked by that sharpening of the debate that led to the ideological alienations of the end of the sixties. That trend found its dubious climax more recently in the so-called *Historikerstreit* (historians' dispute), a controversy spawned by irresponsible or attention-hungry theorizers. It would be regrettable if calls for a "historicization" of National Socialism under the banner or pretext of historical distance—calls that are all too thoughtless in their theorizations—ended up subordinating the rich insights of four decades of research in contemporary history and social science to what is supposedly a necessary process of de-moralizing history. It is only by constantly calling to mind historical experience, especially in its moral dimension, that history can make a serious contribution to the future of liberal democracy, especially in Germany.

History between Ideas of Decay and Progress

I

From the very beginning, the history of political thought has been marked by an ever-shifting polarity. On the one hand it deals with a number of basic questions and with certain recurring key ideas that relate to the central problem of politics, the relationship between the individual and the community. In substance and terminology, most of these ideas go back to Greco-Roman antiquity: democracy and dictatorship, constitution and consensus, freedom and equality, natural rights and human rights.

On the other hand, the history of political ideas deals with the claims of new questions and approaches that are added or opposed to the "classical" key ideas and concepts, challenging or superseding them. Renaissances and revolutions of political thought characterize at least the modern history of ideas. What has recently been described with the phrase "paradigm shift" (Thomas Kuhn) applies also to the struggle for new ways of looking at and thinking in the political realm. It implies, at the same time, that the course of political ideas and the epochs of change in history are determined not by a continuous development and continuation of the "classical" approaches, but by a chain of revolutions in thought.

Weighty examples can be offered for both viewpoints and interpretations. One case in which the basic tension becomes especially clear is the idea of progress. The question of its origin has been subject to debate. Did antiquity and the Middle Ages have an idea of progress? Was it perhaps a key idea, even a logical necessity? Or was it only the great breakthrough of scientific and technical modernity that made possible the dominant role of the idea of progress? That is what Europeans, under the spell of the modern sense of pride in innovation and the progressivism of Enlightenment spokesmen and revolutionaries, came to believe in the eighteenth century.

Careful recent studies have made it clear that older equivalents to the idea of progress existed.[1] And while the idea of progress itself seems not present in these equivalents, they do reveal that a similar way of thought existed in the ancient and medieval worlds. The crucial difference between the ancient and modern notions of progress does not, therefore, lie in the key idea itself, but rather in its historical-political locus and function. Whereas the notion of change, increase, improvement *(auxesis, progressus)* long figured merely as one way of thought among others (indeed was for the most part subordinated to the idea of the cyclical nature of all things and ages), the development in modern times, especially from the second half of the eighteenth century on, is seen as largely dominated by the idea of progress, in fact as virtually identical with it. But this does not mean that the dialectic of decay and progress is unique to modern times, though the most recent survey of the topic perhaps went too far in stating: "No single idea has been more important than, perhaps as important as, the idea of progress in Western civilization for nearly 3000 years."[2]

Of course this general statement—which supersedes older notions that antiquity and the Middle Ages were incapable of the idea of progress and does more justice to the complexity of the idea as well as those periods—is not tantamount to a denial that it was only modern development that brought forth the faith in, and eventually the dogma of, unstoppable linear progress. Antiquity thought only partial progress was possible, and saw itself perpetually exposed to the danger of decay, something even the classical works of the Roman Empire, proud of their own times, did not deny. Only the impetuous expansion and acceleration of the intellectual revolution in the thought of the Renaissance and the Enlightenment, along with the tremendous material consequences of the discoveries and of industrialization, created the seemingly irrefutable and irresistible evidence that helped the idea of progress to triumph not merely in the intellectual constructs of philosophers and historians, but also in the general view of the broader social classes, especially the rising bourgeoisie. The expectation of progress eventually became the "popular" demand of the general public (the *populus*), and the proclaiming of progress served to legitimate political action and the structure of power and authority: the first steps on the road to ideologization.

But even this was not entirely new. The ancient Hellenistic cult of the state and the ruler knew full well how to use slogans about civilization's progress toward a general order of natural law beyond the state, and about a universal history in the spirit of the Stoic philosophy of man. In the Roman Empire, the claim that Rome was the universal guarantor of peace and prosperity, made by emperors and poets, was developed and stylized into ossified propaganda on coins and inscriptions. These spoke of *"progressus"* and of the eternity of the empire and its blessings, trying in this way to counter the assault of the (Germanic) barbarians and the impending decline of ancient civilization. For alongside these positive ideas there had also developed Roman ideas of decay. Beginning as early as the end of the republic, these notions of decay had anticipated the threats to classical civilization. They culminated with Augustine, in the Christian criticism of the pagan empire.

The development of Rome presents a virtually prototypical case of how historical and cultural thought becomes ideologized; it contains many of the elements of the current ideological debates, despite the different premises underlying the problem of progress then and now. Characteristic of all cases is a petrifaction of the debate into conceptual catchphrases and the outbreak of intense dogmatic conflicts. Back then it was the act of elevating the idea of Rome to the metahistorical dogma of a universal mission, which later took on an indispensable function in the Christian sense of mission in the midst of the crises and symptoms of a decaying age. Today we witness the ideological instrumentalization and perversion of political positions, finally almost their reversal, in the old-new conflict between progress and decline.

Thus the crisis of the idea of progress-turned-ideology does not signify its end but rather its transformation; above all it signifies the uncovering of its ambiguity. The challenge to the idea is mounted from two sides simultaneously: from a cultural-anthropological pessimism—the realization through painful experience that humankind and its systems are always incomplete and can be preserved only through strong institutions; and from a messianic-chiliastic delusion of mission and perfectionism—the expectation that paradise on earth can be attained through the revolutionary acceleration and globalization of the transformation of humankind and society, in recent times through a socialization of humankind itself, through socialism. Wedged between these two poles of preservation and change, between ideas of decadence and revolution, are the liberals' evolutionary idea of progress—the notion that the free development of the individual guarantees the constant progress of the economy and society—and the reform conservatives' idea of progress—the conviction that adjustments to the existing institutions lead to greater protection for individuals and the state.

Even as I recognize the crises in the idea of progress, I emphatically note that it represents a constitutive element in the historical development of political thought. It is indispensable not only for the survival of Western civilization but also for human action in history as such—whatever the sociopolitical auspices and beliefs under which it may appear and be used. Its modern forms have taken on world-historical significance since the nineteenth century, especially through the American idea of democracy: humanistic and liberal values, the improvement of living conditions, and the protection of human rights for all have become the common property of Western civilization. But from this we must distinguish the historically limited concretization and instrumentalization of progressivism in certain parties and movements; all the more so since the very history of the word "progressive," which becomes propaganda history in the context of the philosophical and political conflicts of our time, ends up being claimed by the destructive forces of both anarchism and totalitarianism.

II

Time and again the basic problem is revealed in the light of history. It is above all in periods of transition that the two aspects of the idea of progress come to the fore: its substance and at the same time its ability to bear ideology. In the current crisis-debate, a few historical examples may serve to clarify what "progress" might still mean in the future, or come to mean again, if it is distinguished and separated from historical-ideological progressivism.

The great transitions and epochs of change in ancient history—Hellenism as the universalization of Greek thought, and the Roman idea of rule and its Christian transformation in the early Middle Ages—tended to be seen by many contemporaries and critics as retrogressions rather than progress. In fact, the high political standard of Greek democracy as the self-government of autonomous citizens, and later the proud civic ethic of the Roman Republic, gave way to recurring forms of one-man rule. And the spread of civilization's achievements was paid for dearly with a depoliticization of public life by large-scale autocratic systems and the rigidification of political life. With few exceptions, ancient observers were of a pessimistic frame of mind. Polybius may well have interpreted Rome's rise as political progress that broke through the iron cycle of constitutions. But even this Greek admirer of the emerging world empire could not suppress thoughts of the possible decay of such a successful constitution, composed of a combination of monarchic, aristocratic, and democratic elements and thus representing the most balanced constitution ever.

Much the same holds true a hundred years later for Cicero's pride in the Roman Republic in the face of its mortal crisis and a Caesarism to which he himself fell victim. And even Horace and Virgil, poets who sang the praises of a new era, the dawning emperorship of Augustus, were not convinced of progress but tended to be backward-looking in their invocation of Roman history and political morality. Long before the actual decline of the empire that was proud of its civilization, Rome's writers, beginning in the first century A.D., had turned skeptical: the line stretches from Tacitus and Juvenal to Boethius. Later they furnished the greatest Christian critic of the Roman past and present, Augustine, with abundant and convincing arguments for a pessimistic assessment of the direction of contemporary events; in the end, Augustine believed, humankind could be saved only by drawing a distinction between the city of man and the city of God.

To be sure, after its triumph over the pagan past, the Christian notion of history would be torn no less violently between, on the one hand, the assimilation and continuation of Roman imperial traditions both in the papacy and the empire (involving the permanent conflict between state and church, worldly and spiritual power), and, on the other, the chiliastic expectations of a Christian redemptive history. The projection of these redemptive ideas onto the medieval view of history produced a peculiar mix: the existing world became relative while eschatological expectations became absolute; feelings of decline were juxtaposed with visions of a thousand-year empire; pessimistic and optimistic interpretations of Western history arose. These were basic forms of thought, secularized versions of which have reappeared in transitional epochs of modern history.

The secularization of the expectation that redemptive history would run its progressive course occurred on very different levels. In Protestantism, alongside Lutheranism's rather pessimistic tradition toward history Calvinism, in its English and especially American manifestations, became the vehicle of the belief in the sanctified, providential mission of progress of America's New World.[3] This was the belief that with democracy, which combined freedom of religion and economic prosperity, divine providence became visible and active also in the worldly realm: the famous connection between Protestantism and capitalism formulated by Max Weber.

The revival of ancient republicanism in humanistic thinking on culture and freedom, which had started in the Renaissance, benefited from the secularized, individualistic Protestant consciousness of freedom and progress. The benefit was even more tangible in the development of the liberal notions of state and society within the rising bourgeoisie of the Enlightenment.

Many factors—intellectual as well as material—thus came together to bring about this transition to modern times between the sixteenth and eighteenth centuries. The Judeo-Christian notion of man as the center of creation combined with progressive developments in the areas of trade, the natural sciences, and society. The discovery and subjugation of the world could be glorified simultaneously as a divine commandment and a human accomplishment. Of course sharp criticism of the underside of advancing civilization was also voiced, most audibly in Rousseau's exaltation of nature. Rousseau's ideas gave sustenance to the later countermovements of romanticism, and have influenced even so-called alternative thinking today.

History as progress carried out in actual politics: to the medieval mind this notion had something subversive, unworkable about it. For secularized modernity, on the other hand, it became—even if initially with a Christian and especially a Calvinist justification—a self-evident truth, which was opposed only by the unenlightened, the unemancipated, and by despots. After all, the progress of the discoveries and of the sciences had so clearly surpassed everything that had previously existed. The progressive record of education and communication, of the growth of technology and the economy, of material culture and social security seemed irrefutable.

III

In two important areas, however, the notion of progress as never-ending change, because it was deeply problematic, remained controversial and then also bloodily embattled. And it was here that it also sank most quickly to the level of mere ideology: in the realms of politics and morality. These have always been the source of major objections to the almost automatic assumption that material improvement has meant the general improvement of the human condition. The progress of states toward large-scale organizations was not able to solve their basic problem, the management of power: internally it manifested itself as the problem of oppression, externally as the problem of war. In the development of democracy and international law, political progress, understood as progress toward peace (Kant), did in fact produce instruments for the peaceful resolution of conflict. But at the same time it also multiplied the tools of oppression and warfare: from universal compulsory military service to nuclear deterrence. And progress toward the more humane forms of the constitutional state, with a separation of powers and limitations on their exercise, that guaranteed the individual's liberty and human rights, was countered by an abuse of the egalitarian component of democracy; in conjunction with technological developments, it made possible an exaggeration of political equality into a coerced uniformity of society (Gleichschaltung). After brief periods of expansion, liberal democracy was driven back all over the world by modern authoritarian and totalitarian systems into an almost hopeless minority position. The overextension and misinterpretation of the concepts of progress and democracy could lead to ever-new justifications of ever-new dictatorships. The ideologization of the progressive concept of democracy, which in our century has been invoked by the overwhelming majority of despotic states all over the world, points to the profound deficiency and ambivalence of the political idea of progress, its constant susceptibility to justifications of force.

Moral progress is in much the same situation. The deep skepticism of political anthropologists since Thomas Hobbes, whose "homo homini lupus" stands opposed to social optimism from Aristotle to liberalism, seems to be confirmed time after time: we need only think of the brutality of collectivized mass societies, the abuse and erosion of the idea of human rights all over the world, the political exploitation of religions, and the helplessness of the individual in the face of the great machines of manipulation, propaganda, and seduction.

The faith in the educability of (all?) humankind, which ranks among the central elements of modern progressivism, is also suffering constant setbacks. Education is by no means a reliable guarantor of moral-social progress. Since the days of Plato it has also been used as an instrument of political manipulation and ideological deception, and as a playground for an indoctrination which, in the name of the progress of the young over the old, has a destructive and corrupting authoritarian effect.

So where does this leave moral progress? Today its noblest point of departure could be the politics of human rights, which gives a better promise of progress than all lofty admonitions and religious formulas. The idea and history of human rights—whether they are justified by natural law, Christian beliefs, or constitutional philosophy—contain fundamental impulses for an effective improvement of the political and social life of people, and especially for the protection of their personal integrity and freedom, which are also what make them capable of rendering decisions as moral beings. It is precisely here, at their most vulnerable point, that dictatorships should be taken at their word. For today there is in fact hardly a regime that can afford not to legitimize itself with a democratic constitution and concede the existence of basic rights. Everything will depend on whether this claim of basic rights—which has become common property since the rise of the constitutional state—can be effectively enshrined in the political system, can be made legally actionable. The start made by the Helsinki Conference (1975) was undoubtedly "progress" in this direction (with revolutionary consequences in 1989), even if initially it only made the persistent gap between words and reality still more apparent. What is at stake, in the final analysis, is our protection of the concrete constitutional-political realization of human rights. We must not succumb to the ideology of the often-perverted principle, which has been so frequently abused—as in the French Revolution and even more so in the Communist revolutions—and has led to a fatal neglect of political human rights in favor of so-called social human rights in "progressive" dictatorships.

As the ideologies of "emancipatory" progressivism seek to realize the possibility and implement the demands of their respective ideas of progress in the realms of politics and morality, they simply identify those ideas with material or intellectual advances. This had the most disastrous results when politics and morality were equated for the purpose of the totalitarian, futuristic creation of a "new man" and for his subjugation in the name of progress, which is what Communism and National Socialism propagated. In those movements, progressivism as an ideology could justify the most terrible relapses into barbarism, relapses that appeared in the guise of material progress and were clothed in totalitarian promises of salvation by means of an indoctrination that was taken to new heights through technology.

IV

Contrary to the old hopes inherent in the Western idea of democracy, it would thus seem that moral and political development has barely been able to keep pace with technological progress. Either we have ended up with the violent dictatorship of ideological saviors from Robespierre to Hitler and Stalin, for whom even Hegel and Marx laid the groundwork with their equating of history and reason; or this discrepancy has led to the deep skepticism of the ideas of decadence, whose typical arguments, from Rousseau to Nietzsche, are recurring again today. Moreover, despite Kant's emphatic pleas for the idea of peace and a republican and federalist Europe, philosophers have dealt only very tentatively with the actual possibilities of political progress. Most have been either fixated on the question of the perfect form of government (a classic question since the time of Plato) or have considered the development of a democratic theory (in any case always incomplete) to be of secondary concern, while a more precise examination has been left to scholars of jurisprudence and historians. Thinkers like the liberal reform theorist John Stuart Mill and Alexis de Tocqueville, the analyst of democracy, were great exceptions, while the majority of the theorists of progress have tended to focus on society rather than the state.

In actual fact, however, the history of the basic political ideas and forms that led to modern liberal democracy is hardly less important as a motor of change for the idea of progress than the scientific-technological and material developments. Since the time of Locke and Montesquieu, the main principles of these ideas and forms—human and civic rights, popular sovereignty and the principle of majority rule, the idea of liberty and equality, protection of minorities, and separation of powers—have been closely linked not only to the political-social modernization of the West, but also to the scientific revolution of the modern age. The (scientific) idea of balance was also of particular importance. Its translation into politics and the development of the constitutional state implied a form of progress that, to be sure, found little favor in the eyes of progressivist perfectionists, precisely because it aimed at the limitation of power and not at its greatest possible development or at a paradisiac system.

It is no coincidence that liberal democracy was for this very reason attacked by cultural pessimists as well as utopian progressivists. A romantic return to nature (Rousseau) or historical skepticism (from Ranke to Meinecke), a withering away of the state (from Condorcet to Marx and Engels) or technocratic dictatorship (Saint-Simon)—such are the alternatives that have been opposed to the empirical, practical character of liberal democracy. For the empirical quality of constitutional political progress resisted both ideological-eschatological expectations and absolutist ideas of the state. And if some people today doubt the possibility that Western civilization can make further progress, let us only recall the great shortcomings in a world of dictatorships. Such a world knows little progress in human rights; their implementation lags far behind what has taken place in the West.

Of course one can argue that a further perfection of democracy, in its liberal as well as its social aspects, does nothing to impede those tendencies toward self-destruction that allowed the dictators between the wars to overthrow democracy with its own means. But that happened not least because far too many intellectuals and philosophers despised "bourgeois" democracy as a makeshift solution, or dismissed it as a mere transitional form. But success or failure in politically mastering the problems of progress hinges on the balancing function of a constitutional system that is democratic, pluralistic, and based on the rule of law. The hostility toward technology and science that is today spreading in the West does not offer a useful answer either, if it leaves decision making to a dictatorship of ecological experts or places its trust in the anarchical arbitrariness of alternative groups, with their inverted claim of progressiveness—inverted because it is now critical of civilization.

The Western idea of progress experienced its greatest intensification and simultaneously its deepest degradation in the totalitarian-chiliastic ideologies. Humankind cannot do without the concept of progress. Nor can it do without the capacity to understand the abuse and limitations of the idea of progress, the seductions and impositions by the sort of progressivism that, as ideology, has repeatedly taken us down wrong historical paths and has enslaved people; in fact, it threatens to twist the liberating effect of intellectual and material improvement into its opposite. The crisis of the concept of progress in the face of the problems of technological economic development could be seen as an opportunity to unmask its ideological and mass-psychological manipulation as the idol of one-dimensional thinking.

But cultural pessimism, too, has no recipe that would make it possible to reverse industrial society or simply refuse its goods. Both extremes, the idea of linear progress as well as the paralysis of economic growth, threaten to lead to crises that will endanger the very existence of humankind. Yet the formulation of new concepts for the survival of humankind, the changing of its expectations and ideas of happiness, cannot simply be dictated by intellectuals or coercively imposed by dictatorships. The consequences would be anarchy in the former case, despotism in the latter.

Like life itself, human thinking moves between progress and decay. There is an insoluble link between human freedom and the ability to think ahead. It is all about the constantly renewed balance between change and preservation—under conditions, that is, that do not stifle the human spirit but open it up for new solutions. The humanistic sciences—from philosophy and history to the political and social sciences—can make significant contributions to this endeavor.

Thoughts on the Year of Revolution, 1989

The exciting consequences of the historical turning point of 1989 reveal how simultaneously manifold and comprehensive are the great transformations we are experiencing today in the formerly Communist-dominated parts of Europe. Indeed, the very year in which the two-hundredth anniversary of the French Revolution of 1789 was lavishly organized and enthusiastically celebrated witnessed, in the short space of a few months and utterly unexpectedly, a "caesura" of truly historical dimensions and consequences. This transformation—jolting, revolutionary, yet for the most part nonviolent—brought to an end in central and Eastern Europe a ruthless separation of nations and societies that had lasted for decades. At first sight the suddenness of the events seemed miraculous: "Incredible!" was a frequent exclamation from East German refugees in September and October of 1989, who at that time were reaching the West via Budapest and Prague, and later through the wall itself. Many felt that these events, experienced on such an elementary and existential level, meant a profound change full of liberation and redemption, hopeful promises and high expectations.

Caesura and Continuity

Regardless of how we wish to understand the concept of revolution—controversial (and abused) from the very beginning—what took place was, first and foremost, as Helmut Schmidt put it in an editorial (*Die Zeit,* November 8, 1989), a "revolt against oppression and lies" that broke out because of the deep discrepancy between ideology and reality. Taking stock in the summer of 1990, breathtaking results are revealed, in emotional and intellectual-moral terms as well as concrete ones. What is taking place is the overthrow of political systems and social and intellectual structures that had seemed perfectly secure, the collapse of totalitarian dictatorships, and the erosion of the Marxist-Leninist monopoly on truth, with its claim that the communist-socialist utopia would be the final historical certainty.

As Günther Gillessen said, the unification of Germany also "came as a gift of history, not as something earned by a government or as the fulfillment of a great plan. Neither did it come about simply through a German national movement, but as part of a larger international movement of all of Eastern Europe. Unlike in 1870–71, it was accomplished without blood and iron, by the quick determination of Chancellor Kohl, with American support, and the approval of the European neighbors."

On an international scale, this experience has produced, in turn, far-reaching hopes for a solution to existing historical-political problems, at least in Europe. There are voices proclaiming the end of the postwar period, the end of the ideological totalitarian dictatorships (which has long been predicted, prematurely), even the end of history as such through the triumph of liberal democracy (Francis Fukuyama). Of course all this surely exaggerates the importance of the East-West conflict as we have known it, if we think of the current events in the Persian Gulf or the acute problems of perestroika in the Soviet Union. Those are painful demonstrations that the older currents of world history are certainly continuing.

Others speak of a new vitality of nations in view of the erosion of the bloc mentality, the decay of the Soviet empire, and the overextension of the United States. Of course the change from pseudodemocratic dictatorships to liberal and pluralistic democracies based on the rule of law also sets free the ambivalence of the modern nationalism that is inherent in the liberation from communist universalism. Given the rivalry of national states searching for and promising full "identity," it seems hardly possible to avert the dangers of a return to conflicts between nation states at the expense of workable democracies and the interference in democratic reconstruction by nationalistic movements—in sum, a relapse into the interwar period with its primacy of nationalistic over democratic politics. It is probably no coincidence that for some years now the fashionable concept of identity has played an important role. The concept is justified only if it is not couched in absolute terms and if it takes into consideration that every person, whether he or she wants to be or not, is a composite of several identities. Turning a collective identity into something absolute presents a danger whose consequences we have come to know from bitter experience several times, in our century of oppression, seduction, and coercive uniformity.

This old-new problem of the national state can be tackled in the long run only through a federalization of Europe with graduated forms of integration. This, more than anything else, is the task we all face today. To achieve this, the models of the European Community, the Council of Europe, and the Conference on Security and Cooperation in Europe offer (in institutional terms) better preconditions than ever before for a modification of the nation-state principle and the principle of sovereignty. Such a modification will provide the only way in which the historical minority and regional problems can be defused, both in regard to human rights and in socioeconomic terms. This historical problem, which the twentieth century has so far failed to tackle, has not been solved by the events of 1989; instead, it has once again risen to awareness and become topical. In addition, the sudden change from a totalitarian, planned economy to a free-market economy is a challenge that can be met only on a European scale.

"History goes on," said Richard v. Weizsäcker—of course it does, and we hope it will not repeat itself. But we can be sure of that only if an intensive examination of the past takes place in the recently toppled dictatorial states. This type of examination is especially complicated in the still half-dictatorial Soviet Union with its many ethnic groups, some of which are pulling away. But it is also difficult in countries with a "dual" recent past; like the former German Democratic Republic (GDR), they stand in the shadow of a fifty-seven-year experience of dictatorship, both National Socialist and Communist. There will be renewed, bitter, and lengthy arguments about how people behave under a dictatorship and toward it—behavior that ranges from collaboration to withdrawal and all the way to resistance. Until now this question, so critical for our understanding of German history and basic human rights, has been covered up, in the GDR at least, by the label of "antifascism."

A Comprehensive Concept of Totalitarianism

And so what we are in fact dealing with is not simply the end of the postwar period (whose end has been declared many times, beginning in the 1960s) or even a new "clean slate," as some in Germany dreamed of in 1945. Rather, we are dealing with a turning point in the more than seventy-year history of antidemocratic and totalitarian systems that emerged after World War I with the seizure of power by Lenin and Mussolini—that is, Communism and Fascism. This holds also for the much-abused counterforces and opposing concepts of anticommunism and antifascism. The illusions and confusions that have been and still are associated with them were revealed some time ago when Thomas Mann made the dubious statement (in 1942) that anticommunism was "the fundamental folly of our times." Yet the same Thomas Mann wrote to Walter Ulbricht in 1951 concerning the draconian justice of the Socialist Unity Party of Germany (SED) regime: "Communism should avoid being confused with Fascism."

It was to this connection between the two movements that the unjustly attacked debate about totalitarianism addressed itself before and after World War II. After all, that debate also concerned itself not least with the underestimation of Communism in the West. Though false ideologues of détente have tried to minimize the totalitarian nature of Communism and to predict an eventual convergence of the two systems, that totalitarian nature was reconfirmed by the collapse of the Communist systems—as it had been confirmed earlier by the development of the Gestapo state into the Stasi state and the similarities between the two. In a time of old and new fundamentalisms, this experience with totalitarianism also has definite timely importance—if we think, for example, of Arab or Islamic nationalism, of the continuation of the idea of the socialist utopia, especially among intellectuals, and of Communist China, which has nearly a quarter of the world's population.

The era of totalitarian movements has not come to an end, and neither has the possibility of ideological seduction by "political religions" in the service of monopolistic power. Even in what one hopes will be a post-Fascist and post-Communist era, there remain forces and tendencies toward old and new polarization, radicalization, and the creation of utopias.

Problems of Interpretation

To be sure, as we look at the positive aspects of the current transformation, one thing that must give us pause is how difficult it was, right up to the end, to predict what is now happening. Historians, social scientists, and philosophers, just like journalists and politicians, were almost completely surprised by the changes that occurred, by their speed and radical nature— often all the more so if, like researchers on East Germany, they had been studying the topic intensively, in the process grossly overestimating the stability of the GDR and its ability to establish a sense of identity.

Comparing such sudden turning points as a historian of ideas and systems allows one to observe the extent to which the experience of a profound transformation has always rendered people susceptible to misperceiving "epochal changes" as the solution to or even the end of history. From visions of the fall of great empires (as outlined in 1918 by Oswald Spengler and in 1987 by Paul Kennedy, for example) to apocalyptic visions of the end of the state, or war, or even humankind, experience fluctuates between thoughts of decay and thoughts of progress.

Comparable epochal changes are to be found not only in the highly ambivalent course of the French Revolution; striking examples also appear as early as England's Glorious Revolution and in the American Revolution, with its republican self-consciousness and sense of mission. Finally they can also be found in the totalitarian revolutions of Lenin and Hitler, with their eschatological claims. Ancient history, too, furnishes us with examples of such euphoric, seemingly transhistorical elevations of hope for a better world of justice and peace, indeed hope for definitive solutions. We can think of the age of Pericles and his praise of Athenian democracy in Thucydides, or the era of Augustus and the golden age of poets (Virgil), with its idea that the Roman Empire was eternal: and yet both eras were already close to their decline.

How close hope and dejection are to each other in such euphoric moments of history was shown by the Peloponnesian War in Greece and by the invasion of the barbarians in Rome. Likewise, 1789 was soon followed by the incarceration of the optimistic philosophers of the French Revolution (like Condorcet); the triumph of liberal democracy was followed by the terrorist dictatorship of Robespierre and finally by the imperial autocracy of Napoleon.

Realpolitik Instead of Ideology

The ambivalence of those earlier epochal changes, with their euphoria that soon gave way to disillusionment, applies also to our century. Were not the revolutionary events at the end of World War I supposed to be the great hour of democracy? Yet they led to a state of continual conflict between the new nation states, to the rapid smothering of democracy by authoritarian and totalitarian ideologies and systems. And the hoped-for liberation of 1945, despite the enormous changes that went hand in hand with the overthrow of Fascism and National Socialism, did not bring in its wake either the end of previous history or of dictatorships and ideologies. On the contrary: old and new ideals of "one world" accompanied the recasting of Europe and the world following World War II, leading to fateful misjudgments and illusions. In actual fact the renaissance of democracy in Western Europe was able to succeed—one may say unfortunately—only by virtue of the intensely debated determination to pursue a policy of joint defense and European self-assertion in close cooperation with the United States, necessitating a clear separation, even confrontation, of the political systems through the division of Europe and the balance of (nuclear) terror.

The eventual turnaround in the Soviet Union is thus not conceivable without Western rearmament, which confronted Moscow with limits on how far it could go, prompted its withdrawal from Afghanistan, and reinforced its desire for Western economic aid in view of the impending unified European Community (EC) home market. It also gave rise to Moscow's need for security cooperation instead of a politically costly policy of occupation and confrontation. The other essential precondition for the transformations of 1989—the basic striving for freedom and a Western living standard in the East bloc—was already in existence: as was seen on June 17, 1953, in East Berlin, in 1956 in Budapest, and in 1968 in Prague. The difference was that in those days the Red Army did not keep quiet, as it did in 1989.

What made the breakthrough possible was Gorbachev's and Shevardnaze's understanding of what was necessary and inevitable, along with the role played by personalities (in the West, Reagan and Bush, Schmidt and Kohl). And so realpolitik instead of ideology, as Gorbachev put it at the meeting in the Caucasus on July 16, 1990, that was decisive for the united Germany's membership in NATO, did not mean the disappearance or end of politics, but rather the striving for an expedient realization of mutual interests, with the common recognition of the "right of all peoples to freely determine their fate" (joint declaration Gorbachev and Kohl in Bonn on June 13, 1989).

In the current developments, we are thus dealing with changes and continuities, with refuted as well as tried-and-true ideas and values, with qualities of revolution as well as rebirth, as ideological dictatorships are removed and liberal democracies constructed. The renaissance of democracy that is now occurring also in Central and Eastern Europe is building on long-suppressed historical experiences, as evidenced by the speed and irresistibility of the revolutionary events and the implementation of multi-party systems in place of totalitarian regimes. All these things had been demanded in the conflict from the outset of the cold War, and indeed from the beginning of the "bourgeois" revolutions of 1848 and 1918.

The German case, especially, reveals something else very clearly: we are still dealing with the consequences of war and National Socialism. The most recent and (one hopes) final chapter is one that will see the national desire for unification tied into a European-Atlantic framework, with a postnational, human rights orientation and with the defusion of interstate and national antagonisms. The new age does indeed carry much history with it. This history is in equal measures a source of strength and a burden. It is also a learning process with the goal of establishing the primacy of democracy and of Europe. It combines self-determination and the principle of tolerance as the guarantees of civil society, in the pursuit of a peaceful order based on the principle of compromise both domestically (in democracy) and externally (in Europe).

Civil Society

Historians—who tend to be backward looking prophets—can venture to interpret epochs of change in light of comparative insights: of course with the necessary modesty of someone with keen hindsight, and not with the claim to be pointing out the future course, a claim that was put forth especially by nationalist historians of the likes of Heinrich von Treitschke. More appropriate is the critical skepticism of Jacob Burckhardt in *Reflections on History.*

And so far as social scientists are concerned, their claim to be thinking ahead must not be confused with prognosis; this claim remains doubtful, indeed it can have a misleading effect, especially if it is reinforced and vulgarized by the media and mass communications. The reactions of individuals and societies, peoples and states to pressure or seduction—reactions that include so-called self-fulfilling prophecies—can be grasped and interpreted by scholarship at best only after the fact.

Wolfgang Mantl has succinctly outlined what seems politically desirable and up for debate if we are to secure and make use of the great opportunities of the present in a way that will hold out promise for the future. He also identifies what should be avoided and prevented.[1] The unification of Germany is one of the central elements in overcoming the division of Europe, and it also has world-political consequences. It may be a threatening prospect to her neighbors, but it poses no danger if it takes place primarily as a European and democratic process and not, as after 1933, as a path divergent from the West *(Sonderweg)*—quite apart from the enormous economic and social burdens the Federal Republic is taking on.

I repeat: this transformation in Europe is not simply a "miracle," nor should one wait for miracles in the future. In contrast to the breathtaking speed of the changes—which politicians and analysts have been unable to keep up with—what comes next is a further, lengthy testing of the innovations: a process like "drilling hard boards" (Max Weber) or "piecemeal engineering" (Karl Popper), with unpredictable timetables and costs.

We must still reckon with internal and external threats to the kind of open, civil society that achieved a complete breakthrough in all of Europe for the first time in 1989. A look at the member states of the UN and the Third World reveals that this kind of society still remains in a minority position: a continuing problem of economic as well as political and intellectual-moral development. Democracy as a form of government means limited government—through limitations on power, the separation of powers, and supranational ties. It is the always fragile, always contested polity of self-restraint and the understanding that humans are imperfect, just as dictatorship is the form of government that arises from ideological arrogance. The prerequisite for the success of democracy is and remains the possibility of a cosmopolitan, civil society, not the replacement of one ideology by another.

The Janus Face of the French Revolution Today: On Understanding Modern Revolution

I

The image of Janus, the ancient Roman god of doors and arches and the protector of the home, shows a double face. His gaze is turned inward and outward, he is the god of the entrance, to whom all beginnings are consecrated, but at the same time he is also the symbol for the distinction between war and peace. The Janus head describes a double deformity, where twins with two fully formed faces are joined at the back of their heads—something terrifying, a human tragedy, but one certainly found in nature. So much for the ancient historian in me.

If I now speak of the Janus face of modern revolutions, I have this symbolism in mind. It describes the ambivalence, the ambiguity, and the reverse side of the concept of revolution—the fact that it can be used in so many and contradictory ways, which also leaves it open to abuse. Though revolution initially appeared in modern thought as a neutral, scientific concept of radical change, it was then increasingly used in history and politics in a positive, eventually even impassioned way. In fact, when the two-hundredth anniversary of the French Revolution was commemorated not only in France, but all over the world, the celebrations were quite enthusiastic, with the sense almost that this was a world event and world idea. In any case, the celebration was far more emphatic than it had been for the anniversary of the American Revolution, which had occurred a short time before the French, or for England's Glorious Revolution of 1688, even though both of them had paved a far more direct and continuous path toward the liberal, parliamentary-democratic state. By contrast, the much-invoked historic moment of 1789 was quite ambivalent in terms of its consequences, and it remains so to this day.

This ambivalence reveals the problematic connection between the great political and intellectual transformations at the turn of the nineteenth and twentieth centuries, with all their consequences, which have once again become a controversial topic in historical scholarship on revolutions. The English and American revolutions have prior importance not only in chronological terms, and this importance remains a fact even though the notion of the continuity of political development—and the impact of John Locke—has been questioned repeatedly as being a Whig Interpretation, by conservative historians like Herbert Butterfield (1931) or Jonathan Clarke (1985). Hugh Trevor Roper said all that needed to be said about these controversies concerning England's revolution (see *Frankfurter Allgemeine Zeitung*, November 2, 1988).

An outstanding intellectual contribution to what is probably the most important continuing controversy about 1789 and its consequences, the work of the Israeli historian Jacob Talmon (1916–1980), has now become more pertinent and topical than ever before. In the 1930s, Talmon was a young student in Poland studying the French Revolution. Faced with the great terror regimes of National Socialism and Stalinism, he formulated the fundamental idea of his epochal work, *The Origins of Totalitarian Democracy*: namely, that the basic features of this kind of democracy as contained in the ideas of Rousseau, Robespierre, and Babeuf, already pointed toward the pseudodemocratic terror regimes of the twentieth century. Talmon traced this idea in two additional volumes on Socialist and National Socialist utopias (*Political Messianism* and *The Myth of the Nation and the Vision of Revolution*), taking his analysis all the way up to Mussolini, Hitler, and Lenin. In the introduction to the first volume (1951), Talmon juxtaposed the two manifestations of liberal and totalitarian democracy, bringing out the reciprocal relationship of a "totalitarianism of the right and of the left" and of "worldly and religious messianism." Related to this is another aspect that was the focus of Talmon's last, posthumous book: the constant tension and conflict between liberal and totalitarian revolutions.

Talmon was in fact the first to follow through on the basic idea he pursued indefatigably until his untimely death: totalitarian thought and action have a pseudodemocratic character, an insight that went back to his dismaying experiences in the late 1930s. As a concerned historian, he saw in the Stalinist show trials of 1937–38 and in the National Socialist policies of persecution an analogy to the terror phase of the French Revolution under Robespierre. He was referring to the creation in France of the compelling idea and terrible reality of totalitarian democracy, which is in fact the most radical form of dictatorship, all this rising under the banner of a great revolution to liberate peoples and nations. Of course, analogy or chronological precedence does not in any way carry the connotation of "model." In bringing together revolution, democracy, and dictatorship, Talmon united the heterogeneous elements that are of undiminished importance for a modern discussion of revolution that goes beyond its conventional (progressivist) glorification or (reactionary) condemnation.

Above all, this uniting of disparate elements reflects the profoundly confusing experience of the ambivalence of the concept of revolution, the Janus face of modern revolution itself. It reflects the fluctuation of revolution between the greatest liberation and the most abject subjugation of man, with the promise to resolve this contradiction in the utopia of a final solution to the fundamental problems of human life and political order through the identification of freedom with submission, of individual emancipation with collective community. In fact, to this day all totalitarian systems have invoked their own unique revolution, using it to mobilize the masses.

If we now turn to an examination of the classical concept of revolution, we find that its value today is indeed highly contested, on scholarly as well as political grounds. It starts with the problem of historical chronology: there has always been controversy over the application of the term to the religious wars and peasant wars that preceded the great revolutions of the seventeenth to the nineteenth centuries, and also to the authoritarian and totalitarian seizures of power in the course of the twentieth century. Moreover, especially in view of the new socioeconomic and technical forms of change and upheaval in our age of mass society, the conventional understanding of revolution is increasingly seen as scientifically useless or is even cast into doubt altogether.

Apart from objections raised by history and the social sciences, the political questions about the concept of revolution are no less serious and embattled. This applies to the tendency toward a universal generalization of the revolutionary slogan, concurrent with the development of the Third World and its unending series of putsches and dictatorships. But it applies also to the question of the Stalinist development of Communism. Despite its adherence to the Marxist-Leninist claim of revolution, Communism deviated far from its origins and, especially in the Soviet superpower, for decades turned into an ossified state-bureaucratic dictatorship. Is it not the case, then, that we are in fact faced with the obsolescence or dying off of the original idea of revolution and, at the same time, with new forms of change all over the world, whether or not, in the fashion of our times, we wish to call them "postrevolutionary"?

Of course nobody can deny that at least the concept of revolution is now used all over the world, more widely than ever before, as a key political term, indeed as a dominant battle cry or a terror-inspiring slogan. Now, however, it not only describes the abrupt change in the policies of individuals and movements, in forms of governments and social conditions, but it also, and increasingly, refers to the sort of profound long-term changes that were earlier subsumed under the concept of the industrial revolution, and that are today proclaimed in all areas of modernization (not least in the arts)—all the way to the often mentioned revolution in expectations and needs. With the elevation of revolution to a household word, often synonymous with modernization, we can speak, if not of an age of revolution, at least of an age of the concept of revolution.

II

In the history of the great political concepts, that of revolution emerged, of course, rather late. Antiquity understood profound changes in history and politics as a cycle of things both natural and human. And so it was also with the cycle of constitutions, their transformation and degeneration: from the state of nature to monarchy, to tyranny, to aristocracy, to oligarchy, to democracy, to anarchy, which is again a kind of natural state and begins a new cycle. So long as this cyclical theory held sway, the Latin word *revolutio*—"turning back" or "change"—could not evolve the very meaning it would take on in the modern age in conjunction with the idea of progress toward new forms and definitive solutions: the sense, precisely, of "revolutionary progress."

A point of departure were Renaissance ideas about power, in which the word *rivoluzione* (in Machiavelli and others) denoted political conflict, a change in who held the reins of power. Another point of departure is found in the application of scientific concepts to history and politics, beginning with Copernicus's epochal theory of the movement of the heavenly bodies, published in his 1543 work *De revolutionibus orbium coelestium*. It was in keeping with the astrologically inclined thought of the sixteenth century that a quasi-scientific relationship was subsequently established between the upheavals on earth and revolutions in the heavens. From there it was only one more step to the double meaning that revolution took on in the modern age: as an impetuous movement toward new, modern structures and relationships of power, and also a turning back from the corrupt circumstances of the present, a restoration of the uncorrupted conditions of our origin and their projection into a future conceived of in idealized terms, a return to the golden age.

Hence both meanings, as different as they were (one progressivist, one restorationist), contained the idea of an end time, a final order whose new relationships of power would eventually lead to the complete abolition of rule by some people over others. It was the declaration of war on the corrupted present—from a progressive or conservative view—that infused the great revolutions of the modern period with their idealistic fervor and sense of mission, and that was able to rally the masses for or against them: with the result that the political change could be elevated to a great, historically necessary upheaval.

This happened first in seventeenth-century England, where the development of parliament and a party system went furthest in advancing the political demands for constitutional and human rights. While some historians, especially in the Marxist camp, have tried to label the religious wars of the Reformation period as an "early bourgeois revolution," it was the drawn-out English civil war after 1642 that gave the modern concept of revolution a decisive boost. All forms of upheaval that the concept would subsequently come to include were already present: the abrupt fall of the government and the (monarchical) polity along with the execution of the king, rule by parliament and military dictatorship—all the way up to eschatological expectations of final political and social conditions. Finally, the Glorious Revolution of 1688 also contained the positive experience of a successful new constitutional order, which, in its great compromise as a constitutional monarchy with human rights and the separation of powers, sought to put into effect the achievements of limited government.

Characteristically enough, the justification for what was in that sense a successful revolution, one that simultaneously put an end to the radical and destructive consequences of revolutionary fighting, was not only progressivist in nature. The event was also seen as an emphatic return to the genuine, old constitution of England (the thirteenth-century Magna Charta): a restoration, that is, of "original liberty," including the right of resistance in the case of unjust and arbitrary tyranny. John Locke had proclaimed such a right at the end of the Glorious Revolution, and he was to have enormous influence on all subsequent revolutionary and constitutional movements, especially in America and France.

Revolution, advocated or opposed, thus became the great fashionable term of the eighteenth and nineteenth centuries. At first it served the liberal, then the democratic, and finally the socialist movements, as a battle cry and a terror-inspiring slogan for those on the road to better domestic systems and also for the national independence of new states in their fight against foreign rule. When understood as an international concept, it also served the imperialist expansion of the French Revolution into the Napoleonic hegemony over Europe. Finally, today it is in the service of Marxist ideas of world revolution as the liberation from old and new class rule and the attainment of communist world supremacy.

Here, at the latest, is where the different and opposing paths of the modern understanding of revolution diverged fundamentally and in principle. The concept of revolution has always been open to many interpretations and uses, and this has allowed it to be manipulated to this day by the most diverse political currents. Since the end of the nineteenth century, however, two great currents of thought on revolution have emerged above all the others, standing and acting diametrically opposed to each other: a liberal-democratic current, and a totalitarian-democratic one, the latter in truth a dictatorial understanding of revolution.

III

This difference in the understanding of revolution, one of world-historical importance, had actually showed itself to be already present in the character and course of the American and French Revolutions. A striking example is the case of human and civic rights, for the implementation of which these two revolutions had been launched. In America this led to a concrete, practical implementation within the framework of a constitutional and governmental system, with separated powers and safeguards against an imbalance of power. In France it gave rise to the abstract, perfectionist proclamation of ideals that were time and again (from the Jacobins to Napoleon) perverted as ideologies and refuted by the reality of dictatorial rule, in the name of, but in fact contrary to, the principles of liberty, equality, and fraternity.

The political implementation of these two revolutions further reveals the fundamental difference between a parliamentary-representative, pluralistic concept of democracy of the Anglo-American type, and the utopian, violent idea of a democracy fully identical with the people. The latter draws on Rousseau's notion of the *volonté générale* to compel total unity at the expense of the diversity and freedom of the citizens.

Even in the French Revolution, the thoughts of Montesquieu, as earlier those of John Locke, worked in the direction of a representative multiparty democracy that was pluralistic and had a separation of powers. But under the spell of Rousseau, the subsequent course of the Revolution—and after it the radical European idea of revolution held by the socialist Left, as later also by the nationalist Right—unfolded in the spirit of an antipluralist, total integration of society or the nation as the community to which all else was to be subordinated. The result was an institutionalization of the revolutionary one-party dictatorship through seduction, terror, and forced uniformity.

In Germany, where Hegel, then a nineteen-year-old student at Tübingen (with Hölderlin and Schelling), had welcomed the Revolution as a "magnificent sunrise," its terrorist and imperialist perversion soon made the initial enthusiasm give way to a homegrown nationalism. That process was particularly visible in Fichte's quick transformation from an enthusiast of the Revolution to the ideologue of Germanicism. In fact the revolutionary development did not simply replace absolutism, it actually destroyed the road to a liberal democracy, so recently won through struggle, and brought on Napoleonic imperialism—while simultaneously unleashing modern nationalism.

The subsequent development of the totalitarian revolutionary tradition was particularly dangerous and seductive in those movements (like National Socialism) that, under the changed technological conditions and possibilities of the industrial age of the twentieth century, were brutally successful in seeking to establish their own form of revolution by welding nationalistic (racist) and socialist elements and impulses into a totalitarian seizure of power. This was a new kind of revolution, but at the same time one that had affinities to the Communist seizure of power, with its radically democratic as well as totalitarian demands. While the three classic revolutionary states of the West developed in a liberal-democratic direction, the other states, in their attempts at revolution, often got stuck in authoritarian or dictatorial forms.

The truth is that the upheavals of our century cannot simply be understood with the existing philosophical and literary criteria for an optimistic theory of revolution in the classic sense of the English, American, and French models. The distinction between "good" revolution and "evil" counterrevolution is becoming blurred. Events continue to be determined not so much by romanticized popular uprisings in the manner of the legendary storming of the Bastille or the bourgeois revolutions of 1848, but instead by a modern technique of the seizure of power by determined minorities and cadre parties. Modern seizures of power (like those of Lenin in 1917 and Hitler in 1933) can unfold in different ways, can take on and use putschist or pseudolegal forms without thus qualifying themselves from the outset as reactionary or progressive. And an assessment of the antitotalitarian revolutions of 1989 (see the last essay in this volume) raises new problems altogether.

IV

It is particularly revealing to examine the events that, under the battle cry of a "German" or a "national" revolution, led to the most severe rupture in modern German history when the National Socialists seized power. This political upheaval took place in such a radically comprehensive way, with such serious ramifications, and especially in such a stunningly short period of time that it far surpassed the model of Italian Fascism which, for its part, had modeled itself on the French Revolution when it boasted of a new era on its triumphal gateways (even in Libya).

Certainly in some respects—and applying the old scheme—the German case could also appear as a counterrevolution. In addition to the national revolution, the "legal revolution" was invoked to cloak and sanction the countless violations of the law and acts of violence between January 1933 and the bloody purge of June 30, 1934 (with deliberate misrepresentation, the latter was spoken of as the "Röhm putsch" and the "second revolution" that had to be eliminated in the interest of Hitler's legal, authentic revolution). To be sure, Goebbels had declared emphatically that 1933 would strike 1789 from the annals of history. He was referring above all to human rights, which were in fact never violated more cruelly than under Hitler (and under Stalin). But at the same time the National Socialists did this in the seemingly unstoppable manner and the comprehensive claim of revolutionaries who were promising a new order and a new man. The revealing contemporary slogans of "revolutionary inhumanity" they used to numb the public: The end sanctifies the means, and *Wo gehobelt wird, fallen Späne* (roughly, you can't make omelets without breaking eggs).

Of all days, it was July 14, 1933—the day on which the French celebrate the legendary storming of the Bastille as a symbol of revolt against absolutism—that saw passage of a catalogue of radical laws intended to permanently enshrine the National Socialist seizure of power in political as well as ideological terms. Foremost was the establishment of a one-party state through the Law against the New Formation of Parties, but there was also the sanctioning of "confiscation of the property of enemies of the people and the state," which afterwards legalized arbitrary confiscations. There were the restrictive laws on the Constitution of the Protestant Church and the Concordat with the Vatican. Especially ideological and revolutionary in nature were the Law on the Re-formation of the Peasantry and (related to population and race policy) the Law on the Prevention of Defective Offspring, as well as the Law on the Revocation of Naturalization and the Deprivation of German Citizenship. Finally, a Law on Plebiscites established the pseudoplebiscitarian course of the totalitarian one-party regime. What the laws of July 14, 1933, decreed as the "completion of the revolution" was sealed after Hindenburg's death in August 1934, when the army and the civil servants swore an oath of loyalty to Hitler personally. The regime was also pseudodemocratically elevated through the first of those "plebiscites" that were staged with predetermined results on five occasions between 1934 and 1938, as total acclamations of the conformist mobilization of society and as a form of self-affirmation.

Apart from the international policy of appeasement and a domestic trend toward dictatorship in Europe, which brought Hitler success and recognition and fundamentally overturned the balance of power, the underestimation of his revolutionary demands and potential was to have particularly fateful consequences. Because they saw such seizures of power as merely reactionary, contemporaries misjudged their modern, powerfully attractive character, and failed to see that they were populist mass movements with a charismatic leader. Incidentally, this is also true of the "old-new" interpretation of the National Socialist revolution as being primarily an anti-Bolshevist counterrevolution (Ernst Nolte), a view that trivializes its momentous self-conception as a pseudoscientific and biologistic revolution of race war and race domination.

Such misinterpretations were and are possible because, and as long as, the concept of revolution is shaped and colonized by the myth of the good revolution—whether on the French model or following the Leninist version. This is a mythologizing of revolution, an understanding that also, for moral and ideological reasons, angrily rejects the comparability of dictatorships of the Left and of the Right. It has the same logical flaw as the attempt to play down the basic totalitarian features in both variations by referring to the profound intellectual and qualitative differences between them. But the precise ideological difference between dictatorships of the Left and the Right is not a decisive objection, if the loftiest goals are used to justify the most inhuman means—if, that is, the form of rule and its consequences for those who are ruled and affected by it are comparable. With its emphatically revolutionary and mass democratic striking power, National Socialism in Germany proved itself superior to both the democratic republic and the dictatorial competition of the Communists. The Communist dictatorship in Russia and National Socialism drove hundreds of thousands into exile—among them many important Russian and German artists of the 1920s and 1930s; the official art of the regimes was inferior to émigré art, even if it posed for a while as revolutionary art or fed off the latter.

Here again we are confronted with the contentious question about the use of the concept of revolution. One could reject its scholarly use altogether, because its definition is vague and the phenomena that are compared are too different, but also because of its many incendiary abuses (Eugen Weber). One could consider speaking only in the neutral and positivist sense of seizures of power. If one adheres to the current usage, however, which anyway cannot be stopped, that leaves only one option: applying the concept of revolution, despite many differences, to all far-reaching political upheavals, regardless of whether they occur under the banner of a leftist, rightist, or any other kind of ideology, or no ideology at all, and go hand in hand with social changes of varying intensity. Beyond that revolution should also be applied, as it continues to be, to major, long-term, and far-reaching processes of change—industrial and social processes, changes of development and modernization.

It is undeniable that in both respects National Socialism had revolutionary qualities. It is hard to imagine that it would be possible to seize power more swiftly and implement a system of rule more quickly and comprehensively than the National Socialists did. David Schoenbaum has called it a revolution of new means and ends, while Joachim Fest has interpreted the phenomenon of Hitler as a specifically German form of revolution. As a new type of seizure of power, National Socialism has almost typological significance, because in 1933–34 it illustrated with special clarity the various stages of the process in terms of a sociology of revolution, in comparison with the Fascist and the Leninist seizures of power. In all these cases, conscious and emphatic use was made of new instruments of terror, of mass suggestion and mass communication, of control and coercion. Only the February Revolution of 1917 would seem to be a revolution of the older type, along the lines of the classic revolution sociology of scholars like Crane Brinton, Karl Griewank, and Hannah Arendt, for example. Applying a more restrictive terminology, it would make sense to call the Bolshevik October Revolution a seizure of power of the new type. Even with a more broadly inclusive concept of revolution, which as an everyday concept has primarily emotional and polemical meaning, its application not only to Socialism and Communism but also to Fascism and National Socialism can be entirely justified if one considers their epoch-making effect and their aftershocks domestically and in world politics. This holds true even if one doesn't go so far as to speak one-sidedly of an "epoch of Fascism" (Ernst Nolte).

In forming his ideology and program, while he was writing *Mein Kampf*, Hitler was guided from the outset by the idea that the nontraditional, nonconservative, nonbourgeois approach of his movement was the real source of strength behind its effect on the masses, especially among the young generation. In this respect he differed from his left-wing critics and right-wing competitors. Characteristic of this was the fact that National Socialism had success both in traditional circles and in radical circles. Symptomatic was the ambivalence, the inseparable interrelationship of traditional and revolutionary attitudes and convictions. They appeared almost always simultaneously and in combination in most leading figures of National Socialism, as well. We can leave open how much importance should be accorded to the claim of a legal or national revolution, which was a vitally important maneuver for deceiving all groups, from the right to the left of the political spectrum. What might almost be called a dialectical interlinking of the claim to tradition and revolution, domestic and foreign policy, theory and practice—accounts for the extraordinary attraction and effectiveness of National Socialist politics in an age of transition from a society of liberal notables to a democratic mass society.

This characteristic joining of traditional and revolutionary elements strikes me as more important for the political and ideological attraction of the National Socialist system than its frequently invoked "polycratic" structure. What follows are some considerations to support this view.

First, the basic idea of National Socialism, namely the reconciliation of the workers to the national state, went to the core of the problem of the age. It has retained its epochal importance to this day, if we consider the socialism of the developing countries, and the continually propagated "third way" between communism and capitalism.

Second, the basic notion of a racial structuring and grading of human-kind represents a radical alternative not only to the liberal-humanitarian idea of world civilization but also to the prevailing idea of the national state. It is based on the conviction that racism is a world-revolutionary principle that will replace traditional nationalism and will determine the course of history in keeping with the racially superior nation's right to living space *(Lebensraum)*. This is where the idea of mission that informed National Socialist domestic and foreign policy had its roots.

Third, the social Darwinist approach contained in the basic principle of National Socialism exerted its effects, once again, in both directions. As the assertion of the superior right of the strongest, it corresponded to the conservative theory of politics, which essentially holds that men make history. But the basic pessimistic tone of social Darwinism—which also shaped anti-Semitism with its evocation of the supposed threat of imminent ruin through foreign influences—was virtually turned upside down and revolutionized when the theory was made into a politically active ideology: it became the driving force of totalitarian *Machtpolitik* and the racist expansion of power.

Fourth, National Socialist ideas on the structure of society contained a characteristic combination of conservative cultural romanticism and eco-nomic-technological progressivism. Here, too, the ideology of National Socialism profited from strong contemporary trends, which praised indus-trialization and technicalization as a new romanticism and glorified the worker—as in Ernst Jünger's book of the same title—as the embodiment of a new national community. Of course this amounted to a grotesque distortion of the class structure in the modern industrial state. But as an alternative to the by no means realistic ideology of class warfare, it con-tributed significantly to taming as well as mobilizing the population.

Fifth, this combination of opposites appeared almost sloganlike when the most modern mass media were used and the techniques of mass rallies were employed, as for example at highly traditionalist, agrarian-romantic events like the National Farmers' Day (Reichsbauerntag) on the Bücke-berg, but also at the declaration of "total war" in the Berlin Sportpalast.

This body of instruments and techniques included the masterful arrangement of a mass liturgy. It also possessed the qualities and effectiveness of a political religion, with fanatic believers and a pseudo-Germanic or pseudo-Christian leadership cult, which George Mosse has described as a "nationalization of the masses." The grounding of National Socialism in antimodernist, anti-industrial currents of the nineteenth century (as emphasized by Fritz Stern) was actually balanced by the cult of technology and efficiency, which found expression in avant garde undertakings like the construction of the autobahns, the Volkswagen, and the national radio, in the masterful orchestration of public life, and in Hitler's much-admired insight into revolutionary forms of warfare. The rapid switching from one perspective to the other was one of the secrets of National Socialism's success, for it constantly threw the assessments and expectations of friends and foes off balance.

Sixth, the combining of a mystical political religion with the worship of technological success, of an old German peasant romanticism with a modern mass view, or of the Socialist May Day with a National Socialist romanticism of the worker—such a mixture fulfilled its function in uniting opposites and radiating its influence in all directions. That is also true of the concept of a Germanic Reich of the German Nation, which Hitler outlined in a secret talk to future leaders at the Sonthofen Ordensburg in 1937, on the threshold of war. His goals of racialism and the ideology of living space led to a design for rule that was historically dressed up and global in scope. It was no less revolutionary than the impulse of the national state had been 140 years earlier, which had radically transformed states and altered international relations.

The deeply traditional element may be seen in the almost mystical elevation of the concept of the Reich. Yet this vague concept—already during the history of the second German Reich it had swung back and forth with much ambivalence between an old-German, conservative understanding of the idea of empire and an imperial one—was perfectly suited for the plans and dreams of world conquest, which aimed to smash the existing system of states and set up new forms of political life and political organization.

Whatever records of National Socialist thinking, planning, and action we may examine, we will always encounter this fundamental characteristic, which makes it impossible to solve the problem of how to assess this phenomenon by reference to the simple formula that Fascism equals counterrevolution. In this context the following distinction is crucial: while Italian Fascism sought to create the strongest and largest possible state in the spirit of the Roman past, (German) National Socialism saw in the state merely the technically perfect instrument for organizing the superior-race empire of the future that would revolutionize world politics. At stake were not only traditional ambitions of state power in the manner of prewar imperialism but also the claim to be implementing and fulfilling a new world principle. Though some deny this revolutionary claim—in my view, mistakenly—there is no doubt that it mobilized unexpected forces and was put into practice in a way that had never been imagined. It led to the most terrible fanaticism and destruction in all of history. This, too, sets limitations for a general theory of Fascism, and it is precisely National Socialism that does not fit into the theory. For such a theory falls silent in the face of the dimensions that account for the enormous impact of National Socialism and its extreme brutality: the revolutionary aspect of racism, the idea of living space, the totalitarian ideal of domination and of the leader. This is also what continues to lend justification and importance to research into totalitarianism. This research, modifying and carrying on older work— from Franz and Sigmund Neumann to Hannah Arendt and C. J. Friedrich—searches, under changing circumstances, for totalitarian elements that are still active in modern-day movements.

V

As we have seen, it was owing to the conventional and romantic concept of revolution that of all the great changes at the end of World War I and in its wake, only the Russian events were classified as a revolution. The Central European upheavals between 1918 and 1920 were at best a mixture of revolution and counterrevolution, while the Fascist and National Socialist seizures of power were primarily counterrevolutions. This classification reflects not only the helplessness of contemporaries in the face of the specific revolutionary claim of the Bolsheviks and the Communists in general, who used their revolutionary slogans primarily as battle cries (for the revolutionary propaganda of the nineteenth century had done much the same), but it also shows the difficulty in recognizing and explaining the novel phenomenon of a "revolution from the Right." In Fascism and National Socialism, especially, we are dealing not merely with a revolutionary countermovement but with the kind of modern seizure of power first proclaimed by George Sorel in 1907 (who had equal influence on Mussolini and Lenin). Such a seizure of power, using the tools of organization, is able to capture and mobilize the masses through the myth of violence. It takes the stage with all-embracing ideological and pseudoreligious pretensions, and works with the charismatic appeal of an omniscient leader and the binding force of a cultic ritual.

It is this new technique of winning and controlling power—behind which is either the idea of world revolution or war with a focus on the total state—that does make seizures of power from the Left and the Right comparable, regardless of their emphatically opposite ideologies. And this was also the meaning of the concept of totalitarianism that was coined as early as 1923 in the fight against Fascism. Of course, to this day it has met with vehement criticism from those who, for ideological reasons, consider dictatorship from the Left and the Right as incomparable as revolution, putsch, or counterrevolution.

One might ask, under these circumstances, whether it would not be better to avoid the concept of revolution altogether, considering how highly charged it is historically and ideologically and how it has been abused politically. But its widespread use already rules out such a step. At least the concept of revolution should be employed in a way that excludes, as much as possible, preconceived notions and political prejudices. In the more restricted sense it could be used as a value-neutral term for all upheavals that involve far-reaching changes in political structures, and personnel and social changes that cannot be immediately grasped in their full extent or adequately characterized. In the broader sense it could be used as a concept that also describes unforeseen changes, such as anticolonial or cultural and sociological transformations. Moreover, in view of the long-term repercussions of the war and the decisions of the postwar period, we might speak of an epoch of revolutionary movements, especially in the colonial world. The upheavals of World War I and its aftermath have given the epoch its stamp: upheavals in Russia and Central Europe, Fascist and authoritarian seizures of power. This was followed by the decisive event, the seizure of power by National Socialism, that was to dominate the 1930s. Finally, there were the aftereffects of 1945: the political and ideological split-up of Europe and a new division of the world.

And so even in the second half of our century the problem of revolution is as topical and pressing as ever, while the claim to revolution, the revolutionary slogan, is now more widely spread throughout the world than ever before. Of course we can still observe a major difference from the period of the classic revolutions. One can draw the chronological dividing line as early as the year 1917, with its three significant legacies to our own recent history: the Communist claim of world revolution, the entrance of the United States into world politics, and the decline of the European nation-states as the bearers of the liberal-democratic revolution. Alternatively the line can be drawn with the world-political change of 1945: along with the bipolar framework of two superpowers and the division of the world into supranational camps and blocs, it brought, simultaneously, a flood of new states and an endless series of putsches, all of which, like the countless liberation movements, have seen themselves as revolutions. In addition we have witnessed the rise of China and the possible schism within the Communist camp and, finally, the new religious vigor imparted to the concept of revolution through the activization of Islam and other fundamentalist movements.

As we examine the fundamentalist movement, we come face to face once again with the conviction of revolutionaries that they are the true vehicle of the historical process, of a higher power that is creating a new world. "All power to the imagination," was also what the irrational slogans of the students in Paris and elsewhere demanded in the magical year of 1968. In actuality, however, from the time Marxism emerged, the belief in a utopia, a belief that has given the idea of revolution its strength, has been yielding to the realization that long-term processes of universal change and modernization are operating in the direction of a world civilization. The trend is toward the kind of civilization that was foreseen by the Christian-liberal philosopher of history, Arnold Toynbee.

The revolutionary age is continuing and at the same time has been broken. Characteristic of this is the contradictory development of Latin America, which even in most recent times has barely moved beyond the intermediate stage of colonial and developing countries, with a half-industrial, half–agrarian-feudal structure. Certainly the development of the great economic potential that is available especially in Brazil, Venezuela, and Mexico has made noticeable progress, as have social and political stabilization in a democratic sense. The number of palace revolts has declined, and the fall of the Argentine dictator Péron in 1955 was followed by that of other despots. As a result, parliamentary-constitutional regimes became possible in the 1960s, though usually with an authoritarian flavor. The growth of a bourgeois middle class has surely helped these regimes to put down democratic roots.

However, the upper class and the military have continued to vacillate. In addition there is still the radical appeal to the masses from the Left and the Right, with the slogans of both National Socialism and Socialism. That appeal was characteristic of Peronism, and it appeared again during the Falklands war that was launched by the Argentine military regime. Amid the up and down of changing regimes, the call for order and dictatorship could be heard, especially in the 1970s. One example was the bloody overthrow of Allende's leftist regime in Chile by a ruthless military junta, which remained in power from 1973 to 1989. Yet despite economic crises and growing social misery, the Socialists and Communists have been unable to play a more substantial role in most Latin American countries. The conception of revolution, even among workers and unions, has been so thoroughly seized upon by emphatically nationalistic Socialist movements (Right-Left movements, so to speak) that purely leftist revolutionary movements have succeeded only in Cuba (since 1959), briefly in Chile (in 1973), and more recently in Sandinista Nicaragua. The Marxist-Leninist model did not fit, even though the ideological revolutionary propaganda of a vocal intelligentsia, especially at the (neglected) universities, made heavy use of it.

Nevertheless the impact of the Cuban revolution and the influence it radiated were global in scope. In its wake appeared the followers of the highly influential strategy and theory of a political and military struggle for power that was carried on by guerrillas and by means of terrorism. Alongside Maoism, this enormous influence of Castroism on all of Latin America and the Third World, as well as on the Western European intelligentsia, constituted (especially from the end of the 1960s on) an important element of domestic protest movements—ideological and terrorist—against the values of Western democracies and societies.

To be sure, Castro's rule itself was based primarily on the struggle against a demonized U.S. imperialism, which he traded, of course, for economic and military dependence on Moscow and occasionally on Beijing. But as a figure symbolic of the idea of revolution, Castro, together with Che Guevara, at times had unique stature among leftist intellectuals in the West. Alongside the Islamic-Arabic idea of revolution associated with Khomeini, Gadhafi, and the PLO, he remains today a potent force and impetus for revolutionary movements and regimes as far from Cuba as Africa.

All this certainly meant a shift, a change in meaning, possibly a new chapter in the manipulation of the concept of revolution. Its profound ambivalence has become more obvious to us than ever before. Among the catastrophic experiences of the age is this: the great hopes and promises that have spawned powerful revolutionary movements in the name of lofty ideas and comprehensive ideologies have in our century simultaneously caused the greatest destruction of civilization and ever-recurring barbarities and mass murders.

VI

Yet it would seem that individuals as well as nations—under the influence of hard times, injustices, and strong "leaders"—have little capacity to resist the very temptations and illusions that time and again lead to violent oppression. Above all, they appear unable to differentiate between the struggle for freedom and human dignity and the majority of revolutions that result in the exact opposite as they replace the old servitude with a new one, employing in the process the unbroken, old-and-new power of militant ideologies.

In the classical age of revolutions, the important distinction between liberal and dictatorial revolution was already often not made. It is unfortunate that even today too little attention is paid to it, as a look at the UN will show us: of its member states, more than two-thirds, after more or less bloody revolutions, have become dictatorships that lack freedom and human dignity, and promise more revolutions. At the same time all of them demonstratively hold up the banners and slogans of freedom, human welfare, and (especially today) democracy.

What is meant by freedom is thus an essential criterion for judging any revolution—as a movement or a regime. The newest specialized studies of the various concepts and their reality (by van Heuvel and by Repgen) have shown that the totalitarianism of the French Revolution did not replace absolutism; it ousted a representative democracy that had so very recently been won as the result of struggle. To be sure, totalitarian dictatorship in the name of democracy, terror in the name of freedom, virtue, and reason, lasted only fourteen months (during Jacobin rule, from June 2, 1793, to July 27, 1794). But it was already the sort of blood-drenched reality we have witnessed more recently in Iran under the "Islamic revolution."

The way in which Robespierre linked his professed "despotism of freedom" simultaneously with the very concepts of the greatest virtue and the greatest terror was strikingly paradigmatic. In the name of virtue and terror the courts handed down tens of thousands of death sentences, to say nothing of the other victims of this revolutionary step of equating total rule with freedom, national greatness with a humanitarian mission abroad.

In spite of this experience, the idea of revolution as the source of legitimacy for a form of rule in which the utopian goal sanctifies the means has, to this day, exerted its influence as a suggestive model and a myth, indeed as a substitute for religion in many ideologies and political doctrines of salvation. For example, there is the (intellectually highly fascinating) fiction of a perfect identity of state, society, and human beings. This is the totalitarian fiction that such unity is possible, in the sense of a perfect system and a true democracy, of freedom and, simultaneously, submission to society, party, the leader. Needless to say, we have experienced this fiction in a much more enduring form in the leftist and rightist revolutions of our century. It was this fiction that led Jakob Talmon to speak of the almost inescapable "iron law" that "causes revolutionary salvationist schemes to evolve into regimes of terror, and the promise of a perfect direct democracy to assume in practice the form of totalitarian dictatorship."

The Janus face of modern revolutions continues to look at us—it is inviting and encouraging, but also deceptive and warning. For long after the bloody failure of Fascism and National Socialism, and at a time of seemingly unstoppable ideological erosion in the Communist regimes, nationalist or fundamentalist ideas and movements are once again emerging powerfully for the purpose of mobilizing the masses politically and ideologically. And this trend is not limited to the Third World.

The age of susceptibility to political seduction has surely not come to an end, either in the Third World or here, in dictatorships or democracies. The call for freedom is heard more widely around the world than ever before, but as always with the potential for its revolutionary perversion into seemingly voluntary forms of subjection. The warning in Aesop's fable holds true for revolutionary as well as totalitarian seductions: "*Vestigia terrent,*" said the fox outside the lion's den. "I see that many tracks lead into it, but none come back out."

In our "century of refugees" (Kühnhardt) it continues to be a vital distinction whether revolutions end in dictatorial, persecuting states, or whether the number of asylum-granting, pluralistic democracies increases. These democracies do not leave human and civic rights to utopian promises, but strive, through reforms, to safeguard liberty, to anchor those rights firmly in the political culture and the constitutional spirit of the citizens. At least on this point one would hope that some lessons will be learned from the experiences of history, and that we will not glorify only men and deeds, movements and nations—as is, unfortunately, often the case with the French Revolution.

The Ideas and the Failure of Socialism

Today we are facing two important historical and political questions. First: what is the meaning of the accelerating decay of the experiment of socialism? Only a few years ago, especially in the form of Marxism-Leninism but also in various "national socialisms," it seemed to dominate two-thirds of the world's population. Now it is collapsing, especially in Europe, and is in retreat also in the Soviet Union; though, of course, it is continuing in China and parts of the Third World, which means that it still has about a third of the world's population in its grip. Does this decay signify above all an *economically* conditioned, temporary weakness, as de facto underdeveloped states undergo a transition toward modernization and democratization? Or is it the long-term, indeed the definitive decline of a *political* system of previously unknown dictatorial forms, first established (contrary to Marx's expectations) in Russia seventy-four years ago?

Second, and more important: to what extent are we also dealing with the decline of the *idea* of socialism, on which the system was based or which it emphatically invoked? Is this the historical refutation of both the possibility and the idea of socialism itself? Or is it only a temporary, though serious derailment in the effort to implement the "real existing socialism," which can still be carried on or resurrected in a different form? Now, after the de facto collapse, this new form of socialism continues to be proclaimed, sometimes more vigorously than before, as a utopian yet logical and vital necessity, especially in intellectual circles.

The History of an Idea: A Balance Sheet

If we look at the historical place of socialism and its development as an idea, there is a long-standing controversy over whether and to what extent its ideas, cast into such diverse and ambiguous forms, were originally part of the antidemocratic and even dictatorial forces that led to or made possible the age of totalitarian ideologies in our century. It is certainly true that socialism developed from the outset in fundamental opposition to economic and later political liberalism, which was an essential impulse in the antiabsolutist, liberal concept of the state. But at the same time, the ideas of modern socialism, ever since their inception at the end of the eighteenth and beginning of the nineteenth centuries, have been very closely bound up with basic demands of the modern idea of democracy.

And today, after more than 150 years of conflict between democratic and dictatorial currents in socialism, we are witnessing the attempt by hitherto Communist movements and ideologies to lay claim to the concept of "democratic socialism." They do this as a form of disguise, a means of deception, out of genuine conviction or as a chance, after the defeat of 1989, to undo the great schism of 1917.

Of course this maneuver all too easily ignores a century of deceptions and barbarities in the name of democratic socialism. For the problem of democratic freedoms in socialism has been the subject of serious ideological controversies ever since the establishment of the workers' parties. As early as the turn of the century those conflicts paved the way for the differentiation and eventual split of socialism into a democratic movement and an authoritarian-Communist one. Social democracy's self-definition as a nondictatorial, liberal socialism came into its own after World War I in the face of Lenin's dictatorial rule. And its fundamental opposition to Communist-dictatorial socialism, which played itself out in the worldwide conflicts between totalitarian and liberal versions of socialism after World War II, was also underscored by political programs, for example by the 1959 Godesberg Program of the Social Democratic Party (Sozialdemokratische Partei Deutschlands, or SPD) in West Germany. Thenceforth, democratic socialism referred to parties and doctrines that combined their commitment to liberal, constitutional, and pluralistic democracy with their readiness to cooperate politically with the "bourgeois" parties and with their adherence to nonviolent, legal reform pursued in an evolutionary manner.

This emphasis on the democratic and liberal component of socialism, in opposition to authoritarian and dictatorial approaches and driving forces, boiled down to the following questions: how and by what means was society to be changed, and how should its political form be constituted? The Leninist approach, in which the end justifies the means, was rejected. In fact the opposite position was taken: the means "de-justify" the end. This was a decision of fundamental importance, one that, notwithstanding all terminological fluctuation between socialism, communism, and social democracy, deeply concerned all of modern socialism and put it in question.

One cannot simply gloss over this decisive choice between a liberal (democratic) or dictatorial (state) path with the current slogan of "democratic socialism." One of the pioneers of the Polish revolution of 1980 to 1989, Wladyslaw Bartoszweski, went so far as to formulate the dilemma in these drastic terms: "During the Communist period we also lost the Social Democratic ideas." What has remained is the possibility of terminological deception that has political and ideological consequences. Ernst Günter Vetter, in an essay entitled "Der Charme der Heilsgewißheit" (The Charm of Certain Salvation; *Frankfurter Allgemeine Zeitung*, March 2, 1991), counts among the consequences the "repair work to a failed system" undertaken by intellectuals with the help of the slogan of democratic socialism.

In historical terms, socialism sees itself above all as a democratic movement, insofar as it was shaped by the political and philosophical idea of equality, and was linked to the political-social movement of emancipation and to the struggle for political participation by the lower classes. However, there were two fundamental differences between socialism and democratic liberalism: first, the socialist scale of demands and principles, which placed greater emphasis on equality before individual liberty; second, the method of implementing those demands, namely with guidance from the state or through the state. Revolutionary change of the political situation, if it was necessary, was considered a precondition of social reforms and of an equality that was grounded not only in the law but in economic and social life as well.

Most theorists of socialism have worked from the assumption that it is not enough to establish a legal, formal equality. Instead it is imperative to take equality seriously, which is unattainable so long as economic differences operate politically through the dominance of "ruling classes." Thus the starting point for change lies in the economic and social sphere. This is also the case in liberalism. In socialism, however, the emphasis is not on a free and harmonious interaction of social and economic forces, but on the engineering of equality through the economic communalization of the nation. At the beginning of this thinking stands the conviction that humans, as political beings, are socially and economically conditioned, which gives rise to the call for conscious regulation of this conditioning through social and governmental intervention. This means that at the outset there is already a potentially coercive, indeed totalitarian tendency.

Of course the intellectual development and the historical and political unfolding of socialist ideas occurred not only in different stages but also, from the outset, in different directions and systems. Marxism is by no means at the very beginning of this development, nor was it (as it claimed to be) the only viable option—even if it was eventually singled out and used as apparently the most self-contained, consistent, and elaborate formulation of socialist theory. Not only is it possible to trace numerous precursors of socialist thinking as far back as antiquity, to Plato's politeia, but these precursors also contributed important elements to the socialist-communist utopias at the beginning of the modern age, from Thomas More (*Utopia*, 1513) to Tommaso Campanella (*Città del sole*, 1602). All the same, it is, of course, true that only the social transformation at the beginning of the industrial revolution turned socialism into a political force and an "ideology" (in the modern, momentous sense of a political faith), much as it did with modern liberalism and democracy, and in fact more emphatically than either of these two. Here I shall mention only four variants or developmental stages of socialism.

1. After the prelude of the radical "levelers" in the English revolution of the seventeenth century, modern socialism was articulated in the course of the French Revolution in Babeuf's conspiratorial manifesto on the "Republic of the Equals" (1796). This republic was to be achieved through the abolition of private property and through class warfare directed against the attempts to consolidate the waning Revolution on the basis of a propertied bourgeoisie. The basic attitude was this: political revolution means nothing without a social revolution. And so we already read in Babeuf (who was executed in 1797): "The French Revolution is only the herald of another revolution, far greater, far more solemn, which will be the last of them all." It would bring the complete realization of the egalitarian principle—*égalité réelle*—with a community of goods.

To be sure, Babeuf's socialism was basically still backward looking, related to a society and community with an agrarian-militaristic imprint, not forward looking to the new industrial society. Yet his radical conceptions, at once a connecting link between old and new socialist ideas, anticipated important principles and methods of modern radical socialism and especially of Marxism. In addition to the idea of a class struggle and the "final revolution," they included the fundamentally authoritarian and centralist, in fact already totalitarian, character of socialism: for after the successful Revolution, the dictatorship of the revolutionary committee was to be maintained for a long time as a strong regime that would carry out the final implementation of communism in the sense of a genuine and not merely formal democracy.

2. For the time being, however, Babeuf's ideas remained isolated. Only the economic and social changes during the subsequent decades offered more concrete points of departure for socialist thinking. Above all, and this is the second stage, a series of French and English writings (by the so-called

early socialists) formed the bridge to the actual development of socialism. The concept (of socialism) established itself between 1830 and 1840 as a critical response, precisely, to the social consequences of the industrial revolution. In France it was all still rather theoretical; in England it was more concrete, since this is where the process of industrialization had begun earlier and more thoroughly than anywhere else.

Based on his observations of developments in England, Genevois Gismondi, as early as 1819, wrote his *New Principles of Political Economy* as a critique and refutation of Ricardo's liberal optimism that everything would develop harmoniously. He was followed by the early socialist blueprints of Saint-Simon and Fourier, and finally, in 1844, by Friedrich Engels's book *The Condition of the Working Class in England*. Marxism took its beginnings from that work and was thus related to the situation in England. In the meantime, the ideas of Robert Owen (1771–1858)—a philanthropic industrialist devoted no less than the liberals to Enlightenment optimism—were at work in England itself. His tract of 1841 posed the programmatic question: "What is Socialism?" His answer: the reasonable, rational system of a society in agreement with the natural order. But at the same time, Owen started from the thesis that a person is the product of his or her social milieu; accordingly, the first priority was to change the old social system. Initially this was conceived and tried out as an experimental model system, on a small and manageable scale, to improve the living conditions of the workers. But then Owen shifted his sights to the state, which he came to believe should be employed to implement reforms and be held responsible for them. The change he envisaged went far beyond the ongoing English reform efforts. To be sure, Owen, like almost all early socialists, had a strong agrarian-romantic outlook. After the failure of agrarian-communist experiments, like the settlement of New Harmony in the United States, his thinking eventually headed toward a cooperative socialism, and he developed, as Proudhon did later, the idea of the cooperative bank and the industrial credit cooperative. This was the beginning of the cooperative movement, not yet of a socialist organization of production itself, as Marxism would come to demand; this is a basic distinction in the conceptions of socialism. One more point needs mentioning. Owen himself eventually arrived at a social messianism. He believed that the future perfection of the social system would make possible the realization of the kingdom of God on earth.

This moralistic and pseudoreligious direction that the idea of socialism took, the expectation of imminent epochal change, still contained the utopianism of earlier centuries, but at the same time it also formed a bridge to the messianic element that is present in Marxism. Simultaneously Owen exerted a strong influence on the earliest union movement (the Chartists).

The founding of a Workingmen's Association as early as 1836 marked the beginning of an organized workers' movement. But typical of the English development was its reformist thrust. A People's Charter of 1838 demanded above all the periodicity of the Parliament, universal suffrage, and secret ballot, along with equal electoral districts and parliamentary immunity. All these points were demands made by democratically inclined reformist radical liberalism.

3. In France, three names represent a different variant of early (and non-Marxist) socialism: Saint-Simon, Fourier, and Proudhon. All three strove for a reform of society through the economic and social route, though in this case largely without involving the state. The expectation, and subsequently the demand, that the state carry out political democratization and find a comprehensive solution to the social problems arose only in the course of the Revolution of 1848.

The first important representative was Count Henri de Saint-Simon (1760–1825). After a colorful military and social career, which had also seen his participation in the American War of Independence under Washington, he devoted himself to studying the new conditions of the industrial age. His important thesis (anticipating Marx) was that politics was essentially reducible to a science of production, whose aim was to find "the system most favorable to all manners of production" (*On Industry,* 1816). Unlike the socialists who still had a romantic, agrarian outlook, Saint-Simon was probably the first to understand the full import of the new industrial society. He wished to see its problems redressed through an enlightened social policy. He also believed that the national welfare could be decisively raised and secured by means of a massive expansion of production through comprehensive industrialization. In essence it all amounted to a bourgeois system, held together and governed not, as before, by the nobility, the army, and the clergy, but by industrialists, technicians, and bankers. In the future, cohesion and governance were to be put into effect primarily through principles and less so through people. In the old system, Saint-Simon argued, society was largely ruled by people; in the new system it would be ruled only by principles (*The Organizer,* 1820). The idea was of a sort of technocratic dictatorship, essentially placed above socialism and democracy. But it exerted considerable influence on socialism's faith in technology, and especially on Marxism in its Soviet-Communist incarnation of Stalinism (and in fact to this day). Beyond that, in more general terms it influenced industrialism and its progress-inspiring technological projects.

In contrast, Charles Fourier (1772–1837) placed the primary emphasis on a new design for the ideal society, whose structure was once again in the old socialist and agrarian spirit. The population was to be divided into settlements with common land, in such a way that the personal traits of the members of the communities (1,620 in each) would harmoniously complement one another: a communal way of life, a socialist cooperative. Fourier's followers in the United States undertook experiments along these lines, and his ideas had a stimulating effect on the formation of consumer cooperatives. Equal in importance to his romantic intellectual blueprints was his sharp economic and social criticism of liberal capitalism. The fact that it was grounded in real life helped his critique to achieve immediate effect. Here, especially, was a point of departure for Marxism. Contrary to the polemics of its founders and followers (directed also against Fourier), Marxism was definitely only one current among many.

This becomes clearer still if we look at the third French exponent of early socialism, the one-time printer's apprentice Pierre-Joseph Proudhon (1809–1865). As a leader of French workers, his outlook was more strongly directed toward political aspects. His socialism took its starting point, above all, from a critique of the question of private property. A pamphlet of 1840 tersely asked: "What is property?" His answer: "Property is theft"—theft, that is, committed against the "natural" state of communal property. But in contrast to emerging Marxism and in fierce opposition to its dogmatic claim, Proudhon strove for a practical solution, a compromise between the liberal economic theory of his time and the socialist conceptions of society and property. This was to be achieved in such a way that private property, though restricted, would be retained on a small scale. It all amounted to a cooperative solution similar to that proposed by Owen: an economic instead of political revolution. This, precisely, is what Marx saw as "utopian and illusory," for he did not believe that one kind of revolution was possible without the other. Proudhon, on the other hand, believed that a consistent, political democracy and the realization of his liberal socialism would eventually render the state superfluous.

One can see this notion almost as a connecting link between Condorcet's utopianism of enlightenment and progress and the Marxist idea of the withering away of the state. The crucial difference, however, was Proudhon's strict rejection of state socialism, his critique of the extremist position of both liberalism and collectivism. He basically remained (unlike Louis Blanc, for example) a socially liberal reform socialist, who placed his hopes on the cooperative solution, a "mutualism" between the comrades, and the link between small-scale private property and political freedom. These approaches were pushed aside by Marxism, which demanded revolution and the dictatorship of the proletariat. Nevertheless, Proudhon remains important as the embodiment of the emphatically democratic component of socialism. By contrast, other theorists, and then especially Marx himself, endowed the new socialist order with the authoritarian and dictatorial traits that would gain the upper hand, especially in Marxism.

Incidentally, this also applies to the earliest German contribution, Fichte's *Der Geschlossene Handelsstaat* (Closed Commercial State; 1800), which outlined a rigid communal and coercive system as a solution to the economic and social problems of his day. Other conceptions that were essentially state-socialist in orientation—and that leaned not least on Hegel's philosophy—were subsequently developed in Germany by the political economist Johann Karl Rodbertus (1805–1875) and by the true founder of a Social Democratic workers' movement, Ferdinand Lassalle (1825–1864).

4. Of course, these men, too, were soon surpassed and overshadowed by Marxism's overpowering development as both theory and ideology. The basic ideas it built on, and that, in contrast to English and French cooperative socialism, it was able to take to the full logical conclusion of a dictatorial and (totalitarian) state socialism, came to exert a worldwide influence in the political and ideological axioms of Marxist doctrine. That influence made itself felt especially in three ways: as a theory of "scientific socialism," as an international liberation-ideology of "world communism," and as the state doctrine and legitimation of dictatorial forms of government. Marxist doctrine did this with the claim that it was the only correct theory of society, and that it was imperative that it prevail over all other currents of socialism.

Marx early on demanded an alliance between philosophy and the proletariat. With the ethical-philosophical idea of emancipation, he then took the step to an economic-social theory of revolution that was grounded in "political economy" through a radical social critique of both the classical liberal economic doctrine and the idea of social reform. The social misery of early capitalism, especially in the advanced industrialization of England, furnished powerful illustrative material, which Friedrich Engels, Marx's life-long collaborator, had studied in Manchester. With the European revolutions of 1848 came the decisive turn to the revolutionary theory of a proletarian world movement, a theory that pointed far beyond democratic reforms and national boundaries. In trenchant polemics against the "utopian" socialism of the time, Marx and Engels simultaneously developed a grandiose philosophy of history that, in the spirit of the "dialectical" principle, conceived of all previous history as the unfolding and negation of opposites. These ideas received their decisive formulation—one that would dominate all later elaborations of the theory—in the *Communist Manifesto* (published at the beginning of 1848). Written by Marx and Engels at the request of the Communist League, an organization called into life in London by German socialists, this combative tract included a final political and revolutionary appeal that thrust far beyond economics: "Let the ruling classes tremble at a communist revolution. The proletarians have nothing to lose but their chains. They have a world to win. Working men of all countries, unite!"

Of course the last five words, the rousing battle cry of future Marxism, were not Marx's own, they had already been the motto of the *Communist Journal,* which had appeared a year earlier. At first the manifesto also had only limited practical impact. Especially in Germany, the revolution of 1848 was a thoroughly bourgeois-liberal revolution, not a proletarian or socialist one. However, the manifesto supplied not only the economic but also the overall political starting point of Marxist doctrine—a theory in which all three of Marx's approaches were now combined: philosophy of history, economics, and political revolution.

The Core Ideas of Marxism

We have now arrived at the core of the socialist ideology, an ideology that has not come to an end, just as history itself has not. The basic idea of the *Communist Manifesto* was this: the history of all hitherto existing societies, and thus of all states, was the history of class struggles; the content of this history was the battle between opposing sides, which resulted either in the revolutionary reconstitution of a society or the common downfall of the contending classes. And so we read: "The modern bourgeois society that has sprouted from the ruins of feudal society has not done away with class antagonisms." But it did simplify them, reducing them to one great confrontation: bourgeoisie versus proletariat. There were now only two great hostile camps that confronted each other.

For the moment the bourgeoisie, ruling like a class, dominated the modern state and its government—which was nothing but the bourgeoisie's "committee"—as well as the tremendously growing means of production. The inevitable consequence, however, would be a great increase in the size of the proletariat, which was becoming conscious of its power and would eventually unite into a coalition against the bourgeoisie. What set the proletariat fundamentally apart from earlier social movements was the fact that it was no longer a minority movement: "The proletarian movement is the self-conscious, independent movement of the immense majority, in the interests of the immense majority." As it would turn out, however, this was the fundamental fiction of Marxism. Its consequence was the demand for total revolution. For the proletariat, the lowest stratum in the current society, could not rise up "without the whole super-incumbent strata of official society being sprung into the air." That smashing of official society would also overturn all previously existing laws, morality, and religion. According to Marx, all these things had to be unmasked as class-based prejudices and vehicles for the interests of the bourgeoisie.

At first the revolutionary struggle would occur on a national level. Later, however, it would become increasingly important to emphasize the common, international goals: the formation of the proletariat into a class, followed by the downfall of the bourgeoisie and the conquest of political power. The basis of and tool for this political struggle was the socioeconomic revolution, especially the abolition of wage-labor and private property. Private property was "the final and most complete expression of the system of producing and appropriating products, that is based on class antagonisms, on the exploitation of the many by the few."

Marx was mistaken in his expectation that the proletariat would ever achieve an "immense majority": neither in his day nor later did it ever amount to the 90 percent he prophesied. Moreover, the social stratification in the modern states was and has remained much more complex: the concise, twofold scheme of bourgeoisie and proletariat was in no way grounded in objective analysis. It was, instead, a matter of struggle and faith. Also a matter of faith was the vision of the future that Marx offered: after the revolution "the proletariat will use its political supremacy to wrest . . . all capital from the bourgeoisie, to centralize all instruments of production in the hands of the State, i.e., of the proletariat organized as the ruling class; and to increase the total of productive forces as rapidly as possible"—at first "by means of despotic inroads," but eventually through the disappearance of political power as such. Political power, as the organized power of one class to oppress another, would eventually be swept away.

This idea of the withering away of the state in the "true democracy" had already appeared in Marx's "Critique of Hegel's Philosophy of Right" (1841–42); it was philosophical in origin before it was translated into an economic revolutionary movement. To be sure, Marx and Engels subsequently did little to develop and elaborate this theory of the state, which is of particular importance for the history of political ideas. The economic and social problems remained in the foreground, while political aspects were considered subordinate, in the sense that the state and politics were merely instruments in comparison with the necessary, deterministic process of revolutionary emancipation and thorough upheaval in the economic sphere. This was the source of the great uncertainty of a socialist theory of the state; for the later splits and manipulations—especially in support of the Communist form of rule under Lenin and Stalin, Castro and Mao—it offered almost any desired point of departure between democracy and dictatorship.

Marx himself fell short of providing an answer to the question of what form the state would take. He outlined not the final political conditions but only the revolution itself, with the famous theory of the dictatorship of the proletariat: "Between capitalist and communist society lies the period of the revolutionary transformation of the one into the other. Corresponding to this is also the political transition period in which the state can be nothing but the revolutionary dictatorship of the proletariat" (*Critique of the Gotha Programme*, 1875). This was almost an aside, and yet it concerned *the* central problem of political Marxism: its fatal relationship to dictatorship.

The subsequent elaboration and development of Marxism occurred—from the second half of the nineteenth century to the great schism between dictatorial Communism and democratic socialism after the end of World War I—in constant conflict with rival theoretical currents and between the concrete political forms taken by Socialist workers' parties. From their permanent adopted home in London and Manchester, Marx and Engels tried with varying success to intervene in the formation of socialist programs and parties. But above all, Marx tried to provide the scientific basis for his theories through laborious, detailed studies: first in his *Critique of Political Economy* (1859), then in his major work *Capital* (volume I, 1867; volumes II and III published posthumously in 1885 and 1894).

In these works he developed, above all, two basic principles: historical materialism and the dialectic method, though of course both had already appeared and been used in the *Manifesto* and earlier. The basic thesis of historical materialism was the claim that the entire social, political, and mental life process was conditioned by the "mode of production of material life." When, "at a certain stage of their development, the material productive forces of society come into conflict with the existing relations of production" and property relations, the result is social revolution. In the wake of the economic upheaval, the entire "superstructure" of ideologies—along with their legal, political, religious, aesthetic, or philosophical forms—is transformed in the same degree in which people become conscious of this process and fight it out. History is seen as a succession of contending antagonisms pushing for a resolution—ending, finally, in the definitive victory of socialism over capitalism.

This historical scheme was shaped by the dialectic method: having taken it from Hegel, Marx claimed he had made it real by "turning it inside out," "setting it from its head onto its feet." Hegel's basic idea was that the various stages of development, pushed to the extreme, would eventually change into their opposite; from that conflict would result a higher synthesis, which would once again produce its antithesis, and so on. Marx and Engels developed this scheme into a theory of the "general laws of movement" of human society: the point of transition always comes into effect with the awareness of the economically conditioned change of circumstances (thus Engels in *Feuerbach and the End of Classical Philosophy,* 1888).

Socialism had now reached that point. According to Marx, the conflict between the inexorable expansion of production and the obsolete legal system of private ownership of the means of production found its expression in periodic, intensifying economic crises. It led inevitably to a tremendous sharpening of the conflict between the growing masses of the have-nots and the increasing concentration of capital in the hands of a few. In fact, socialists should promote this crisis in the interest of the revolution, instead of trying to ameliorate it through reforms. After all, in the end that contradiction of the capitalist system would explode the capitalist system as such, and with it the principle of private property, which had turned into an utter injustice: "The expropriators will be expropriated" (*Capital* I). Its place would be taken by a new principle, the "communalization" of the means of production in the sense of participation by all workers. The chaotic production and distribution of goods would be replaced by a "planned, deliberate organization." All people would become lords; true freedom would lie in the perfection of their emancipation as the main driving force of socialism. In the end there would finally occur, as Engels described it in 1878, the "leap of mankind from the realm of necessity into the realm of freedom."

Here, too, a fundamental ambivalence in Marxism emerges. On the one hand it emphasizes the "necessity" of the revolutionary process. On the other hand, it is clear that this doctrine has a voluntaristic character, for it is the object of conscious "struggle." This ambiguity also marks the ongoing conflict between theory and practice in the historical development of the growing Socialist parties, between their theory of revolution and the practical reforms that prevailed for the most part—until the tension resulted in the splitting off of Communism. Of course these contradictions could not retard the enormous continuing influence of Marxism outside of Communism. A seductive power was found to lie in the theoretical claim of socialism and the popularizing of a socialist faith—in its rousing slogans and the new scientific terminology—that made socialist politics look like the definitive solution to all problems—precisely what our century of ideologies demanded.

Criticism of Marxism has focused on three points in particular, which have remained relevant to this day.

1. Marxism employs a number of quite unproved and vague basic concepts, yet at the same time, contrary to its own principles, it exempts itself from any ideological criticism.

2. What appear to be very empirical and revealing analyses and prognoses do not square with the increasingly complex reality and subsequent development of the Western industrial societies, to which those analyses and prognoses refer.

3. The simplification into a theory constitutes the strength, cohesiveness, and impact of Marxism as socialism, but also its weakness: as a "science," which is what it wants to be, it repudiates the basic, comparative, and pluralistic approach and the questioning that are part of any science. It rejects the openness and freedom of science, thus losing the ability to control and correct itself.

More specifically, what turned out to be wrong with Marxist theory was the assumption that the truly dismal condition of the working class (proletariat) under early capitalism would get progressively worse as long as capitalism lasted. In reality, and contrary to the principles and prognosis of Marxism, social reforms, social legislation, and a mixed form of economy with the continuation of private property have changed the situation profoundly in what is now the welfare state.

The theory of the unstoppable process of economic concentration, the growth of the proletariat into an immense majority, and the imminent demise of capitalism proved likewise premature and simplistic. In reality capitalism continued to develop vigorously and expansively, most clearly in the highly industrialized United States, the very country in which socialism as a political movement was much less able to develop than elsewhere. In reality, the twentieth century has seen an increasing "leveling" of society, precisely by means of economic progress and social reform. The road toward an affluent society in the welfare state, and the creation of forms of political participation, defused a sharpening of class differences in the highly industrialized countries. Revolutionary expectations applied more to "underdeveloped" countries, where, of course, agrarian structures, not industrial ones, predominated.

The same is true for the theory about the disappearance of nationalism, the authoritarian state, bureaucracy, and the class society: neither the strengthening of socialism into a great political movement after the turn of the century, nor the victory of Communism in Russia and its more than seventy years of totalitarian state rule has made these prophecies come true or validated the deterministic character of the Marxist historical process. Marxism has remained essentially even more of a utopia than the "blueprints" of the utopians that Marx and Engels so strenuously opposed. What was proclaimed as the imminent "socialist revolution" as early as 1848 occurred only seventy to one hundred years later, and then, of all places, in countries like Russia, China, Cuba, and Vietnam, which did not meet the preconditions for revolution as Marx had defined them. These countries had neither a fully formed bourgeois society nor industrial capitalism; instead, they had a primitive agrarian feudal society that only Communism sought to lead by force into the industrial age.

And so to this day the most diverse political currents invoke Marxism, in spite of the repeated failures in trying to implement it. Its intellectual attraction in theory and practice stretches from orthodox-deterministic to activist ways of thinking, from international to national-Communist forms, from economic to psychological, literary, and cultural theories. But of course the socialist dream has always had a tendency to turn into a totalitarian political religion. Contrary to what Marx believed, the situation of the proletariat has been profoundly transformed not by scientific-revolutionary and dictatorial socialism, but by democratic and reformist socialism. At the same time, the totalitarian elements and the deep contradictions of Marxism benefited not only the future tyranny of Communism, but also the use and "abuse" of the idea of socialism as such by nationalist movements. For among the great ideologies and secularized salvation doctrines of the twentieth century, it was the very combination of socialism and nationalism that became (in opposition to Marxism) a totalitarian force of the first order.

As Europe enters a period of transition at the end of our century, a century that has witnessed, not least, German dictatorships from the Left and Right, the potential of radical right-wing and radical left-wing ideologization—joined to conspiratorial ideas driven by anxieties and fear of the enemy, to nationalism and extremism—certainly remains virulent, particularly in times of political, economic, and social crises. As of yet, totalitarian socialism, the historical legacy of the first, strongest, and most politically far-reaching variant of totalitarian thought and belief, has by no means simply vanished. This is true even though there is now little or no talk of Communism; instead its former protagonists, in a grotesque turnabout, now speak with equal ardor of democratic socialism. And now, as in the early years of socialism, there are again emphatic invocations of the Enlightenment or the great French Revolution. To be sure, the radical phase of the French Revolution was already driven by the claim that it was implementing the sole truth and virtue. And it did so through violence and terror, the terror of virtue. In actual fact, Communism, by presenting itself as the sole guardian and executor of both Marxism and Leninism, has always opposed and suppressed democratic policies of reform as "revisionist" deviation, as a degeneration or betrayal of true socialism. This, precisely, was Lenin's position, which has been maintained to this day and is only now slowly beginning to crumble. Lenin, the cultically elevated leader and idol of world Communism, decisively expanded Marxism. His main contributions were two theories and a corresponding practice:

1. The anticapitalist theory of imperialism, which successfully inserted itself into the liberation struggle of colonial peoples, concealing Marxism's own imperialist doctrine of revolution behind peace propaganda and movements of world peace.

2. The totalitarian party-theory of the avant garde. It argued that the violent revolution was to be carried out by a minority of professional revolutionaries (in the sense of Sorel's contemporary theory of the elite, which also inspired Mussolini), replacing Marxism's original idea of a majority revolution, which was also associated with the industrialized countries. Lenin moved the theory of the dictatorship of the proletariat, in Marx a transitional phenomenon mentioned only in passing, squarely into the center of his ideology. In the so-called democratic centralism, it was shaped to fit a small, activist minority, and was elevated to a permanent state.

The democratic claim of socialist revolution operates in Leninism to this day with the deceptions and seductions of a totalitarian concept of democracy: structurally in the system of soviets (councils), which quickly became an institutional facade, and intellectually in the claim that it is realizing the true interests of the people (the proletariat). But its effect has been a dictatorship of "the" party and "its" state, that is to say, of a totalitarian bureaucratism (Wolfgang Leonhard). Instead of the promised withering away of the state, the state was strengthened in dictatorial ways. This was allegedly only the first phase, but in reality it was a permanent dictatorship.

Still, what characterizes Communist socialism is, at the same time, its ability to change. Even today, after the system's (partial) failure, we must always bear this in mind. At one time it was able to find agreement, despite differences in origins and goals, with the techniques and practices of the National Socialist system, and not only in 1939. Especially in the policies of Stalin, who succeeded Lenin and completed his work, the bloody dictatorship at home was, simultaneously, the revival of the nationalist and imperialist traditions of the Russian colonial empire. These traditions were now under the banner of socialism, even if this contradicted Marxist premises and Lenin's prophecies of world revolution. Marx and Lenin, it was said, had been wrong; hence there was now socialism in a single country, along with its coerced development into a national, industrial state. In ideological terms this "erection of socialism" was marked by a power-political, irrational myth of struggle and victory, by a pseudoreligiously legitimated nationalistic imperialism that postured as a doctrine of human salvation. Still, the theoretical and rational premises—distorted almost to the point of being unrecognizable—proved attractive, especially to intellectuals. Their influence could be seen in their fellow travelers of the 1920s, and can be found today in the socialist claim of antifascism. That claim is cultivated in an arid and arcane scholarly world of textual analysis, and it testifies to the need for a socialist faith. But in view of the fact that the act of invoking Lenin has always been effective (even Gorbachev has done it), we must bear in mind that the Stalinist theory of dictatorship—as blunt as it was in its authoritarian vision of the state and the party—certainly grew almost seamlessly from Lenin's totalitarian understanding of dictatorship. This is true even if we take into account that Leninism was violently expanded whenever the leadership felt the need to do so. Lenin was "adapted" to current needs. Under Khrushchev it was adapted in the conflicts with deviants from Yugoslavia to China, and it was adapted later in the Brezhnev-doctrine after 1968.

In any case, the close bond between the Leninist and the Stalinist theories of rule is undeniable, and the latter is inseparable from the former. That is why Gorbachev's attempt to build his reforms on a "true" revival of Lenin is so contradictory, and I believe (in March 1991) that the contradiction cannot be resolved.

Perspective

I have now arrived at the third and final part of my reflections: the current perspectives of the idea of socialism.

In looking at the historical and political balance sheet of (1) early socialism and (2) socialism in power, we must always bear in mind the ambivalence in all ideas of socialism: on the one hand they carry the old seduction in the guise of utopia; on the other they represent the reformist and corrective strength of liberal democracy. In this context the experiences of the impetuous year 1968, and their ideological consequences down to this day, are particularly instructive as an example of the recurring longing for socialist utopian and redemptive thought, for a political religion, especially among intellectuals. Since that time, utopian and fundamentalist movements—in part old, in part new—have responded to the recurring demand for de-ideologization with wave after wave of re-ideologization. The apparent or partial opening of Communism made it easier to project what were at first rather unfocused desires and expectations of social and cultural revolution onto a higher form of "socialism," which no longer wanted to be, or could be, described as a totalitarian monolith. There seems to be an irony of history here: at the same time that non-Communist socialism within the Social Democratic parties of the West began to detach itself from the dogma of Marxism in ideological terms, new waves of ideologization turned the concept of socialism in all its breadth and depth into the global battle-cry of youthful rebels in Western countries and the Third World.

Communism itself did not remain unaffected by these developments. However, the official criticism of Stalin's tyranny (which began with Khrushchev's well-known "secret speech" at the Twentieth Party Congress in Moscow in 1956) usually stopped short of touching on ideology and the one-party system: only the "cult of personality" was open for debate, not the basic totalitarian structure of Communism. Still, this modest self-criticism in Communism that began in the 1970s fed old and new hopes in the democratic aspects of Marxism as well as Leninism. And beyond all the violent actions of Soviet Communism at that time and later, it spurred hope in its democratic development and its capacity for compromise, hope in its "human face." This was true of the revisionist and national variants of Communism in Moscow's Eastern European satellite regimes, as well as of the special road taken by Titoism, Maoism, and Castroism.

The progressive decentralization and de-Stalinization of world Communism freed it from some long-outdated dogmatic shackles, though it did retain the essence of the socialist faith, the belief that it was the final stage of total democracy. There was movement in other areas as well. The Catholic Church under Pope John XXIII opened itself to talks with the Communist parties. European Communist parties, particularly in France and Italy, invoked a special national "coloring," at times took a new course of democratic cooperation, and along the way also insisted on ideological independence: this was the so-called Eurocommunism. This trend was particularly evident in the case of the Communist Party of Italy, with its emphatic invocation of Antonio Gramsci as the "Italian Lenin." Gramsci's version of democratic communism, which he developed in Fascist prisons, became influential among intellectuals, even though Gramsci and his followers unquestionably adhered to the basic Leninist positions.

To those willing to believe and those enamored of revolution, who could not find a home in the moderate Social Democratic parties, the worldwide Communist transformation of the past two decades offered new and exciting possibilities for identifying with socialism as a quasi-religion. One could associate Communism at will with revolutionary movements and personalities of the most diverse kinds and backgrounds, without necessarily having to defend the Soviet Union and its policies. At times it seemed that the more distant the cause, the more attractive it was. What was fascinating about the violent "cultural revolution" in China were the radical rebellion against the people's own cultural identity and the idea of "permanent revolution," which Maoism, especially that of the students, sought to carry all over the world. Castro and his Latin American followers aroused enthusiasm for their use of the (Maoist) guerrilla theory, with its (agrarian-Communist) struggle against the (capitalist) metropolises; an entire body of literature was produced about that struggle and used as manuals for European terrorism. The long, drawn-out conflict of the Vietnam War impressed sympathizers with the successful partisan struggle of a nationalist Communist movement. The hegemony of the West was deeply shaken by that success, which was also daily served up on our television screens in a masochistic display.

All this occurred not so long ago, at a time when it was not so much social and economic problems but rather the need for re-ideologization demonstrated clearly, time and again, the virulence of socialism. I will mention only the Cultural Revolution in China as one example during the past two decades. In spite of the socialist reality in the Second and Third Worlds, socialism often seemed to be stronger than other ideas, indeed it seemed to be *the* idea of political thought. In all this, the vagueness of the concept became still more confusing and at the same time more open to manipulation through the unique African, Asian, and Latin American forms it assumed. Thanks to the shifts in political terminology, it did not matter much that, in every single case, dictatorships claiming to bring liberation and democracy were established by militant elites using violent means and acting in the name of socialism.

To an ideological way of thinking, the differences between democracy and dictatorship, between pluralism and totalitarianism become irrelevant, so long as the primary need—a feeling of redemptive safety—is met within a closed community and a political faith. This is precisely the promise that socialism has held out since its beginning—something that has been repeatedly demonstrated after brief interludes of de-ideologization. The cult of revolutionary heroes—of the likes of Castro, Che Guevara, and Ho Chi Minh but also usable non-Communists like Nasser and Allende and numerous African liberating dictators from Nkrumah to Gadhafi—continually reinforces the romantic stamp given to socialism in the Third World.

Finally, the fascination of the exotic and the mobilization of political sympathies have been given an enormous boost by the possibilities of rapid mass communication that developed with the global spread of television. The phenomenon of "telecracy" has now taken on crucial importance, especially for the spread of political ideas. Telecracy refers to the visual information provided to the masses, information that seems direct and irrefutable, but is in fact quite deceptive, subjective, open to manipulation at will, and hardly verifiable. What we see must be real, right? The question about the power *of* political ideas is now joined by the problem of power *over* ideas and how they are politically presented: in the future, every history of ideas will have to pay attention to this shift in the way intellectual and ideological influence can be exerted.

In conclusion let us ask once again: are we witnessing the collapse of socialism as a system or its immortality as an idea? An idea that has survived failed programs and experiments, along with their inhuman consequences, because it concerns itself not with socialism as a state but with the utopia of a better world, indeed the best world, a utopia the world supposedly cannot do without? What persists is the old danger of ideological thinking. By focusing on goals, it devalues the importance of actual political structures and the means and ways of obtaining those goals. In reading the Western catastrophe literature from the 1970s and 1980s with eyes critically focused on ideology (I am thinking of the apocalyptic tone of books like the 1982 collection edited by Walter Jens entitled *In letzter Stunde* [In the Last Hour] and R. Jungk's 1977 work, *Der Atomstaat* [The Atomic State]), one is reminded of the feeling of hopelessness that once made so many intellectuals in the period between the world wars receptive to the ideologization of thinking. Ideologized thinking is an escape from reality. It can take on pseudoreligious features, lead to the ideological undermining of an open society, and weaken its resistance to dictatorship from the Left or the Right. Conservative nostalgia and a retreat into nature or the past can join hands with various other currents: with a nostalgic Marxism; with the struggle against large, anonymous bureaucracies and multinational companies, and in support of community models that are soviet-democratic and anarchistic; with a sharp criticism not only of capitalism but in part also of the real existing socialism of the Soviet system.

Anticapitalism from the Left and the Right, by now a fixture of the critique of civilization that is more than one hundred years old, lives on as the romantic declaration of war against the consequences of progress. Of course the alternative of the Left, socialism with a "human face," remains an illusion so long as it clings to the one-sided Communist vision and thus to dictatorship. Authoritarian nationalism as the alternative of the Right, at one time reduced to absurdity by National Socialism, offers once again the explosive combination of romantic-ethical and economic-technocratic currents. Both alternatives, however, are confronted by the basic question concerning a humane relationship between ends and means. Marxism and nationalism, social utopianism and antitechnological neomysticism—they all evade the central question that only pluralistic democracy, with its constitutions and rules of the game, seeks to answer: how can a political system realize humanistic values without fundamentally violating them in the process of their implementation? This is precisely what has happened in the case in Marxist socialism, with its continuing violation of real-life humanity in the name of great humanistic values.

The question of power, too, works itself out very differently in open and closed systems. The struggle for power is surely a fundamental political reality. However, the regulation of power in the most peaceful, manageable, and controllable way possible is just as surely a central criterion for differentiating political systems. Power, like fear, is among the basic drives of politics: from Thucydides and Machiavelli to Hobbes and Montesquieu, Max Weber and Ferrero, the examination of history and politics through the lens of the theory of power has lost none of its importance. However, a political anthropology that recognizes power and fear as "natural" basic drives, and freedom and justice as their civilizational regulators, will accord the highest importance to securing and safeguarding these humane controls.

Thus the struggle over values is and remains primarily a struggle over the methods of politics—and neither chiliastic nor catastrophic visions and counterformulas, no matter how extreme, can trivialize this struggle. The critique of civilization and its perversion in National Socialism, and Marxism and its perversion in Stalinism, offer a lesson in what humans are capable of or can be led to do if they place political goals above means, the total idea above respect for the rights and interests of their fellow man. After the debacle of Communism in 1989 to 1991, it would appear, in fact, that the survival of a socialism that wants to be more than the social and liberal welfare state depends most likely on the deceptive trick of separating the idea from its implementation to date: we need only recall the renaming of the Communist Party in Germany and Italy as the Party of Democratic Socialism. No matter how much an ideology has been refuted historically and politically, what persists is the ideologues' ancient art of legitimizing the function of the idea as a utopia, regardless of actual experience. Utopian thinking is not imperative (as von Friedeburg believes); what is imperative is that we renounce it (as Nipperdey has said). An optimistic Joachim Fest already sees, and brilliantly describes, the "end of the utopian age" in the "broken dream" of the great ideologies. But I think Raymond Aaron was right when, at the end of his life and after earlier prognoses of de-ideologization, he spoke, with some discouragement, of the persistence, indeed the "immortality," of ideologies (*Memoires*, 1982).

Those ideologies include, above all, socialism—as an idea and as a matter of faith. With its longing for social justice and emancipation, it appeals to humanity's general need for intellectual guidance and the idealistic elevation of reality. With the secularization of political and social thinking, this need can be met all the more by political religions.

These are also the future weak points of liberal democracy, contrary to what some would like us to believe, with the euphoric and unhistorical prognoses of the "end of history" through the victory of freedom in the epochal caesura of 1989.

As an antitype to the technological development of the world, and as a stand-in during crises of meaning and direction brought on by greater insight and information, ideology has time after time had the power to attract followers and challenge the attempt to order the political and social life of the citizens in accordance with human rights and the civilizing of force. Such an attempt seeks to make possible the kind of "good life" and moderate government that the political idea of freedom has opposed, since Aristotle, to the ideologies of the perfect society and totalitarian rule. Its success or failure depends on the citizens' readiness to resist such ideological seduction, and on society's ability to counterbalance the fallibility of humans and their world with constant efforts on behalf of a system of peaceful compromise. It also depends on the ability to see this not as a necessary evil, but as a value greater than the promise of paradise on earth, which has been used since time immemorial to justify inhuman force and to destroy liberal communities.

But if ideological thinking is continuing—as I am afraid it is—much will continue to depend on the place socialism will occupy in the give and take of ideas and slogans. The critical issue continues to be this: will socialism present itself as a doctrine of salvation with an ongoing tendency to become totalitarian, and thus represent a constant danger to freedom? Or will it act as a social corrective, and thus be part of a liberal order with a viable competition of ideas and forces in the spirit of pluralistic democracy?

Reflections on the Problem of Power

I

In times of unexpected change and far-reaching transformations of states and societies, of ideas and patterns of behavior, such as we are currently witnessing in those parts of Europe that were long under Communist rule, the need for political explanation and conceptual understanding gives new life to old, classic key words of history. In the language of the "epochal turning point" *(Zeitenwende)* of 1989–90,[1] as during earlier revolutionary periods of transition, historical lessons and ideas about loss of power, power vacuums, shifts of power, and changes in power—though hopefully not again of dictatorial seizures of power—are once more playing a prominent role. This is particularly true as contemporaries, finding themselves at central historical junctures, raise questions about the direction and interconnection of the events. A rational interpretation and assessment is difficult at the present time, owing to the pace and complexity of the events. In a manner both urgent and vague, the concept of power calls for the examination and assessment of dynamic processes that are part of the nature of politics.[2]

Among the key concepts of history and politics, indeed of culture as such, there is hardly one more central and important, but also more vague and contradictory, than the concept of power. With an innocuous linguistic derivation from the verb "to be able to, can" (from the Middle English *poër* and the Latin *posse*), the word "power" has taken on a rather demonic connotation. It often goes hand in hand with concepts such as rule, force, coercion, superiority, leadership, influence, and authority, in all social relationships and also in human dealings with nature.

Proponents of depth psychology, such as Alfred Adler (1926), thus regarded power as a basic drive behind human action and the mastery of the environment in the broader sense. Of course the striving for power, "this most prominent evil of our civilization," was to be counteracted early in childhood to make it controllable through coexistence with others and through a sense of community.[3] From the 1880s, highly influential philosophers, such as Friedrich Nietzsche, elevated the "will to power," in a manner as radical as it was misleading, to the main driving force in all living things. But they also demanded that it be revalued as part of the self-discovery, self-mastery, and personal power of the individual (as Nietzsche understood his "superman" in *Zarathustra*).[4] The philosopher Eduard Spranger (1921), on the other hand, stylized the "power person" type into an expression of a "form of life": a person can be superior "through his intelligence and actual knowledge, through the economic and technical means which he commands, through inner wealth and the consequent personality, or, finally, through a religious power and value certainty which others recognize as his being filled with the spirit of God."[5] But from there it is not far to the charismatic leadership and the ideologies and fundamentalisms of today.

In an even broader sense, one finds relationships of power beyond politics in all spheres of life, be they based on traditional positions and roles (in the family and professional life), on material and intellectual superiority, on the possession of better information or command of knowledge ("knowledge is power"), on a special gift for organization and efficiency, or on the kind of information that can be used to blackmail and coerce people, as happens with the "state security" in totalitarian systems. Finally, such relationships can be based in a very elementary sense on the creation and use of fear and terror as well as admiration and glorification. In view of all this, the English mathematician, philosopher, and social critic Bertrand Russell declared straight out "that the fundamental concept in social science is Power, in the same sense in which Energy is the fundamental concept in physics."[6]

However, the assessment and evaluation of the phenomenon of power is *not* scientifically neutral, as the comparison with the concept of energy in the natural sciences suggests. Rather, it remains highly subjective and controversial. Let us recall two opposing positions. In one camp are historians like the liberal politician Lord Acton. In 1887, writing about history, freedom, and power, he penned his now-famous moral verdict: "Power tends to corrupt. Absolute power tends to corrupt absolutely."[7] The eminent Swiss cultural historian Jacob Burckhardt, reflecting on the modern power-state from Louis XIV to Prussia-Germany, took that verdict even further in his posthumously published *Reflections on History* (1905).

In 1870–71, on the occasion of the first German unification, he remarked that "power is of its nature evil, no matter who wields it" (Basel lecture, "On the Study of History"). Power, he goes on to say, "is not stability, but a desire, and ipso facto unsatisfiable; it is therefore unhappy in itself and doomed to make others unhappy."[8]

Different from, indeed opposed to, these verdicts that are grounded in morality, culture, and religion is Max Weber's well-known definition. Weber looked at power sociologically and analytically, in a deliberate effort to reach an understanding of power that was value-neutral and relative. Of course he did so with the significant sigh of admission that power was "sociologically an amorphous concept": "Power is the probability that one actor within a social relationship will be in a position to carry out his own will despite resistance, regardless of the basis on which this probability rests."[9] In Spranger, on the other hand, this is understood, especially intellectually and ideologically, as "the ability and in most cases also the will to place one's own sense of value into others as a lasting or temporary motif."[10]

In view of the moralistic as well as relativistic conceptions of power, the political and legal dimension of the problem of power, that is to say the question of legitimacy, takes on special significance. Blaise Pascal, the seventeenth-century French mathematician and philosopher, phrased it sharply when he said: "Right without might is helpless, might without right is tyrannical . . . We must therefore combine right and might, and to that end make right into might or might into right."[11] In our own time, finally, it was put more tersely by Dag Hammarskjöld, the former secretary general of the UN who died in a plane crash in the Congo in 1961: "Only he deserves power who every day justifies it."[12]

These very different quotes address a basic dilemma: as an elementary concept, power, unlike rule and authority, can get by without recognition from those it affects. And yet, how effectively and for how long power is exercised depends at the same time, and quite fundamentally, on the capacity of power to legitimate itself: that is to say, on its capacity to institutionalize itself, to be restrained and restrain itself, to civilize force and rule. All these things the democratic constitutional state, in particular, seeks to accomplish.

If we look for insight into the ambivalence of the phenomenon of power, the fact that it is unavoidable but must be restrained, the history of 2,500 years of political thought since Thucydides offers countless attempts to describe and define it. Of course, with the transformation of historical contexts these attempts always turned out to be inadequate. The question of power has surely remained a controversial one in the modern tensions between state and society, economy and technology, culture and morality, for in each area power is situated very differently and works itself out in very different ways—it is, precisely, amorphous and difficult to channel.

In its recurrent revolutionary transformations, our century of democracies and dictatorships, ideologies and movements has given rise to conflicts and shifts in the realm of power politics. Despite the historical lesson that the essence of politics is the striving for power, and despite all efforts to come up with an exact sociological conceptualization of power, those conflicts and shifts remain difficult to predict, let alone control. If the unexpectedly rapid European upheaval of 1989 has once again shown that historians are only backward-looking prophets after all, the reason lies in the complexity of the phenomenon of power and in the difficulty of interpreting it. We can see this in all the great transformations of our century, be they political-military, socioeconomic, or ideological. In 1914 and 1917–18, 1933 and 1939, 1949 and now 1989: what occurred at each time were decisive and yet rather unpredictable shifts in power. Today the shifts are marked by the collapse of Communism and the Soviet power, with, once again, world-political consequences.

Yet in spite of—or precisely because of—the fact that the concept of power presents such difficulties, there are concrete and practical reasons that an analysis of power is indispensable. This is the case even if such an analysis is put in question by conceptual and scientific as well as political and moral reservations, or is declared to be obsolete from the standpoint of both a normative and a positivist political science. (Incidentally, it is unfortunate that Max Weber, too, for all the perspicuity of his political sociology, dealt mostly with the problem of legitimacy and authority, and for the most part avoided the problem of power.) However, since neither the concept of power—a central one in all languages—nor the thing itself can be eliminated, there is a danger that we become immobilized between ignoring the phenomenon of power and demonizing it. Unfortunately this is happening even in the historical and social sciences, in spite of the fact that the modern state—since the time of Machiavelli and the rise of the modern state in the sixteenth century—has been explicitly understood (and glorified or demonized) as a "power state": that is, as a sovereign entity with a command of power that is self-justified and wholly autonomous, a state with its own *raison d'état*.[13] In his book *Dämonie der Macht*, Gerhard Ritter, drawing on the opposition between "the power state and utopianism" at the beginning of the modern period and using the examples of Machiavelli and Thomas More, located the divergence in modern constitutional thought between a secular and a religious justification of the state in the early sixteenth century. He also saw that divergence as the confrontation of realism and moralism, or of power and ideology.[14]

However, such an examination of politics, which is focused primarily on power, is also found in classical historiography. Examples are Thucydides' famous Melian dialogue and his keen analysis of the Greek civil war as a struggle for power by the Greek polis and the erosion of its power. Later we encounter it in the work of Tacitus on the decline of the Roman Republic.[15] The analytical examination of politics in terms of power thus goes hand in hand with the rise of political thought as such.[16] It is a constituent part of every political anthropology, regardless of whether such an anthropology is, in the final analysis, a pessimistic expectation of humankind's submission to power or a more optimistic assumption of the human capacity to control and tame power in politics and society.

From the time of Aristotle, power, understood as the dynamic force in politics and individuals, has thus been considered a central category of thought concerned with philosophical as well as political systems.[17] That being so, the very general and diffuse character of the phenomenon of power and the sociologically highly amorphous concepts associated with it, demand all the more insistently that we make them more useful as a sociological category, on a lower level of generalization than even in Weber. Doing this requires—in addition to continuous reflection on historical experience—a differentiation of the various spheres and levels of power, with respect to the factors and typical patterns in its formation, the degrees of its consolidation and mode of operation, the interlinking of power structures and their transparency, and the possibilities for controlling those structures.[18]

This is also unquestionably the place to raise the crucial question about the relationship between the economy and power—that is, about the economic component of power in history, society, and politics. This component has become dominant especially with the socialist critique of capitalism and with Marxist theory, that whatever happens in the realm of power in the age of the industrial revolution has an economic cause. From the end of the nineteenth century on, this controversy also imparted a substantial thrust to anticapitalism from the Left and the Right as well as to economic anti-Semitism.

It is certainly true that the definitions of economic power are particularly controversial: not only in the sense of the old-new debate of capitalism versus socialism and a basic conflict between hostile systems—between democracy and dictatorship—but certainly also within the framework of the market economy itself, with its variations and mixed forms. On one side of the debate is the critique of shortcomings and imbalances in the social sphere, which are attributed to free-market power factors; this is at the same time also an eminently political discussion. On the other side is the liberal attitude, which holds that these defects are the short-term effects of abuses of power and will be compensated for in the long run by market mechanisms: the famous "invisible hand" of Adam Smith.[19]

Similarly, modern econometricians, like Wilhelm Krelle, following the lead of the classical theorists,[20] have identified a scientifically ascertainable economic law, pure and simple. This law will prevail in the end, as it has now in the triumph of the social free market economy over the state-directed planned economies. According to this view, there are definitely a number of "points where power can intervene in the economic sphere"[21]: for example, by influencing the information system, the social and institutional structures of society, the decision makers' command over material means and the technical and organizational knowledge ("technology") at their disposal. These "influences of power" are said to be able to affect economic processes (similar to the way they work in politics) from production to distribution. However, they bring with them the danger of influence monopolies in the economy and in politics.

But in contrast to the role power plays in politics and society, in the economic sphere it seems more possible to calculate the correctness and efficiency of measures that are taken and decisions that are made. As a result, it is not necessary to accept power as an irrational, elementary force; instead, it can be relativized as a correctable datum and employed as a part of the system, as it were. Added to this is the importance that innovative research conducted by large companies (which are anything but powerless) can have for the economic and technological developments in the interest of the collectivity. Thus the use and abuse of power are to be measured using the criteria of power's effect on progress and market justice, in the sense of its economic performance on behalf of society.

In politics pure and simple, the question of power cannot be solved or controlled in the same way, by invoking a correctness that carries the virtual force of a law. Instead, in politics power must be recognized and taken into account above all as an unavoidable basic drive. The situation is different in the economic sphere. For a long time, two models for how to solve or restrain problems of economic power have confronted each other in theory and practice: state-directed centralism versus social balance through competition; monopoly versus pluralism; concentration of power versus the division of power. To put it differently: on one side is the notion (which tends to be pessimistic) that prime importance belongs to the restraint of economic power through the state. In this model, concepts like finance capital, banks, major shareholders, company power, and multinationals, and also unions and mass media, are used as scare words in many different ways, to complain about the unequal distribution of power. On the other side, as in the theory of political liberalism, is the notion (which tends to be optimistic) that in spite of all crises, the abuse of economic freedom and power in the market is the lesser evil—provided it can be corrected (to whatever extent necessary) by legal, social, and now also ecological provisions, and that progress in productivity can develop with the least amount of interference.

At present we are witnessing the epochal failure of planned socialism—in economic as well as ecological and political terms. The road toward failure began in the 1950s, when performance and living standards started to lag behind those in the West, and it eventually led to the revolution of liberty in 1989. In the final analysis, this revolution has also provided an answer to a debate that has been going on since the world economic crisis of 1929 to 1933: contrary to the socialist-communist conception of economy and democracy, it is now clear that a free market economy and political freedom, despite whatever need exists for correction, balancing, and control, are not only compatible but actually dependent on each other. Economic power, too, can be restrained through counterpower and a distribution of power, and especially through competition in goods and services. But it cannot be restrained by state power that is bureaucratic-authoritarian or even dictatorial-ideological, for that would mean putting the fox in charge of the hen house. This has been made clear in an impressive and catastrophic way in the countries of Eastern Europe (including the GDR), countries we can, after all, characterize as bureaucratic dictatorships.

It has been our experience that the renaissance of the liberal democracies of Western Europe rested on the concurrence and interaction of political and economic freedom. It established a stable and humane order by eliminating or containing (after 1945) the nationalism of the power-state, contrary to what happened in 1918. In the East, meanwhile, the elimination of allegedly capitalist power structures through antiliberal measures resulted in a socioeconomic fiasco, which has now exploded (in democratic fashion) even tightly structured dictatorial systems through the domestic "revolt against coercion and lies" (Helmut Schmidt).[22]

These topical connections between power and freedom also reveal, from the perspective of political science, that in the age of modern democracy two concepts, in particular, should be part of every discussion on the problem of power: *trust* and *balance*. They make their appearance both in support of and as countermeasures to the exercise of power. In the blueprints produced by socioeconomic thought as well as by political systems, ideas about the creation and loss of trust correspond to how power and the actions of power are conceptualized. Even sober, indeed pessimistic, theorists of power, like Thomas Hobbes in the seventeenth century or Machiavelli in the sixteenth century, emphasized this close relationship between power and trust—trust, that is, in people and institutions. Whereas Machiavelli composed The *Prince* as a handbook for the ruthless exercise of power, in the *Discourses,* devoted to the lessons of Roman history, he advocated a liberal republic, one in which the concentration of power was to be prevented and the rule of law safeguarded. Machiavelli, however, accorded great importance to trustworthy individuals precisely because he considered the people's capacity for political judgment to be unsteady. Hobbes's arguments were more pessimistic still: since man is a wolf to man, mere self-preservation requires that he be subjected to a strong, nonpartisan state. This is the opposite, then, of the separation of powers, but with an emphasis on institutions and the securing of private freedom. That emphasis can be taken in a totalitarian or a liberal sense.[23]

In the subsequent discussion on power, an important role has been played, since John Locke, by trust in institutions in addition to trust in people. It has been a factor in the protection of both power *and* liberty, and has functioned, not least, as a force that counters the dangers of charismatic or plebiscitary leadership. Such dangers are inherent in the ideas of Rousseau, but also in those of Weber. By contrast, in dictatorships the organized mobilization of trust—though here, of course, not as voluntary trust but as "obligatory" trust (G. Schwan)[24]—makes possible the typical replacement of all controls on power, especially in totalitarian systems, with the notorious approval rate of 99 percent.

Finally, according to Karl Popper's famous book of 1945, the great alternative of an open society as against a closed one aims in theory and practice at a fundamental loosening and transparency of power.[25] It opposes all attempts to concentrate power in a closed system. It rejects efforts to monopolize and mystify power. These efforts eventually give rise to the claim that state and society are functioning perfectly: that there is total trust and complete agreement, that the people and the leader, rulers and ruled, the party and the state are identical—the typical totalitarian syndrome.[26]

Today the role of the media in all of this has unquestionably become more important than ever before. Alexis de Tocqueville, in his book on American democracy (1835), had already pointed out the ambivalent meaning of public opinion. In modern mass democracy, it is not only a tool of liberty but also a means of exerting pressure if public opinion pushes for confrontation and increases political and social power through a manipulation of trust.[27] Given the current extent of the media's ability to influence public opinion, this applies to an even greater degree to closed political systems that have a coercive monopoly of opinion created by the threat of punishment. This remains true despite the increased possibilities of countering this monopoly across borders and regimes: let us recall the role of Western television in the GDR, of Western radio in the Eastern bloc, and earlier also of BBC transmissions into a Germany dominated by the National Socialists.

The other principle that is important for the question of power is *balance:* that is, the idea of safeguarding liberty by dividing power. Balance appeared in Montesquieu's doctrine of the separation of powers (1749), and was subsequently applied in the American Constitution as "checks and balances," faithful to Montesquieu's famous dictum: *"le pouvoir arrête le pouvoir."*[28] The concept was based on a quest for balance, as skeptical as it was optimistic, that influenced constitutional thinking beginning in the seventeenth and eighteenth centuries, especially in the wake of progress in the natural sciences. The idea of balance became important first and most obviously in foreign policy, in the conflicts that were sparked by the drive for excessive power. But eventually it also became important in the growing sphere of economic relationships, where balance was sought through competition instead of monopoly, through the market instead of the state. Something similar was taking place in domestic political and social relationships, as well, where the pluralism of associations and parties took the place of autocratic and monocratic power structures, and, in the politics of the state, where federalism counteracted centralism.

The theory of pluralism has become increasingly important to the political and social discussion of power since the 1920s (Harold Laski), but especially in response to the experiences with dictatorships before and after 1945 (Ernst Fraenkel). After all, the Fascist–National Socialist and the Leninist-Stalinist conceptions of dictatorship, while they proclaimed themselves to be popularly democratic or superdemocratic, always categorically rejected, and in part bloodily suppressed, pluralism and the separation of powers.[29] This fact demonstrates that pluralism as a means of balance involves not only formal principles but also value principles of democracy and freedom. Contrary to the devaluation of "formal democracy" in favor of "substantive democracy," which has again become popular since 1968, it is therefore the *pluralistic* structure of democracy that guarantees its ability to both use and control power in a way that is appropriate for and respectful of human beings. For what determines the difference between dictatorship and democracy are not simply the ideologically expressed goals but, above all, the means used to attain them: democracy not according to what humankind ought to be but according to what it really is. Of course, above the pluralistic interests of people should be a canopy of moral values—though not of an allegedly disinterested moralism, which serves, above all, the ideology of dictators.[30] This structural decision to pursue balance through pluralism, federalism, and the separation of powers (that is, in terms of both vertical and horizontal structures),[31] constitutes at the same time a fundamental *value* decision in favor of the limited exercise of power by all sides on the most diverse levels of political, social, and economic processes and institutions. For the attempt to protect liberty through institutions can function only if the balance and division of power is secured through links to a corresponding liberal-democratic constitution.

This applies, finally, to international relations as well, which are marked by a continually growing interdependence of nations and states. Here the problem of power and its restraint has been seen from the perspective of the theory of sovereignty and the balance of power, especially since the creation of international law in the seventeenth century (Hugo Grotius).[32] The idea of collective security, so often disappointing in the past, has gained importance after the catastrophes of the two world wars. At the same time, the most recent upheavals in Eastern Europe and in Germany have given a strong impetus, above all, to the idea of order and peace through federalism and transnational ties—in the sense of a political containment and integration of the egotisms of national states on a European level.[33] Another impetus has come from fears (particularly on the part of the British) of a renewed predominance by the reunited Germany, though such fears should, of course, argue for an even greater willingness to pursue European integration.

It is certainly true that the long-time doubts about the theory of the separation of powers are not unfounded, insofar as we are dealing with a schematic model that has been attributed (not entirely correctly) to Montesquieu (who saw the model in less precise terms than his legal interpreters do). The efforts, in particular, to define a new demarcation of the separation of powers from the perspective of realpolitik—undertaken, for example, by Ernest Barker, Karl Loewenstein, and Dolf Sternberger[34]—were meant to do justice to the changed circumstances of power in the modern state of parties and associations, without violating the fundamental principle of control and balance in the power process. The general principles of a division of power among different bearers of the state's sovereign power, and especially of the independence of the judiciary, remain relevant under the changed structural conditions of modern parliamentary democracy, to which Montesquieu's model no longer fully applies. What is now of fundamental importance is the de facto division of power between the government and the opposition. Federalism—which is once again attracting increasing attention after the excesses of the centralist theory of the state—also contains an important element for a new understanding of the separation of powers: now there is talk of a vertical *and* a horizontal division of power.

In an age of totalitarian and monopolistic tendencies, the federalist principle has shown itself to be more important than ever. It was not merely an episode of the eighteenth and nineteenth centuries. Rather, it embodies an ongoing "discovery" of political theory and practice, whose prehistory can be found far back in the idea of the mixed constitution. To be sure, the principe of federalism was associated with a specific historical period and with a specific social class, the bourgeoisie. In fact this association made possible the decisive breakthrough of the idea of the separation of power, and it reflects the great contribution that was made by liberal theory. But none of this deprives the principle of federalism of its universal, continuing, and fundamental importance under changed conditions of social and political life. Much the same holds true for the reinvigorated, universally valid ideas of human and civic rights, which originated in the same historical-political and philosophical-moral context.[35] It also holds for the idea of the citizen, which as a *political* concept goes beyond the merely social, transitory concept of the bourgeoisie and in the liberal democracies of today has once more taken on a central role. After a long period of disgrace, the concept of the citizen is now experiencing an almost inflationary use in the political vocabulary of nearly all parties and movements.[36]

Of course, the same problems and dangers that we can observe in the expansion of the state's function also arise here: liberal formulas are being adopted and their meaning permanently altered. An egalitarian society has fewer opportunities for individualistic and differentiated diversity, and thus understands it less. It was this diversity that gave rise to the concept of the citizen and, along with it—as was already the case in the classical concept *(polites, civis)* and later, especially, in the early modern concept— to the need for a conception of politics and the state in which power is limited and divided. The threat to an open, pluralistic community—one in which power is limited and which sets limits on power by virtue of this openness and pluralism—can come not only from the great antibourgeois, antiliberal surges of the 1920s and 1930s, with their renewed, impetuous resonance in the ideological protest movements since the 1960s. It can also arise from domestic trends on the road toward developing the support systems and administrative structures of the welfare state, with its centralist patterns and the concentration of power in associations and the bureaucracy.

Until 1989 this internal threat was joined by the external front of the avowedly monolithic states, in which the division of power was not only implicitly altered but was abolished outright by the deliberate and emphatic character of the system itself. This dual assault from inside and outside rendered the situation of the liberal democracies dramatically uncertain in a time of global confrontation between liberal and totalitarian conceptions of power. At the same time, however, it made even clearer what is at stake if the principle of separation of powers itself is questioned, and what constitutes its lasting meaning beyond changes in external forms.

The conflict over the separation of power and the legitimation of power reflects an old problem of political theory: the tension between unity and diversity, between the individual and society. Aristotle stated this problem in *Politics* (II.2), assigning the principle of unity to the family and the principle of diversity to the state. Since that time, and right up to the recent formulation in the works of Karl Popper, the history of political ideas has been permeated by a confrontation between open, pluralistic conceptions of society and the state, and closed, uniform ones. The latter have been advocated especially within the framework of Platonic, Hegelian, and Marxist traditions.

This distinction opens a view onto a problem at the core of all theories of the state: the sharp opposition between empirical community and ideal state. The closed, perfectionist, totalistic conception has always been predominant in the thinking of influential political philosophers. For a long time it impeded and discredited the development of a theory of the state and society that was empirical, pluralistic, and based on a separation of powers.[37] The truth is, if the diversity of human existence and the variety of ideas on how to shape political communities are to be given adequate and humane consideration, we need a theory that is far more sophisticated, complex, and, of course, realistic. Representative democracy with a separation of powers is a mature and at the same time complicated and fragile fruit of human civilization and the capacity for political understanding. It demands that the community be shaped through ordered compromise and not by the power of the stronger. It calls for state power that is based on the regulated distribution of power and the conscious renunciation of force, and for limitations on majority rule through minority rights.

This is a challenging prospect, and it represents the more difficult path. Since Plato's blueprint of the politeia and the great utopias of the state, since the time of Rousseau's *volonté générale* and the modern versions of total democracy, and finally in the National Socialist and Communist totalitarian dictatorships, the conception of a social order based on an absolutely fixed, uniform principle has had a dominating, suggestive, and seductive power over all composite, open, and mixed forms of social and political life. Time and again victory has gone to the "reduction of diversity [*Vielfalt*] to uniformity [*Einfalt*]" (Fritz Stern), to the "totalitarian temptation" (J.-F. Revel).[38]

Political terminology, too, has corresponded to and followed this dominant trend. Its key concepts concern the search and demand for a *consensus omnium* (universal consensus), for the realization of a professed common will and common weal and eventually of a complete identity of the
people and the government. And this is also invoked by the power philosophy of the great ideologues. Instead of engaging in the laborious balancing
of power day to day, they seek the complete abolition of diversity and
division. Their goal is consensus through plebiscitary acclamation instead
of through voluntary cooperation and plural representation. Consensus
either as communal coercion or as voluntary consent: time after time the
dispute over the acceptance or rejection of the separation of powers has
been decided by these two alternatives. Under the totalitarian fiction, the
question about concrete structures and their institutions becomes a
"merely formal one," since the absolute goal justifies the means.

The invocation of a higher legitimacy turns practical politics, the regulation of the domestic question of power, into a mere doctrine of functions.
Though modern dictatorships use the vocabulary of the constitutional
state, their claim that they possess a revolutionary legitimacy that is derived from their "substantive" final goals, that they are pursuing true
freedom and perfect justice, pushes aside the question of the concrete
constitution. The perversion of concepts becomes apparent in the transformation of such genuinely democratic and liberal ideas as political contract
and popular will, representation and parliament, parties and unions. Basic
notions of liberal democracy were taken over by the closed, totalitarian
theory. The one-*party* state with (manipulated) election results of 99.9
percent—a contradiction in terms because it substitutes a *part* for the
whole—began its triumphant advance around the world.

However, the principle of the separation of powers can never be reconciled with the claim of leadership put forth by old and new dictatorships,
with autocracy and totalitarianism. It is true that we see this principle
being weakened and challenged in modern democracies: by the strengthening of the executive at the expense of parliaments, by the blurring of the
boundaries between the powers through the power of associations and
party monopolies. However, the difference between the democratic and
totalitarian conceptions of power, a difference that cannot be obscured,
revealed itself as recently as 1977 in the emphatically modernized and
democratized Soviet constitution: its legalistic and pseudodemocratic declarations were always relativized with reference to the hegemony of the
party and the "power and authority of the Soviet state."[39]

The first and most important step in the practice of every dictatorship,
whether or not it has a constitution, is always the total concentration of
power, subject to no controls. These are the typical signs: parliament is

coerced into line; a *single* party assumes absolute leadership, whether in the name of the national community or the proletariat; all social and political organizations function as channels to transmit the will of the leadership. What such a system lacks is space for the interplay of government and opposition. As the classical scheme of the separation of powers becomes increasingly controversial, this interplay becomes all the more important in the system of separated powers. The true character of a system, which is often obscured, is revealed by the question concerning the division and control of power.

It was a grave misjudgment of this fundamental difference when recent studies of the Third Reich and, in a different way, studies of the development of Communism advanced the claim that these systems were by no means monolithic and therefore were also not totalitarian.[40] This argument was part of a fashionable campaign against the concept of totalitarianism as such. Seeking to reverse the accusation of dictatorship that had been leveled against Communism, in a broader sense this campaign also contributed to a blurring of the fundamental difference between democracy and dictatorship. In reality, totalitarian dictatorships are never able to eliminate the persistence of conflicts over competency and power, or of changing divisions of power. But they do put forth the absolute and ruthlessly enforced claim that they can, at any time, intervene in and decide the outcome of the processes from a central control center. To describe National Socialist rule as a mere "polyocracy" or a pluralism of powers, as a new school of interpretation is doing, ignores the fact that a kind of "authoritarian anarchy" is unquestionably part of the nature of totalitarian regimes.[41] Hitler and Stalin, as the highest arbitrators, so to speak, used the chaos of leadership and government offices to maintain their autocratic positions all the more effectively: monocratic rule through polycratic means.

This kind of authoritarian anarchy has about as much to do with democratic pluralism and the constitutional separation of powers as the old motto of *divide et impera* (divide and rule). Politics has always tried to follow that motto, which thus says nothing about the nature and quality of a regime. A distribution of power has existed at all times and everywhere: in tribal and feudal systems as well as in bureaucratic and party states. The crucial point is whether such divisions of power are constitutionally guaranteed as a regulated system, whether they are institutionally and politically secured, or whether they are unregulated, arbitrary, illegal, and instantly revocable forms of a power struggle between individuals and political groups. This, then, is the fundamental question that remains: can the citizen rely on a guaranteed separation of powers that has a limiting effect on power, or will he remain subject to the dictatorial whims of a "power Darwinism," and be coerced or seduced into placing his trust in the monopolistic claim of a totalitarian leadership, come what may?

The idea of the separation of powers thus proves to be a decisive advance in the history of the theory of the state, one that is highly relevant today. We are dealing here with a principle that runs counter to and resists the deceptive dream of the perfect state and social order, because that dream has always led away from freedom and toward despotism. It does not promise a final solution to the problem of power, as there is no such solution. Churchill's view, that of all the bad forms of government, democracy is the least bad, applies particularly to the constitutional separation of powers: among all the ways of organizing power and rule, it is still the least objectionable. Its superior legitimacy is grounded in the fact that it recognizes and protects civic freedom and diversity. It ameliorates the evils of power—and without power, human coexistence is impossible—by controlling the excessive growth of power, which, in the name of political perfection, destroys that very coexistence.

II

European, and especially German, history offers compelling historical and political examples of the problem of power in the concrete relationships between the state, society, and the economy. I shall examine some of these here.

Concurrent with the rise and crises of the national power state came the headlong development of political parties and social associations as they struggled to participate in power while state and society were undergoing a process of modernization and eventually democratization. After World War I that development was already leading to the great controversies over a radical reshaping of the political structures under the new slogans of economic democracy, emancipation, codetermination, and self-determination. The fight was about and against the old bastions of power: the political, military, and socioeconomic establishments, and also the primacy of foreign policy and the *raison d'état*. This conflict permeated the three major periods of the modern German constitutional state: the Empire, the Weimar Republic, and the Federal Republic. It was also present during the National Socialist dictatorship, though there it was frequently suppressed or ideologically distorted and perverted under the banner of a so-called national socialism, and violently abolished in the führer principle and in the ideology of the pseudoegalitarian national community and the friend-foe ideology of the totalitarian state.[42]

"Politics is fate," Napoleon once said to Goethe. In our own century, Walther Rathenau, an entrepreneur, writer, and politician all in one, countered that with his dictum: "The economy is fate." The question about the interconnections between politics and economics, their reciprocal relationship, and the primacy of politics over economics is particularly controversial when it comes to historical turning points and talk turns to economic causes and responsibilities. Recall the ongoing debates over the power-political role that economics played in the outbreak and war aims of World War I, in the revolution of 1918 and the inflation of 1923, and especially in the world economic crises of 1929, with the seizure of power by National Socialism and its subsequent expansion. The role of economics appears again at the end of the Third Reich, and in the course of reconstruction after 1945, with the historic decisions of the Marshall Plan, monetary reform, the European Coal and Steel Community, and the European Community. Today we are faced with the economic causes and motives behind Gorbachev's policies and the most recent upheavals in Central and Eastern Europe.[43]

In all these cases, the question about the power-political role of economics and economic actors has been answered in very different ways. Serious historical reflection can and must exclude two extremist viewpoints from consideration. One is the picture-book approach in which only the free decisions of good or evil statesmen matter. The other is the economistic, mostly Marxist-influenced simplification that turns political decisions into a function of socioeconomic interests and power relationships. As a result of the latter view, history appears to be a series of relentless manipulations or even conspiracies by dark powers. As it is, the penchant for *conspiracy theory* is widespread not only in popular history but also, and particularly, in discussions about power. The great ideologues, who have always seen secret string-pullers as being key figures in the history of power ("the secret powers"), exert their influence on scholarship—or at least like to appear in emphatically scientific dress. Of course, they do so with a thoroughly unscientific, monopolistic claim. One need think only of the exclusive truth of so-called scientific socialism in Communist parties and states, or of the conspiratorial role that ideological interpretations of history from the Left or the Right have ascribed to capitalists, Jews, Freemasons, or finance capital—all this in our own "enlightened" century. These views have had the thoroughly unscientific consequences of radical persecution and destruction of certain classes and races under totalitarian revolutions and dictatorships, where the political or "racial" enemies were equated with the social and economic enemies, and were expelled or exterminated because they were regarded as the source of all evil.[44] The extreme danger posed by such monocausal myths about history and power becomes particularly clear in times of crisis and upheaval. At such times they can be used to mobilize the masses and justify state crimes, in that social and economic needs and interests are (or can be) related directly to political and ideological confrontations, and are (can be) instrumentalized and ideologized for power-political purposes.

However, the question about the tangible influence of economically powerful actors on politics, and of politically powerful actors on the economy, confronts us not only when the connection between political, ideological, social, and economic revolutions comes to a head in such dramatic fashion. In comparatively normal times, too, we are continually confronted by it. At the same time, we also face the question of to what extent the socioeconomic condition is part of the political condition—the classic question of both liberal theory and the critique of capitalism. The picture is rather confusing, even without the extreme positions of an ideological view of history. Since history is often anything but clear and reliable, people repeatedly seek refuge in the great simplifiers. Four great currents of historical interpretation, in particular, confront each other as rival explanations. They offer quite divergent analyses and interpretations of and answers to concrete problems of power.

There is *economic history,* which investigates the meaning of economic processes and trends, and also the economy's capacity to act with respect to politics. It has in tow *social history,* which focuses on the consequences of economic processes for society, its stratification, and its relationship to the state. Of course social history, in recent times a particularly strong and often trendy current among historians, tends to underestimate *political history*—that is, the autonomy of political actions. This amounts to a reversal of the earlier dominance of political over social history. Finally, there is *cultural history.* Depending on how culture is conceptualized, it sees political, social, and economic factors in equal measure as determined by and linked to intellectual impulses and accomplishments.

Yet it is precisely this *diversity* of approaches, questions, and methods of historical research and explanation that makes possible a scientific clarification of the problem of power; elevating any one of the approaches to an absolute position obstructs it. Even if the economy can become fate, and not least so in the socialist systems, the relationship between economic and political power cannot be determined in the sense of a simple causality or even a direct dependence of one on the other—and we are not even addressing the importance of psychological factors in both spheres. Instead, the relationship between the two reflects the complexity of the motives and values that determine how politics can be implemented and how it must be corrected, and that sometimes cause the failure of politics.

As an example to support these insights, I will use one of my own areas of research: the Weimar Republic. In spite of the growing distance in time, many battles are still being waged in this field of scholarship. Today the crisis of the Weimar Republic—a process of shifts in power, from the loss of power to a power vacuum to the seizure of power—is regarded as a completed story that has been examined with almost anatomical precision and is now more than half a century old.[45] Yet at the same time it forms an immensely topical point of reference for discussions about the lessons of history, in Germany and abroad. For it is not only in Germany that the period of world economic crisis, with its disastrous consequences and the downfall of most new democracies in Europe at the time, in particular the highly developed Weimar Republic, is considered a general, exemplary experience. How, then, are we to define the anatomy of developments between 1930 and 1933, the relationships between economic and political crisis? How are we to rank the various power factors, and what led to the decisions that were made?

It all begins with events that have a predominantly international and economic explanation: in particular, the crash of the New York stock market in October of 1929, and the pressure exerted on the German economy by questions about reparation and credit. Added to these were the psychological pressures of unemployment and fear of inflation; to this day they have set specific and very narrow limits on economic policy in Germany. But at this point it was the *political* factors that were assuming increasing importance against the world-economic backdrop of a crisis in credit, a slump in sales, and critical levels of unemployment. The first decisive event was, in fact, the fall of the government of the Great Coalition at the end of March 1930. The two wing parties were unable to agree on the level of unemployment insurance: on one side were the German People's Party (Deutsche Volkspartei, or DVP) and the industrialists, on the other the unions and the Social Democratic Party (Sozialdemokratische Partei Deutschlands, SPD). The SPD went into opposition and cleared the way for presidential government; that is to say, it released its grip on power. Thus began the state of continual political crisis and the road to a power vacuum, in which governing was possible only by emergency decrees. This situation amounted to a dismantling of the parliamentary form of government, eventually providing a point of entry for authoritarian and totalitarian parties opposed to the system, "movements" from the Left and especially the Right.

However, of particular importance for the development of the political climate, which in Germany eventually led to the acceptance of National

Socialist dictatorship, were the *psychological* effects. Chancellor Brüning's policy was based on two basic ideas, both of which turned out to be questionable: first, the idea that a quasi-dictatorial method of government was superior to the parliamentary method in solving the technical problems of the economic and governmental crisis of 1930 to 1932; second, the firm belief that the economic course of choice was deflation and austerity, despite the domestic political problems that course entailed. The fundamental decision for a deflationary policy was also motivated by foreign policy considerations: the expectation was that Germany could rid itself of reparation obligations by giving economic proof of its inability to pay. But in the final analysis, it meant that preference was given to a bureaucratic instead of a political solution to the crisis. The catastrophic consequences of that decision—economic collapse and mass unemployment, domestic political polarization and radicalization—overtook all concrete solutions (whether or not they were beginning to take effect), for the simple and sole reason that the political crisis was now running away from such solutions. After 1930, all German governments were fundamentally deluded in believing that the political process could be temporarily excluded, neutralized, or arrested, so that the economic solution could be arrived at in a clinically precise way, as it were, within a politically sterile environment. The result was a loss of power and a power vacuum, and this gave rise to the common refrain: Where is the power? In the end, the time factor proved decisive: the cancellation of reparations and genuine recovery in the economic situation beginning in the summer of 1932 came too late for an impatient populace; *after* the political decision had been made, these developments benefited only Hitler.

Only if one recognizes this basic problem can one understand the chain of power-political causes that led to the end of the Weimar Republic. That end was not brought about simply by the often-demonized support Hitler received from industry and business, which became truly relevant only after the NSDAP (Nazi party) had already grown into the largest party as a result of the political response to the crisis. Moreover, the important role of individuals—Hindenburg, Papen, Hugenberg, and others—must also be seen solely against this political background; that is, against the abdication of power by the democratic parties and the acceptance of the radicalization of public life due to the underestimation and neglect of domestic political power factors in favor of a supposedly non political, purely technical solution to the crisis. That situation left the political field to Communists and National Socialists, both mortal enemies of the Republic. The political parties, as well as economic organizations and the unions, were subsequently paralyzed or deceived by the supposed lack of democratic alternatives. The fact that the nontotalitarian parties declined to fulfill their power-political obligations, using the presidential solution to withdraw from responsibility in the economic crisis, explains the unexpected ease with which the National Socialists subjugated them, or with which the parties carried out voluntary *Gleichschaltung* in 1933. What came together in that process were illusions and self-deceptions, and of course the determination and power-focused efficiency of the National Socialist crisis policies that were subsequently pushed through. In fact since the 1930s, since the fundamental work of John Maynard Keynes (1936), the belief that crisis problems have a predominantly economic solution through "deficit spending" has become the foundation of our economic-political civilization. As we now know, this optimism is exaggerated. The global dimensions of the world economy overtax the tools and devices of economic policy and are unable to prevent new economic crises.[46]

The historical lesson we are left with, in view of the current crises in liberated Eastern Europe as well, is this: political and economic crisis management must work together in the modern state. If that state is simultaneously a welfare state and a liberal democracy, its economic policy must at all times be embedded within general political measures to combat the crisis. But this does not mean that I am advocating a one-sided primacy of politics. Socioeconomic conditions are of fundamental importance, especially in a democratic state dependent on the vote of the electorate. These factors of the crisis were neglected in important ways in the years 1929 to 1933. The deflationary course proved an excessive burden on the population; the promises of an upswing that began in 1932 took hold too late; too little consideration was given to the political-psychological consequences of a policy of austerity. But the simplistic notion of "the" economy that commands and controls politics was also taken to absurd lengths at the time—especially since quite divergent interests existed, from the various industries, to trades, to agriculture. What triumphed in the end was the noneconomic, political-ideological command movement of National Socialism. The expectation of bureaucratic experts as well as theorists of Fascism from the Left and the Right that Hitler would come to grief over the economic incompetence of his movement turned out to be mistaken. The true power factor, namely the totalitarian movement, was once again underestimated.[47]

This brings us to a problem that is decisive for any liberal form of government: the multiparty system. This system is the recognition of the freely organized representation of interests and their effective articulation in terms of power politics through social organizations, pluralism, and codetermination. The fundamental difference between democracy and dictatorship emerges nowhere more clearly than in the free development and leading role of diverse, independent associations. Within and through these associations, the various interests and abilities of social forces can be given an effective political voice. While the reciprocal relationship of economics and politics constitutes a general problem in all political systems, when it comes to free associations, we are dealing with a complex and sensitive phenomenon. Like the liberal and pluralistic constitutional state, which is the precondition for their existence, they are a product of highly advanced civilization. The alternative is autocracy: either the autocracy of the preliberal, absolute state from above, which constrains the political and social forces of movement; or the autocracy of the antiliberal dictatorship of one party, which is based on a coordination of the economy and society in the service of totalitarian goals or personal whims. The result is either a planned economy, a command economy, or a war economy.

We must always bear in mind this vulnerability of liberal democracy, especially today when we hear self-confident talk about its victory over the socialist systems, or about the end of history.[48] Of course neither is true, for we must bear in mind two factors, in particular. First, there are the realities and constraints of international politics, as can be seen now in the crisis in the Middle East, but also in the various nationalisms that have outlasted the end of the conflict between the two systems. Second, history *will* go on. Especially in our age of liberal democracies, this is assured—by natural necessity, so to speak—by counterforces and challenges that are constantly emerging and always go hand in hand with conflicts about power and conflicts involving the use of power.

The fact that the pluralistic constitutional state ranks so high on the scale of civilization means, at the same time, that it is an extremely complex entity, as vulnerable as modern civilization itself.[49] This form of government, like modern civilization, is all about the refinement, indeed the overcoming, of the primeval form of society and politics: the mere rule of the stronger. It is about continuous balance, and the division and taming of power to preserve freedom. Therein lies the *political* role that all participants in the social process play—economic partners, employers and employees, unions and industrialists, consumers and producers. Their associative organizations make possible power in this sense, and at the same time they offer protection against arbitrary power, against anarchy and autocracy in equal measure.

From the very beginning the unions have put forth the lofty claim that they have a broader political calling that transcends mere special-interest politics. They bridge the gap between themselves and the parties—which, after all, act as representatives of the common good *(pars pro toto)*—by claiming that unions, as representatives of workers and employees, act and speak on behalf of the great majority of the population. But unions, too, are confronted with the problem of how to deal with minorities inside and outside their organization, who challenge their all-inclusive claim to represent the workers collectively and who feel patronized by them (as, for example, is currently the case in the conflict over work hours). Quite apart from the fact that only some of the workers are unionized, the unions' claim to power could contain a threat to the pluralistic understanding of power in a liberal state and society, most sharply in the confrontational weapons of strike and lockout. If unions are such broadly encompassing organizations (which is the case—of course not without corruption—in all Western countries, with the possible exception of the United States, where they are limited to mere interest groups), besides consumer groups and other interest groups they must have their counterparts in similarly comprehensive associations of employers. These associations can counter the power of numbers with their own economic importance.

This, it seems to me, is the eminently political dimension of highly diverse organized interests that are able to solve the inevitable conflicts over distribution in a socially agreeable way. Two problems must be considered with regard to associations and interest groups: first, the problem of how to control the excessive power of associations, and second, the problem of a relapse into a corporate state, which, through economic councils or central, overlapping committees that share in decision making, can impair parliamentary democracy. An example of the latter is the dubious idea of a soviet state that emerged in 1918 Germany; again and again, as after 1945 and 1968, it has caused considerable confusion, also as the idea of a "third way."[50]

The recent past offers abundant examples of the decidedly political significance of economic associations and free enterprise for a liberal conception of the state and society. In like manner it also provides examples of the threats to such a conception. As a prime example of the latter, one can consider the discussion over *Mitbestimmung* (codetermination), and its importance and limits within the discussion about power.[51] It is an eminently historical-political topic, transcending the forms of mere economic organization and demonstrating in exemplary fashion the possibilities inherent in the political dimension of the economy—and, of course, the dangers when economics becomes politicized. On the other hand, the first major case of direct cooperation between industrialists and unions, employers and employees, the Central Association of 1918–19, made a significant contribution to overcoming the revolution in the economic and social as well as political spheres, and consolidated the principle of autonomy in negotiating wage rates.[52]

An important strand, especially in the German tradition, emerges here: the development of forms of cooperation, and the channeling of conflict through regulated compromises on the part of employers and employees and through institutionalized conflict resolution. "Codetermination instead of class struggle" is the catchphrase of this particular tradition, which was eventually developed and elaborated to a far greater degree in Germany than anywhere else. It regards itself as a constructive, homegrown alternative to the ideology and practice of a syndicalist policy of class struggle. As a result, it was, and still is, condemned by socialist-Marxist theoreticians as revisionism or reformism, the delusion of "employer-employee partnership." Outside of Germany, including in the southern European countries, it has barely taken hold. Even in tried-and-true parliamentary democracies like England's, the policy of codetermination has long been looked upon with skepticism.

But the model of cooperation, either admired abroad or mistrusted as "typically German," also has serious power-political consequences. The continual strengthening of the power of unions and of the policy of codetermination can lead to a change of power relationships in the spheres of economic and social policy. We have also learned from the experience of the universities how enormous the problems can become in terms of jurisdiction, structure, and function, if codetermination is pushed right up to the threshold of parity, or even beyond it (as in the infamous three-part parity, or *Drittelparität*). The magic words are participation and democratization, or simpler still: participatory democracy. Just as codetermination often forms a counterposition to parliamentary democracy in the political realm, its continuing development and generalization is a consequence or secondary phenomenon of the seemingly unstoppable strengthening of the social and egalitarian principle at the expense of an appreciation of liberal values.

Deliberalization experienced its first high point in the statist-authoritarian regimes of the 1930s and 1940s. Of course, after 1945 there was a remarkable renaissance of liberalism in Western Europe. In contrast to Communist state-socialism, a regeneration of the free market economy and of social policy took place, contradicting gloomy predictions about declining late capitalism and the late bourgeoisie that had been pronounced since the turn of the century. The vitality and appeal of basic liberal views took on new importance as an antitotalitarian alternative. Its influence also penetrated deeply into the conservative and socialist camps. This occurred because the liberal principle was linked to the social principle; that is, it was combined with the corrective of social justice and thereby adapted to the needs of industrial mass society and the rising classes. From John Stuart Mill to Friedrich Naumann, there had been an early current that anticipated this development.

The social-liberal corrective, which did much to spread bourgeois values among the working class, did not take hold without repercussion for the liberal state. It amounted to a social shift in power. What happened next—in part because of the pressure to form coalitions with social-democratic parties and ideas—was the sort of strengthening of the role of the state that had already been latent in the idea of a social market economy, and even more so in the shift from private to governmental social security. In Germany this development could follow in the footsteps of Bismarck's social security, and in America, of Roosevelt's New Deal. The economic shift initiated a political shift in the role of the state: even under liberal auspices it changed the social space and restricted the individual's freedom of responsibility in favor of a broad social safety net. Sociologists spoke of a "social democratic century" (Ralf Dahrendorf), though now, to be sure, they are prophesying its end.[53] The qualitative change that accompanied the quantitative, equalizing advance of codetermination was apparently the price that had to be paid for the German form of cooperative conflict resolution, which was relatively successful compared with the development in other countries. Of course, its precondition remains a renunciation of sharp ideological positions and strategies. The policy of codetermination is basically incompatible with a Marxist or syndicalist conception of socialism, just as the theory of the single party is incompatible with parliamentarianism, or the totalitarian idea of socialism with democracy.[54]

However, preserving the precedence of a cooperative model over an antagonistic economic and social theory—within the framework of a politically and socially demanding system that channels economic and social power into the narrow path of a viable policy of codetermination—requires that the power-political dangers inherent in codetermination be avoided. Those dangers are: growing rigidity, bureaucratization instead of responsibility, a nonexistent or shrinking capacity for accommodation and decision making, and corporatist petrifaction. These are all obstacles to an economic life that has a social dimension and that possesses the greatest possible flexibility and orientation toward opportunity and the free market.

This is also where the importance of the control of power through the policy of private ownership and competition comes into play. One of the creators of the social free market economy, Walter Eucken, boiled it down to this formula: "Just as private ownership of the means of production is a precondition for the competitive system, the competitive system is a precondition for ensuring that the private ownership of the means of production does not lead to economic and social abuses."[55]

In this sense there is need for the state to deliberately shape the framework of economic life.[56] What is not needed is that the state socialize the economy, which has so often failed economically as well as politically, or that it pursue the dream of an economic democracy that tries to simply equate economic and political ways of functioning. On the contrary, it is precisely the preservation and promotion of competition through strict competitive rules that simultaneously serves the cause of democracy. The goal is not total "democratization of the economy and society," which can lead to dysfunction, but a moderate democracy through competition on many levels, economic and political, as Joseph Schumpeter, for example, described it so impressively in his work *Capitalism, Socialism and Democracy* (1942).[57] We are talking about "democracy by competition" (including between suppliers and consumers) as a check on economic as well as political power, a check that is democratic on a very basic level. This check operates in conjunction with a strict safeguard of competition and the requirement that private property be socially responsible (Article 14, section 2 of Germany's Basic Law). The welfare state then compensates for what freedom cannot accomplish.[58]

At the end of our century of ideologies, what is the situation of the socialist ideology, which in its Communist form, even after the end of Fascism and nationalism, led to the justification and implementation of an extreme concentration of power and renounced the separation of powers? What had happened after 1918 and 1945 was repeated after 1960: another global expansion of the idea of socialism. In the wake of decolonization, it captured nearly the entire Third World and became a global idea of the future, with Lenin as the idol in the post-Stalin global era. It was much like a gospel of salvation, with its partly doctrinal and scholastic, partly romantic and nostalgic quarrels over which socialism was the "real existing" socialism and which the authentic one. It didn't matter how often the socialist utopia of freedom from all forms of rule was refuted, or how often people had to experience and suffer its totalitarian consequences. In actuality socialism functioned as a utopia, as a pseudoreligious ideology of power to legitimate dictatorial rule that sought to be as all-encompassing as possible.[59]

Despite the warning examples from the Communist world, the idea of socialism proved powerful and attractive because it spread simultaneously on three different levels of argumentation and agitation: on the economic level (the anticapitalist argument), on the social level (the egalitarian-community argument), and on the political level (the centralist, statist argument). But the economic solution of anticapitalism did not work, the egalitarian claim led to "equal" unfreedom for all, and centralism prevented vital social diversity as well as genuine federalism and pluralism. This, too, the upheavals of 1989 have made clearer than ever before.

The main difficulty with the debate over capitalism versus socialism lies in the fact that socialism, from the very beginning, has embodied the most diverse, even contradictory meanings. The spectrum of socialist ideas stretches from Bloch and Havemann to Biermann, Bahro, and the Eurocommunists, from collectivist-planning fetishism to the individualistic slogan of emancipation. To be sure, nearly all political and social movements have sought to participate in some form or another of socialism, even if they have tried to distinguish "social" from socialist, and without exception all of them have invoked a keyword or magic word like "solidarity." Disastrous reminiscences of the 1920s spring invariably to mind. Back then, too, the substance and meaning of the concept of socialism became blurred. It was manipulated almost at will by radical movements, with the well-known result that the greatest manipulators of words and ideas triumphed in the name of National Socialism. This intermediary form of a supposed "third way" between capitalism and socialism has enjoyed renewed interest especially in the Third World, where it is called Arab or African Socialism, or is directly called National Socialism.

The alternatives emerged most clearly and hence most effectively once again in the classic confrontation between socialism and capitalism. That confrontation was seen as a worldwide clash of systems and, at the same time, particularly by the younger generation, as a confrontation between the old and the new, the past and the future. Socialism had the advantage in that it was seen as part of the wave of the future. The alternative to it was devalued—eschatologically, as it were—as "late capitalism." But it was all a dream, the socialist illusion. Today it strikes us as all the more paradoxical—a bad dream—because historical and contemporary experience has shown that socialist solutions to economic and social problems do *not* result in innovation and vitality that hold promise for the future. Instead they tend toward paralyzing bureaucratism and the administration of scarcity and decay.

What has made the capitalism-socialism debate so otherworldly and unrealistic is the fact that, in reality, mixed forms combining private and public economic elements existed everywhere, except in the politically and coercive Communist systems. In our Western societies a kind of convergence has taken place: we can observe a tendency toward a socialization of liberalism but also a liberalization of socialism. This has brought itself to bear most effectively in the idea of the social free market economy, especially in the Federal Republic. The social and the liberal elements were combined, but the principle of the free market economy remained the bedrock element, and it exerted its influence on socialist economic ideas. If along the way some even spoke, paradoxically, of "free market socialism" or the "socialist market," that too showed that historically obsolete and politically exhausted concepts were being replaced. What is called capitalism today has moved far from the Marxist image and its dogmas. In fact, the concrete development of economic and social relations within the framework of a liberal-social democracy proved so successful and attractive that it left the old scheme of capitalism versus socialism far behind. Yet that old scheme continues to haunt industrial society. In fact from the 1970s on, it experienced a revival in Western Europe as a campaign of ecological anticapitalism. That campaign has given impetus to the Green movements and has left its mark particularly on the universities.

One of the ongoing tasks of the representatives of a liberal and social common sense is to resist the attempts and temptations to re-ideologize the debate. Such efforts are again on the rise, especially in the economic sphere. Their starting point is the still enormous gap between West and East, north and south. Even in Europe, and definitely in the Third World, that gap impedes the development of an economic and social system that is simultaneously liberal and social, and it constantly reopens the old fronts of the socialism versus capitalism debates. There is much work here for a sensible, structure-oriented developmental policy that should and could be more than mere developmental aid. Such a policy should contribute to making an open society politically feasible and workable, even in countries that are structurally different.

One important reason for the seemingly anachronistic persistence of ideological positions from the nineteenth century and their reappearance in our modern industrial society was the continuation of the cold war, the battle between systems. No policy of détente and no amount of economic cooperation could remove the basic principle of the Communist "policy of coexistence," namely that the two economic systems were *ideologically* incompatible. This fundamental challenge was not altered by political and economic agreements even in the age of détente. In the field of human rights, it became instantly apparent, time after time, how fundamental the difference was between liberal democracy and socialist dictatorship, and how irreconcilable were the liberal and totalitarian views of humankind and society. Let us hope that the great upheavals of 1989 have also brought changes in thinking. Relapses are still possible.

III

I will now try, briefly, to carry these lessons and thoughts further and to summarize them in the form of theses.

1. To begin with, one might distinguish between various forms of power and its limitations. On one side are the natural limitations of geography,

the inherent potential of power and its overextension (for example in the case of Hitler, where the overextension caused the collapse of his power into nothing). On the other side are the conscious, deliberate limits to power, for example with respect to economic interests and rules or laws. In particular, there is the deliberate political (self-) limitation of power through the legal system, through constitutions and international law, through decentralization, federalism, the separation of powers, and balance.[60] But in all of this it is essential to emphasize the principle of the state's democratically legitimated monopoly of power. The private and social accumulation of power is a problematic issue. By contrast, the monopoly of power by public authorities remains the critical prerequisite in the modern state, as it seeks to maintain peace, protect the weaker, resist organized crime and terrorism, and defend against all forms of civil war. Expressions of state-exercised power include the use of direct or indirect coercion, the setting of norms, voluntary loyalty (in a democracy), and the use of authority or "structural force" (a highly controversial notion), particularly in dictatorships.

However, the implementation of political majority decisions must, not least, respect the right of opposition, which constitutes a central component of every democracy based on the rule of law. The protected right of opposition now takes the place of the right of resistance. In my view the right of resistance can and must exist only in and against dictatorships; in democracies, opposition has been or should be made a reality. At the same time we are faced with the plurality of power in private or social hands, as well as a large sphere in which they compete for power. Time and again this raises the question of the internal sovereignty of the state with respect to mass organizations and organizational elites, economic federations and large companies, critiques of multinationals from the Left and of large-scale economy and large companies and unions from the Right. The slogans of the party-state or association-state play an important, though often exaggerated, role here. On the other side of this is the institutional separation of power and governing, in which "parliaments, governments, parties, special interests, and the mass media exercise power in the sense of diverse influences."[61]

2. These kinds of analyses are concerned with the quantitative weight and structure of power relationships. By contrast, the *socioethical examination* focuses on the influence of the power factor on the quality of human existence, and on the relationship between power and responsibility from the perspective of humanistic and religious values. Criticism of the social repercussions of the exercise of power by the state as well as private sources was formulated most trenchantly by Marxism in its critique of capitalism, which traces everything back to economic power relationships. In contrast,

a doctrine of state and society that is oriented toward ethics and human rights, and that eventually finds expression in pluralistic democracy based on the rule of law, emphasizes "that political power is not self-justified but is granted temporarily and must protect social coexistence and serve the preservation of peace."[62] Here democracy always means only a "timely limited contract of government" (Theodor Heuss).[63]

3. The *linking* of power to the conscience of the individual, to basic values, to firm constitutional and legal norms and public supervision, is intended to prevent the abuse and arbitrary exercise of power. The separation and distribution of power (through federalism and parliaments) is supposed to ensure that power can be controlled both vertically as well as horizontally. However, the democratic limits on power also mean that the struggle over the power to make political decisions can in fact take place according to the rules of free competition. The consequences of a concentration of power and its exercise through bureaucratization are revealed by the extreme example of a total surveillance state like the GDR: an omnipresent power apparatus, the preponderance of administration over economics, the power of blackmail through the activities and files of the Stasi (state security). But the more indirect power of the mass media, which seek to promote information and transparency, also conjures up dangers of the political monopolization and manipulation of information and of the public and private formation of opinion, a trial of strength over influence and control that can best be objectified through disclosure and impact studies.

The discussion about *new forms of exercising power* that go beyond the traditional spheres becomes particularly intense in the face of technological progress. The possibilities for and fears of an abuse of power in violation of the responsibility of social and scientific ethics reach from nuclear physics, to data processing, to issues involving the ecology and biogenetic engineering. All these issues are now related to the survival of humankind as such and thus transcend the old power question of limited states and societies.

4. In this respect, in particular, it is essential to recognize not that the phenomenon of power is ethically neutral, but that it is *simultaneously an ambivalent impulse and a danger* in human history. Of course this recognition must not take the form of a general evocation or exaggeration of the problematic nature of progress as such. Instead it should be expressed through the concrete examination, in each individual case, of the circumstances surrounding a decision and the various spheres in which it takes effect, along with the experientially and intellectually tested countermeasures for balancing and limiting power. At the same time, however, there must be an indispensable acceptance of power and its use in shaping

private and public life and its role in the genuine progress of humankind. For the opposite of too much power, namely a loss of power and power-lessness, would mean both dysfunction and ineffectiveness; that is to say, nothing other than a renunciation of a responsible and effective management of these kinds of political and economic problems. And today, more than ever, the future of a world of growing populations depends on the technical and scientific solutions to these problems.[64]

5. The social, economic, and political development toward greater complexity and increasing needs does in fact bring with it a *growing "need for decision-making,"*[65] whether we like it or not. And the situation is now further exacerbated by ecological problems, which, characteristically enough, are emerging with particular urgency in dictatorial systems, after having been hushed up for so long. Today, in a time marked by regionalization and federalization, especially in the European Community, the modern state confronts new spheres in which power and its constraint are called for. These spheres relate to the organizing and balancing of an enhanced capacity for decision making on various levels, in a centralized or decentralized arrangement. Complexity, efficiency, time pressure, democratic participation—all these factors simultaneously impair and demand the use of power and authority. In a power vacuum, power and authority will be seized by ambitious individuals, who then become uncontrollable (as happened with von Papen and Hitler in 1932–33). In any case, the use of power and authority frequently wavers between too much and too little.

This seems to confirm the belief of the many pessimists among the critics of democracy, who, in view of the "chronic lag of reality behind the structurally anchored expectations,"[66] lament either (from the Left) excessive decision-making power or (from the Right) the lack of decision-making power. In so doing they repeatedly shift the focus, intentionally or not, to dictatorial solutions and dreams of omnipotence. In this respect, too, we have surely not reached the happy end of history, as some believe in their overoptimistic assessment of the crucial year 1989. They elevate the victory of liberal democracy to an eschatological level, and even imagine that the end of all ideologies has arrived.[67] The problems that remain, and not only in the discussion of power, ensure that political systems will continue to rise and fall, that social and economic crisis will recur, and that the threats to liberal democracies will persist—and with them, disastrous ideologies. And at all times, terrorism, which is, after all, partly ideological,[68] is among the abiding risks of power and a threat to those who wield it: the security problem of leaders as the obverse of power.

6. Of course social and political interactions are frequently marked less by a dramatic and violent use of power than by institutionalized and thus regulated and controlled power relationships.[69] Except in the case of war

(and civil war), the risks of power manifest themselves precisely in the *abuse of legal, institutionalized power.* This is what happened in the modern seizures of power beginning with Lenin, Mussolini, and Hitler. They were carried out largely as pseudodemocratic or pseudolegal revolutions. Moreover, they laid claim to a higher legitimacy for their use of power, which was actually a dictatorial and totalitarian use. In fact, with the help of manipulated "consent," indeed agreement, they presented themselves as guarantors of freedom and peace, of order and efficiency, by suppressing conflict instead of solving it through compromise and the orderly settling of differences. From this perspective, too, the upheaval in Eastern Europe is a (naturally) protracted, late return from the Communist dead ends of 1917 and 1945 to the normality of a legitimate, democratic system of power, which has been violated for so long by the pseudodemocratic abuse of nearly all institutions. Our century, as Luhmann believes, surpasses "all previous ones in the degree and efficiency of the abuse of power," and in the "impotence of the old remedies against the abuse of power, beginning with the right of resistance."[70] But as our century draws to a close, it does show once again the validity of the old, classic struggle against the abuse of power. For it was and is the effective invoking of the ethical and political values of human rights, and the demand for a state based on the rule of law, that contributed, alongside the economic crisis, in very important ways to the loss of confidence and the collapse of the totalitarian power systems and their "age of ideologies." This is what happened in 1945, and it is happening again in 1989.

7. In liberal democracy, however, the problem is usually not an excessive *consciousness of power,* such as one might find in dictators, for example. Instead, we can frequently observe that those who possess power think, or at least profess, the opposite: namely, that they don't have any. The reason for this could be that the demonization of power can lead to its opposite, "forgetfulness of power" *(Machtvergessenheit),* with its own attendant dangers.[71] Alternatively, because others have more power, the power in one's own hands can seem diminished and insignificant. One final example of this phenomenon: when the old question about the "governability" of democracy became a central topic of discussion in the 1970s, it was due to the politicians and those in government, who were groaning under the flood of tasks and complaining of an increased narrowing of the room within which they could take action. (Pressure also came from a financial and economic recession after the oil crisis of 1973 and from the gloomy predictions from the Club of Rome.) On one occasion in 1976, Helmut Schmidt, then head of the West German government, was reminded of his strong position of leadership in the "chancellor democracy." In response, Schmidt, who was more qualified for the position of chancellor than

anyone since Adenauer, insisted that he had at most a 5 percent margin for decision making: everything else was already planned for and unchangeable, in the budget as well as in political planning. On Schmidt's part this may have been a misjudgment of what he could do, or an understatement that is reminiscent of his abdication of leadership authority in his party, which he left largely to Brandt and Wehner. All the same, it is certainly true that since the Brandt era, the government and the state, under intense pressure from the demands of the 1968 movement, have been marked by the phenomenon of "overload" (the international catchword for the overburdened state).[72]

"Powerlessness" is frequently professed by politicians, but not only by them. Contrary to a widespread perception, economic and social leaders, too, frequently tend to underestimate their power. In contrast, our own contemporary history certainly offers many examples of the importance attached to the political role of economics. The basic criticism of the "system" of parliamentary democracy has always been a criticism of the society of free competition, which is quite rightly regarded as the foundation of every pluralistic polity. However, systemic criticism of this kind brings with it three dangers: first, as a critique of pluralism, it opposes the system of free associations; second, as a critique of capitalism and monopoly, it infers from the concentration of economic power that the free market has entered its final, "late capitalist" stage; third, the demand for unlimited participation that it has raised seeks to delegitimize representative and even hierarchical organizational structures. In the process, these dangers have unsettled the society and the economy, schools and universities, all of which have, in addition to codetermination, technical and educational functions that are quite primary.

We are left with the important lesson that the value-oriented competitive democracy, especially from the perspective of power, is most likely to create and maintain the space in which individuals can develop in joint responsibility and, as citizens, make the state their own. And civic freedom as the basic requirement of humane thinking and conduct always presupposes the simultaneous use and limitation of power.

As is the case with freedom, the value of power depends on the (necessarily limited) use we make of it. Like the pluralistic state, the social free market and the policy of competition are, and will continue to be, imperfect answers to the problem of power—though less imperfect than all the other answers (to once again rephrase Churchill's well-known saying). If it is at all possible to provide a more lasting check on the primeval right of the stronger, with its egotism and tendency toward arbitrary power, and turn it into something positive, it is probably only constitutional democracy that can accomplish it. The system does so through the separation of powers, peaceful conflict resolution, protection of minorities, and the reciprocal control of power. Only in this way can it create the space for intellectual freedom, and for that reason, despite all its shortcomings, it has every right to be considered the highest expression of political culture. For it offers the chance to realize and maintain a humane existence—and to civilize power, which, contrary to Jacob Burckhardt and others, is not simply "of its nature evil."

The Dissolution of the
First German Democracy

When yet another change of government took place at the end of January 1933, the twenty-first change in the short, fourteen-year history of the Weimar Republic, few contemporaries realized that it had unleashed events that would deeply affect not only German politics but the course of world politics as well. Even today, more than half a century later, there are still major differences of opinion regarding this momentous turning point in Germany's recent past, indeed in the twentieth century as such—differences not only among surviving politicians of that period, participating observers, and contemporaries who merely went along and suffered, but also among historians, social scientists, scholars of constitutional law, political economists, psychologists, and philosophers. In thousands of books and articles, they have sought to describe and explain how it was possible that in 1933 a people with a great culture and an advanced civilization had delivered itself, voluntarily it seemed, into the hands of the destructive despotism of a group of power-hungry fanatics. A group whose führer had many years earlier openly outlined his radical and nihilistic goals, leaving no doubt about the totalitarian character of his future rule.

Quite clearly, it is not enough to reason in general terms about the character of the German people, and to discover, in a historical excursus from Luther to Bismarck to Hitler, the German susceptibility to dictatorship and a mentality of subservience, as was done in the initial horror after 1945. Of course, the opposite tendency has been equally unsatisfactory: that of emphasizing primarily the common European responsibility for Hitler's rise and for the uncommon burdens on the Weimar state, or of gathering together all the diverse arguments that seem to indicate the inevitability of the National Socialist seizure of power, from an alleged conspiracy of monopoly capitalists all the way to the dangers of a Communist revolution. For the course of events refutes the fundamental belief inherent in both explanatory models: that the Hitler regime was historically unstoppable and politically irresistible. In fact, nearly a century after the emergence of National Socialism in Austria and Germany, more than seventy years after Adolf Hitler's attempted coup, and more than sixty years after he came to power, what I was compelled to conclude in my book *The German Dictatorship* (1969) is still valid: "Though National Socialism has been exhaustively investigated, it remains a controversial subject to this day." The same applies to the origins as well as the preconditions and circumstances of its political rise in the Weimar Republic. To the very end there were alternatives other than the triumph of a movement that was never able to win a majority in free elections.

But the road that led to January 30, 1933, at the same time brings up the larger, more lasting theme of democracy and the seizure of power in the question that is central to our times: how can a totalitarian dictatorship establish itself within a parliamentary, constitutional state? Alongside the historical facts of the German development, we must also consider Europe's historical experience in the twentieth century with the crisis in democracies and the emergence of authoritarian dictatorships. Two perspectives are of equal importance: the uniqueness of Germany's development into the most comprehensive and radical totalitarian dictatorship of its time, and the more general trends of modern European history that made it possible or aided it. Among those trends is, above all, the rise of totalitarian ideologies from the Right and the Left before and after World War I. Next there is the great front of antidemocratic movements in Europe in the 1920s and 1930s. We must also add the political weakness and economic crisis of the old and especially the new democracies of the time, few of which survived. And finally, in particular, there were the new techniques of political seizures of power in the twentieth century. After the opening bang of the Russian Revolution of 1917, totalitarians triumphed over liberal democracies in the pseudodemocratic, ideological mass revolutions of Lenin, Mussolini, and Hitler.

Although the Weimar Republic, born from the collapse of the Empire, was confirmed as a parliamentary democracy in 1919 by a large majority of the freely elected National Assembly (the vote was 262 to 75), it was not a stable state. The monarchy had bequeathed the republic a grave military defeat, and had left it no choice but to conclude a peace agreement that posed an extreme threat to its economic and political development from the very outset. Wide segments of the population were quick to blame the new political order for the existent difficulties, which were the result of the legacy of the old regime, four years of war, and the conditions of a harsh peace settlement. Memories of a happy prewar period joined with the desire to have, instead of the cumbersome, lusterless parliamentary democracy, if not the lost Empire at least a tighter leadership of the state. As early as a year after the founding of the Republic, in the first Reichstag elections of 1920, a bare majority voted for parties who were critical of or even hostile to the republican constitution. That same year the government succeeded in quashing the Kapp-Lüttwitz putsch, an armed coup attempt led by reactionary members of the military. However, attempts to overthrow the government by left-wing and right-wing radical movements three years later, in the stormy year of 1923, were fought back only with great difficulty. In the meantime, the catastrophe of inflation ravaged most of all the middle class, the pillar of the state. Reparations and the occupation of the Ruhr region brought the German economy as a whole to the brink of collapse.

Five years of crisis were followed, however, by five years of calm and stabilization, during which time political radicalism receded. The fact that people were getting used to the Republic, the successes of Gustav Stresemann's policy of rapprochement, and the prospects of reconciliation at home and abroad held out the promise of continuity and security. After a long stretch of governing by weak, frequently changing minority cabinets, the elections in May 1928 were a defeat for the opponents of the Republic and reduced the National Socialists to a splinter group with 2.6 percent of the votes. There was success, even, in forming a Great Coalition. Headed by the Social Democrat Hermann Müller, it was able to govern for two years with a strong parliamentary majority, longer than any of the other twenty Weimar cabinets. There was little to indicate that only three years later the Republic, without any external threat, would deliver itself unconditionally into the hands of its destroyers. After all, despite all shortcomings and difficulties, the Weimar state had already survived the crises of the postwar period and constant attacks on parliamentary democracy by enemies from the Left and the Right a decade longer than Italy, for example.

In actuality, the first German democracy stood, as it were, in the middle, between the older Western democracies and the contested establishment of states and democracies in Eastern and southern Europe. Later, with the impression of the failure of the Weimar Republic and the particularly radical nature and destructiveness of the totalitarian system of National Socialism still fresh, emphasis was usually placed on the persistent political crisis and almost inevitable dissolution of the first German democracy. Yet it is quite clear that the state and society offered better preconditions for a workable system in Germany than in Italy and most other new democracies, which sooner or later fell victim to the antidemocratic, authoritarian currents of the 1920s and 1930s. The German case, in particular, had some very specific conditions and aspects in terms of its history and structure.

Of course, at the same time it represents such a clear and compelling example of how a modern democracy is established and subsequently succumbs to crisis and dissolution that it has to this day attracted special attention around the world as a "typical" case.

A host of very different answers have been given to the two great questions of German democracy: why did it fail, and why was a man like Hitler able to attain total power? A critical appraisal of the answers shows that a simple explanation is not possible. All arguments and inferences that are based on a single main cause or causal formula are headed down the wrong track. This is the problem with the following six explanatory approaches, which I will very briefly indicate. The *economic* explanation is too one-sided in bringing out the economic crisis. Inadequate is also the *institutional* argument, which places the primary responsibility on constitutional defects. *Sociological* interpretations focus solely on the instability of the petty bourgeoisie, while *ideological* ones do the same for Germany's authoritarian tradition. No less one-sided are, of course, the *Marxist-anticapitalist* arguments about a historically necessary crisis and the *mass-psychological* emphasis on the role of propaganda and mass suggestion.

The depth of the crisis as well as the national and social footholds of the antidemocratic movement were quite similar in Italy and Germany, the two "latecomer nations" of the nineteenth century. An essential difference lay in the *individuals* involved. In Germany a Social Democratic president, Friedrich Ebert, headed the Weimar Republic in the critical years between 1919 and 1925. Only during the second half of the Republic did the state have the kind of leadership at the top (in the person of the pre-Republic Marshal Paul von Hindenburg) that made it possible for power be handed over, albeit reluctantly, to a man like Hitler. All Hitler had to do was to stand at the gates with sufficient strength and menace while simultaneously offering himself as a useful partner. The situation of the Italian monarchy in 1922 was politically very different from that in Germany at the same time. It is rather more comparable to the German situation of 1932–1933: an interesting case of deferred analogy.

Surely the notion that the Weimar Republic was doomed to fail, if not immediately then certainly in the long run, because it had serious structural flaws stemming from the unfinished revolution and the strong continuity of predemocratic elements in the state and society, would be too simplistic. Against all expectations, the Republic survived even the crisis year of 1923, with its catastrophic events that could have brought down a democracy with firmer roots. But the main problem was and continued to be this: the German democracy, regarded as a result of the unexpected defeat in World War I, was and remained anything but popular. A year after the Weimar Constitution was adopted, at the first Reichstag elections of 1920, the parties who were its main pillars had lost their majority. There was growing support for the extremist parties of the Left and the Right, who waged a bitter struggle against the Republic. The Communists saw democracy as the result of a betrayal of the working class by the Social Democrats and the unions, a betrayal through compromises with the capitalists, the army, and the old ruling class. The Right denounced democracy as the product of a betrayal of the fighting front by the revolution at home (the legend of the stab in the back), and simultaneously as a foreign diktat over Germany. The Republic was an "un-German," imported form of government, as the right-wing opponents of democracy incessantly claimed.

Thus either the "capitalist class" or the "November criminals" was held responsible for the German misery by the two poles of antidemocratic agitation that opposed the Republic powerfully and suggestively from the very beginning. For the Right, the political and ideological confrontation with Weimar went something like this: on one side were national interest, good Germans, and social justice ("work and bread"); on the other side were the Republic (the product of treason), a foreign democracy, economic misery, and a dishonorable policy of fulfilling the provisions of the Versailles Treaty. The Left, meanwhile, used the slogans of social revolution and antimilitarism to fight the Republic as a bourgeois-capitalist system. And so the negative teamwork of the Republic's enemies from the Left and the Right was active not just from 1930 on, but from the very beginning of the Republic, no matter how bloodily the hostile camps fought each other under the slogans of revolution and counterrevolution. Versailles and revolution were the great slogans of agitation, in 1919 as well as 1933. This great antidemocratic potential, which regarded itself as the "true" Germany, was always present. Hitler, like the war-propagandist Mussolini, did not have to invent or create it—he merely seized on it with maniacal determination and became the most radical champion of the antidemocratic surge.

One must acknowledge this fatal encirclement of the democracy by its enemies if one is to do justice to the achievements of the republican parties and politicians. In truth, the Weimar Republic was not foreign or imported. Instead, it represented the breakthrough of a democratic tradition that had been smothered by the glorification of realpolitik and the strong state of the Second Empire. At the same time it amounted to the resumption of a supranational tradition of a "cosmopolitan" culture and society transcending the narrow focus on the nation state. The Weimar Republic was essentially an attempt to combine the Bismarckian state with 1848 and 1789: this accounts for its character as partly national-conservative, partly liberal and socially forward-looking. This became visible in the very brief, very rich cultural development of the "golden twenties," which was not least a breakthrough of prewar currents in new form: the outsider became the insider, as Peter Gay described it in his fascinating book *Weimar Culture* (1968). The ambivalence of that development found expression in the "rise and decline of the avant-garde" (Walter Laqueur, *Weimar: A Cultural History,* 1974), in the revolutionary and reactionary traits of a hectic time of new departures, which lasted barely more than ten years and ended in the destruction and self-destruction of 1933.

In this respect, too, it holds true that the Weimar Republic was in nearly every way a republic of the minority, a state subject to everyone's reservations, excepting the brief months during which it was founded. This was the fatal significance of the Versailles Treaty: signing it under coercion put an end to the initial period when the Republic enjoyed the approval of the predominant majority of the population. But there was also a large number of Germans, especially in the broad middle class, who wavered and did not move permanently into the antidemocratic camp either after Versailles (as the rejection of the reactionary Kapp-Lüttwitz putsch in 1920 proves) or in the crisis year of 1923. Options and alternatives definitely remained open. Moreover, the mixed character of the Weimar Republic, which combined conservative with liberal and social traits, could also work as an integrative force.

That potential for integration could only be realized, however, if there were external progress and an improvement of the international situation, which would gradually lift from the Republic the stigma of being the Allies' helper in carrying out the provisions of the Versailles Treaty (the so-called fulfillment policy). Moreover, this progress would have to be translated into domestic politics, so that an effective government and socioeconomic stability could refute the previous experience that democracy was to be equated with crisis and chaos. This, precisely, was the real significance of the interim period of "normalization" from 1924 to 1929. International treaties improved the Republic's stature, a respected foreign minister (Stresemann) embodied its growing prestige, the economic progress was obvious. The impact of the onset of the world economic crisis was therefore all the more momentous. From the end of 1929, the plunge in productivity and the tremendous surge in unemployment altered the economic, social, and psychological situations in most ominous ways, and in short order also destroyed political life. One cannot compare this with the crisis years of 1920 to 1923. Those years had brought internal strains every bit as severe, and external strains even far more serious. However, thanks to the leadership of President Ebert, the Republic had been able to weather that crisis without damage to the democratic system. But now the task of leadership fell to a legendary, glorified (though militarily defeated and politically poorly educated) imperial field marshal. Elevated to the status of an "ersatz emperor," as it were, by the plebiscite of a slight majority in the 1925 presidential elections, Hindenburg, despite his formal loyalty to the Republic, remained filled with a deep disdain for civilian and especially republican politics. Once the crisis had begun, he let his advisers—above all the agile General Kurt von Schleicher, State Secretary Otto Meissner (who outlasted all changes of government), and his son Oskar von Hindenburg (who was "not provided for in the constitution," as a contemporary joke had it)—push him steadily down the road of authoritarian, extraparliamentary experiments in governing.

One foothold for these experiments was Article 48 ("the dictatorship paragraph") of the Weimar Constitution, which had been fatefully left without the intended safeguards. It empowered the president to pass emergency decrees and to enforce the executive authority of the Reich against recalcitrant state governments. Though the Reichstag could demand that these measures be rescinded, the president ultimately had more leverage by virtue of his ability to dissolve the parliament. Moreover, since he also had the right to appoint and fire the chancellor and the ministers without the participation of the Reichstag, he could practically govern without any parliamentary checks. During the Ebert era, these three interlinked presidential powers, which the National Assembly of 1919 had added to strengthen the Republic, could certainly also work to the advantage and in defense of the democratic system. But from 1930 on, in the hands of Hindenburg and his advisers, they made possible first the forcing back of the Reichstag, then the authoritarian experiments of Papen and Schleicher, the takeover of Prussia, and finally (in 1933) the terrorist means by which a minority government under Hitler seized power.

Already, the overthrow of the Great Coalition and the appointment of Brüning in the spring of 1930 had been engineered deliberately above the head of the Reichstag. This meant that the Reichstag was relieved of the responsibility for compromise and constructive politics precisely at a time of crisis. Shortly thereafter Brüning prematurely dissolved the Reichstag, which did not want to go along with his course of authoritarian government by emergency decrees, thus restricting its role to one of merely tolerating what the government was doing. The subsequent Reichstag elections in September of 1930 confirmed, through the enormous increase in the number of National Socialist deputies (from 12 to 107), how disastrously ill-timed Brüning's decision had been. The startup support that Alfred Hugenberg's German National People's Party (Deutschnationale Volkspartei, or DNVP) had given the Hitler movement since 1929, against the warnings from thoughtful conservatives around Graf Westarp, had more than succeeded.

Thus in the spring of 1932 the democratic groups, in a political about-face, came to believe that only Hindenburg's reelection could stem the surge of the totalitarian movements. When the newly re-elected president withdrew his support from Chancellor Brüning a few weeks later, it led to the rupture that removed the last remnants of parliamentary coresponsibility. The appointment of Franz von Papen—a renegade politician of the Center Party—as chancellor, without parliamentary backing, brought the experiment of a "party-free authoritarian state" to its climax. Simultaneously, of course, it did the same for the rise of the National Socialists: a series of elections brought on by Papen's abuse of the presidential power to pass emergency decrees and dissolve parliament produced in July of 1932 a destructive majority for the totalitarian parties of the Left and the Right. Three months later, however, the elections of November 1932 showed a first, sharp drop in the National Socialists' mass following.

Schleicher, Papen's successor, made a last-minute attempt, at the end of 1932 and the beginning of 1933, to break off the authoritarian experiment and defuse the situation of imminent civil war by trying to split the National Socialist German Worker's Party (NSDAP—the Nazi party) and gain the support of all nontotalitarian groups. But his moves came too late. Meanwhile his offended predecessor, Papen, took the initiative more quickly. With a frivolous overestimation of his own capabilities, he hoped to carry out his ambitious plans for a restorative and authoritarian restructuring of the state by striking a deal with Hitler. In conjunction with the DNVP and Stahlhelm, he opened the door to power for the "Bohemian corporal," who had so far been steadfastly kept from it, and whom Hindenburg held in low esteem.

The fact that Hitler was appointed chancellor and vested with the full presidential powers at a time when his party was in a deep crisis makes the decision of January 1933, and the intrigues of the Papen-Meissner group that was substantially responsible for it, one of the most momentous mistakes in history. It was a doubly absurd decision in view of the fact that at the end of 1932 the low point of the economic crisis and of unemployment had already passed, the problem of reparations had found a solution favorable to Germany, and further revisions of the Versailles provisions were in the offing. The upswing, whose ground had been laid during the Republic, now worked to the full advantage of National Socialist propaganda and the Third Reich's message of salvation.

In fact, Hitler's breakthrough to power was made possible only by a series of personal intrigues and deception tactics. He never won much more than a third of the votes in free elections and this blocked the legal road to power via a majority party, which Hitler had set out on after the failed putsch of 1923. When a noticeable decline of the National Socialist share of the votes (from 37 to 33 percent) in the elections of November 1932 coincided with the first signs that the economic crisis was on the wane, it seemed that the National Socialist reach for power was moving once again into a distant and hardly attainable future. The result was tension within the heterogeneous mass party and the danger of a split. In this situation, the eighty-five-year-old President von Hindenburg took the advice of his closest circle, in particular of the ambitious and thoughtless ex-chancellor Franz von Papen, and appointed Hitler to head a coalition government of "national concentration." The calculation was that the conservative majority in the cabinet (eight conservatives as against three National Socialist ministers), with the help of Hindenburg and his vice chancellor, Papen, would be able to tame the dynamism of the Hitler movement and use it for its own goals of an authoritarian or monarchic reform of the state.

This proved a grandiose miscalculation. The National Socialists, once in control of a few key positions, such as the chancellorship, the Reich Interior Ministry (under Wilhelm Frick), and the Prussian Interior Ministry, which also gave them control of the police (under Hermann Göring), were quickly able to overwhelm such plans. They did it through a series of pseudolegal, partly violent manipulations that were dressed up with the catchphrase of the "national rising" and with nice-sounding Christian-national slogans. Since he still did not command the majority in parliament or of the voters, Hitler, using the dictatorial power of the willing president (Article 48 of the Weimar Constitution), passed a series of radical decrees in February and March of 1933. Their purpose was to make public opinion receptive to National Socialist propaganda (under Joseph Goebbels), eliminate the basic rights, force the states into line, and subject all of public life to a permanent state of emergency. The unscrupulous exploitation of the unsolved Reichstag fire (February 27–28, 1933), and an Enabling Act (March 24, 1933) that was forced through with deception and threats, completed this process. The original coalition of right-wing parties was now transformed into a total seizure of power by the National Socialists. With parliament's self-elimination, Hitler's dictatorship was legalized. The "coordination" *(Gleichschaltung)* or subjection of associations and unions, the dissolving of the parties, and the "cleansing" of the administration occurred with a rapidity that eclipsed by far the model of the Fascist seizure of power in Italy.

Domestic and foreign policy misjudgments on the part of his opponents made it easier for Hitler to pursue this course. The strong political Left was divided within. While the Communists contributed substantially to the destruction of the Republic with their obstructionism, finding themselves often in an unholy alliance with the National Socialists and even fighting the SPD as their main enemy, the Social Democrats and the unions were nearly paralyzed in the face of the deceptive National Socialist strategy of legality. The weapon of a general strike was not activated—its use seemed too doubtful at a time of such great unemployment—and the positions of power that the opponents of Hitler held were quickly crushed by the dictatorial regime of decrees and the violent party-armies of the National Socialists. By the time the reality of the "legal revolution" became apparent, it was too late for open resistance. On July 14, 1933, the one-party state was declared. All that remained was the path of "illegal" resistance, a path full of sacrifices. It was taken by some of the workers, later by some in the Church and in the middle class, and in the end in the military. It held out little promise of success. By this time the totalitarian führer-state had been consolidated. An apparatus of propaganda, threats, and terror had been set up, and it secured the consent and fear of the population as the foundation of the new Third Reich.

Among the many and various methodological and substantive approaches used in international scholarship of the past fifty years to explain and interpret the momentous events of 1933, it is well worth considering the relationship between democratic and dictatorial elements in the transformation from the parliamentary Republic to the plebiscitary führer-state. Regardless of whether we are discussing the revolutionary character of the upheaval, the economic and social interconnections, the role of action-taking or hesitating individuals and parties, the structures of the constitution and power, the problems of political culture and ideology in the crisis of the state—or whether we place greater emphasis on the process of dissolution and the assault of the seizure of power—we are always dealing with one basic question: how was it possible, especially under the political conditions of the twentieth century, for a liberal state based on the rule of law to be transformed into a totalitarian regime? Transformed, that is, in an apparently legal way, indeed through the use and abuse of democratic processes (a change in government, the empowerment of the state through the president and the parliament) and finally by plebiscitary consent, all within a few weeks or months?

The twofold question about the dictatorial elements in the democracy that (still) existed between 1930 and 1933, and about the democratic or pseudodemocratic elements in the dictatorship that followed in 1933–34, makes one thing clear: democracy and the seizure of power were closely related. However, in spite of the frequently emphasized continuity, what happened was not a "mere" radicalization but a deep rupture that eventually marked and sealed the overthrow of existing conditions. A development that had begun with a supporting device in the problematic presidential "reserve constitution," and its subsequent abuse and transformation into broad emergency powers in accord with Article 48, culminated on

January 30, 1933, when dictatorship became the foundation of the government. At the same time, the democratic principle was transformed from a basic constitutional principle into an acclamatory and plebiscitary instrument of manipulation for totalitarian rule over the state and society.

8

Liberalism in the Century of Ideologies

I

The history of liberalism is the history of the transformations it has undergone and the challenges that have been mounted against it. If we seek to understand the current "crisis of liberalism," reflected perhaps in the state of the Free Democratic Party (FDP) after the change of government in Bonn (1982), we must first of all become aware of this historical fact. It applies especially to the ups and downs of political liberalism in the past one hundred years.

A century ago, the inroads that the state and its legislation had made into increasingly broad areas of society and the economy already posed a dual challenge to the development of liberal theories. On the one hand, they interfered with the classical notion of a completely free, and thus virtually automatic, upward development: with the rise of economic interest groups and labor unions, group and state political interventions gained in importance during the last quarter of the nineteenth century. Indeed, the liberal parties played a prominent role in this process, contrary to their original principles. On the other hand, rivalry with the still powerful conservatives (and their agrarian policy) and with the emerging socialists (and their social policy), forced the liberals to amend their pure doctrine. These corrections had, in fact, been foreshadowed in the emphatic "social liberalism" of John Stuart Mill (1806–1873). From the turn of the century they drastically altered conceptions about the role of the state and the demands placed on liberal democracy.

Liberalism had risen with the modern idea of progress, but now the belief in its future universal validity suffered noticeable setbacks. This applied not only to economic laissez-faire liberalism as such, but also to the convictions that freedom takes political precedence over equality, the individual over the collective. The pressing social questions of the day, an expanding imperialism, and the nationalism that led to World War I were political challenges that went far beyond the basic individualist and rational axioms of liberalism.

On the one side there were dire warnings, not least in England, of an imminent collectivization that threatened to overwhelm the liberals; even in the land of John Locke and Adam Smith, liberals were forced onto the defensive. As early 1884, the influential sociologist Herbert Spencer, in a book with the alarming title *Man versus the State,* deplored the increasing parliamentary transgressions against the principle of the free market.

On the other side, humanitarian as well as nationalist sentiments, in the face of the headlong industrial and political developments, were compelling even liberal theoreticians to justify or even advocate state measures that delivered increasing blows to their credo that the state should act as merely a night watchman, and also to their belief in the free development of society.

It became apparent that liberalism and humanism, individual rights and human rights, were inextricably intertwined: the necessary reforms aimed at the evils of industrialization and the abuse of power required ever new interventions in free development. The liberal dilemma was evident. Just as the conservatives were caught between reaction and continuity, and the socialists between revolution and democracy, the liberals were caught between their economic and political postulates. And in each case the solution to the dilemma amounted to a strengthening of the state.

II

The fallacies and disappointments surrounding liberalism led to a variety of attempts to adapt and modernize it. Every social or national modification, however, robbed liberalism of a piece of its persuasive consistency, which simultaneously reinforced the impression of critics from the Left and the Right that the liberal and bourgeois age was coming to an end. In England, which had a two-party system, it proved possible longer than elsewhere to prevent the decline of liberalism into a mere party of class and special interests, and to integrate the social component of the movement. On the Continent, however, the divisions and struggles over which direction to take were already well under way. Before and, particularly, after World War I, liberal theory was either narrowed down to special-interest politics or transformed into general postulates, and separate liberal parties were rendered dispensable to the extent that liberal ideas were taken over by other democratic parties.

In Germany, the social implications of liberalism were taken up especially by the Protestant pastor and "national-social" politician and journalist Friedrich Naumann (1860–1919). Among his friends were Max Weber and Hugo Preuß, and his students eventually included Theodor Heuss. Naumann attached great importance to education in the broad sense of an "education of the people," and also to the religious component of social affairs. In his view, social justice and participation by all citizens—both politically and in the fruits of progress—were among the obligations of the liberal idea under the conditions of his time.

The attempts to reconcile liberalism with the social and national elements of the time came, of course, at the expense of the clarity and rigor of its identity. Long before its contraction to the level of party politics, liberalism thus got caught, along with rationalism and individualism, in the grinding wheels of doubt and in a critique of capitalism and civilization. Those currents furnished the irrationalism and collectivism of anarchists and authoritarians with the ammunition they needed to destroy the idea of freedom and progress.

The liberal "revisionists" at the turn of the century were concerned with giving full consideration to humankind's social nature, as well as to its nonrational needs and susceptibilities. Naumann's social idea of the nation contained a critique of laissez-faire industrialism and its social consequences; through open-mindedness toward the powerful social current he tried to win it over or save it for liberal democracy. He wanted to prove that a renewed form of liberal democracy was modern and open to the social and national dimensions of humankind, that individualism and socialism could be reconciled. "From Bebel to Bassermann"—from the Social Democrats to the National Liberals was Naumann's slogan of political coalition. Behind it stood more than mere party politics: namely, the liberal conviction of the compatibility of these philosophies on the basis of a democratic "people's state."

The state not as a merely negative limitation, but as a positive tool for securing liberty in both its individualistic and civic-social dimensions: this represented the decisive transformation toward a political modernization of liberalism. Of course this also opened the possibility of a new threat to liberalism from more tightly organized, etatist mass movements on the Left and the Right, once the increase in the state's responsibilities and spheres of competence was accepted, and was indeed sanctioned with liberal, civic-rights justifications. In the educational system, in cultural and social policy, in the relations between employers and employees all the way to collective bargaining, and in the combining of the principle of private property with the principle of the common good: everywhere there occurred a shift from the idea of economic freedom to the political idea of the constitutional state, an idea that also increasingly embraced elements of the welfare state.

This meant, of course, that the fundamental differences that had set liberal principles apart from conservative as well as social democratic ones were leveled out and relativized. In the union of liberal principles with etatist and social trends lay a chance for a workable democracy. But at the same time, the adoption of conservative and social-political concepts deprived the liberal credo of some of its original force; it muddled the great "issues" and postulates that had accounted for its persuasive power. In a time of political ideologies, and in comparison with more consistently self-contained socialist and etatist ideologies on the Left and the Right, with their clearly outlined images of the enemy, liberalism appeared to have less coherence as a worldview. Greater tolerance toward other currents, an essential characteristic of liberalism, was, of course, in keeping with its name and self-image. At the same time, however, it made liberalism appear to the broad populace to be inconsistent and compromising, devoid of principles and opportunistic. And with the war economy and the postwar crises, its economic theory, too, seemed increasingly less valid.

III

The great moral substance of the liberal idea—the principles of civic and human rights, of political control of power and violence, of national and international cooperation—had found expression in Woodrow Wilson's theoretical ideas on politics. But like Wilson himself, that moral substance fell victim to the disappointments over the wartime and postwar developments. Liberalism, which had given rise to modern democracy, could not hold its own in the competitive struggle of ideologies. It was identified with democracy's problems and crises, while the great left-wing and right-wing ideologies, riding the waves of criticism of democracy, satisfied the need of the masses for a political faith.

Added to this situation was the ambiguity that the concept of liberalism itself had acquired in the course of the nineteenth century, and in particular since the ideological confrontations at the turn of the century. The narrower concept of liberalism referred, above all, to the intermediate position of the liberals between conservatism and socialism. In sociological terms it referred to the bourgeoisie, in political terms to a nonradical reformism. In that narrower sense liberalism continued to be equated with capitalism and as such attacked, in particular by Marxists. Marxists even saw fascism as growing seamlessly from liberalism: the Marxist "theory of fascism" was a deliberate distortion of the universal political and humanistic substance of the idea of liberalism. It narrowed that substance down in social and economic terms, turning liberalism into the selfish dogma of special interest, the battle cry of laissez-faire, and into a capitalist conspiracy whose goal was the (fascist) destruction of socialism.

By contrast, the broader concept of democratic liberalism described— above all in the United States, where no socialism of any consequence has developed—the basic idea behind a libertarian and pluralistic democracy. It was politically and intellectually a broader conception, capable of incorporating social-democratic trends and classes, and of forming the counteridea to autocracy and dictatorship, to authoritarian and absolutist-totalitarian movements and systems. This democratic liberalism demonstrated its "ideological" strength in its opposition to communism and fascism. Unlike its counterpart on the European Continent, it stood its ground in the totalitarian period between the wars. After 1945, it made possible the reconstruction of democracy in Europe and formed its intellectual foundation.

The core ideas of this democratic liberalism, apart from the freest possible economy and society, were the preservation and further development of democratic institutions, of free elections and legislatures as well as the separation of powers, and also of national self-determination and a social morality that was aimed at freedom and equality for all, not least for minorities and the disadvantaged. Such a broad democratic philosophy could see itself as progressive in the sense that it promoted a stronger social and economic policy on the part of the state. That view has been evident in liberalism's development since Franklin Roosevelt's New Deal, when "liberal" first tended to mean "Left." But a "neoconservative" direction, as seen in the 1920s and again the 1970s, is also part of the more general notion of liberalism, though it has increasingly and sharply dissociated itself from the left-wing, welfare-state oriented, or more radical conception of liberalism. In any case, the broad concept of liberalism has not been narrowed down to class politics. Instead, it has been above all antidictatorial, anticollectivist, antiracist, and antitotalitarian in orientation. Conceived of as a defense against state intervention and for the preservation of democratic institutions, it has regarded itself in this sense as being the high point and quintessence of the Western political tradition, indeed as the secular form of Western civilization.

This double meaning in the modern idea of liberalism is reminiscent in many ways of the ambiguity of the modern idea of progress—with its economic and social, political and cultural dimensions and ambivalences— with which liberalism has been intimately associated. Both ideas share the belief in humankind and its potential, the conviction that the human order can be improved not only materially but politically and morally as well, and the idea of liberty and human rights. But after the turn of the century, at the moment of its highest development, this faith confronted its fiercest challenges, especially from Communism, Fascism, and National Socialism, the great movements of "illiberalism" (Fritz Stern). In the interwar period, the ideas about masses and elites offered by the critics of liberalism gained the ideological upper hand over the liberal ideas of freedom and compromise.

IV

It took the experience of dictatorships and the Second World War for the basic antitotalitarian attitude of liberalism, as well as of democratic socialism and of Christian-democratic ideas, to find common ground and create a more lasting basis for cooperation between individualistic and communitarian ideas. This cooperation was able, in the interest of (liberal) freedom and (social) reform, to break the absolutist claim of the ideologies, and to provide a better safeguard for the existence of a liberal and social democracy. This generalizing of liberalism, its integration into all democratic parties, turned a concept that had often been declared dead into the foundation of the revived liberal-parliamentary democracy of the West.

In contrast to the period between the wars, after 1945 the component of freedom within democracy was formulated in more definitive constitutional terms, which also enhanced our ability to deal with freedom on a theoretical level. This was accomplished not only through a more substantive emphasis on basic rights but also, above all, through the further development of the idea of pluralism. The notion of democracy as the agreement to simultaneously tolerate and restrain different opinions and ambitions signals more clearly than mere formal constitutions and institutions (which could resemble one another outwardly) the difference that sets democracy apart from all forms of dictatorship. Pluralism also means that the common will is not determined in an authoritarian or totalitarian manner by the state, but is based on and determined by the readiness to set voluntary boundaries on the plurality of ambitions and forces; those boundaries are drawn at precisely the point where the existence and workability of this plurality, its freedom and reciprocal tolerance, are threatened or denied. Conversely, only where this basic agreement is accepted can the democratic state grant the multitude of aspirations full play without endangering itself. The controversial step of banning parties, for example, is taken precisely when extremism calls the pluralistic system itself into question.

The fundamental notion that the state is the plurality of its citizens contains the ancient insight of Aristotle, in his rejection of every monomorphic theory of the state. A basic agreement by all citizens means that the pluralistic principle is accepted, not that all citizens have identical views or that all political currents are fused into one in relationship to the common good, which is what is desired in the fictions and coercion of modern dictatorship and "totalitarian democracy" (J. L. Talmon). It means that differences are settled freely, and that some interests can prevail over others, provided they can line up a majority behind them. What remains important is respect for people who hold different opinions, for the outvoted majority, as is so aptly expressed in the famous English phrase "to agree to disagree." What is at stake is the very principle of discussion and compromise in the political process. Given the apparent impossibility of reducing all views and interests from the outset to a single formula, as dictatorships demand, liberal democracy is existentially founded on the historical experience and realization (which needs to be conveyed not through political indoctrination but through political education) that only the unobstructed settling of differences of opinion and different interests can give rise to those points of agreement that render individuals capable of striking compromises that enhance the common welfare.

V

One prerequisite for the liberal-democratic theory of pluralism was, of course, the progressive broadening of equal rights to all strata of society. But equality and emancipation, first in the liberal-bourgeois sense and then in the socialist sense, could also endanger the component of freedom in democracy. Therein lies the inextricable relationship and the permanent tension between liberal and egalitarian principles, a situation that reflects the diversity of human beings and their interests. Democracy seeks to render those differences capable of compromise without abolishing them by force. All criticisms of modern democracy, and in particular the attacks on its pluralistic structure that have arisen from theoretical debates since the 1960s, are a rebellion against the impossibility of abolishing the antagonistic relationship between the principles of majority rule, freedom, and equality.

This has had far-reaching consequences not only for the theory of full political equality, but also for the social structure of modern democracy and for its egalitarian tendencies. Transferred from the political to the social idea of equality, those tendencies have been carried as far as the revolutionary consequences of totalitarian, coerced uniformity. The shift toward an egalitarian understanding of democracy is visible in the progressive social elaboration and extension of basic rights in the liberal-democratic constitutions: the postulate of social and material equality has penetrated deeply into the legal and political realm.

This has set the stage for the great confrontations between liberal and egalitarian conceptions of democracy that have been unsettling our century. The social foundations of democracy are changing; the welfare state, the all-providing state is advancing, and along with it the criticisms about the excessive or inadequate realization of equality. The controversy over the egalitarian conception of democracy is marked, on one side, by warnings of "leveling" tendencies and gloomy pessimism about civilization, and on the other by revolutionary demands for redistribution and restructuring. The controversy always heats up when crises, generational rifts, or conflicts over social emancipation demand that the liberty-equality balance be modernized or adapted. This happened in the second half of the nineteenth century and after the two world wars. More recently it has been happening since the late 1960s, and under the Third World's pressure for emancipation.

Yet these ever-recurring antagonisms, and the irresistible advance of elements of the welfare state within democracies based on freedom and equality, are the consequence of and price we pay for the modern all-citizen democracy's function of absorbing and transforming new political elements. Modern democracy did not create these problems, as antidemocracy critics, especially before and after the First World War, have claimed, nor has it failed to solve them, as radical-egalitarian, socialist maximalists have charged to this day. Rather, it seeks to absorb and channel the effects of the industrial-technological revolution and the population explosion, no matter whether these are directly or indirectly related to the development of democracy. Above all, by strengthening and universalizing the demand for liberty and equality, it also seeks to direct the rapid social change into a peaceful form that counteracts crisis, chaos, and dictatorship.

VI

This is the significance of the struggle of ideas waged over the ever-recurring need to balance the relationship between freedom and equality: achieving a balancing to support the strain in that relationship, to translate it into constitutional politics, and to cope with it in terms of conflict theory. The idea of the "social free market" and the formula of the "social constitutional state," which were established as the foundation of the West German constitutional system, contain the tension and the compromise that characterize modern democracy. The debate over the relationship between legal and social equality, over the consequences of pluralism and individual freedom, remains a permanent issue in the theoretical and political disputes about an exercise of power that is capable of managing conflict, and about different conceptions of democracy. But the debates take place within the framework of a liberal system of compromise. The real threat to democracy has always come from the rejection or denegration of this system by critics who oppose it.

Needless to say, the profound shift from liberal to social democracy amounts to neither the refutation nor to the end of democracy's basic liberal conceptions. To be sure, a society of increasing social and economic complexity leads perforce into a web of dependencies, state interventions, and postulates of economic democracy. Yet neither a soviet or corporate state nor a system based on orthodox-liberal ideas conforms to the advanced state of modern society. Instead, the countermodel is a pseudoegalitarian authoritarianism or totalitarianism, whose promises of equality have proved either fictitious or destructive. For the political surrender of democracy's principles of freedom, majority rule, and supervision ultimately leads to the loss of the essential equality of the citizens.

There are, thus, reciprocal principles that support and presuppose each other in spite of the tension between them. They form the three basic conditions for a workable state that can get by with a minimum of political force and offer a maximum of peaceful conflict resolution. First: democracy is majority rule, in which all votes are equal and free. Second: democracy accommodates to the largest extent possible the pluralistic as well as egalitarian needs of the citizens for freedom of movement and equality of opportunity. Third: democracy is not, however, a radical, coerced uniformity and absolutism of the majority, because it remains committed to the protection of the individual and the minority, which is not a fixed entity and might become part of the government itself.

This is a structure as rich in tensions as it is exacting and complicated. But only liberal democracy is able to translate into politics the moral endeavors that are among the highest fruits of human cultural evolution: to develop and yet restrain oneself, to control by institutional means the constant temptation to abuse power, to resist the age-old imposition of the will of the stronger, and to counterpose to the barbaric "nature" of the exercise of political power a political culture of voluntary cooperation or compromise, born of informed self-interest yet bound by mandatory rules and enshrined in constitutional law. The idea of liberalism—at the core of this limited government, this liberal-democratic, moderate conception of the state—remains indispensable in a state based on political parties. In modern history, liberalism has been a decisive impulse behind the civilizing of government and the domestication of violence. The modern state can dispense with it only at the price of freedom and by inviting the prospect of dictatorship.

THE
LEGACY
OF
NATIONAL
SOCIALISM

Authoritarianism and Totalitarianism: The German Dictatorship and Austria in the Antagonistic World of European Nationalisms

I

Beginning in the early 1920s there arose, within the changed system of European states, a confrontation that seems more characteristic of the period than the alternative between revolution and counterrevolution that was invoked in 1918. I am referring to the confrontation between democracy and antidemocracy.[1] This confrontation also highlighted the differences between old and new democracies—between the states of western and northern Europe, on the one hand, and those of central, eastern, and southern Europe, on the other—and brought out the differences between the victorious powers and the countries that had lost the war or were unhappy with the victory, including Japan and Italy. These trends, especially after the world economic crisis in the 1930s, then played a decisive role in the formation of political fronts, a process in which the maelstrom of authoritarian and totalitarian movements at home intensified in foreign affairs into the events that laid the groundwork for World War II.

Along with the nationalistic debate over revisionism, it was the debate over democracy that drew up the great camps within and between states, politically as well as ideologically. World War I at first produced a jolting expansion of the external and internal spheres of activity of modern democracy. This applies not only to its geographic spread across Europe but also to the expansion of institutions and constitutions, the development of parties and associations, the pushing through of political equality in the vote for women, and the efforts to safeguard civic freedom and political participation. But with this expansion and deepening of the hoped-for and proclaimed "democratization" of Europe, the great structural problems of political modernization became apparent (much as they did after the World War II when democratic forms were transferred to the Third World).

These problems existed even in the older democracies, and their intensity and gravity could be inversely proportional to the absence of the historical, social, and intellectual preconditions that had made the rise of modern democracy possible and had helped it put down strong roots in a few states of western and northern Europe, in Switzerland, and in the United States. Its experimental adoption by or transfer to states in central, southern, and eastern Europe depended on the extent to which it was possible, through favorable political and institutional measures as well as social reforms, to expand the narrow popular support for democracy, the basis on which the democratically minded politicians and parties could prove the worth of the new system. As difficult as this pioneering work might have seemed in the misery and chaos of the postwar period, the obvious superiority of the democracies in the war, along with the avoidance of revolution outside of Russia, provided a positive impetus. Clearly the old systems were exhausted, and the radical revolutions from the Right and the Left went against the great yearning for freedom and a just order when all they did was replace the old, predemocratic system with a new, dictatorial one.

Much depended on what kind of image and inspiration the established "classical" democracies would be able to convey. It was all but inevitable that they, as the victors, would be held responsible for postwar misery and injustice, and that the harsh peace treaties would not exactly improve this sentiment. Thus, whether the restructuring of Europe could also be secured on the basis of the domestic constitutions of the various states depended all the more on the internal qualities and attractiveness of those democracies. For that reason all eyes were on France, England, and the United States. Not only had they decided the war and the postwar order, they also were the decisive players in the debate over democracy.

Of course the policies of the Western powers were substantially shaped by the fact that after the war their divergent peacetime interests reemerged strongly once again. France was primarily interested in security, England in restraint and political distance from European politics, the United States in a withdrawal from world politics. The result was a restoration of the power politics of national states and a quick dashing of hopes for a League of Nations and European unity, and eventually even a naked, feeble policy of appeasement toward the dictatorships. It was all the more significant that, in contrast to the Western European states, the introduction and development of democracy in the rest of Europe went hand in hand with the establishment and rise of extremely hostile movements and ideologies. These struck a revolutionary or reactionary posture, and all had one thing in common: an antidemocratic thrust. This applied to the Iberian countries, which had kept out of the war; it applied above all to the newly established states in Eastern Europe, even if they stood on the side of the victorious powers; and it also applied to the states that were particularly traumatized or disappointed by the war, and in which the economic and social problems at the same time took on a special driving force: Germany, Austria, and Italy. In all these cases there was a close, reciprocal connection between the crises of democracy and growing antidemocratic movements.

After the October Revolution in Russia had given a signal from the Left, it was in Italy that the signal of an equally emphatic "seizure" of power from the Right first manifested itself. Of course Mussolini, too, came out of a revolutionary socialism; in fact his Fascism was, in its structure and impact, much more complex than the leftist slogan of "counterrevolution" suggested. What happened was this: in the bosom of the antidemocratic movement, there developed *simultaneously* the two loaded concepts that were marked by seduction and terror and that remained highly contested in the conflicts of the century: Fascism and totalitarianism.[2] Italian postwar politics, unsettled by the confusion of revolutionary and nationalistic, procommunist and anticommunist slogans and aspirations, saw the first victory by one of the new mass movements. With their combination of conservative and progressive, anticommunist and state-socialist goals, a combination that appealed to all classes, these movements fought above all against liberal democracy. They were the truly new phenomenon of the interwar period, out of which a new form of dictatorship would arise: totalitarian dictatorship. But the importance of these highly ideologized mass movements and "absolutist-integration parties"[3] lies in the fact that they made possible a renewed, final excess of national-imperialistic power politics in Europe—and then led to its deepest fall. The special contribution of Fascism to modern history was, in fact, the unexpected discovery—unexpected especially to the Left—that anti-Marxism and antiliberalism side-by-side, in fact precisely in combination, could prove highly attractive to the masses. But that presupposed the magic formula of National Socialism. As an alternative equally to Marxism and capitalism, to liberalism and Communism (against "Red Front and reaction"), National Socialism offered the masses national *and* social fulfillment in national-revolutionary garb.

National Socialism in Germany expressed this claim clearly and radically even in its name, and it should by no means be understood simply as German fascism. Its "revolution from the Right" (Hans Freyer)[4] meant more than the simple counterrevolution of which leftist opponents spoke in such fateful underestimation. Their verdict was shaped and dominated by the myth of the "good" revolution that was based on the French model or even the Leninist all-encompassing claim, and more seldomly on the moderate American ideal. Liberal observers, on the other hand, hesitated for moral and intellectual reasons to apply the concept of revolution to the

National Socialist type of seizure of power, even if they rejected the exclusive Marxist and Communist claim to the good or true revolution, which still today draws the simplistic distinction between right-wing putsch and left-wing revolution. It is certainly true that the National Socialists saw themselves as the great counterblow to the French Revolution. When they seized power in 1933, Goebbels declared emphatically: "With this the year 1789 is struck from history."[5] But at the same time they spoke not without reason of their "legal" as well as "national revolution." To misjudge or underestimate this would be tantamount to the sort of flawed understanding we find in the critique of totalitarianism that invokes supposed differences between Left and Right dictatorships. However, even qualitative differences in the intellectual and moral spheres do not amount to a decisive objection to the concept of totalitarianism, if the forms of ideologized one-party rule and their brutal consequences for those they rule and persecute are similar. In Germany, National Socialism, with its revolutionary and simultaneously pseudodemocratic striking power, proved superior in the battle against the Weimar Republic. It prevailed against the dictatorial competition from Communism and, after 1938, from Fascism as well.

II

We are thus confronted in the 1930s with three different manifestations of the antidemocratic movement and forms of rule. There was the Fascist nationalist imperialism of the Italian type (of course in reality only a *"totalitarismo imperfetto"*).[6] What set it apart from other, imitative Fascisms was its strong emphasis on the total state and on the Roman imperial tradition. Then there were the two pronounced totalitarianisms in the Soviet Union and the Third Reich. Not only were they aiming for a more radically oppressive regime, they were also based on a pseudoreligious kind of total ideology. In the former case, that ideology was revolutionary in class terms and on a global scale; in the latter it was social Darwinist and revolutionary in racial terms. Finally, there was the wide field of authoritarian dictatorships, which Austria, in the shadow of both Italian Fascism and German National Socialism, joined after 1933–34. The fact that Hitler and his anti-Semitism had come from old Austria, and that National Socialism itself began in that country produced an ambivalent and tense situation.

How realistic, then, was the claim of these "authoritarian regimes" that they were realizing, beyond the great total dictatorships *and* beyond the supposedly decayed democracies, the often envisioned "third way" between the fronts of democracy and dictatorship, capitalism and socialism?

Looking at the more recent scholarship from Juan Linz to Alfred Ableitinger, it is important, as it was with the use of the concepts of fascism and totalitarianism, to recognize, first of all, the significant differences that existed from one country to the next.[7] The polymorphic concept of the authoritarian state is anything but exact; it comprises a great many forms of predemocratic and postdemocratic regimes. But the conditions that gave rise to them seem in the 1930s comparable in many ways: against the background of deep division in political and social life, malfunctions in the party system and parliamentarianism were felt to be, or were propagandized as and dramatized as being, crises of national legitimacy. Justifying themselves as the inevitable emergency form of government necessary to save the state from a loss of power and a power vacuum, from civil war and existential crisis, the authoritarian regimes at the same time saw themselves as a separate way, a third way: this was the case in 1932 in both Germany and Austria. It is certainly true that the mentality of authoritarianism belongs to the world of dictatorships and to the establishment and sanctioning of nondemocratic ways of governing. But authoritarian government is actually more reminiscent of the ancient Roman type of emergency regime, which was of limited duration and had a restricted sphere of competence. It is thus as far removed from the revolutionary and ideological way of thinking of modern, totalitarian dictatorships as it is from the liberal-democratic way, no matter whether the authoritarian view of order has a more tradition-oriented or a more technocratic cast. The authoritarian regime is all about the preservation (or enforcement)—with dictatorial support—of class-related, economic, or military positions of power. Totalitarianism, on the other hand, is about the pseudodemocratic mobilization of all citizens in the service of a revolutionary, monopolist movement, and about a quasi-religious ideology with a claim to exclusivity.

Authoritarianism can be under the banner of the Left or the Right, the private economy or state economy, defensive or developmental policies. It can arise from the crisis of a democracy or from predemocratic, feudal, and absolutist conditions: it all depends on the maturity of the political and social institutions in a given state, on the level of material and intellectual culture, on the forms of religion and morality. The great variety in the forms that authoritarian regimes can take—this, too, a contrast to the claim of absoluteness in fascist or totalitarian ideologies and regimes—is matched by the noticeably reduced role of or the absence of a revolutionary ideology and party. For while declared "leaders" or elitist groups lay claim to the exercise of power in authoritarian regimes, they do so without the possibility of mass suggestion and without redefining morality in the pursuit of utopian and chiliastic goals.

In fact, authoritarian regimes are often rather defensive in nature. They tend to suppress pluralism (a step that is inimical to freedom) as well as radical ideologies. They lean toward a position in between totalitarian dictatorship, which mobilizes the masses, and a democratic opening of politics. Their dictatorship is legitimated by a combination of arguments about tradition, order, and protection: the goal is to strengthen and elevate a state authority that draws its support one-sidedly from certain social strata or groups, the military, the churches, and existing hierarchical structures.

A well-known example of theoretical legitimation in the case of Austria was the model of the "true state" that Othmar Spann outlined as early as 1920 to justify a *Ständestaat* (corporate state) as an alternative to egalitarian democracy.[8] While the National Socialists were critical of it, it served as a starting point for the pioneering thinkers of an organic and holistic unification and amalgamation of state and society. In this vision, conservative-antiliberal and Christian-social ideas were combined with corporatist ideas about the organization of a guided economic order and occupational hierarchy. This Austrian *Ständestaat* as it existed between 1934 and 1938, hovering at the edge of civil war and assuming an intermediate position between Fascism and National Socialism in terms of the political coercion it exerted, was thus deliberately opposed to democracy. But it was also emphatically antitotalitarian, seeing itself as a defensive regime in need of an authoritarian structure—whether such a structure was regarded, in Spann's sense, as the ideal for the state or only as an extended emergency regime. Until 1938, this regime was home to critics of National Socialism and to refugees from Germany who were fleeing political and racial persecution. After the annexation of Austria, they had to flee once again or were dragged off (like Eugen Kogon, for example, at one time a doctoral student under Othmar Spann) into German concentration camps.

Closer to Fascism than to National Socialism, but sharing the anticommunist and antiliberal stance of both, all authoritarian regimes of the interwar period sought above all to strengthen and stabilize the state in pursuit of national integration. After all, they were faced not only with the threat of Communism or National Socialism but also with nationalist and revisionist tensions with neighboring states, and with the pressure and weight of the great powers, who had to be seen as a threat. Such were the fears of the "small states." At that time authoritarian powers in Europe took advantage of them, as today they do in Latin America (now invoking the specter of "U.S. imperialism").

Authoritarianism's opposition to both liberal democracy and totalitarian dictatorship, along with its claim of a third way under authoritarian guidance, accounts for the vagueness and haziness of the constitutional programs that sought to move beyond the emergency regimes. In Germany, for example, there was Papen's failed concept of the "New State" in 1932; in Austria there was the Dollfuss regime's constitution of May 1934.[9] Alfred Ableitinger has rightly described the basic characteristic of the authoritarian regimes in Europe as "factually usually quite pragmatic, ideologically focused primarily on rejections. Evidence of this is the fact that they were, almost without exception, established in the wake of the world economic crisis after 1930, often by forces that had previously been part of the government and that now ventured to transform themselves into authoritarian regimes or regarded such regimes as unavoidable."[10]

The following stages were characteristic of this process, as seen in Austria between 1932 and 1934: the elimination or self-elimination of parliament through the resignation of all three presidents; a further dismantling of political and constitutional controls; the repression of opposition and resistance by means that included the violation of basic rights and the use of military force; censorship of the press; prohibition of assembly and of the right to strike; the setting up of so-called detention camps for political opponents and people the government did not like; a prohibition of political parties directed against Communists and National Socialists (as early as May and June of 1933) and also against the republican Schutzbund and the Social Democrats; the banning of parties or their self-dissolution, and the establishment of a unity movement, the "Patriotic Front."[11] Thus here, too, as in the Weimar Republic, we find the classic case of the "decay of power in a democracy." Of course, at the same time the fundamental difference from the totalitarian development in Germany becomes apparent once more. The Austrian "unity party" remained a coalition of competing elites without a mass following. The restructuring toward a corporate state tended to amount to a bureaucratic authoritarian state, not least in the "treatment of workers, which wavered between suppression and appeasement."[12]

Moreover, the fact that the Dollfuss-Schuschnigg regime was unable to win loyalty by means of a separate national ideology capable of mobilizing and integrating the masses had to do above all with the continuing strength of the pan-German idea, fears of the Third Reich notwithstanding. This idea remained virulent in all political camps, enjoying greater popularity than the artificial affinity for Italian Fascism that was cultivated by the corporate state, particularly by Starhemberg's Heimwehr (Home Defense League). Italian Fascism was, in any case, burdened by Austrian memories of the two countries as wartime enemies and by the problem of southern Tyrol. Still, until 1936 Mussolini's regime was undoubtedly an effective counterweight to the power of Nazi Germany (especially after the murder of Dollfuss in 1934). After 1936 the precarious balance was increasingly lost, replaced by the preponderance of Germany in the Berlin-Rome axis.

III

We have thus seen some of the characteristics of the authoritarian surge that, in an age marked by dictatorial seizures of power in Russia, Italy, and Germany, overwhelmed so many states in Europe. The states that fell victim to it were particularly those that had emerged from World War I new or profoundly altered and that could become "trouble spots of world politics" (Herzfeld)[13] owing to their own weakness as well as the influence of the great powers and their eventual intervention. Within a decade the surge swept over nearly all of central, eastern, and southern Europe. Through the fragility of the postwar order, it was already a harbinger of a new war. Characteristically enough, however, the issue was no longer primarily one of traditional diplomacy and the politics of influence; instead, domestic social and political-ideological tendencies and changes were playing an increasingly important role.

In the face of the weakness of the postwar democracies, the problem of national self-determination emerged with particular starkness, as did, simultaneously, the betrayed hope of liberal optimism. That optimism had led many to believe after 1918 that the full realization of the right of self-determination in the new states would automatically lead to a better international order. The connection proved to be much more complicated and profoundly contradictory—like the relationship between nationalism and a new international order, and between self-determination and democracy as such, which were prematurely regarded as identical.

To be sure, the space created by the retreat of Russia, the collapse of the Austro-Hungarian Empire, and, earlier, by the amputation of Turkey, offered many peoples the first chance for national self-realization. The flip side, however, was a problematic economic and political fragmentation, exacerbated further by the impetuous nationalism of the decidedly "young" nations. Mixed settlements, multiethnic states, and contested borders created trouble spots, and the democratic principle of self-determination had the potential to quickly transform itself into authoritarian and dictatorial claims to power. The domestic tensions thus created were joined by socioeconomic problems, especially in regard to agrarian reform. Radical agrarian reform was demonstrated in the neighboring Soviet Union; however, its implementation also touched on the problem of minorities and created new conflicts.

In other respects, too, the conditions and circumstances for a new state were singularly unfavorable. This worked primarily against democracy, which had been prematurely regarded as a virtually natural consequence of national emancipation. Economically the new states were for the most part weak, having few industries and a strong dependence on the larger nations, which they needed as a market for domestic agricultural products and as a source of industrial goods. This dependence remained virtually unchanged, but at the same time it was politically—and emphatically—rejected. The multitude of new customs frontiers further exacerbated this problem, and establishing a new state with new institutions created additional expenses. The states' budgets were weak to begin with, and were under strains that made democracy difficult even for "victorious states" like Romania, Yugoslavia, Poland, and Czechoslovakia. The situation was worse still for the defeated and territorially reduced countries like Austria, Hungary, and Bulgaria. Added to this was their lack of experience with the complicated workings of a parliamentary democracy, since most of the new states had previously been ruled by authoritarian monarchies. Finally, the persistent nationalist ethnic and revisionist conflicts intensified the instability that accompanied all young states from their birth and favored the rise of "little dictators."[14] Only two of those states, Finland and Czechoslovakia, were able to last until 1938 in a more or less democratic form.

Unfortunately the various authoritarian regimes we must now examine (they number at least ten) can be discussed only briefly. They are: the new Baltic states and Poland under Marshal Pilsudski; a territorially drastically reduced Hungary under Admiral Horthy; the new Yugoslavia of Serbs, Croats, and Slovenes, who had never before formed a single state; an expanded Greater Romania with its semifascist Iron Guard, as difficult to govern as Yugoslavia; Greece under General Metaxas; and, finally, Portugal under Salazar and Spain under Franco.

The three Baltic republics of Estonia, Latvia, and Lithuania owed their existence to the collapse of Russia and their protection by the German troops, who had initially tried to win the Baltic for Germany. In 1919 Germany had even planned an independent "East Germany" stretching from East Prussia to Latvia. Dependent on the goodwill of the Western powers, the new states strove for democratic constitutions and agrarian reforms. But pressure from Russia soon increased again, even though that country had at first formally recognized the newly established states (in 1920).[15] Problems involving minorities and borders existed especially between Lithuania and Poland regarding the old Lithuanian capital of Vilnius, which Poland had occupied in a surprise move in 1920. In 1923, the League of Nations accepted this as a fait accompli, and in the same year Lithuania indemnified itself by annexing the German Memel region. That move turned the region into a potential crisis area, which played a role in the revisionist conflicts right up to World War II. From 1934–35 at the latest, authoritarian regimes were in control in all three states, and in spite of the differences between them, they all suffered the same fate. At the decisive moment in 1939–40, Lithuania would derive no advantage from its close, special relationship with the Soviet Union. Nationalism was their tragic, paradoxical fate, for the same force that had helped them attain statehood made them politically fragile, because it gave them little capacity for cooperation.

Even shorter was the duration of democracy in Poland. The country's Western orientation and its importance in the French security system against Germany did not change the fact that people in Poland believed they could survive the persistent tensions with Russia only with the help of an authoritarian government. The country's democratic constitution of 1921 existed on paper only; the conflicts within the parties and national groups did not permit democratic processes to develop in a normal way. The administrative system came from three different state traditions to which Poland had been subjected during a long period of foreign rule: those of Prussia, Russia, and Austria. In addition, there was the problem of national minorities: of 29 million inhabitants, 18 million were Poles, but there were also 4 million Ukrainians, 3 million Jews, 1.5 million White Russians, 1 million Germans, 100,000 Lithuanians. What is more, a strong anti-Semitism existed in Poland as well as Rumania, and it could be used by the government to divert attention from domestic problems.

Above all, the problems with agrarian reform were what caused conflicts in Poland and in 1926 provided an opportunity for a putsch by the universally admired national hero Marshal Pilsudski.[16] Of course he soon disappointed the hopes and expectations of democrats and reformers; over the years the regime's veiled military dictatorship drifted increasingly to the authoritarian Right. In 1935, the year of Pilsudski's death, it launched a new constitution, which gave the president and the government dictatorial powers. It was a half-authoritarian, half-constitutional dictatorship of the sort that became almost the norm in Europe in the 1930s. These conservative and semimilitary authoritarian regimes, which presented themselves as alternatives to democracy, fascism, and Marxism, spanned the range—in each case in a special form—from Hindenburg-Papen-Schleicher via Dollfuß-Schuschnigg, Horthy, and Metaxas, to Salazar and Franco.

In Poland, as elsewhere, the invocation of a great national tradition failed to produce a workable political solution. Instead it strengthened the antidemocratic camp. The country's overestimation of its position of strength benefited for a time from the weakening of Russia and Germany. However, it was not Poland's role as France's ally in controlling Germany that proved decisive. The decisive factor turned out to be the same as it had been at an earlier point in history, namely the cooperation between Germany and Russia (in 1939). This virtual geopolitical dependence on its two powerful neighbors, which goes so deeply against the Polish desire for independence, was the cause of Poland's dilemma and repeated failure in its struggle for freedom, after 1919 as well as after 1939 and 1945, each time in a different way.

Particularly intractable problems interlocked in the development of the successor states to the Hapsburg Empire. Hungary's path, after the adventurous intermezzo of Béla Kun's Soviet Republic (1919), was the first to lead to an authoritarian regime, that of Admiral Horthy. Horthy considered himself a "regent" of the monarchy: a fiction with which Hungary justified its claims to a restoration of its territory—to the great outrage of its neighbors. Horthy's supposedly provisional regency lasted in fact almost to the end of World War II. The constitutional forms made little difference to the continuity of an aristocratic and authoritarian regime, which early on aligned itself with the trends of Fascist and National Socialist policies and became a pillar of the authoritarian wave in the Danube region.[17]

The states that had profited most from the territorial reduction of Hungary, Romania, and Yugoslavia, also took over more of its problems than anyone else. Characteristic was the question of minorities and the problem of development in the Greater Romanian Monarchy, which was created as a reward for Romanian participation in the war on the side of the Allies, and which turned out to be particularly difficult to govern. In 1930, King Carol II, who was tainted by rumors of scandal, returned from self-imposed exile. He played the hostile parties off against each other and, during the ensuing quick succession of governments, tried to launch a personal dictatorship, which put Romania on its path into the camp of the Axis powers even though it was anything but a revisionist state. Parliamentary and democratic institutions and processes were not able to take root. After 1933 the anti-Semitic movement of the Iron Guard also prepared the way for the transition to a semifascist führer dictatorship, which was finally put in place in 1940 by Marshal Antonescu, with Germany's blessing.[18]

Different in its end result, though no less troubled in its course, was the fate of the newly established state of Yugoslavia, which built upon the Serbian monarchy. The enmity between Serbs and Croats, who had never before formed a common state, proved ruinous to any productive development. A federalist solution did not materialize. The fatal shooting of Stephan Radic, leader of the Croatian Peasant Party, by a Serbian deputy during a heated session of parliament in 1928 signaled the end of the parliamentary-democratic system, which was already functioning with difficulty and stumbling from one cabinet crisis to the next. In 1929 King Alexander I suspended the constitution. The dictatorship outlasted his assassination in 1934 in Marseilles, and the efforts by the new regent, Prince Paul, to restore constitutional conditions of government were swept up in the maelstrom of the general dictatorial current in Central and Eastern Europe.[19]

Greece and its system of government were overshadowed by unsettled relations with its neighbors: first with a Turkey under authoritarian rule, in a conflict that led to the serious defeat of Greece in Asia Minor, and subsequently with Fascist Italy, which announced its ambitions in the Adriatic and Mediterranean in a number of actions. As in all the smaller states, a grand idea was simmering in Greece: that of the Great Hellenic Empire. A 2,500-year-old memory emerged with new vigor in the period of political change after World War I. After frequent changes of monarchic and republican regimes, the returned king, George II, finally dissolved parliament in 1936 for an indefinite period and transferred power to a quasi-dictatorial regime under General Metaxas, a regime based on emergency powers of martial law.[20]

The great variety of socioeconomic and political preconditions and forms that led to dictatorship militates against the use of a general concept of fascism, the sort of concept that is used to this day in ideological or thoughtless oversimplification. This applies, for example, to the course of events in Spain and Portugal.[21] Like the dictatorship of Salazar and other variants of the authoritarian surge, the development of the Franco regime during the Spanish civil war and in the decades following it cannot be explained with a general idea of fascism. Only the Falangists, whom Franco occasionally used, were a Fascist movement, but they were never able to win a larger following, let alone gain control of the system. For that, not only did they lack the indispensable charismatic leader after the death of the young Primo de Rivera in 1936, but also the circumstances that gave birth to the Spanish regime were not very favorable: the anti-democratic military putsch did not have a Fascist mass movement behind it, and the conservative powers retained full control of the authoritarian dictatorship they established. The case of Spain (as also that of Austria) shows with particular clarity how false is any explanation that sees Fascism merely as the executive organ of reactionary or capitalist powers: what made the relevant movements and regimes Fascist or National Socialist was only, and precisely, the fact that they were able to set themselves apart from those "reactionary" powers and implement their own goals.

In Spain the situation was, in this regard, fundamentally different from that in Italy or Germany. The Spanish struggle was not about great ideological goals, but purely and simply about the restoration and safeguarding of the predemocratic, prerepublican system, the conservative establishment. And that it was Franco who became dictator was almost an accident. The various scheming and conspiring politicians and generals considered Franco only after the leaders of first choice had all been killed. It was the Spanish–Latin American tradition of the *caudillo,* the successful general, that was picked up. Moreover, the inclusion and restructuring of the Falange within the framework of an all-embracing national movement, something Franco saw to in August of 1937, makes clear the distinctive flavor of the Spanish dictatorship. As a politician who tended toward caution on the international stage, Franco was the opposite of the mass demagogues in Rome and Berlin, with their ideological-revolutionary way of acting. His stance during World War II made this even clearer, though during the civil war, of course, Franco had accepted any and all help from Italy and Germany.

The Spanish version of antidemocracy, Franco's dictatorship, certainly did not fail to have an effect on the Latin American countries: its influence can be seen in political movements from Peronism to the Latin American military regimes of today. Within the European framework, however, it was a special case. Its importance lies in the fact that the Spanish civil war could be seen as a prelude to World War II, as the dress rehearsal for the ideological fronts that ended in the triumph of the new dictators. As a dictatorship, however, the Franco regime was far removed from the ideological and revolutionary extremism of the Right, nearly as far as the regime of Portugal's Salazar. A return to monarchy was Franco's final answer to the question about the goal and direction of his system.

As for the Salazar regime, it is uniquely interesting that this variant of the authoritarian surge—which seemed quite comparable to other attempts at establishing corporate states when it first appeared in 1932—lasted until the 1970s, like a fossil from the antidemocratic era, indeed from the predemocratic idea of political order. Of course the old-new dictatorships of Latin America—as well as the authoritarian structures in Communist Eastern Europe—show that it was not merely the remnant of a distant past.

The agony of democracy in the 1930s proved to be a heavy blow to the hopes and expectations that had been tied to the realization of national self-determination. It became clear that it was not inevitable, or even likely, that self-determination would lead to the establishment and strengthening of democratic systems. The relationship between nationalism, the nation-state, and democracy was much more complicated than contemporaries, with an optimism that was still part of nineteenth-century liberalism, had assumed. No later than the mid-1930s, the grave structural problems—minority conflicts, economic crises, questions of agrarian reform and of an industrial middle-class policy, and added to these a fear of revolution and

Communism—had led to authoritarian-dictatorial systems everywhere, which were also unable to solve the problems. What is more, the illusion of the third way discredited the idea of democracy itself by implying that democracy was viable only under the exceptional conditions that prevailed in the developed Western states. At the same time, the chaotic conditions offered the great powers an opportunity to intervene and shifts the balance of power, which posed a threat to the European system of peace and order as a whole.

However, the example of the new democracies after World War I also demonstrates that it is not possible simply to infer a political susceptibility to dictatorship from a level of socioeconomic development. Susceptibility took quite different forms. There were the underdeveloped or semideveloped countries in the Balkans, and to some extent Italy, Poland, and the Baltic states also belonged in this category. These authoritarian or even Fascist regimes could present themselves as dictatorships promoting development, precisely because viable political and state infrastructures were lacking. Such dictatorships, however, never attained the political perfection of the totalitarian regimes. More developed countries with higher living standards, threatened by a deterioration of those standards or by far-reaching structural crises as a result of the war and continuing modernization, were also vulnerable. This was the case with Germany and, especially, Austria. Austria, with its great tradition of statehood and culture, found itself—as the "result of subtraction" (Robert Musil), so to speak—in search of a lost role. To be sure, the preconditions for the development of parliamentary democracies were better in these more affluent countries. However, at the same time they had tendencies that were more radical, because they sought greater perfection. And they had currents leading toward a reactionary or revolutionary change of the postwar situation, currents that could be organized in a totalitarian fashion.

IV

The history and failure of Austria's first democracy was thus definitely part of the authoritarian surge, but it was so in a special way, because it was bound up with the German problem and subsequently confronted with the German move toward an emphatically totalitarian dictatorship. After the prohibition of *Anschluß* (annexation) to Germany, the rump Austrian Republic, barely viable in economic terms and kept afloat by loans from the League of Nations, managed with great difficulty to bring about a certain consolidation by 1931, in the end under the leadership of the Christian-social Monsignor Ignaz Seipel.[22] In view of the continuing question of *Anschluß* and the economic problems, it was, in particular, the confrontations between militant Right and Left movements, with their quasi-military organizations, that prevented a calmer, integrative development of the country. At the same time there was an upsurge of anti-Semitic sentiments, which Hitler had already absorbed to the saturation level during his years in Vienna.[23] Political enmity, strikes, and violent demonstrations repeatedly took the country to the brink of civil war.

In particular the two camps confronting each other were the agrarian, right-wing, authoritarian Heimwehr under Prince Starhemberg, who was friendly toward Fascism, and the republican Schutzbund (Defense League), whose main base of strength was in Vienna. The approximately 60,000 members of the Heimwehr, and the 90,000 members of the Schutzbund (who were armed) dwarfed the Austrian army, which had been reduced to a level of 30,000 men. In 1927, the acquittal of militiamen accused of murdering a Socialist prompted Viennese workers to launch an assault on the Palace of Justice, which was set on fire; the bloody unrest lasted for three days.[24] In the following years the Heimwehr, for its part, repeatedly threatened to call for a march on Vienna; following the Fascist model, it would do away with the weak, despised parliamentary democracy. In 1931, a putsch attempt took place in Graz. At the same time the plan for a tariff union with Germany was again blocked by objections from France and the Little Entente.[25] All these crises and humiliations were points against the democratic Republic. Finally, in 1931 and 1932, respectively, the Republic, in return for the approval of urgently needed credit, was compelled by the Lausanne Protocol and the International Court to permanently renounce any union (even an economic one) with Germany. At the time Germany was still a democratic country (in any case, it was not yet National Socialist).

This was the situation when the rise of Austrian National Socialism shattered the already precarious balance between the hostile camps of Socialists, Christian-socials, and Pan-German nationalists, and with it parliamentary democracy—not least under growing pressure from the German development toward dictatorship. It is true that democratic options remained viable longer in Austria.[26] In the elections in November of 1930, 90 percent of voters still cast their ballots for the three founding parties of the Republic; in Germany at the same time, a third of the electorate was already voting for the totalitarian Right and Left, and in 1932 those votes made up a majority. But in both countries, the final option of a Great Coalition was dismissed—in keeping with that old, popular illusion that dictatorial, state-of-emergency solutions were superior to democratic ones. Moreover, personnel factors played a disastrous role: in Germany, for example, there was the fall of Brüning and Otto Braun at the hands of the Hindenburg camarilla; in Austria, the deaths of

Seipel and Schober, both of whom died in the same fateful year of 1932 (and both in August). Similar to what happened in the Weimar Republic by means of presidential dictatorial powers, in Austria the pseudolegal "putsch in installments" (Peter Huemer) occurred as a "putsch of small steps" (Manfred Welan), through the "authoritarian Trojan Horse" of an old Enabling Act for a War Economy (dating from 1917).[27] Thus the dictatorial regime came to power not via a majority but through the abuse of emergency laws—from the self-elimination of parliament (March 4, 1933) to the bloody suppression of Socialist resistance (February 12, 1934) and the National Socialist putsch attempt (July 25, 1934).[28]

Contemporary history in Austria is still left with some difficult questions of interpretation that concern all political camps. To what extent was the corporate state an emergency solution, and to what extent was it a separate path to dictatorship? How is one to assess the role of those from the Christian-social, conservative, and nationalist camps who paved the way to the corporate state and entered into coalitions? What was the importance of the Italian pressure for a Fascist restructuring of Austria? Where, apart from the left-wing radicals and right-wing radicals, were the political counterforces? To what extent was the opposition aimed at the state as such or only at an authoritarian regime? Finally, what can be said about the authoritarian conception of the state, according to which a dictatorially abbreviated decision-making path guaranteed more efficiency than democratic paths, once we take into account the costs of false decisions—subject to no control and supervision—that are made in dictatorships? And is it in fact true that the experiment failed only or primarily because of the German ultimatum and occupation in 1938? Wedged in between the National Socialist and Fascist regimes, Dollfuss and Schuschnigg steered a course that sought to repress the Socialists and initially also the National Socialists (until 1936)—only to succumb in the end, with no alternative to offer, to the Pan-Germanic coup, amidst the cheers of a deceived majority of the population. The end of the drawn-out intermediate authoritarian stage—experienced as self-surrender, liberation, or occupation—demonstrated simultaneously the seemingly irresistible advance of ideological forces and the close intertwining of power factors in domestic and foreign politics.

One of the favorite ideas of Hitler, the expatriate Austrian, was to have the seizure of power in Germany followed immediately by a National Socialist revolution in Austria. Even more than in the case of his anti-Versailles revisionist policy, he could draw for this on strong Pan-German sentiments on both sides of the border and within all social classes. The Pan-German idea was not a National Socialist invention but an intellectual and political force that had remained alive since the end of the old empire, and that had received a new boost by the collapse of the two empires in 1918.[29]

But the National Socialist initiative immediately imparted its own meaning to the idea of a Reich of all Germans. Hitler strove for his specific *Anschluß* of Austria not in the federalist sense of the liberals of 1848 or of the democrats and social democrats of 1918, nor by way of a peaceful revision of public and constitutional law. Instead it was to be achieved by absorbing Austria quickly and forcibly into a centralized state of imposed uniformity. German politics interfered in Austrian domestic affairs beginning in the spring of 1933, through massive support for the Austrian National Socialists. At the same time Germany put Vienna under tremendous economic pressure by responding to defensive moves on Austria's part with a closing of the border and a tourism boycott, which had a devastating impact on the country.[30]

This development prompted resolute responses from both France and Italy. Faced with the menacing German policies, the authoritarian Dollfuss regime leaned closer to Mussolini. It suppressed the Austrian National Socialists and also sought to realize its alternative of a corporate state with Italian help, in the process, of course, brutally eliminating the Social Democrats. Agreements between Vienna and Italy and Hungary, as well as a solemn declaration by England, France, and Italy on February 17, 1934, affirmed the independence and territorial integrity of Austria. The National Socialists responded with preparations for the putsch and assassinated Dollfuss on July 25, 1934, only a short time after the bloody consolidation of the National Socialist regime in Germany on June 30, 1934.

Though the Austrian National Socialists' rash attempt at seizing power failed and the German leadership was still able to extricate itself from the affair, Hitler's policy became noticeably isolated by the setback of 1934.[31] After the assassination of Dollfuss, not only the plan for *Anschluß* but also a close alliance with Italian Fascism seemed to have moved into the distant future. But at this point Franz von Papen, in spite of the murder of his closest friends and the loss of his post as vice chancellor in 1934, did what he had done in 1933 when Hitler seized power in Germany: he acted as a conciliatory mediator, this time as the "special envoy of the Führer" in Vienna. He was still seen as the advocate of an authoritarian state, not a totalitarian one, which only reinforced the illusions about German intentions. Then, once Mussolini turned away from the Western powers in the Abyssinian War of 1935–36 and the Spanish civil war of 1936 to 1939, with a shift in the focus of Italian policies to a Mediterranean mare-nostrum imperialism, the annexation of Austria offered itself as the first, virtually risk-free phase of German expansion.[32] The right of national self-determination, so long as it conformed to the National Socialist idea of living space, provided the most effective pretext for this move. And the authoritarian Austrian regime itself, not very popular to begin with, was now outmaneuvered by Europe's retreat before Hitler's Pan-German policy. Decisive for the ultimatum of Berchtesgaden, to which Schuschnigg had to yield, was the report from Philip of Hessen—the Italian king's son-in-law, who had been dispatched to Rome—that this time, unlike in 1934, Mussolini would not take any action. In response Hitler telegrammed his thanks from Linz (March 13, 1938): *"Mussolini, ich werde Ihnen dieses nie vergessen!"* (Mussolini, I will never forget this!).[33]

With Hitler's successes in his policy of rearming Germany, Versailles was past history, and it seemed unlikely that the Western powers would intervene on behalf of the relic of a broken system. In Austria itself, the feeble semidictatorship of Dollfuss's successor Schuschnigg was not able to stop National Socialist activities even with initial prohibitions and persecutions. Unable to popularize a policy of its own, it even drew the enmity of both the Left and the Right. In this isolated situation, the Austrian chancellor, despite a number of warnings, accepted a formal invitation from Hitler on February 12, 1938, to his retreat at Berchtesgaden, located on the border between the two countries. There he let himself be intimidated into appointing a National Socialist minister of the interior, Arthur Seyss-Inquart. Belated attempts to resist German pressure and preparations for a plebiscite on Austria's independence drew another ultimatum from Hitler. In a hasty action, Seyss-Inquart took over the chancellorship, and on instructions that Göring phoned in from Berlin, he opened the border to the waiting German troops.

On March 13, 1938, Hitler proclaimed (first in Linz, and two days later on the Heldenplatz in Vienna) the "reunification" of what was to be called the Ostmark with the Reich. A subsequent totalitarian plebiscite, which showed 99 percent approval (on April 10, 1938) legalized the action. The entire action was carried out under the rather technocratic names of *Anschluß* and *Gleichschaltung,* encountering virtually no resistance. Of course there were also swift actions by Himmler's arrest units, and the pogromlike, ruthless persecution of Jews and political enemies. What took place was the brutal transition from an authoritarian to a totalitarian regime; representatives of the corporate state felt the blow of Hitler's revenge.[34]

Hitler had returned to Austria; his work, as the propaganda proclaimed, had been completed. The international reaction confirmed the optimistic predictions of the dictator, who only a year earlier had forsworn any further surprises. In England, which pursued its policy of appeasement, an inclination to show understanding for the action prevailed, despite a disapproval of the methods used. The desire to have peace in international affairs and to maintain the empire ranked ahead of European issues and impeded England's taking a stand for the values of Western democracy. France, shaken by the Popular Front and its own governmental crises, remained nearly immobile, focused entirely on domestic problems. Mussolini, who had kept quiet, willing or not, received Hitler's exuberant telegram of thanks. Congratulations arrived even from Chiang Kai-shek.

The year 1938 was also decisive in that immediately before and after the *Anschluß,* the leadership structure in Germany itself was radically transformed through a further Nazification of its personnel. The "authoritarian" partners of the seizure of power in 1933—conservatives, German nationalists, technocrats—were eliminated. Generals Blomberg, Fritsch, and eventually Beck went down; in the Foreign Ministry, Neurath had to make place for the likes of Ribbentrop; and in economic policy Hjalmar Schacht had to yield to the yes-man Walter Funk.

Thus the establishment of the "Greater German Empire" took place as a virtually unchallenged victory of National Socialist policies. Its consequences were unforeseeable: it did not mean, as contemporaries believed, the end of revisionism, but the beginning of expansion. Hitler's next step, the absorption of the Sudetenland, was evidence of that. It could still invoke the ethnic-national ideology, but no longer a "merely" revisionist one. Moreover, the military orders of May 30, 1938, already indicated October 1 as the concrete date for Hitler's "irrevocable determination to smash Czechoslovakia in the near future through a military action."[35]

The catastrophe of World War II was beginning to loom on the horizon, along with the inhumanity of its National Socialist originators: Austria in 1938 witnessed, with the transition from authoritarian to totalitarian politics, the first radicalizations of the persecution of the Jews and the concretization of the Third Reich's Eastern European imperialism, which had a geopolitical and racial basis.

V

The events between 1934 and 1938 reveal the blending of the two powerful currents of the time: the radical-nationalistic current and the authoritarian-dictatorial current. A comprehensive ideologization of politics, coupled with us-them thinking *(Freund-Feind-Denken)* and scapegoat anti-Semitism, paved the way in the 1930s for the fateful exacerbation of the situation in the heart of Europe. Some glorified its violent, power-political "resolution" as the fulfillment of legitimate demands for self-determination, others suffered it as a calamitous subjugation. Far too many, however, accepted and supported it as a seemingly unavoidable historical fate. To be sure, the development from 1933 to 1938 cannot be understood in isolation as a German and Austrian phenomenon. It forces us to look at the European landscape of crises and dictatorships in the 1920s and 1930s. But nor can placing it historically within the authoritarian and totalitarian surge of dictatorship amount in retrospect to a convenient relativizing of the events—either politically or morally. We are left with the driving, leading role that National Socialism, with its uniting of the idea of the Reich and the nation, played in the radicalization of the situation beyond Germany's own borders. This caused the inhuman intensification of the authoritarian and Fascist forms of dictatorship into a totalitarian system of rule that eclipsed everything that had gone before—most certainly Fascism, which National Socialism after 1938 increasingly subordinated to itself in political and military as well as ideological and racial terms. And in one crucial way National Socialism went beyond the inhuman collectivization and show trials of Stalinism: in the racially based policy of identifying and exterminating the enemy.

The pogrom of 1938, and only a few months later the occupation of Poland, revealed those traits of the regime that truly differentiated it from other tyrannies. They showed that it was far more than merely anti-Bolshevist and antidemocratic in the sense, for example, of Nolte's theory of Fascism, and also that it went far beyond the contemporary justifications (by Carl Schmitt, for example) of authoritarian emergency regimes.

And so, in the end we must emphasize the primary importance of the German and Austrian components, especially in a comparative analysis of the general European situation and the circumstances of the political system. The reason a dictatorship of this kind could come to power first in Germany, and then expand first into Austria, even though similar intellectual, social, and political currents had existed in many countries since the turn of the century (nationalism, anti-Semitism, socio-imperialism), has to do, not least, with two complexes of facts and ideas.

First, National Socialism itself was primarily a German phenomenon, not a "Fascist" one (just as Fascism was genuinely Italian), no matter how much of an inspiration Fascism may have been at times. It was based in particular on a brutalization of political thinking and acting, on a distorted understanding of what politics was, which one might identify as the perversion of German idealism and desire for order by World War I and the crises in its wake. George Mosse has described this "brutalization of politics" in a recent essay on "the political Right, racism, and the German *Sonderweg*."[36] Of course the controversial theory of the *Sonderweg* (special path) applies only insofar as it refers to the consciousness of having a special destiny, which was marked by the "crazy ideas of 1914" and then by the bitter disappointment of 1918. An inability on the part of the Germans to deal with the defeat, a feeling of having been treated unfairly by history, the legend of the stab in the back: these symptoms of national distortion nourished everything that Hitler later called *Mein Kampf*, and that he used in the most fundamental way for his early agitation in postwar Munich.

Second, this German ideology of the war that was not lost, with which National Socialism then stood and fell until the end of 1945, drew strength not only from its "negative" thrust—anti-Marxism and anti-Bolshevism, which were, after all, not uniquely German—but also from a linking of emphatically "positive," programmatically progressive ideological elements. Beyond an extreme "*völk*-ish" nationalism, it drew on a racism that differentiated itself from the colonial-apartheid racism of other countries (and of Fascism) by the pseudoscientific and biologistic justification of its Aryan claim to rule over and destroy others, which was necessarily directed against other peoples and races. Broadened from anti-Semitism to anti-Slavism, this racism got tied into the expansionary theory of living space, which was no longer defined only geopolitically but also in terms of natural law and race. With this "irrevocable" (to use National Socialist terminology) ideology and its ruthless implementation, which did not admit of compromises (unlike anti-Bolshevism, as evidenced in the Hitler-Stalin pact of 1939 to 1941), Hitler was not merely an anti-Lenin (Nolte), and National Socialism was much more than merely the negative image of Bolshevism, no matter how effective the opposition to and simultaneous imitation of Communist policies of rule and oppression may have been as a form of propaganda.

Finally, what was missing in Germany (and later also in Austria), more so than anywhere else, were political and humanistic-moral forces of resistance. Those that did exist obviously did not have enough support in history, religion, and culture to ward off the totalitarian seduction and sustain an effective resistance. Too many contemporaries failed to take seriously soon enough the innermost driving forces of National Socialism (especially social Darwinism, the ideology of living space, and biological racism), underestimating them or trivializing them as mere ideological eccentricities or trimmings. And yet these forces were what unleashed the totalitarian energy and gave it a quasi-scientific, indeed a "moral" justification, very much in the sense of a higher morality and a totalitarian faith, without which, in the final analysis, the crimes of the Third Reich cannot be explained. That is why it is imperative to establish precisely the essential differences between the concepts at the root of the problem of dictatorship in modern history and politics. They should make it clearer how the coming together of tradition and revolution, of fear of Communism and a sense of mission, of authoritarianism, Fascism, and National Socialism, opened up the misguided path that Germany and Austria took between 1933 and 1938, a path that led to the catastrophe of World War II.

And in the context of a colloquium fifty years after the fact, it remains as important and urgent as ever, as part of the exploration of the culturally effervescent but politically gloomy period between the wars, to shed more light on the intermediate position that Austria held for a time between Fascism and National Socialism. For Fascist Italy, this period was in fact simply an era of dictatorship. For Germany it meant, with the totalitarian rupture of 1933, the confrontation between constitutional democracy and a dictatorship that was far more radical than Fascism. For Austria, however, the period divides into three different phases, resulting in a special complexity and an overlapping of historical experiences: democracy, authoritarian regime, National Socialist rule. What Austria had in common with many other states in Europe was the path from newly created democracy to authoritarian regime, along with the problems of nation-state identity and socioeconomic viability. Its fall from an empire to a reluctant single republic was exacerbated by its location between two revisionist and eventually highly ideologized great powers, to which it had partly historical, partly national ties. As a "democracy in the shadow of imposed sovereignty" (Walter B. Simon)[37] it struggled with the structural problems of modern party-state parliamentarianism, problems that even the older democracies had great difficulties in tackling.

In contrast to back then, today Austria has found its identity as a state. The German case is more complicated: here the division of the nation is at the same time an important factor in the debate over the National Socialist past. Both Austria and West Germany, and also the GDR, which has been trying to simply avoid the problem through an anti-Fascist but not antitotalitarian dictatorship, are left with the burning moral questions raised and left behind by the rise of the National Socialist dictatorship and the destruction it wrought. That dictatorship signaled a crisis of Europe and its values, but it was above all a German dictatorship, and unfortunately even a Pan-German one. We are left with the warning lesson of what humans are capable of if they escape from the problems of the day and from rational political thinking into the ecstasy of totalitarian ideology and power politics. At the beginning of our revolutionary age, two hundred years ago, Edmund Burke remarked (in 1784): "A people never gives up its freedom except in some act of folly." Our century needs those bitter experiences of voluntary disenfranchisement; it must not suppress or forget them. In an age of all too many dictatorships, right down to this day, those experiences have been paid for by the many victims of violence and illusions. Let us recall the words of Benedetto Croce: "History is the only true criticism one can make of the facts of humankind."[38]

Totalitarianism as Concept and Reality

I

It remains imperative to carry on the interdisciplinary discussion about the concept and reality of modern totalitarianism, in spite of all the hostile objections. Over the past decades the concept itself has come under suspicion of being a mere outgrowth of anticommunism and has been attacked, in the Western world, as unscientific. Alongside the old and new controversies over East-West détente, the renewal of the "historian's quarrel" *(Historikerstreit)* in Germany over the comparability of Communist and National Socialist tyrannies and dictatorial regimes has also played a role in this.

However, when we are dealing with the reality of totalitarianism, and especially then, there is no place for the kind of breathless polemic that appeared during the *Historikerstreit,* which strikes me as excessively personalized and politicized. Totalitarianism is by now a long and richly faceted historical experience that must be taken into consideration if, amid the tangle of sentiments and resentments, systems analysis and dogma, we wish to probe its substance and problems. Since the 1960s, the word "totalitarianism," more so than almost any other key word in contemporary history, has instantly called forth the most intense political and ideological reactions—comparable, at best, to the similarly charged concepts of antifascism and anticommunism.

The controversy over the concept and reality of totalitarianism is in fact among the great contested themes of our century. It is certainly not a product or legacy of the cold war after 1945, as is often claimed today. Instead, it began with the formation of right-radical and left-radical ideologies as political religions at the turn of the century, eventually finding its first conceptualization with Mussolini's seizure of power in Italy in

1922–23. It is thus as old as I am, and it has accompanied the lifetime of my generation.

Driven by the simultaneously democratizing and mobilizing effects of World War I, this controversy flared up and became "tangible," demanding a conceptual term, when the new revolutionary dictatorship of Lenin in the Soviet Union was confronted by a dictatorial alternative—Fascism. Using similar means, regardless of whether they are seen as revolutionary or counterrevolutionary, Fascism laid claim to power in a total, "totalitarian" sense, not only over state and society, but even over the thoughts and beliefs of its citizens. First coined by the democratic opponents of *il duce* as a form of criticism, the totalitarian concept was adopted by Mussolini himself: *"Tutto nello stato, nienti fuori dello stato, feroce volontá totalitaria"* (Everything in the state, nothing outside of the state, a ferocious totalitarian will) was Mussolini's slogan.[1]

Since then, however, discussion has repeatedly revolved around the following issues: can the concept be used in a scientific way at all, or is it merely a battle slogan? Is the concept limited to a specific historical and political constellation (and to specific states)? If so, is it still relevant and topical after the end of the Fascist and National Socialist systems and the transformation of Communism after Stalin? Of course the real controversy revolves around the drawing of comparisons. It is this that ignites the quarrel, insofar as comparison between the Left and the Right makes possible the use of totalitarianism as a battle cry. It calls forth political and moral outrage when the analysis of totalitarianism either reveals that movements and regimes that seem to be diametrically different and mortal enemies are in fact comparable phenomena, or when it discredits them.

However, to my mind the decisive point in the question about relevance is the fact that totalitarianism accompanies, indeed is intimately linked to, the rise of modern democracy. As Gerhard Leibholz has said, it is *the* political phenomenon of the twentieth century. When a historian like Jakob Talmon, in his extensive investigation, goes all the way back to the radicalization of the French Revolution and to Rousseau to find the concept of a "totalitarian democracy," his line of argument might be open to debate. But it is certainly illuminating to read Alexis de Tocqueville, the keen observer of the rise of egalitarian mass democracy. For totalitarianism was undoubtedly the word Tocqueville was looking for when he wrote one hundred fifty years ago, with regard to the future: "I think, then, that the species of oppression by which democratic nations are menaced is unlike anything that ever before existed in the world; our contemporaries will find no prototype of it in their memories. I seek in vain for an expression that will accurately convey the whole of the idea I have formed of it; the old words *despotism* and *tyranny* are inappropriate: the thing itself is new, and since I cannot name it, I must attempt to define it."

Today we can name the thing. And we should not again hesitate to do so only because some forms have been changed or veiled, and because it is inconvenient to call something by its name and in so doing expose oneself to the accusation, in particular, of being anticommunist.

II

Let us begin by examining the nature of these new, totalitarian regimes. They can no longer be grasped using the classical types of despotism and autocracy, nor are they mere throwbacks to traditional predemocratic forms of rule. Instead, as apparently total-democratic dictatorships, they constitute something quite new.

The authoritarian wave of the interwar period, the call for a "strong man," the great leader, was one precondition for the rise of these regimes. The other was the increased possibility, created by the technicalized age of the masses, for encompassing and making uniform the life *and* thought of all citizens. For in contrast to the older, conventional (so to speak) dictatorships and military regimes, these regimes now laid claim to all-embracing rule and total submission, indeed to a perfect *identity* of leadership and party movement, of the nation and the individual, of the general and the individual will. This claim can be implemented and enforced only if extremely harsh political controls and terror are legitimated by the fiction of such a system of complete identification, and if the belief in *one* absolute ideology is made obligatory—supposedly as "voluntary" consent but in fact on penalty of death. The Marxist-Leninist dogma of class warfare, or the Fascist–National Socialist friend-foe doctrine of a war between peoples and races, were such totalitarian ideologies. They justified all acts by the government, even mass crimes and genocide, regardless of whether they were committed in the name of the will of the people, the party, the leader, or whether they were given a pseudodemocratic and pseudolegal or revolutionary and messianic-chiliastic cast, as in the myths of a future classless "workers' paradise" or a "Thousand-Year Reich." Also of importance was the role of pseudoreligious needs and manipulations in a period that saw the decay of and a vacuum in religious values: thus the fervent belief in Adolf Hitler or Stalin, and also in symbols and rituals of mass events that were intended to convey the emotional experience of community.

Totalitarianism aimed at the elimination of all rights of liberty that were personal and prior to the state, and at the obliteration of the individual. To be sure, it was nowhere fully realized, but it was implemented to such a degree that it could ask normal citizens to perpetrate the most horrible crimes. At the same time, however, these regimes created the impression that they could realize the true destiny of humankind, indeed true democracy and the perfect welfare state, far more effectively than all previous forms of state and society. This power of seduction was spread better than ever before through the means of modern communication technology and propaganda. All the differences between Communism, Fascism, and National Socialism aside, each case shows three great, characteristic tendencies.

1. Fundamental is the striving for the greatest possible degree of total control of power by a single party (organized in a totalitarian fashion) and its leadership, the leadership being endowed with the attributes of infallibility and the claim to pseudoreligious veneration from the masses. Our century has taught us that power can be seized by such a totalitarian party not only in the "classic" way, through the revolutionary putsch of a militant minority (as in the Russian October Revolution in 1917). It can also be seized through the undermining, abuse, and pseudolegal manipulation of democratic institutions (as in the pseudolegal seizure of power by National Socialism in 1933). All other parties and groups that represent political and social life are subsequently either destroyed through the use of bans or terrorism, or they are coerced into line through deception and threats of violence. In other words, they are reduced to a hollow existence in phony elections and sham parliaments, as in the Communist "people's democracies," with their single ticket of a "national front."

2. The total one-party state bases itself on a militant ideology. As an ersatz religion, a doctrine of salvation with a claim to political exclusivity, this ideology seeks to justify the suppression of all opposition and the total *Gleichschaltung* of the citizenry in historical terms as well as with reference to a future utopia. The historical background, political designs, and ideological doctrines of the various totalitarian systems might be very different, yet Russian Bolshevism, Italian Fascism, and German National Socialism have in common the techniques of omnipresent surveillance (secret police), persecution (concentration camps), and massive influencing or monopolizing of public opinion. The unconditional consent of the masses is manipulated using every available tool of propaganda and advertising. According to findings of recent work in mass psychology, the goal is the creation of a permanent war mood directed against an enemy that is defined in absolute terms. In this process both the "positive" needs of the masses for protection and feelings of enthusiasm and their "negative" fears and obsessions are mobilized and used to consolidate power. The tightly controlled need for movement, excitement, and entertainment is satisfied with rallies and parades. The one-dimensional organizing of all spheres of life conveys at the same time a feeling of security, compelling the submis-

sion of the individual to the community, the collective. The state replaces constitutional legitimation with a system of pseudolegal consent and pluralistic elections with acclamatory plebiscites. With its claim to complete control over the life and beliefs of its citizens, the total state denies any right to freedom, any final meaning and purpose outside itself; it thinks of itself as the only, binding "totality of all purposes."

3. They all shared an essential component of the ideology of totalitarian rule: the myth that a total command state is much more effective than the complex democratic state based on the rule of law and limited by numerous controls and checks. The totalitarian ideology invokes the possibility of total economic and social planning (Four- and Five-Year Plans), the capacity for quicker political and military reaction, and the *Gleichschaltung* of political-administrative processes and increased stability by means of a dictatorial running of the state. However, the reality of totalitarian governing bears only a very qualified resemblance to this widely held notion. Constant rivalries within the totalitarian party and its controlling bodies, an unresolvable dualism of party and state, and the arbitrary actions of an uncontrolled central agency overloaded with authority—all this counteracts the perfecting of a command state constructed after the model of the military command structure. In this coercive system, partial improvements are bought at the expense of a tremendous loss of freedom of movement, legal order, and humanistic substance. In the final analysis this also reduces the professed ideals of security and truth to absurdity. The failure of Fascism and National Socialism, and the political and economic problems of modernization within post-Stalinist Communism, reveal that totalitarian systems of rule by no means guarantee a higher resistance to crisis and a more effective "order." Instead, a coercive system not subject to any control renders the exercise and consequences of concentrated political power immeasurably more costly in the long run than the seemingly cumbersome process of separating powers and striking compromises in a democratic state governed by the rule of law. This was demonstrated again more recently by the catastrophe at Chernobyl (a monopoly of information, a lack of supervision, and manipulation of the population).

III

These experiences, to which was added that of the Stalinist system in all of Eastern Europe, formed the basis of the decidedly antitotalitarian consensus that made possible the reconstruction of liberal democracy after World War II, especially in Western Europe and West Germany. But then came the new conflicts of the 1960s and 1970s. As the deterrent experience of the old totalitarianism was waning, the new generation of 1968 considered it not only possible but virtually necessary to dismantle Western society's antitotalitarian defenses as such. Even when it didn't go so far as to question the need for authority itself, this revisionist trend suppressed or trivialized, in any case, the fundamental difference between the political systems of democracy and dictatorship.

At the same time, an effort was made in the discussion about terrorism to remove the limitations from the concept of force, to wrest the monopoly of force from the democratic state. This was not simply a harmless thought experiment, for it could lead to a dangerous self-disarming. The ideologically motivated tabooing of the very concept of totalitarianism was part of the self-endangerment and weakness of democracy in the seventies.

It was not the disappearance of pseudodemocratic dictatorships but their multiplication on all continents that led some to stop calling them by their true name. This applies especially to the Communist systems. They had always rejected being called totalitarian (while simultaneously, without any qualms, condemning any "reformism" aimed at the omnipotence of the system). Now they very much enjoyed being "de-totalitarianized," so to speak, in the name of détente and cooperation, even though the monopoly of the party and the secret service, the nomenclature and the ideology changed only to some small degree and not in any fundamental way.

Thus the seventies were marked above all by a controversy over the concept of democracy. The conflict with totalitarian forces and tendencies was displaced by the euphoria of détente. Another phase began toward the end of the decade, when an intensifying economic crisis coincided with the final climax of terrorism and the appearance of ideologies and movements critical of Western civilization. The upsurge of alternative and ecological convictions, together with pacifist and neutralist movements and the revival of a supposed third way *between* the fronts, beyond parliamentary democracy and industrial society: all this brought to the fore a "whiff of totalitarianism," as Kurt Sontheimer has said, a political and moral rigorism that was to some extent reminiscent of the self-destructive currents of the twenties and after.

Our problems have taken on a different cast again today: we no longer live in a time of confident de-ideologization, but in one of new uncertainties and philosophies of anxiety. Thought no longer revolves, as it did in the 1968 movement, around optimistic ideas of progress that had once given rise to liberal and socialist notions of emancipation, nor around ideas of national-imperialist expansion. Now at issue is a critique of culture and society marked by antistate ideals of community. The complaints about an excessively rational, progress-oriented society nourish neo-idealist and irrational utopias of the perfect life.

Totalitarian movements have always known how to make use of such needs and yearnings. In the eighties these movements have been appearing once again in pseudoreligious form. Not only is one-third of the world's population subjected to Communist systems, which continue to be based on totalitarian claims and fictions like that of the identity of the regime with its people. The advance of fundamentalist movements, like the revolution of Islamic revival, and the successes of sects in Western democracies reveal the strong potential of ideological seduction. That potential has been resurfacing or arising for the first time throughout the world, out of the crises of orientation in the wake of secularization and modernization. Two-thirds of the world's people are ruled by dictatorships, and one-half of those by totalitarian ones. We have not yet reached the end of our century, which has been called, with terrible justification, the century of totalitarianism.

IV

Three topical points of departure make clear the enduring relevance of the totalitarian temptation.

1. The continuing technicalization of our life is also perfecting the techniques of surveillance and manipulation: mass media and information technology in the computer age can endanger liberty in the bureaucratic welfare state, which is taking on rising expectations and thence also greater authority. Therefore, more than ever before, everything hinges on the political system, for we continue to experience the dialectic of pluralistic democracy and totalitarian ideology that is contained in the idea of consensus (Ulrich Matz). It shows itself in the recurring revivals of Rousseau, with their antipluralist faith in the true common will, in the true rule of the people as an alternative to or transformation of "mere" party democracy.

2. The late totalitarianism in the Communist system is still powerful enough, despite challenges to the ideology, to quash any opposition from dissidents should it wish to. A new study on Soviet law and Soviet reality (by Otto Luchterhand) makes clear that while economic and social rights are given special emphasis in the law, there is a wide gap between theory and practice with respect to those particular rights. The gap is even more pronounced with political rights. Rigorously restricted freedom of opinion, secrecy of judicial acts, the duty instead of the right to participate, acclamation instead of election, the absence or perversion of the concept of human rights, a glorification of state power instead of its limitation, restrictions on religion or its monopolization by the state, psychiatric clinics for dissidents instead of habeas corpus, threat of the Gulag instead of fair trials, the extreme inequality of the privileged class, and the terrorist

persecution of dissidents: instead of civic rights what exists is a state of submissive subjects, a state that continues to be dominated (in quite a totalitarian fashion) by the party's monopoly on truth and the demand for complete dedication to the system. The liberalization that was so often expected and hoped for remains subject to recall at any time, even if the forms of rule are becoming more refined. And yet no ideology is more widespread than the cult of Leninism. It rules over a large part of humankind and influences revolutionary youth and liberation movements on all continents.

3. All ideas and movements with an absolute, unilateral objective are today also potentially totalitarian, if the goal is seen to justify the means and if the movements spread the belief that there is one key to solving all problems here on earth. With a one-sided, fanatical sense of mission, and with social-utopian, potentially violent theories of perfection, they undermine today, as they always have, pluralistic democracies and their methods of free parliamentary politics based on mutual tolerance. Democracy is self-constraint, ideology is presumption—and unfortunately the latter repeatedly gains the upper hand over the former, for time and again the ideology of "true" democracy brings about a disastrous "turnabout from emancipation to despotism" (Klaus Hornung). The decisive, doubtful question that remains is whether people truly possess an urge for freedom and are able to cope with freedom, or whether they continually look for leaders, systems, and ideologies that relieve them of freedom and take them into their service. In other words, does humankind seek a political religion that will take away the uncertainty about good and evil, meaning and meaninglessness? In that search, the belief in progress and superstition, the cult of science and anxieties about life can form peculiar mixtures: the Stalinist terror and above all the Nazi persecution of the Jews are perfect examples of what pseudoscientific madness is capable of, if it obtains totalitarian instruments of rule and places the total idea above respect for human rights.

Moreover, if the fundamental difference between democracy and dictatorship is downplayed, even for such laudable purposes as détente and peace, it creates what Alexis de Tocqueville saw as a characteristic precondition for totalitarianism: namely the fact that it can appear to be an optimal synthesis of both principles, the democratic and the dictatorial. We need only think of the Marxist and Leninist concept of democracy and its linkage to the dictatorship of the proletariat and the single party. Or we can think of the very characteristic blending of democratic and dictatorial elements in the pseudolegal transition from the Weimar Republic to National Socialist totalitarianism with its emphatically plebiscitary claims to legitimacy; the paradoxical "legal revolution" of National Socialism is not least an expression of this deceptive double track. Who would want to argue that the pseudodemocratic, pseudoplebiscitary threat that democracy poses to itself has become obsolete today? It is as alive as the global virulence of the leftist, Leninist version, which continues to be professed by reform Communists right down to Gorbachev. The totalitarian threat or seduction has not come to an end. Democracy continues to be dependent on the refusal to surrender the experiences it has had with totalitarianism since Lenin, Stalin, and Hitler.

V

I shall conclude with a few summary comments on the current discussion about totalitarianism.

All justifications for getting rid of the concept of totalitarianism are inadequate, so long as we do not come up with a better word for this phenomenon: to call it authoritarian or fascist does not quite capture it and is even more vague and general.

The rejection of the concept comes primarily from those to whom it may very well apply—just as, conversely, we hear talk of "democracy" especially where no such thing exists.

The intensification of power occurs through the removal of all dividing lines between state and society and through the highest possible degree of total politicization of society—in the sense of Trotsky's statement that Stalin could say with every right, *"La société c'est moi."*

One could raise the objection that totalitarianism is more of a tendency, a temptation or seduction, rather than a definitive form of government, and that, semantically, the word tends to be evocative rather than descriptive. This, indeed, is the reason for the difficulties of classification: totalitarianism as a nightmare, a syndrome instead of a clearly defined system. But for all that, it is no less effective and oppressive to those affected by it.

The attempt over the past two decades to get rid of the concept of totalitarianism has certainly failed, as any list of the alternative concepts will show: for example, neofeudalism, restricted pluralism, welfare-authoritarianism, and so on. These are either unusable or are in turn too vague and general. In any case, they fail to fully encompass or cover the area that this phenomenon occupies in the comparative study of power. A centralized, monopolistic ideology and a mass party are absent in authoritarian dictatorships. At the same time, the expectations of a post-totalitarian Communism after Stalin have proved illusory, as have the hopes for a smooth transfer of democracy to developing countries. The need for a concept of totalitarianism remains, and this also answers the question of whether it would be better, heuristically, to get rid of the concept or refine it.

Refining the concept would mean, at the same time, learning from history. In contrast to contemporaries like Alexis de Tocqueville and Karl Marx, and to the generation of World War I, we are today aware of the threat that democracy poses to itself and can put up a timely defense: not least by not hesitating to give the totalitarian phenomenon or tendency its proper name. The very name that Tocqueville was searching for remains indispensable for as long as the possibility of ideological seduction and a pseudodemocratic justification of totalitarian dictatorship persists. The power and attraction of ideological thinking rests on what is in this case a pseudoreligious human need for the absolute; that is, for a "true democracy"—a democracy that promises a utopian solution to all problems by abolishing the opposition and conflicts between the government and the governed, between poor and rich, interests and norms, power and spirit.

Incidentally, whenever ideological thinking takes over, the very foundation of our humanities and social sciences is in jeopardy: namely, the possibility for freely expressed and pluralistic criticism not least of one's own political system. The possibility of being seduced or blackmailed by pressure or the pull of a current exists not only in politics. It is also found in scholarly and scientific thought, speech, and writing—and especially in the vanguard of totalitarian systems, often long before they are implemented, as fellow travelers discover afterwards in a painful way. The tabooing of the concept and reality of totalitarianism repeats the underestimation of the experiences of our century. It trivializes Talmon's insight that "designs of salvation through revolution develop into terror regimes, and the promise of a perfect, direct democracy in practice takes on the form of a totalitarian dictatorship." Thus, what is at stake in the current dispute over the topical relevance of totalitarianism is the defense of liberal democracy against old and new seducers.

11

Resistance in "Right Dictatorships": The German Experience

The Tradition of the Idea of Resistance

Whenever we remember the events that led to the end of the first German democracy and to the establishment of the most terrible "Right dictatorship" in history, one question arises with great urgency: what are the possibilities for resistance to such a disastrous development?[1] For the fact is that the irruption of the National Socialist dictatorship in 1933 occurred with such stunning speed and in such a seemingly irresistible manner because clear and effective resistance was not offered soon enough.

The question of resistance is as important as ever. Critics of our modern-day democracy have derived from it, with increasing vehemence, a right—indeed a duty—of resistance by combining the claim of civil disobedience with spectacular breaches of the legal system. It is all the more important to ponder the painful lessons from the resistance movement against National Socialist rule in Germany and Europe. The first lesson is this: resistance is difficult but imperative in a dictatorship that violates human rights; it is easy and pernicious, however, in a constitutional democracy that allows and accepts legal opposition. Since time immemorial, a people's right to resist usurped or arbitrary and unjust state power has been postulated as a human right and a right of freedom that is prior to and above the state, from the tyrannicides of antiquity, to medieval doctrines of resistance, to the great revolutions of modern times—in England, America, and France—and the totalitarian dictatorships of the twentieth century. The problem of resistance is one of the basic questions of political thought and action, of political morality and the conduct of citizens.

Of course, with the rise of modern democracy the problem presents itself in a different way than before, for this form of government emphatically recognizes the crucial existence and function of a political opposition. The great achievement of liberal constitutional development has secured the realization of human and civic rights while eliminating the need to invoke resistance to the state.

But at the same time the irruption of modern dictatorships raises new problems. It forces us to differentiate as well as compare the problem of resistance in Communist and anticommunist dictatorships, in authoritarian and totalitarian systems of the Left and the Right, in military dictatorships, and in dictatorships in the Third World and developing countries. In all events, for all these forms of dictatorial regimes from the Left and the Right, it holds true that the question of resistance is fundamentally different from a claim to resistance in a democracy with secure rights of opposition.

Moreover the simple division into Left and Right dictatorships is, of course, a questionable one, if we think of the mixture of conservative and revolutionary traits in Fascism and National Socialism on the one hand, and of the bureaucratic-authoritarian tendencies in postrevolutionary Communism since Stalin on the other. Without addressing this basic question of totalitarianism scholarship, in the discussion that follows I will examine the theme of resistance using the most important historical case and prototype of a radical Right dictatorship with leftist components, National Socialism, and the resistance against its totalitarian rule in Germany and occupied Europe.

Opposition Groups in the National Socialist State

As soon as we begin to think about the problem of German resistance, 1933 becomes and remains the decisive date. What took place then was the pseudolegal transition from democracy to dictatorship, which cast the old question about resistance to tyrannical rule in a new light at that time. The opposition to a state that had fallen into the hands of a dictatorial party in an apparently legal, indeed pseudodemocratic way (through emergency decrees, the Enabling Law, and plebiscites) had to overcome incomparably greater difficulties than the almost classic resistance that arises against a violent putsch and open usurpation, or against the coercion of a totalitarian occupational regime, as was the case in Eastern Europe and East Germany after 1945. The National Socialist slogan of supposedly "legal" and simultaneously national (people-supported) revolution was designed precisely to confuse minds and weaken all opposing forces. This influenced the character and hampered the chances of any opposition to the regime, which had attained comprehensive power over state and society in an extremely short period and through pseudodemocratic manipulation. Lacking, for the most part, were the intellectual and social preconditions that could have supported the clear formation of opinions and decisive measures in the face of the National Socialist seizure of power. In contrast to what had happened in the West, as the modern idea of the German state developed after 1848, the old tradition of the right of resistance to arbitrary power was suppressed and overlaid by the bureaucratic structure of the patriarchal state. This emerged with particular clarity in the problem of the oath that all military personnel and civil servants were required to swear in 1933–34 to Hitler himself rather than to the constitution.

The tradition of a patriarchal state also explains the erroneous assessments that paralyzed a more general resistance to the National Socialist seizure of power. The basic problem of 1933 for Weimar politicians and parties, who wavered in their assessment of the National Socialist movement, was determining the extent to which they would be able to influence or even control the National Socialists through collaboration, and the point at which resistance would be unavoidable—thus all to little thought was given to whether and in what form resistance would still be possible when the time came. The illusions of the unions, the inattention of the Social Democratic Party (SPD) leadership, the futile accommodation of the bourgeois parties, and the isolation of the German Communist Party (KPD): each in its own way reflects this problem. In the process, the moment was missed when it would still have been possible to operate from the old positions of power.

It was only as the parties were dissolved and democratic positions and rights were rapidly lost that scattered centers of resistance formed. They, too, were still impeded by the belief that Hitler would soon bring himself to ruin, and it would be necessary to survive only a brief period of oppression. Yet the tens of thousands of Germans who were politically persecuted and prisoners in the concentration camps, which were instantly set up, attest to the potential strength and willingness to sacrifice on the part of those Germans who did immediately take a stand against National Socialism.

If we speak of resistance, we must distinguish very different groups that opposed National Socialism or certain aspects of its regime; these groups emerged at different times with different methods and goals. To begin with, there were the old political opponents from the Left and the center, who were soon joined by disappointed conservatives; subsequently opposition from the sphere of the churches grew stronger; to this we can add individuals from the bureaucracy and the economic realm; finally, the military moved into the center of oppositional planning and action in 1938 and again after 1942–43. The evaluation of the resistance is so difficult and controversial because it can involve very different criteria: should the main emphasis be placed on the motives, the chances of success, or the political goals? The choices one makes here determine how one assesses the leftist, bourgeois, ecclesiastical, conservative, and military opposition, and how one looks at their relationships to each other and their tactics toward the regime.

In any case, here we already see the great, fundamental difference between a situation of resistance amid the dictatorial oppression at that time and the presumptuous proclamation of resistance today, that is to say in a constitutional-liberal democracy. We can only hope that the current democracy will not put itself at the mercy of its enemies in a similarly defenseless and illusory way, after having granted them the freedom to march against it. The problem of 1933, the all-too-easy subversion and conquest of democracy by dictatorship, was grounded, precisely, in the fact that in Germany, as in other countries of Europe, there existed a large and destructive fundamental opposition to *democracy*. It was present throughout the entire history of the Weimar Republic, from the putsch movements between 1919 and 1923 to the street battles between 1930 and 1933. In contrast, the power of resistance to *dictatorial* movements and regimes was much weaker, both before and after 1933.

What needs to be addressed is the basic question of the relationship of resistance to democracy and dictatorship, and the great social span of the actual resistance to Hitler. The discussion after the fact has suffered from the restrictions placed on it by politically, socially, and ideologically determined approaches to the history of the resistance. To this day, four main approaches have shaped the interpretation. There are, to begin with, the two rigorous views that, first, the Communist resistance and, second, the conservative and military oppositional faction should be excluded from the start; the former because it amounted to "treason," the latter because it was no more than disagreement with the regime. Such an anticommunist or procommunist restriction of the concept of resistance is unhistorical. Both forms of resistance constituted a threat to the National Socialist leadership and its totalitarian claim to power. Moreover it would amount to a misjudgment of the political-moral dimension to see the resistance as only "antifascist" and not primarily as antitotalitarian, directed against injustice from both Left and Right dictatorships: one thinks of George Orwell's self-critical words of 1944 that leftist intellectuals all too easily made the mistake or succumbed to the illusion that they "wanted to be antifascist without being antitotalitarian." Instead, what holds true especially for our problem of resistance in Right or Left dictatorships is this: if you talk about fascism, don't forget totalitarianism.

However, the fact that the National Socialist regime, after it was firmly installed, could no longer be overthrown without the force of arms, does not justify the third approach, that of limiting the perspective to military resistance. Such resistance was entirely absent in the first half of the Third Reich, and after 1938 it can be seen only in conjunction with the political forces of opposition. Fourth and last, the claim that a popular movement against National Socialism emerged only in the churches, and that especially the Catholic Church stood nearly united in opposition, is as problematic as the counterthesis of a Communist mass movement against Hitler. To be sure, opposition from the churches—very important but at the same time in many ways ambiguous—was also a political matter; but only in a few instances did it move beyond the defense of its own positions and interests and become political resistance. At the same time, those who have criticized (not always without good reason) the illusions of the conservatives (including the blueprints for a new state that came out of the Kreisau Circle, for example) overlook the fact that a popular uprising did not seem possible at any stage of the Third Reich, while an overthrow from the top, as was eventually attempted, especially on July 20, 1944, presupposed contacts with the bureaucracy and parts of the establishment. Of course, stating this does not amount to a disavowal either of the moral aspects or the spiritual and social problems of such attempts.

It is not possible to speak of a unified resistance movement at any point during the Third Reich. Certainly the many different political and intellectual forces that sooner or later avoided or even resisted *Gleichschaltung* drew closer together at various points. But in terms of their conduct and plans, the differences remained considerable, and after the end of the regime those differences reemerged in very concrete ways. Still, the extent of the opposition within Germany in the prewar period was far greater than the state's organized demonstrations of unity sought to suggest. Given the mass arrests of political opponents, the murder of thousands because of active opposition, and the terrible collective persecution outside the legal system through the concentration camps, we must put the number of acts of resistance higher than the National Socialist regime would have had us believe. The secret surveillance reports of the Gestapo present a picture that is quite different from that presented by the regime's propaganda.

However, it was a big step from nonconformism on the part of many individuals, which in itself is a political matter under totalitarian conditions, to disobedience and finally active resistance. The fact remains that prior to all later forms of opposition from churches, the military, the bourgeoisie, and the conservatives, the first resistance was put up by those who felt the terror of the National Socialist regime "earliest and most strongly, and who were simultaneously regarded by the regime as its most dangerous enemies: the organizations of the workers' movement" (Reichhardt). It is, of course, difficult to get a grip on this resistance. Often we get only sweeping references to the persecution of leftists and to the activities in emigration, while a comprehensive account of this widely dispersed, faceless opposition is hampered by a lack of sources. Under the conditions of totalitarian rule, the conspiratorial activity of leftist resistance groups had to remain under the shroud of illegality and anonymity; their documents are thus more meager and often less informative than those generated by the bourgeois and the conservative opposition. Though records of innumerable trials, especially from the early years, do reveal the breadth and continuity of this "silent revolt" (Weisenborn), they, too, frequently offer only a distorted picture of what the administration of "justice" under National Socialist direction wanted to present as an image of the enemy. Moreover, in many cases the persecution occurred outside of the judicial system altogether, in the sphere of the SS state and the concentration camps.

If the opposition from the Left, split into Communists and Social Democrats, was already too weak to set in motion an active popular resistance to National Socialism, this was even more true of all the other political and social groups. They lacked the experience for the formation of underground cells and organized resistance, which was at least part of the tradition of the parties of the Left, above all the KPD. Over the years, as it became clear that an expansion of the illegal groups into a mass movement from the Left was failing, and that the only alternative was individual oppositional activity among a few like-minded people, an increasing resignation took hold on the Left. At the same time, however, the bourgeois camp made a growing number of attempts to use its own positions of power within the state or society as starting points for opposition and for a change of the regime. Such starting points first became visible in three places: in the partial resistance of the churches to *Gleichschaltung,* in the misgivings in liberal and conservative circles about the reality of National Socialist rule, and, finally, in the criticism voiced by those in the military who were disillusioned by Hitler's brinkmanship and by the war course he was pursuing, a criticism that made itself felt for the first time in the crisis situation of the summer of 1938.

The Motives and Organization of Opposition

The varied motives and forms of these opposition movements can hardly be encompassed in a single formula. They arose from liberal or conservative traditions, from religious or humanistic ideas. But the decisive impulse for breaking through the paralyzing and intoxicating spell that had been cast over all of German life was the anguished conscience aroused by sights of tormented fellow human beings, of persecution and terror. It was individual moral indignation that, beyond the boundaries of collective concern, took people of the most varied backgrounds from participation to resistance. The turning point may have come first in the personal sphere, in view of the immediate and urgent task of helping people who were being persecuted and deprived of their rights. A subsequent step was contact with like-minded people, and a realization of what was really happening behind the propaganda of uniform and controlled information and news. Finally, even more risky, and hazarded only by a few, was the step to political conspiracy, to the organizing and planning of active opposition, to contacts with other individuals and groups of the resistance.

The external dangers of oppositional activity were joined by the inner, psychological impediments of an authoritarian mentality among the German middle class. The decision to resist had to be made in terrible loneliness in the midst of mass coercion by the regime. It meant enduring the constant strain of suspicion and silence, endangering family and friends, and being isolated from the great majority of one's own people. Unlike the situation for those joining later resistance movements outside of Germany in occupied Europe, this decision could not draw support from the proud consciousness of national duty. Instead it meant opposing the general patriotism in one's own country. The churches, insofar as they were able to avoid complete *Gleichschaltung,* were the most likely to offer a certain measure of support, but of course that was not always the case. And furthermore, opposition by the churches did not in itself amount to *political resistance* in the stricter sense, so long as it was directed not against National Socialist "authorities" but at the preservation of ecclesiastical autonomy and freedom of teaching. In the subsequent years, moreover, the fronts were often blurred, and many compromises and concessions were made that restricted active opposition even within the Confessional Church. The result was a sort of truce; only a few individuals consistently took the road all the way to the political resistance movement.

This fact was revealed by the largely ambivalent attitude toward the Jewish question. Criticism of the Aryan paragraph did not impede the persistence of a traditional anti-Semitism. Protestant and Catholic objections to euthanasia (1939–40) were not joined by an equivalent protest against the Jewish policy; the reaction remained limited to individual actions or relief measures. Ecclesiastical statements of general import were rarely hazarded, major exceptions being the "Resistance Synod" of Barmen in 1934, as well as the memorials, proclamations from the pulpits, and pastoral letters during the following years. And in October of 1943, the Protestant Confessional Synod (meeting in Breslau) openly denied that the National Socialist state had the right to pursue its policy of annihilation and declared: "The divine order knows no such terms as 'eradicate,' 'liquidate,' and 'useless life.' The destruction of human beings, merely because they are the family members of a criminal, are old or mentally ill or belong to a foreign race, is not a 'wielding of the sword that has been given to authority.'" This also applied to the "life of the people of Israel," and to the claim that one was only following orders: "We cannot let superiors relieve us of the responsibility before God."

However, even most of those closely involved with the resistance from the churches were unable to cope with the following three problems in particular. First, in the debate over the oath to Hitler, only a few were able to transcend the traditional loyalty to the state. Second, when it came to war, the churches for the most part fell back into the attitude of 1914 to 1918 and placed patriotic duty and prayers for victory above earlier scruples: as early as during the Sudeten crisis of 1938, the Lutheran bishops distanced themselves from the Confessional Church. Third, the "fight against Bolshevism" proved to be an argument of tremendous power even in circles critically disposed toward the regime. Nationalism, anticommunism, and a pseudoreligious disguising of National Socialism neutralized much of the possible opposition against the regime in both Protestant and Catholic thinking. Only individuals made the breakthrough to a condemnation of war, or framed the situation of the Germans in terms of a choice, as Dietrich Bonhoeffer did, "either to accept the defeat of their nation so that Christian civilization might live on, or to accept victory and in the process destroy our civilization."

Theologians like Bonhoeffer and the Jesuit priest Alfred Dep also made it to the very front line of the political resistance movement, and were actively involved in the plans for an overthrow of the government and a new political order. Of course the churches as such were not able to bring themselves to explicitly approve of such efforts; revolution and tyrannicide stood in a tense relationship to basic beliefs of Christianity and the churches, and the dilemma of violence and guilt remained unsolved even in resistance to the dictatorship. But among the conspirators of July 20, 1944, Christian motives played an essential role, alongside moral-humanistic ones and the liberal and socialist idea of democracy. To the very end, those in power saw the actual or potential resistance of the churches as a particularly serious obstacle; in the census of 1940, 95 percent of the population still declared formal membership in some church. It was among the regime's most important goals to eliminate this threat after the victorious end of the war.

It remains true that reservations about the regime exerted a greater influence in the churches than elsewhere. Following the "struggle against the churches" in the early years of the regime, the policy of ideological *Gleichschaltung* had limits when it came to the churches, despite organizational restrictions, prohibition of the press, the imprisonment of prominent leaders like Niemöller (since 1937), a dismantling of theological faculties, and threats against all priests who read the oppositional statements of the Confessional Church or Catholic pastoral letters from the pulpit. The response was illegal activities and organizations, especially in the divided Protestant churches.

But the further consolidation of the National Socialist regime restricted both the socialist and the ecclesiastical resistance to a very narrow space. There was no hope of a popular uprising or of mustering enough strength on one's own to bring about change; only contacts with those who held social, governmental, and military positions of power created footholds for exerting influence on the regime's political and military decisions. It became clear that the possibility of setting in motion a popular oppositional movement in a totalitarian dictatorship and getting it to do anything effective is very slim, and that the masses are ill-suited for illegality and resistance. Consequently the antitotalitarian sentiments arising among the civil servants and the military, circles that were in the beginning by no means democratically minded, took on increasing importance. Characteristic in this respect was the ceaseless activity of the lord mayor of Leipzig, Carl Goerdeler, who until 1931 tended to be German-national, and subsequently emphatically independent. After his demonstrative resignation in 1937 in protest over the removal of the Mendelssohn monument in Leipzig, he pursued his efforts in three directions especially: he attempted to influence the leadership of the state through memoranda; he established contact between the various circles of an emerging middle-class and conservative opposition; and he brought his influence to bear on the bureaucracy.

Eventually, with the growing realization that a revolution from below was out of the question, and that only a coup at the top was possible, the resistance began to shift its attention to the army. The Wehrmacht was anything but prepared for this. Against the hopes of many conservatives, it had accepted the seizure of power, the murders of generals von Schleicher and von Bredow, and the oath to Hitler without any protest. Hitler had been able to placate the old-style officers with initial assurances of the military's autonomy. Added to this was the presumed overlap of military and National Socialist interests: rearmament and the elimination of the restrictions of the Versailles Treaty were goals for the sake of which the military was willing to accept the practices of National Socialist rule as mere aberrations. Then, after the debacle of 1934, the Wehrmacht was hardly in a position to act as a separate power group. At the most, military resistance could be a partial movement, the efforts of a minority that could temporarily occupy important positions and make important contacts, but could never accumulate sufficient influence in the top echelons of the military. This fact shaped its form and its limited possibilities.

It became clear that the German military tradition did not offer a viable basis for political resistance: such resistance remained dependent on the individual initiative of intellectually and morally independent officers. Its roots lay not in the tradition of the Reichswehr, but in the decision of conscience on the part of individuals. However, for far too many that became a reason or pretext for avoiding the question by taking refuge in mere obedience and refusing to participate in resistance to the very end, against their better conscience. Still, in the summer of 1938, a first military opposition that formed around Chief of Staff Ludwig Beck had contact with resistance plans in which, for the first time, nearly all political camps were involved. The conspirators, who were planning to change the regime at the moment of the expected military-political crisis, had contacts that ranged from leaders of the SPD and the unions all the way into the upper civil service and the semicivilian secret service of the Wehrmacht.

From this time the active conspiracy was centered in a group formed in the Abwehr (counterintelligence) section of the High Command of the Wehrmacht (Oberkommando der Wermacht, or OKW). The people in this circle had the keenest understanding of the real situation, and the driving forces were the then-colonel Hans Oster and later the Reichsgerichtsrat (high court attorney) Hans von Dohnanyi. Central to the plan was the arrest of Hitler the moment he gave the order to start the war and the Western powers responded with their own declarations of war: the conspirators figured that the start of war would frighten the German population, and would give the undertaking broader support, thereby avoiding the risk of civil war. Once Hitler's criminal and catastrophic course became obvious, the resistance hoped for support from the middle class and military, which was authoritarian-minded, so that the refusal to follow orders would not seem like sabotage and treason. The experience of November 1918 was a warning backdrop to these expectations.

There were two dangers the conspirators were trying to avoid: a civil war, whose outcome would be uncertain in view of the power of the National Socialist party; and a reverse stab-in-the-back legend, which could poison a future new order with the claim that the army and the opposition stabbed Hitler in the back in the face of victory. How justified these fears were was later shown by the defamation of the attempted assassination of Hitler on July 20, 1944, the success of which would only have put an end to a war long lost and would have saved millions of lives.

With Hitler's triumph at the Munich conference in 1938, the ground fell out from under all these plans. During the next three years the regime rushed from victory to victory. Its prestige not only weakened the ranks of the opposition and rendered a counteraction nearly hopeless, it also meant a coup would have been burdened with the dreaded consequences of civil war and the legend of the stab in the back. All this made the participation of those in the military, which was problematic to begin with and endlessly hesitant, decidedly more complicated. Added to this was the increasingly tight security around Hitler during the war.

Opposition during the War

At this point a political-moral problem emerged: when and how should and could the opposition have recourse to force? The churches, which with few exceptions rejected the justification of acts of violence, including the killing of Hitler, were not alone in clinging to their fundamental objections to the use of force. Many bourgeois and conservative opponents of National Socialism, from Goerdeler to the Kreisau Circle, were also undecided about this problem and left the issue of an assassination attempt to the military men, most of whom, for their part, clung to their oath and military obedience. This impeded not only the practical preparations for a coup, but it also seriously obstructed communication among the various oppositional groups; eventually it decisively hampered the putsch attempt itself. To the very end, the conspirators relied too much on subterfuge and surprise. The putsch plan of September 1938 remained the basic model: first, secure military support for an action involving as little bloodshed as possible; second, win over the population by providing information on the criminal character of the Hitler regime and the catastrophic course it was pursuing.

The war both complicated and assisted the opposition. On the one hand, it became increasingly difficult to differentiate between National Socialism and Germany. The appeal to patriotism was stronger than people's misgivings about the regime. Added to this were the increased regimentation in time of war, extensive surveillance, and a general acceleration of the tempo of life. On the other hand, the war demanded a greater degree of improvisation and pragmatism, and it promoted tendencies toward a loosening and opening of the governing structure in the civil as well as the military sphere, all of which was favorable for the organization and spread of resistance. Above all, there was an instant surge in the importance of the Wehrmacht, which, despite its failures, had maintained a certain distance from the party and the SS. In addition, many civilian opponents of the regime were now placed in military positions. From the outbreak of the war, Oster, under the protective umbrella of Admiral Canaris, was admitting men like Dohnanyi and later Bonhoeffer into counterintelligence.

In the situation before 1939–40, before the widening of the war, this group tried to maintain contacts with the Western powers, and Oster attempted to furnish final proof of the sincerity of the opposition by passing to Holland the dates for Germany's attacks on Scandinavia and France. This attempt—which, like all foreign contacts, has been condemned to this day by critics of the opposition as treason against the country *(Landesverrat)* and has even been used for a new stab-in-the-back legend—was an expression of Oster's unconditional opposition to the regime and of his determination to risk everything to end the war and overthrow the regime. Crossing the line from treason against the government *(Hochverrat)* to treason against the country *(Landesverrat)*, a line that was in any case blurred under the dictatorship, was justified by the realization that Hitler was about to attack five neutral countries, whose inviolability he had explicitly guaranteed.

Oster had political as well as moral reasons for his action. He was only too well informed about the unscrupulous preparations for National Socialist aggression. If high treason presupposes the intent of harming one's own country, then the law was also, in this unusual situation, on the side of the person who tried, with all means available, to fight against the breaking of treaties and the destruction of the law. High treason and breach of oath can no longer be valid accusations in a tyrannical state that itself violates all obligations toward its own citizens and toward neighboring states. However, Oster's deed was, at the same time, a very concrete and desperate attempt to save the confidence of foreign countries in the German opposition, a confidence that had been shaken since the outbreak of the war. The attempt failed because the opposition's warnings were not taken seriously, and because the military efficiency of the German operation led to an unexpectedly swift and complete victory in the West.

Hitler's new triumph changed the situation fundamentally. His victory over France also marked a profound defeat for the opposition, and the beginning of the most difficult period for a resistance that had to try to hold its own amidst the frenzy of the victorious dictatorship. The previous contacts with the West and the hopes for a quick end to the war and a revolution at home were destroyed. Isolated, and without any prospect of winning over the population, the opposition was left with little more than the moral position, the ground having been cut from under its possibility of external success. Thus the degree of continuity with which the opposition was organized and expanded over the following years seems all the more remarkable, and it contradicts the later claims that German resistance was only spurred on by fear of defeat, a kind of last-minute panic. That may be true for some of the military representatives. But it certainly does not apply to those who bore the burden of the perilous fight against

Hitler and his seemingly invincible regime at a time of the greatest successes of the Third Reich.

Two problems, above all, determined the subsequent development of the resistance. First there was the fact that every victory of German arms reduced the domestic political prospects of the opposition to the same degree that it expanded the foreign policy claims of the opposition's national-conservative wing, including the Foreign Office. The second problem had to do with the discussion about the political and moral implications of an assassination of Hitler, without which it did not seem possible for the opposition to realize the most pressing goals: removal of the regime, an end to the war, the restoration of law and freedom. This was the consistent position of Dietrich Bonhoeffer. Against those who had misgivings, he declared as early as 1942 that the guilt of National Socialist Germany no longer admitted of any "way out by means of foreign politics." The acts of the resistance were, rather, an "act of penance" and had to be made clear as such. For Bonhoeffer, as for Julius Leber and Helmuth James von Moltke, unconditional surrender was unavoidable. Going beyond the views of others in the Kreisau Circle, Moltke, at the end of 1943, considered the "unquestionable military defeat and occupation of Germany absolutely necessary for moral and political reasons."

This realization also brought about the attempt by the students of the opposition group "White Rose," after 1942 and 1943, to rebel against the political failure of the German educated class. But this kind of resistance remained isolated and was condemned in most institutes of learning. Against the background of the German tradition, scholars and intellectuals were as little equipped as generals for the struggle against conventional patriotism and loyalty to the state. Fear of persecution and of the stigma of treason frightened those who should have known better because they had day-to-day contact with the political and military spheres or with the intellectual-moral world.

The Right of Resistance

Finally, we are faced again with the question of whether resistance in a dictatorial and tyrannical state, which perforce must take on the stigma of illegality and violence, can be in any way related to the claims of an antisystem opposition in a democratic state based on the rule of law. The current protest movements like to reduce the problem to the antistate argument that, because political rule supposedly amounts to "structural force," it justifies counterforce. What this neglects is the decisive frame of reference within which resistance to dictatorship is legitimated: the demand for the restitution of constitutional conditions and human rights.

When we examine the rise of all too many dictatorships in our century, right down to the present, we note that the use and abuse of ideology and religion are among the most important elements in the conflict between political systems—especially in all the attempts to suppress freedom and law in the name of a perfect society that, according to the promises of the totalitarian salvation doctrines, will bring paradise on earth. This totalitarian temptation through political religion and radicalism, through pseudoreligious ideologies and the pseudopolitical manipulation of faith, poses a danger even under the profoundly altered conditions of our own time. From 1933 to 1945, thanks to such a use of ideology, a nominally Christian nation was unable to counter the three great evils of National Socialism: the merciless persecution of all who had fallen out of favor, and especially the Jews; militant imperialism; and political-racial mass murder.

As much as one can regret the political and social misery in most developing countries, there are not only historical but also political and moral reasons that warn against any hasty equating of the situation of resistance in the Nazi period with the power conflicts and the "liberation movements" in the Third World. Christian impulses of love for one's fellow humans and of social justice can easily be utilized and abused by movements that themselves have dictatorial methods and goals. And in the struggle over fiercely contested political issues of the day, activists, invoking the failure before and after 1933, are too quick to elevate one-sided opinions with chiliastic pathos to the level of final truths. The German experience with the acceptance of "movements" that justify violence or dictatorship with lofty goals also serves as a warning against underestimating political religions that strive for one-sided rule under a Christian or non-Christian banner: rule, that is, over the state as well as over people's thoughts and souls. We should reserve the concept of resistance for the struggle against the kind of totalitarian threat and deprivation of rights that a courageous group of German citizens tried to resist back then.

It remains important to make a fundamental distinction between resistance undertaken to defend a profoundly violated constitutional state and to protect mercilessly persecuted people, and efforts aimed at revolutionary upheaval in the name of perfectionist, future utopias, made without any regard for how many victims it will cost. Of course there are fluid transitions from one to the other: in the resistance to Hitler, as well, the goal could not be a mere return to previous conditions or socialist utopian dreams. This fact put a question mark on the designs of the constitutionally and socially conservative opposition groups, as well as on the dictatorial counterconceptions of the Communists. The object was the restoration of a liberal and social state based on the rule of law; the liberation of the law from arbitrary abuse in the service of superhuman and inhuman goals pursued by the Right and the Left. One may very well argue that a right of revolution exists, and that the breakthrough of modern democracy was due largely to revolution. Germany, the land of the failed or missed revolution, certainly has some ground to make up in this discussion; the 1989 "revolt against coercion and lies" (Helmut Schmidt) in the GRD is a hopeful sign.

But the failure of 1933 and of the opposition in the Third Reich contains, above all, the lesson that the political culture of a modern state depends on the moral and the constitutional establishment of the right of opposition. In Germany, unlike in the Western democracies, a self-evident tradition of the right of resistance was interrupted when, after 1848, a national, authoritarian state was established in a revolution from above. Neither the Weimar Republic nor the Federal Republic were able to pick up the thread of a secure, self-evident conception of the state and citizenship. The experience of totalitarianism shows that two things must be avoided: a relapse into the protective spheres of the authoritarian state, and the outbreak of radical antisystem movements, which would mean a return to the extreme polarizations of the Weimar Republic.

Both forms of behavior go against the painful lesson of the failure of the first democracy and the painful story that the resistance has left us. The sacrifice of those who bravely resisted the pull of seduction, the opportunism, and the uncritical enthusiasm for power and success, those who, attacked and lonely, took upon themselves persecution and death, cannot be judged by the fashionable "capitalist-socialist" or "reactionary-progressive" alternatives. The overriding aspect of the resistance seems to me to be that it demonstrates the old conviction, long buried in Germany, that politics must make possible two things simultaneously: the construction and consolidation of a constitutional democracy, and also criticism of every biased and unjust exercise of power. Certain forms of government suppress such differences of opinion, whether in the name of a supposedly conflict-free society, under the banner of an authoritarian state, or in pursuit of the victory of a militant ideological movement that believes itself the sole repository of truth and invokes (for example, in military or ecological questions), in the alleged interest of the people, the exceptional right of resistance against parliament and constitutional state. Such systems violate the basic law of any politics worthy of the human race.

The dead of the antidictatorial resistance are witnesses to the idea of the moderate and liberal state founded on the separation of powers, an idea that Western politics has been striving for ever since the age of Greek democracy and the revolt against tyrannical power. They reconnect us to this great international tradition, renounced by Germany with her anti-Western cult of the state. And this is all the more remarkable as most of the resisters were women and men who, against the background of the problematic tradition of German ideas of the state and a consciousness of being special and different, were not naturally inclined toward democratic sentiments and revolutionary acts. They "put back into the German vocabulary" the words "resistance" and "tyrannicide" (Wilhelm Hennis). They rose above the German metaphysics of the state, the belief in the state as the highest good, by finding their way from an antidemocratic to an antidictatorial understanding of resistance and joining the ranks of the European struggle against Hitler. The fundamental lesson left by the German resistance to the Right dictatorship is that the state, authority, and the nation are no longer absolutes, that values transcending the state, as well as a humane political process, are the first points of reference for the loyalties of the citizen, and that the overriding consideration should be not the state, nor some oath or order of society as such, but an alert constitutional understanding and a democratic consciousness. Therein lies the deeper justification for a resistance to one's own state that has been condemned and vilified as illegal and traitorous.

Thomas Mann once called politics part of the human condition. The significance of resistance lies not in separating politics and morality and considering them in isolation from each other; it lies precisely in the close connection between the two. In recent German history, and in the interpretations of the resistance against Hitler, the one has often been played off against the other. The old question about the relationship between law, justice, and force confronts us time and again. The answer given by the resistance was not that force as such was justified, which is often carelessly talked about; it was that those in the resistance were willing to take on themselves the odium and sacrifice of force, to restore right and justice against an inhuman and criminal tyranny.

The Place of World War II in History

I

In contrast to the lengthy discussion about the responsibility for World War I, there cannot be any serious question about who bears responsibility for the fateful events that led, fifty years ago, to World War II after the German attack on Poland. Fundamental responsibility lies with Hitler and his National Socialist regime, no matter how the role of other states and politicians should be assessed.

Walther Hofer, in his pioneering work of 1954, the making of which we contemporary historians in Berlin witnessed (the fifties, much underrated today, did much for our working through of the recent past), said that we should not speak of the outbreak of World War II, but rather of its "unleashing." Historical and political scholarship, drawing on archives that are increasingly accessible and, one hopes, soon also drawing on the Soviet archives, has essentially confirmed Hofer's view. In the process it has subjected the conduct of the Soviet Union, Poland, the Western powers, Italy, and Japan to critical scrutiny. To be sure, there have been repeated attempts, not only in Germany, to exonerate Hitler's policies of rule and war or even to revalue them through historical myths. But like the effort to resurrect the legend of the stab in the back by defaming the resistance, these attempts have been limited for the most part to sectarian circles. However, this does not mean that the potential popular impact, to this day, of such deliberately apologetic or emphatically revisionist endeavors should be trivialized. In any case, contrary to right-radical (Hoggan) and sensation-mongering efforts (A. J. P. Taylor, David Irving), the "question of war guilt" is not open.

Nor will the *primary* responsibility that lies with German and National Socialist policies be altered by reference to the West's policy of appeasement, or by the role of the pact between Hitler and Stalin, which is finally no longer a completely taboo subject on the Soviet side. Of course this does not relieve us of the task of determining the historical place of World War II, that is to say, of examining the longer-term national and international conditions, the political system, and the ideological circumstances of the disastrous policy that, together with the illusions and mistaken assessments by contemporaries, made Hitler's war of conquest and annihilation possible.

Andreas Hillgruber sees the historical place of World War I as the "end point of a development of the European state system that spanned more than one hundred years."[1] It finalized the collapse of the barriers that the Congress of Vienna had set up in Europe in 1814–15, after Napoleon's great hegemonic war, against the unfettered power politics of nationalism and imperialism. The American diplomat and historian George F. Kennan has, even more pointedly, called World War I, in view of its consequences, "the great seminal catastrophe of this century."[2] To this day, and with good reason, scholars have emphasized the fundamental significance of the war between 1914 and 1918 for Europe and for the world as a whole. This view has been expressed in the broad assessments by Hajo Holborn, Felix Gilbert, and James Joll, as well as in the quite divergent interpretations by Ludwig Dehio, Fritz Fischer, and Michael Howard.

What, then, is the historical place of *World War II?* To what extent was it a continuation of World War I or even its repeat? To what degree was it an intensification of that development, to what degree an entirely new dimension? Was it a rupture in the development or its continuity in terms of results and repercussions?

In fact 1914 marked not only the end point of a preceding epoch but also the beginning of a momentous new development. In 1918 one already encounters everything that would make our century the century of the persecuted and oppressed: the confrontation between government of laws and dictatorship; the era of economic and political crises and breakdowns; the age of ideologies, with their claim to total implementation; indeed "the rivalry between totalitarian nationalism and totalitarian Marxism" (Hugh Seton-Watson),[3] the age of left-totalitarian and right-totalitarian seductions and the unprecedented mass crimes they made possible or even legalized. But it also became the century of the struggle for democracy, of the great resistance movements, of the battle for freedom and human rights!

World War II made it possible to carry out what had been fatefully present in 1918 in embryonic form. Whatever existed as a thought or a ferment, as a technical possibility or an extreme consequence, the war took to the point of "implementation" *(Durchführung)* in the brutal sense of

National Socialist language. At the same time, the historical differences between the two periods are certainly evident. It is true that 1914 marked a time of profound crisis—indeed, in many ways, the end of the nineteenth-century world of progress—not only because of the persistence of old regimes that were still monarchic and feudal in character (Arno Mayer),[4] or because there was a tendency to let oneself drift in the current of the movements (Hillgruber). The year 1914 already seemed to be the "crisis of the age of the bourgeoisie," as the slogans from the Left and the Right proclaimed. At the same time, however, contemporary prognoses spoke just as emphatically about a future world of universal democracy, the irresistible advance of socialism, or a new Caesarism under the banner of nationalism that was now to be brought to its completion. Behind the much-quoted spirit of new departure in the "ideas of 1914," with which the war began, were two things: the fall from the self-idolization of old Europe to its self-destruction, and simultaneously the impulse for a new wave of modernization and for revolutionary changes in the material and intellectual worlds.

Thus the course and consequences of World War I revealed, suddenly and terrifyingly, phenomena and trends that, though initially largely mis-interpreted, would constitute the true beginning of our modern era and represent the fundamental causes and parameters of World War II: the Russian Revolution and the Communist seizure of power; America's entry into world politics; the spread and simultaneous crisis of liberal democracy; the radical change in colonialism and imperialism; growth problems of capitalism and socialism's universal pretensions; social change and emancipation movements; nationalism and racism; and, finally, the possibility for authoritarian and even totalitarian dictatorships of hitherto unknown intensity. The latter are inconceivable without World War I's "brutalization of politics," which George Mosse has described in light of Germany's development in the twenties and thirties.[5]

Added to this is the fact that the final triumph of the European nation-state principle and its exaggeration coincided with the crisis of the traditional concert of European powers, with the "collapse of the European state system," indeed with the "end of the European era" that Hajo Halborn (1954) and Felix Gilbert (1970) noted in their retrospective assessments. True enough, after World War I Europe's previously dominant role in world politics was diminished by the growing weight of outside powers, primarily the United States, then also Japan, and even more so by the internal weakness of Europe, which affected both the victors and the defeated. Indirectly, despite peace treaties and the League of Nations, a potential state of war continued. And with the end of World War II, the "reduction" of Europe's position ended in Europe's division and dependence on two outside superpowers, the United States and the Soviet Union, and in the alternatives of liberty or subjection, as Alexis de Tocqueville had prophesied a century before.

In view of this interconnectedness of the two world wars, some have even spoken of a mere "interwar period," indeed of a modern version of the Thirty Years' War between 1914 and 1945. Correct in these assessments is the fact that World War II was to be, above all in the mind of Adolf Hitler, the man who unleashed it, the reversal in world politics of the German defeat in 1918 and a correction of the Pan-German and imperialistic shortcomings of the German Reich. This interpretation highlights not only the fundamental differences in the events that led to the wars but also the similarities in the structure of the two world wars. It includes the fact that the classic separation of domestic and foreign politics was increasingly relativized, and indeed abolished. Previously this had taken place only in the age of the great revolutions, especially the French Revolution. This loss of distinction between the two spheres of politics came from both the endorsement of an *open diplomacy* (Wilson) and the breakthrough of the ideological politics of a (world-)revolutionary age (Lenin).

Moreover, World War I was conducted with the extensive use of domestic-political and intellectual weapons, and with a psychological warfare that proved to be a lasting inspiration for Hitler. Thus the year 1914, with its exacerbation of the conflicts into economic, social, and ideological confrontations, already constituted a watershed for the great, contrary currents of the century. The high point of this development was reached when two profoundly different visionaries and utopians, Wilson and Lenin, appeared on the stage of world history in 1917 and 1918. However, they were immediately followed by the two ideologists of World War II, Mussolini and Hitler. This completed the deployment of the great, antagonistic political camps of the twenties: democracy, Communism, Fascism, and National Socialism.

II

The fact that the period since 1914 forms an interconnected epoch is revealed in the intertwining of national and international history, and also in the rise of social-scientific ways of thinking. History now has to deal with the growing complexity and interdependence of states and societies, with overarching movements, parties, and groups. Above all, it must deal with the permanent conflict among democratic, authoritarian, and totalitarian trends and regimes, among liberal, conservative, and revolutionary conceptions of politics—a conflict that is sharpened by ideology and grounded in socioeconomic realities and mass politics.

Along with this development, an older problem, one that points to the religious and revolutionary wars of the early modern period, entered into a new phase. In an earlier age, wars and diplomacy were pursued by high-handed monarchs. With the transformations of population policy and economic policy in the wake of the industrial revolution, however, confrontations were no longer between individual governments and rulers but between entire nations. There were now states that conceived of themselves as nations. Their foreign policy—during the trend toward general democratization and the increasing weight of "public opinion," of parliaments, parties, and interest groups—was now fundamentally determined or influenced by domestic politics.

This new situation profoundly altered the character of international politics: internal movements, sentiments, and ideologies became increasingly important for international relations. And it was precisely the dictatorial systems, no matter how authoritarian or totalitarian their internal structures might be, that could not and did not wish to escape these new, mass, "democratic" conditions of political motivation and action. On the contrary, in the interest of strengthening the dictatorship at home, they even placed special emphasis on what had become an indissoluble link between domestic and foreign policy, either by pursuing the internal *Gleichschaltung* and mobilization of the population with a view toward what was, in the final analysis, an unlimited, utopian expansion, as the National Socialists did, or by using what was at first a "defensive" foreign policy in the name of "peaceful coexistence" to infiltrate and undermine the policies of other states, as the Soviet Union, for example, did with its combination of class warfare and peace propaganda.

The central question of why a National Socialist dictatorship prevailed in Germany, of all places, must also take into consideration a dense, interconnected web of different factors that cannot be reduced to a single cause. Any monocausal approach would miss that web of interconnections, no matter how suggestively it might be grounded in current theories of capitalism, fascism, or socialism, and no matter how seductively ready it might be to offer final explanations.

Though politics was still marked by the struggle for hegemony in Europe, it was now, in addition, a struggle over ideological revolutionization. The modern economy, with its technicalization, particularly of warfare, had unleashed massive forces. It had placed at the state's disposal the means to mobilize and direct those forces, means that could be abused by dictatorial regimes. Inherent in the colonial competition of the powers and the imperial claims of the nations that had "come too late" (Germany,

Italy, and Japan), were forces that were intensified, after the first explosion of 1914 and in the crises of the postwar period, by the appearance of radical, pseudoreligiously fanaticized movements with dictatorial claims. These movements were marked by an even more intense development of technical potential and the power of numbers, by a maximum application of domestic-political, economic, and intellectual-psychological means, and finally, by an ideological radicalization of the will to destroy that far eclipsed even that seen in World War I.

It was fateful that the intellectual and moral handling of the new conditions was not able to keep pace with the expansion of politics internally and externally. Despite an upsurge in the idea of democracy and peace, nationalism and imperialism continued to be the powerful and influential standards and models, no matter how much the circumstances and forms of politics were changing. The discrepancy between the new world situation and the old thinking in terms of the power state was further exacerbated to the degree that the democratic slogan about the right of self-determination of peoples was perverted into an argument for intolerance, into a means of oppressing minorities. This had already taken place at the time of the dubious peace treaties of 1919. As a result, at the very moment that the idea of self-determination was being realized, it lost, under the pressure of war psychosis, its original intellectual-moral and democratic value.

The extreme consequence of this tension between a changed world and the unbroken power politics was the exaggeration of ideologized national imperialism, which culminated in Fascism and National Socialism. Its origins, like the rise of its leaders, lay in the prewar and war years around 1914: in the overheated and Machiavellian power politics, in a radical friend-foe ideology domestically and internationally, in a naturalistic conception of politics, including the belief in a necessary expansion and rounding out of an autonomous "living area." Such ideas, hatched (like anti-Semitism) in the 1870s and 1880s, were the breeding ground from which Hitler, in particular, drew his weltanschauung with monomaniacal consistency.

III

The explosive power of these trends came to the fore when the United States, which had decided the outcome of the war and which, through President Wilson, had emphatically demanded a new order that transcended the nation-state, abruptly withdrew and left European power politics once again to its own devices. The result was a vacuum, a relapse into nationalistic rivalries, and this placed a fateful burden on the peace treaties, the reparations, and the reintegration into Europe of the defeated

Germany. The passions of war waned too slowly to allow the League of Nations to change from an alliance of the victorious powers into an effective instrument of politics transcending the nation-states.

Thus while France and Great Britain sought to solidify the outcome of 1918, the front of the dissatisfied grew—those defeated countries who were not willing to accept the situation, and those, like Italy and Japan, who did not feel satisfied with their share of the victory. Frequently the fault lines of diverging opinion ran right through the states, and it was this that contributed to destabilization, especially in the new democracies. It intensified the persistent conflict until it was nearly a form of civil war and eventually drove the states to a new readiness for war. The disappointment over the new order of 1919, the failure of European solutions, and the relapse into national power politics coincided with the serious economic crises that affected the victors as well as the defeated, as a result of the war. Political radicalization and the confusion of intellectual and moral standards continued to spread. These trends led some to a resigned withdrawal from realistic politics (as in the growing pacifism in Great Britain and France), and others to the fanaticization of revisionism and irredentism (in Germany, Italy, and the Balkans).

How was it possible that after decades of an increased safeguarding of peace, of seemingly definitive humanitarian advances in the abolition of slavery and the taming of war, there followed the most unbelievable relapses into barbarism: World War I followed by World War II, by genocide and internal oppression, work camps and concentration camps, total war through the involvement of the civilian population, exile, deportations, and mass expulsions?

This development, too, had been prepared in the 1870s and 1880s. So far as ideas are concerned, lasting importance attaches to the stirring events of the Paris Commune of 1871, and to the great economic crises of the period of rapid industrial expansion in Germany between 1871 and 1873, which resulted in a radical critique of capitalism. One result of this was an intensification of socialism in the antiliberal version of Marxist doctrine, with the slogan of the dictatorship of the proletariat. Another was a racial sharpening of nationalism and anti-Semitism. This resulted in extreme biologistic-Darwinian theories of society. Instead of class warfare, these theories elevated the struggle between peoples, the friend-foe relationship, and the "right of the stronger" to basic principles of politics. Both of these extreme ideologies—Marxism and racism—invoked the radical insights and theories of modern science, indeed they took the stage with the claim of scientific infallibility.

It was this front of antiliberalism from the Right and the Left that condensed into an explosive mix in the critique of civilization and the accompanying cultural malaise. It radically questioned the ideas about liberal progress and democratic forms of compromise, and declared war on them. The intellectual midwives of the totalitarian ideologies exerted their influence to the Left and the Right: as with, for example, the ex-Socialist Mussolini, who became the founder of Fascism during the war, whom Marx and Nietzsche served as idea donors. On the other side of the political spectrum, the conflict over a reformist versus a revolutionary conception of socialism brought forth, during the same period, a radical, violence-affirming version, with which the French philosopher of violence, Georges Sorel (1908), had already influenced the Russian champion of dictatorial one-party socialism, Lenin, with world-historical consequences. In this situation the first modern war of the masses—World War I—eliminated existing structures, standards, and inhibitions even more rapidly, or made them morally pervertable. Lenin and Hitler, in particular, understood not only the external impact of the war but also its inner, intellectual-psychological significance. An intellectual-political vacuum had resulted. In this vacuum it was possible to pursue, with far greater success, the mobilization of social-ideological "movements" beyond the existing parties and organizations, and to bring them to power as seductive alternatives to the existing, semi-absolute monarchies and to the only half-successful new bourgeois democracies: this happened in 1917 in Russia, in 1922 in Italy, in 1933 in Germany.

Hitler's seizure of power in 1933, the most momentous totalitarian seizure of power next to the October Revolution of 1917, formed the climax of an authoritarian surge that overpowered the still-weak, crisis-ridden democracies in most of the newly established states of the postwar period by means of a cult of the strong man: in Hungary (Horthy) and Poland (Pilsudski), Portugal (Salazar) and Spain (Franco), in the Balkan states, in Austria, in Greece (Metaxas). Among all these antiliberal and antidemocratic ideas and currents of power, National Socialism was, of course, the most radical in theory and practice. It was as consistently and comprehensively totalitarian as its Communist counterpart. It was no doubt close to Italian Fascism, and it borrowed some forms and slogans from it, but it differed in its extreme racist goals. And with its ideology of the collective nation, a homophobic ideology, it moved closer to the Stalinist way of rule than the emphatically "antifascist" sympathizers of Communism were willing to admit.

While the twenties had still seemed open and filled with the possibilities of intellectual and political diversity, the thirties were now overshadowed and dominated by two great camps. Despite the hostility between them, both were, above all, declared enemies of pluralistic democracy and its values, countering the achievements of liberal and humane politics with the seductive power and mysticism of a socialist or nationalist community. Most young European democracies wavered between the two and collapsed under the pressure of economic and national crises. Increasingly it seemed to be demonstrated that democracy was viable only in exceptional cases, and that the future form of state and society would be marked by these Caesarist leadership figures, as not only Oswald Spengler but also Max Weber had expected.

IV

In the interconnected web of the epoch's forward-pressing and destructive forces, the actual prehistory of World War II begins with the year 1933. That year was the real beginning of the "German catastrophe," which was not only a political and military catastrophe but a moral one as well. After his seizure of power, which was facilitated by a misjudgment of National Socialism by the Right as well as the Left, Hitler set out on two paths simultaneously: that of protecting his regime through an apparent readiness to negotiate and a wooing of international recognition, and that of alternating threats, surprise actions, and faits accomplis. Through the interplay of these two methods, the Third Reich was able to survive a dangerous early phase. From 1935 on, in possession of a consolidated position of power at home and with a demonstratively enlarged military and economic potential, it then prepared for the violent thrust outward with its policies of alliances and rearmament.

Historical scholarship, through a critical examination of these interconnections, has refuted a claim put forth in the memoirs and apologies of participants in the events: that Hitler developed what was initially a justified revisionist policy into a destructive policy only during the course of the following years; that he was steering a fairly reasonable course until 1938. An assessment of his pseudolegal seizure of power was distorted at the time by the apparently positive accomplishments of Nazi social and economic policy. In like manner, the apparent continuation of a peaceful revisionist policy, the deceptive (because temporary) shelving of the plans for conquest, and the loud proclamation of a peaceful course in Hitler's official declarations made it difficult and confusing to evaluate National Socialist foreign policy. In Germany, as abroad, the illusion persisted that the responsibility of government would make Hitler reasonable and that he would not return to the equally dilettantish and unbridled plans contained in the National Socialist program for the future. The policy of appeasement, which determined the behavior of the Western powers right to the threshold of the new war, arose from a faith in the possibility of a peaceful containment of Hitler's foreign policy though contacts and concessions; in much the same way, the illusion of taming Hitler had been the undoing of the domestic politics of the Weimar Republic.

In contrast, Hitler was flexible yet tenacious in pursuing the path that, despite the seemingly "polycratic" conditions and contradictions of the regime, led his dictatorship step by step to an absolute freedom of action, to a total revision of Versailles, and eventually to an unrestrained reach for hegemony in Europe and plans for world supremacy. The outlines of his first goals appeared as early as 1934 and 1935. There was, above all, the dissolution of the collective system of the League of Nations, achieved through pacts with single states, the isolating of France through a front of alliances with Fascist Italy and if possible with "Germanic" Great Britain, and at the same time a Pan-German expansion through pressure on Austria. Hitler left no doubt that the final purpose of his domestic policy, conceived in totalitarian terms, was to be a function of his new, expansionist foreign policy. In *Mein Kampf*, as in the famous speech before the Industrialists' Club of Düsseldorf in January 1932 and in lectures to generals and civil servants, party functionaries and economic leaders before and after 1933, he unmistakably emphasized that the National Socialist policy of rule would first create the prerequisites for such a foreign policy in terms of an intellectual, organizational, and military readiness to pursue it. Alongside the old foreign policy, reduced to a mere instrument, this new foreign policy, which was not taken seriously by the decisive actors in international politics, began immediately after the seizure of power to intervene in all spheres of political life. On the road to war, it became, in turn, a means of total rule at home based an unlimited dynamism and military striking power.

Though this discussion comes back to *Hitler* time and again, it should not be understood in the sense of those popular theoretical debates, such as "men make history" versus "the Third Reich as a polyocracy." Such statements push theories to exaggerated heights. Reasonable scholarship has always emphasized that structures and individuals are interconnected. The real, or perhaps artificial, controversy over whether Hitler was an omnipotent or a weak dictator was recently best clarified by Manfred Funke and Hermann Graml. After a careful examination of the debate and the facts, Graml reached the following conclusion: "Leaving aside the sole special case of Austria, all of the more important foreign policy actions of the Third Reich go back to decisions by Hitler, decisions that were not directly or decisively influenced either by persons or groups or by situations and developments. The dictator acted freely and alone, subject only to the constraints he himself had created with the National Socialist program and with his fixation on that program."[6] No matter how important it is to examine systems and structures (since my early studies of the Weimar

Republic, I, too, have considered such an examination to be essential), when describing the developments leading to World War II, the focus must rest above all on Hitler, his ideological fixations, his political will, and his decisions. This approach has been used by historians from Alan Bullock to Eberhard Jäckel and Norman Rich.

And amid all the learned discussions about missed chances and alternatives, one thing remains clear: there was no real possibility of avoiding the war if, and so long as, Hitler was able to make the decisions. His goals and style of rule admitted of no other way—whether or not the way the events actually unfolded or their timing was exactly as he wanted. The development of the war outside of Europe is also connected to this, as Japan's exploiting of the circumstances between 1931 and 1941 shows.

Hitler benefited from what seemed an almost unstoppable crisis of democracy in the thirties. An "authoritarian wave," a march toward national dictatorships, increasingly determined the European scene. The promises and ambitions of these dictatorships exerted a growing pull, they disturbed the politics between states and exacerbated the general uncertainty and instability. Also, increasingly, parliamentary democracy seemed to demonstrate that it was unworkable. Almost nowhere did it appear able to accommodate the political and social tensions of the "mass age" in a stable and simultaneously adaptable system. Even in the democracies that were fortified by tradition, Great Britain and France, there were disruptions, long governmental crises, and divisions. At the same time, the consolidation of the Communist system in the Soviet Union, and even more so the noisy rise of the Third Reich, exerted a growing influence on the wavering neighbors. The outward projection of power, the infiltrating of neighboring states, and the apparent successes of domestic unification had a paralyzing or seductive effect on friend and foe.

Beginning in 1936, a redefinition of the spheres of interest in Europe emerged. Hitler recognized Italy's claim to the Mediterranean; Mussolini, Germany's goals in Central and Eastern Europe. Only their shared ambitions in southeastern Europe harbored problems, as was later shown in Italy's policy toward Albania and Greece. The ideological and propagandistic basis for the "Berlin-Rome Axis" was an anticommunism dressed up with pathos and popular appeal. The "battle against Bolshevism" had acquired new arguments with the Soviet intervention in Spain. This was given institutional form by the conclusion of the Anti-Comintern Pact between Germany and Japan in November of 1936, which was later joined by Italy, Spain, and other states. This heralded an expansion into world politics of the National Socialist ideology of struggle.

And while the Western powers clung to their indecisive, unsuccessful strategy of appeasement, the German-Italian alliance quickly made its influence felt in all directions. Belgium withdrew from the French alliance system and eventually entrusted itself, as did the Netherlands, to Hitler's guarantee to respect their national integrity. Poland had been keeping to a pro-German course since 1934. Revisionist-minded states like Hungary and Bulgaria, and even Yugoslavia, hitherto so closely tied to France, drew closer to the Axis. Only Czechoslovakia and the Soviet Union were left for a Western defensive system. The Soviet Union had been watching the passivity of the West with indignation and suspicion, but in that time of Stalin's policies of coercion and terror, it was almost completely focused on domestic politics and confined itself to criticism and declarations. An East-West front against the Axis was prevented by mutual distrust.

This was the backdrop for the two decisive and interconnected developments that eventually made possible the unleashing of the war: the concessions of the Western policy of appeasement, on the one hand, and Stalin's Machiavellian about-face, on the other. These cleared the way for the subsequent, swift unfolding of National Socialist power politics. Hitler's goals and tactics, in contrast, hardly changed. His tried-and-true sequence of actions was this: extensive demands first for a revision of the existing situation and then for a geopolitical rounding-off of territory, and finally an imperial claim to rule; secret planning and a successful surprise strike; emphatic assurance that this was the last act in the realization of the German right of existence, and that there would be no further demands against the party concerned. This process was repeated again and again.

The West's policy of appeasement was inextricably tied to the course pursued by the British prime minister, Neville Chamberlain. His ambassador in Berlin, Nevile Henderson, whose memoirs bear the resigned title *Failure of a Mission,* lived to the very end with the illusion that it was possible and imperative to tame Hitler and ward off the threat of the Axis by giving in to reasonable demands. This was a fundamental fallacy, one that further reinforced Hitler's self-confidence and urge for conquest. It is true that in good faith the "appeasers" could point to the fact that Germany was apparently not seeking to drive its intervention in Spain to a warlike expansion. Moreover, Hitler initially impressed Henderson and Chamberlain with gestures of friendship and peace, and repeatedly affirmed his old concept of a German-British alliance. On the fourth anniversary of the seizure of power, January 30, 1937, he solemnly declared before the Reichstag that the politics of surprise was over, and a visit by Lord Halifax to Berlin in November of 1937 was marked by similar assurances. At the same time, however, the Axis was strengthened by a pompous visit by Mussolini to Berlin in September of 1937 and by Italy's joining of the Anti-Comintern Pact, and the other partner, Japan, reactivated its warlike operations in China with the occupation of Shanghai and

Peking. Great Britain, and at its side a hesitant France, remained willing to see in Hitler's signs of compromise a validation of their wait-and-see attitude, even though the compromises were only protective maneuvers in Hitler's feverish rearmament policy, the extent of which the poorly armed appeasers nevertheless tended to overestimate.

V

In the momentous secret conference on November 5, 1937 (recorded in the famous Hoßbach protocol), Hitler confirmed his "irrevocable decision" to bring about the "solution to the question of space" as early as possible, beginning with the "lightning-quick" smashing of Czechoslovakia and Austria. In the Spanish civil war, as the dictators saw it, a dress rehearsal was already under way for the great *ideological civil war* that was to prepare the decisive course of future world politics. At this point it also became apparent to keen observers what sort of inhuman threat the totalitarianism of the Right and the Left posed. And so the perspective of that period produced two of the most powerful analyses of the totalitarian threat: George Orwell's vision of horror and Jacob Talmon's comparative critique of ideology. The British writer Orwell (1903–1950) took part in the Spanish civil war, an experience that led to his conversion from leftist beliefs. The Israeli historian Talmon (1916–1980), to whom we owe the historically comprehensive account of the intellectual origins and consequences of "totalitarian democracy," tells us that in those days, as a student in Poland, he was influenced first and decisively by three experiences that reminded him of the terrorist phase of the French Revolution: the Spanish civil war, the Stalinist show trials, and the National Socialist persecution of the Jews. Orwell's self-criticism from the year 1944 remains valid to this day: the leftist intellectuals, he said, made the mistake or succumbed to the illusion that they "wanted to be anti-fascist without being anti-totalitarian."[7] And until his untimely death, Talmon repeatedly emphasized that he traced his insight into the pseudodemocratic character of totalitarian thought and action precisely to his dismaying experiences at the end of the thirties.[8]

In fact this historical interconnection was subsequently confirmed in dramatic fashion. The surprising and yet quite characteristic pact between Hitler and Stalin in 1939 caused the distinction between a Left dictatorship and a Right dictatorship to recede behind the dictators' shared will to conclude a temporary pact of conquest and bring about a totalitarian transformation of the state system. In the rapid intensification of European politics through Hitler's pressure on Poland, the attitude of the Soviet Union assumed decisive importance. The Soviet Union had been feeling isolated and deceived by the Western powers ever since the Munich conference. Although of course a major reason for this isolation was those large-scale, bloody "purges" and show trials with which Stalin had sealed a fifteen-year-long process of totalitarian *Gleichschaltung* and consolidation of his autocratic rule.

In the rest of Europe, which followed the almost unbelievable events in Moscow with dismay, doubts grew as to whether one could form a front against Hitler with this kind of Soviet Union, which did not seem to be much better than the Hitler system *at that time*. These doubts were further reinforced by the fact that the bloody purges were expanded to include even unpopular members of the Western Communist parties and participants in the Spanish civil war. Stalinism extended its reach into all countries of Europe with intrigues and murder, not to mention the elimination of Communist émigrés in Moscow itself.

The National Socialist regime, which contributed to the show trials with information from the secret service, must have been happy with both the weakening of the Soviet position, militarily as well as politically, and the breakup of a potentially broad anti-Hitler front, which had seemed a possibility ever since Germany's withdrawal from and Moscow's admittance into the League of Nations and the policy of the Popular Front in France. Here Hitler's plans worked: in the decisive months of 1939, the Western powers were no longer able to bring Moscow into their camp.

Of course, in all of this Stalin's fear of an agreement among all Western powers at the expense of the Soviet Union and of a deflection of the German dynamic toward the East was certainly combined with his own revisionist and expansionist demands: toward Poland, in the Baltic, in Rumania and Finland, eventually even in the direction of the Mediterranean. There is no reason that it should not have been possible for Stalin's totalitarian regime suddenly and radically to change fronts, even if the Soviet Union's ideological opposition to the Third Reich was so sharp. Added to this was tradition of German-Russian cooperation (up to and including a cooperation between Reichswehr and Red Army, and between SD and GPU, the German and Russian secret services), as well as Germany's strategic desire to avoid a war on two fronts. The efforts by the Western powers to include Moscow in their system of guarantees were also unsuccessful because the Soviet Union responded with broad demands for passage for her troops, which her neighbors, understandably fearful of infiltration and annexation, were unable to accept.

When the Western-oriented Foreign Minister Litvinov was replaced by Molotov in May of 1939, the alternative of a Soviet-German alliance moved to the fore. Economic negotiations had begun in April in Berlin. Nationalist Socialist enemy propaganda shifted its sights from Bolshevism to the democratic "plutocracies," and Hitler's final plan to attack Poland eventually led to a surprisingly quick agreement between the declared mortal enemies. While the British and French negotiators were still in Moscow, Ribbentrop, on the night of his arrival on August 23/24, 1939, went straight to the Kremlin at the invitation of the Russians. In the presence of Stalin, he and Molotov signed the momentous "nonaggression pact" that caught the world by utter surprise and cleared the way for Hitler. In fact, in a top secret supplementary protocol, he sealed the German-Soviet community of interests with a precautionary division of the expected spoils: Finland, the Baltic (and Lithuania, in the German-Soviet "friendship pact" four weeks later), the eastern half of Poland, and Bessarabia were to fall into the Russian sphere of interest. With this, Hitler offered Stalin more than the Western powers, out of respect for the independence and sovereignty of the states involved, could ever have discussed.

And so the gates to World War II had been thrown open. The true character of the Hitler regime emerged: its main goals were not the defense against communism, as National Socialism had proclaimed with such great success, but racism and a policy of conquest at any price. Ribbentrop explained to Stalin that the Anti-Comintern Pact, too, was "essentially directed not against the Soviet Union but against the Western democracies."[9] Molotov's interpreter at the time, Bereskov, has recently told us that Moscow even considered that joining the three-power pact of the Axis and Japan was a definite possibility as late as November 1940.[10] The super-Machiavellianism of the Hitler-Stalin pact was accompanied by a complete reversal of enemy propaganda into friend propaganda on both sides, the sort of thing that is possible only in totalitarian regimes.

This, especially, reveals that, contrary to the notion of theorists and interpreters of Fascism, National Socialism should by no means be defined primarily as (popular) anti-Bolshevism, but in its ideological core (probably less popular and thus underestimated) as racism and anti-Semitism. A complete about-face, like the Hitler-Stalin pact together with the subsequent friendship treaty, was utterly unthinkable with regard to Hitler's Jewish policy: beyond all considerations of tactics and self-interest, Hitler clung fanatically and murderously to the goal of a biological war and the final annihilation of the Jewish people.

VI

The beginning of World War II was as different from World War I in its outbreak as it was from its course and consequences. Only a generation separated the two European catastrophes, and memories of the first had a profound influence on the thinking and behavior of those involved, on the strategy and tactics of the actors. The nations were also more deeply conscious of the magnitude of the events than they had been in the surge of enthusiasm in 1914. This was true not least for Germany. The rigorous *Gleichschaltung* of public life, its systematic penetration by comprehensive propaganda, even the admiring recognition of Hitler's successes and the widespread conviction that the policy of revision was legitimate could not prevent the fact that a majority of the population reacted by no means enthusiastically to the outbreak of war, a moment that had long been feared and had been averted time and again.

The mood in the rest of Europe was even less warlike; convictions about standing up for a just cause against the violation of treaties and against aggression and oppression gave the British and French the feeling, at best, that the war was a bitter necessity. No one, of course, could have foretold the duration and extent of the conflict, the psychic and material burdens it would impose. One thing only was certain: far more so than the struggle between 1914 and 1918, this was a war over domestic forms of rule, a war of weltanschauungen, of propaganda and truth, one that would decide not only the distribution of power but also the future face of Europe, its intellectual and moral values. And so it eventually reached a pitch of intensity and a scope that far eclipsed everything that had gone before. The fact that the fronts of power politics, nation-states, and societies were crossed and intersected by a conflict of political ideologies and moral loyalties made this clash far more elemental than the propaganda battle between the democratic West and the authoritarian Central Powers in World War I. It is noteworthy, however, that in both cases the position of Russia disturbed the pattern of confrontation: the alliance with czarism in 1914 had rendered the Western claim of democracy dubious; the pact with Stalinism contradicted, first, in 1939, the National Socialist campaign against Bolshevism, and then, after 1941, the Western Allies' crusade for freedom. But despite many seductions and lapses, there were demonstrative decisions by individuals and groups for the freedom and rights of the individual beyond mere power politics. These decisions confirmed the intellectual and moral substance in a world of nations and states that was believed to have long since been given over to the "decline of the west" (Spengler) and the "revolution of nihilism" (Rauschning).

What was new, what was deeply terrifying *and* simultaneously liberating in this war, emerged in the radical confrontation between *terror* and *resistance*. This definitely played a part in determining the war's historical place. The crisis of National Socialist wartime rule, in the wake of its greatest unfolding in 1941, exacerbated two fundamental trends: the Third Reich's policy of terror and annihilation, and the internal resistance and the future cooperation within and between the occupied countries of Europe. Even after the war expanded into a worldwide conflict through Japan's attack on Pearl Harbor, in Roosevelt's thinking it was the struggle against Hitler, the decision in the European war, that would determine the future of the world. The war was conducted as a struggle for the survival of the constitutional democracies of the Western type against freedom-opposing totalitarianism. Indeed it became a "crusade" against the destroyer of Christianity and morality, against the tyrant: a war of ideologies that often made national-political boundaries recede into the background and reached the level of intensity of a religious or civil war.

National Socialist propaganda also left no room for doubt about the nature of the struggle. The battle against Bolshevism was at the same time declared to be a battle against the plutocratic democracies, for behind both, National Socialist ideology saw the phantom of "world Jewry": the obsessions of *Mein Kampf* formed an ideological framework that was set up in absolute terms.

The result of this "superwar" was that resistance movements against the occupation as well as against their quisling governments intensified in the occupied countries of Europe, and that the concept of "treason," along with the values of patriotism and nationalism, got caught up in the gray area of supranational ideological conflicts. At the same time, volunteer SS troops of non-German background moved into the Soviet Union; they were elevated to the status of pioneers of the SS empire, to which especially Himmler's plans of a "new order" were tailored. The horrifying realities of a future state of the Germanic elite were alluded to in Hitler's "table talks" at the end of 1941 and the beginning of 1942: the opening and development of the conquered territory from the North Cape to the Alps, from the Atlantic to the Black Sea, with autobahns and Germanic fortified settlements; Berlin as the gigantic "world capital" with the new name "Germania"; what remained of Russia as an enormous military training area and colony, where the native population would be prevented from procreating and left to wither away, where their schools would be closed and "they would no longer be allowed to learn more than at best the use of traffic signs" and what was needed to understand German orders; if necessary the population, concentrated in ghettos, would be annihilated with a few bombs, "and that takes care of the matter."[11] These ghastly visions of domination and destruction were confirmed by the actual *practice* of rule in the occupied countries, particularly in the East.

The most horrible consequence of this policy was reached in the inhumanity of the war and occupation in Eastern Europe, in the exploitation, enslavement, and murder of millions of Slavs and Jews. The systematic murder of the Jews, in particular, was not merely a wartime tactic or an act of terror. Neither individual judgment nor political conflict, neither public intimidation nor considerations important to the war played a decisive role in this policy. The monstrous acts of annihilation were grounded in the biologistic madness of National Socialist ideology, with its perversion of moral values; they stand out sharply against the terror of revolutions and wars in previous history.

VII

The deceptions, secrecy, and threats with which the policy of annihilation was carried out confused the resistance to it and made it more complicated. The outcry of the world came late. Organizations of moral authority, like the churches, also failed to take a clear stance: in part out of fear and opportunism, but also because they were susceptible to the antidemocratic, anti-Bolshevist, and anti-Semitic slogans of National Socialist ideology, which sought to impart a historical meaning to the brutal actions. The nearly unresisted implementation of the monstrous crime of the "final solution" can be explained only in part by the infamous perversion of values with which National Socialism, in the spirit of a misunderstood Nietzsche or Machiavelli and a biologistic social Darwinism, turned against the moral world of the West, against Western civilization. This moral perversion provides a profound look at the capacity for and suscep-tibility to barbarism that modern man in the advanced twentieth century possesses. As a reaction to the Enlightenment and to the liberal culture of this very modernity, it fulfilled the gloomy prophecies that had already been made by such nineteenth-century critics of the belief in culture and progress as Heinrich Heine or Franz Grillparzer. Heine (in 1834) spoke of the German thunder that would one day convulse the world like nothing ever had in history, Grillparzer (in 1849) of the "path of modern man from humanity via nationalism to bestiality."

And yet there were many outstanding examples of protest and resistance against the brutality of the totalitarian policy of rule and annihilation in Europe. Victims of persecution were hidden and transports were sabo-taged. Early on in the Netherlands (February 1941), a strike against the deportation of Jews took place. Rebellions occurred in the concentration camps of Eastern Europe: the great, tragic uprising in the Warsaw Ghetto at the beginning of 1943 was put down by the SS only after a long and bloody fight.

It is true that resistance became a threat to National Socialist rule only after the crucial military decisions had been made. The totalitarian system of National Socialism could not be toppled from the inside—just like the Stalinist dictatorship, both before and after the war. For those involved and affected by it, it was terrible to see how little internal resistance was able to accomplish, and how helpless the outside world—from the Allied powers to Pope Pius XII—was in the face of the news that was getting out from 1942 to 1943 on about the Nazi regime's policy of annihilation. More could have been done to save Jews and to sabotage the functioning of National Socialist rule. In the two dominant countries, too, in Italy and Germany, tens of thousands of people had to suffer for their beliefs in camps and prisons during the prewar years, even before the lights of freedom were extinguished in the rest of occupied Europe. And yet resistance was everywhere continuously at work.

Effective attempts to challenge the totalitarian system required, of course, the help of insiders, of officers, civil servants, economists. This was demonstrated especially at the turning points of German resistance, in 1938 and in 1943 and 1944. We can speak of a "mass" popular opposition, which the Communist history of resistance, in particular, has claimed for itself, only in the final years. Prior to that the Communists, while making great sacrifices, based their underground strategy on dubious generalizing judgments of "fascism" and its "monopoly-capitalist" nature. As a result of these views, they could do little against the mass effect of National Socialist slogans and against the skillful techniques of rule that operated with simultaneously reactionary and revolutionary means.

In addition, the Communists in all countries had to follow the directives from the headquarters in Moscow, where policy was anything but geared to reality. The vacillation of positions and tactics, which followed the prevailing interests of Soviet foreign policy, reached its nadir between 1939 and 1941, when the Communist parties had to stop their antifascist propaganda, and the French Communist Party did not support France in the war against Hitler's Germany. This made all the more important, especially in the darkest period from 1939 to 1941, the role of Great Britain, which for an entire year stood all alone in the fight against National Socialism. One can hardly exaggerate the importance of the broadcasts of Radio London for a discouraged Europe divided up by Hitler and Stalin in 1940 and 1941.

The turning point came with the German attack on the Soviet Union and America's entry into the war. Resistance movements now developed in all those countries that were suffering from the brutally intensified German policy of coercion. As more "foreign workers" were conscripted by Germany, and as the political and economic consequences were felt all the more strongly, resistance and guerrilla groups began operating after 1942 in all of Europe, under different political banners but all with great sacrifice. The remembrance of these actions, carved in stone in so many monuments, would play an important role in the postwar period for the recovery of national self-confidence and the development of the idea of Europe, and also of course for Communist rule.

However one might assess the details of the history of the "other Europe" and the "other Germany," the fact that they existed was the great pledge at a time when the depressing experience of the decline and helplessness of the old world overshadowed everything. In the words of James Joll: "But perhaps the significance of the European Resistance lay not so much in the actual strategic or material achievements but rather in the psychological experience which it provided, the continuity it gave to national life, and the basis which it offered for reconstruction after the war. Its importance was as much moral and political as it was military."[12]

VIII

What, then, does this mean for the historical placement of World War II from the perspective of the developments that followed it?[13] In contrast to the history between the two wars, of which we believe we have a clear view in retrospect, this question definitely addresses unfinished contemporary history as contested in a bipolar world, a history to which I should like to address a few points.

1. The irrevocable failure of the National Socialist attempt at unlimited world power no longer permits a policy of self-deception as in 1918. And with the mutual deterrence in the atomic age, which also began, in fact, in 1945, with the first and so far only dropping of atomic bombs on Japan, another continuation of the war has become essentially unthinkable. The result, of course, has been a drawn-out "cold war" in the divided Europe. During the course of the cold war there could be little doubt that the long-concealed end of the European age had come. Europe still remained in the center of events, though it was no longer the subject but the object of world history. Obscured one more time after 1918, denied one more time in the persistence of colonial rule and the outward reach of the dictators, this change of the world-political constellation now appeared final. But the fact that it was two antagonistic world powers—so opposite in political, social, and ideological terms—that decided the fate of Europe contained, at the same time, in its future division, a new starting point for Western European cooperation and democratic integration.

2. The "fresh start" of 1945, a decisive reference point especially in the shaken world of German intellectuals and historians (Friedrich Meinecke, *Die deutsche Katastrophe* [The German Catastrophe]; Alfred Weber, *Abschied von der bisherigen Geschichte* [Farewell to Past History]) existed, however, more as a moral idea than as a political reality. Serious prewar and war problems persisted, as the following three examples illustrate.

The (Pan-)German question of the nation-state, a problem of European politics since the nineteenth century and taken to explosive heights in National Socialism, was suspended by the division of Germany between the political-ideological world blocs. The result was that the question of unification was overshadowed by the demand for liberal democracy and subordinated to the question of the political system. Moreover, in power politics terms, the only solution that seems realistic is to overcome this division on a European level.

The East-West conflict, which since Lenin's seizure of power in 1917 has been part of the history of the Soviet Union and of the Western responses to revolutionary and totalitarian challenges, expanded globally with the participation of the United States in world politics after 1945. The result has been a bipolarity of international politics, which, despite all changes, has been predominant until today (1989).

The problem of imperialism and colonialism also goes back to a decades-long process of transition that began with the challenge to European supremacy in World War I. The definitive emancipation of the new nations as a result of World War II led, at the same time, to a conflict-laden transfer of Western concepts of the nation-state and industrialization, of democracy and, unfortunately, even dictatorship, to all parts of the world.

3. The great decisions of the second postwar period were not made at peace conferences like the one in 1919 and 1920. Rather, they were the result of a process of international politics, which in Europe stretched over five years to the Korean War (1950), and which after another five years led to the complete consolidation of the blocs in the East and the West. But that did not amount to the one-sided primacy of foreign policy. On the contrary. The interweaving of domestic and foreign policy, of ideological and socioeconomic motifs emerged in the very division of Europe. By now, no state in Europe can entertain the illusion that it alone determines its history: interdependence is the fate and at the same time the opportunity of the second postwar period.

4. In contrast to the history of crisis after World War I, there were three great experiences that determined the reconstruction and the political understanding of the changed world after 1945: the experience of totalitarian dictatorship and the vulnerability of democracy; the notions of modern war, which is waged against civilian populations, and ideologically motivated genocide; and the sobering disappointment over the behavior of the Soviet Union in 1939 and again after 1945 in the division of Europe. Communism seemed less and less to be an interesting experiment or a new utopia, and more and more to be a threat to the very freedoms whose existential value Europeans had just come to realize more directly than every before, after their experience with the Hitler regime.

This situation produced almost by necessity a scale of values, something that had largely been lacking in the period between the wars. The concept of the "free world," later dismissed as a mere slogan or an empty formula, described something very real back then, with a dual meaning: liberation from the yoke of National Socialist rule, as well as defense against new dictatorial threats.

5. For the first time in the history of Europe, a unanimous opinion about the value of liberal democracy and the community of European interests began to take shape. For the time being, this could take place only in the West—and against the backdrop of a profound exhaustion and a mood of crisis, which shaped the many analyses and interpretations of writers, philosophers, and theologians. But the experiences with dictatorship and war created, at the same time, the preconditions for a democratic European policy, preconditions that were totally different from the ideas and thinking of the first postwar period. This did not happen overnight, however. The tenacious traditions of national and ideological politics lived on as mighty fossils of political life and beliefs. The intellectual and normative decisions that were made, reflected in the constitutions, books, and discussions of those years, and not least in the abrupt break with Communism made by Western intellectuals, brought about the creation of a common European and common democratic conception of politics. Far more strongly and generally than previous political thinking, this conception was convinced of the primacy of freedom and human dignity, of the importance of a balance between individual and social rights, of the absolute value of pluralistic democracy over all monolithic ideologies and systems. Whenever a dictatorship was relaxed, such ideas were also articulated in the larger Eastern Europe, from the Prague spring to Solidarity to the idea (still unclear) of a "common European house."

6. Under the pressure of the great events, and in the face of the compelling bipolarization of the world by the superpowers, the states of Europe were left with a politically reduced importance. But this also compelled them to a deeper political reflection, which had been lacking before and after 1918. The peoples of Europe were forced to contemplate the limits to nation-state power politics. Intellectuals were forced to contemplate the fundamental difference between democracy and dictatorship, instead of engaging in arguments about "bad" democracies and "good" dictatorships, and instead of flirting with the latter because of their ideologically perfectionist visions of the future.

Thus 1945 was a great refutation of the political illusions and fictions that had emerged in the wake of modernization and the belief in revolutionary progress. More so than ever before, the faith in an inexorable and automatic improvement of humankind in respect to morality and culture had been shaken; it was confronted by the experience of Auschwitz. But Communism as the embodiment of antifascism was equally inadequate, for contrary to its moral and ideological claims, the inhuman concentration camps continued in the Soviet Union. At the same time, the critique of culture and the mood of cultural malaise, now that the fears of decline had come true in a different way than had been expected, could no longer count on strong men or ideological salvation; instead there was an immense exhaustion and a sobering, a need for de-ideologization. A "skeptical generation" was now looking for something to hold on to outside of or beyond the traditional ideologies, to bring about not the great revolution but feasible reform, and above all to protect its own physical and moral survival.

7. However, the apocalyptic view of the war that had just ended, and of the war that seemed a possibility in the near future, was also a strong incentive to avoid a continuation or repetition of the great errors of thought and action that had marked the first half of the century. The great refutation of these errors and a more realistic conception of political freedom, of human dignity and the moral value of democracy: these were the positive aspects of the catastrophe that, going beyond national differences, made possible a sort of basic consensus of the free world. Even the defeated nations, Germany and Japan, were included in this consensus surprisingly quickly. This, too, was very different from what had taken place after World War I—though it took place, of course, only where self-determination was granted.

The construction of a free Europe closely linked to the United States: this was the political idea that had been missing after 1918. It included the concrete establishment of those values that were to strengthen and unite Europe against despotism—which it had just suffered through and survived but which threatened it once again—and to protect the democratic freedoms saved from Hitler. A stroke of good fortune lent a helping hand: namely, the economic boom in Western Europe, which even the actors in the Marshall Plan (developed in 1947) had not expected. It took that part of Europe from abject misery to new prosperity within a few years. This, too, formed a strong contrast not only to the socioeconomic crises in the twenties and thirties, which had contributed so heavily to the ruin of democracy, but also to the obvious inability of the Communist systems to realize the promised social and economic progress. Seldom in history has the interaction of socioeconomic and political thinking come to the fore in such a striking manner.

8. The immeasurable consequences of the war, murder, and oppression after 1939, the results of totalitarian power politics and homophobic ideology—above all the responsibility of the German dictatorship—surpass

everything that has gone before in human history. The historian committed to accurate memory will be especially mindful that the totalitarian experience of our century must never be forgotten. But he or she will also note that liberal democracies in Europe have been able, for the first time in history, to break the vicious cycle of threats and counterthreats of war and occupation, and to establish on a voluntary basis supranational organizations that serve to protect and realize human rights.

Almost without exception, wars in our century have been and continue to be started by dictatorships. Whatever one may think about the debated primacy of foreign policy, when it comes to safeguarding peace, prime importance belongs not only to international politics and ideologies but also, above all, to the domestic structures of states and societies, their protection against dictatorial rule as well as against relapses into narrow nationalism. That lesson, too, is part of the effort to determine the historical place of World War II. Its politically binding warnings and lessons include an understanding of the necessity for a federatively united, democratic Europe. Such a vision was already alive in the resistance movements against Hitler's totalitarian Europe—especially in France and Italy, but also in the German resistance, as for example in the plans of the Kreisau Circle.

At a time when the idea of Europe is making liberating advances, and in a world in which totalitarian force is still at work (as we look at Beijing), one legacy certainly remains relevant: the renunciation of war must be inseparably linked to the renunciation of dictatorship and totalitarianism.

The Dual Challenge of the Postwar Period

In view of the current upheavals in Central and Eastern Europe, there is once again talk of the "end of the postwar period," as there has been so often since the 1960s (as, for example, in Ludwig Erhard's governmental declaration of 1965).[1] But what does that mean? The end of World War II and the German dictatorship were experienced simultaneously as destruction and salvation, and soon also as the continuing threat to freedom from another dictatorship. The dual German catastrophe of 1933 and 1945 was followed, with unexpected rapidity in the midst of the great decisions of 1948 and 1949, by the establishment of a second German democracy and at the same time, of course, by the division of Germany and Europe. At that time, the future President Theodor Heuss, at the conclusion of the constitutional deliberations of the Parliamentary Council in Bonn on May 8, 1949, said of the Germans' situation that May 8, 1945, remains "for all of us the most tragic and puzzling paradox of history. Why? Because at one and the same time we were both saved and destroyed."

This dual challenge of the postwar period concerned international power relations and ideologies as much as it did the moral thought and political culture of the era. As ambivalent as the feeling was for the starting position in 1945, the developments and decisions of the first decade have remained decisive to the present day, in terms of their intellectual and material consequences. That the *Zeitenbruch,* or epochal turning point (W. Mantl), of 1989–90 has in fact brought the long-proclaimed end of the postwar constellation seems doubtful, despite the most recent euphoria—as doubtful as the current emphatic pronouncements about the "end of ideologies" and even the "end of history." Such periodic diagnoses, wearing the dress of philosophy of history, pass too hastily over what is the real fundamental question: to what extent do the challenges and consequences of the new beginning in 1945 continue and in fact are only now becoming fully apparent in terms of German and European politics, even if the conflict between democracy and dictatorship is now entering into a new stage? The postwar period may be coming to an end (or be declared over), but many of its fundamental questions and answers remain. They remain not merely as historical lessons, but as old and new challenges in a time marked once again by the fundamental historical problem: Europe and nationalism.

No "Zero Hour"

The world-historical caesura of 1945 had a decisive influence on the subsequent fate of Europe, the rise of the superpowers, and the end of colonialism. It was equally momentous for Germany's often-fractured history as a nation and a state in the middle of Europe. The end of the National Socialist dictatorship, which in the twelve years from 1933 to 1945 had demonstrated the full extent and horrible possibilities of a modern totalitarian system of rule, left behind a devastated land, a destroyed state, and a political and intellectual-moral vacuum in the heart of the Continent.

Those countries in Europe, Africa, and Asia that had been occupied and exploited by the Axis powers of Germany and Italy, or by their Asian ally, Japan, experienced May 8 and August 14, 1945 (the surrender of Japan) as liberation. While the Resistenza in Italy and the emperorship in Japan provided a certain political and cultural continuity, in Germany the resistance to Hitler had failed; the road to the bitter end had become unavoidable. And so the leading German historian, Friedrich Meinecke, entitled his book on Germany's recent history *The German Catastrophe*. The sociologist Alfred Weber (the brother of the great Max Weber) noted no less tersely the *Farewell to Past History,* and the philosopher Karl Jaspers spoke of *The Question of German Guilt* (all three published in 1946).

The road that brought Germans from the total defeat of the German Reich to the Federal Republic of Germany reveals the heavy and painful burden that rested on all Germans after the unspeakable crimes of National Socialism. Yet the collapse of their existing state opened an early chance for a new beginning, as they sought to make use of the existential political experiences and urgent lessons of the most recent past.

The situation in 1945 was marked by the guilt and misery of a people, the better part of which had succumbed to the totalitarian seduction of the Hitler regime. The Germans had not been able to rid themselves of their criminal leadership. Even the few who, after several failed assassination attempts, tried to eliminate the government as late as 1944, in a nearly hopeless situation, tended to be seen at first not as heroes, like those in the resistance in the countries occupied by Germany, but as traitors. Then, after the war, all power lay with the unlimited occupational authority of the Allies, who had agreed on a comprehensive control of Germany at the conferences at Yalta (February 1945) and later at Potsdam (July to August 1945). Thus the expectation that this starting position, later so frequently referred to as the "zero hour," would give rise to an autonomous domestic purification and a radical political renewal of Germany crashed head-on with the political realities of the day. Political decisions and measures came from outside and above: the so-called de-Nazification and demilitarization, the prosecution of the perpetrators, and the restricted political life in the four occupation zones and in Berlin.

However, it soon became clear that the Allies were unable to find a common line in their occupational policy. Two factors in particular changed the situation fundamentally within a short period. First, the fact that the Western powers and the Soviet Union could not come to an agreement on their policy toward Germany led almost inevitably to the first conflicts of the "cold war," when the Soviet policy of domination and *Gleichschaltung* in Eastern Europe as well as in the Soviet occupation zone (SOZ) in Germany increasingly eliminated those whose thinking was allegedly not true to the Communist line, and eventually imposed Communist regimes everywhere. Second, the internal political and economic development of the other three zones, after a temporary period of dismantling, was oriented toward Western democracy's liberal ideas of social order and freedom. In spite of the restrictions imposed by the occupying powers, these Western ideas soon proved far more attractive to the Germans than the coercive Communist new order in the East. As a result a stream of refugees was soon heading for West Germany. In addition to the well over 10 million who were expelled from the separated German territories in the East, these refugees included nearly 3 million inhabitants of the SOZ-GDR, who kept leaving until the building of the Berlin wall on August 1961 abruptly ended this "voting with the feet."

These factors proved stronger than all original plans, which had provided for and expected a much longer period of joint Allied occupation and for other solutions to the German problem.[2] Almost without any time for reflection, the defeated and guilt-ridden country was drawn into bipolar world politics, between East and West, which had taken the place of the great anti-Hitler coalition of 1941 through 1945. The process of erecting a new state began sooner than had been planned. Though the caesura of 1945 was a break in the history of the German nation state, it was not a "zero hero" in the sense of providing a pause for thought or even freedom of choice; rather, it was a moment when new constellations were formed with compelling, far-reaching consequences and decisions were made that determined the future course of the nation.

For Germany this gave rise to the possibility, despite the burden of Hitler's legacy and the great destruction caused by the war, of entering more quickly than expected into a period of reconstruction, in which the enemies of yesterday became the allies of today. In all of this, neither the Nuremberg trials of the National Socialist war criminals nor the million-fold and yet superficial de-Nazification of the citizenry led to a full confronting of the most recent past, let alone to the often invoked mastering *(Bewältigung)* of the past, which is hardly possible in the literal sense. For the Allies as well as the Germans, the original attempt at "reeducating" the German people—which was in any case controversial as a collective enterprise—made such an abrupt transition into the phase of including the new German state in the Western political sphere that many internal problems in the new German democracy could not be credibly solved by the time the Federal Republic was established. Moreover, the simultaneous establishment of the German Democratic Republic meant not only the painful division of the nation, but also the continuation in its eastern part of dictatorship under a different banner.

What did succeed, even if at the expense of the division of Germany and Europe (a long-lasting division, as it would turn out), was a solution to the central problem over which Western policy after World War I had come to grief: namely, replacing what the Germans felt was a repressive, negative policy of control with what was in fact a positive control, as it were, of the German problem within the framework of European integration. And so the worst aberrations of German history and the worst defeat of the German state turned, in the western part of the country, into a successful reconstruction of the economy and society, of liberal democracy and international, indeed supranational, forms of cooperation.[3] Of course one-fifth of the Germans, those in the "German Democratic Republic," a state with coerced uniformity under Soviet domination, continued to live under the yoke of dictatorial politics.

Thus for the great majority of Germans, the importance of the immediate postwar period lay in the unhoped-for chance that the end of dictatorship and war gave them for another try at the democracy they had gambled away. Germany also had to continue to bear the historical responsibility for the crimes of the Hitler regime, above all for the systematic murder of millions of Jews and the unleashing of the greatest war in the history of the world. But in contrast to the painful history of the Weimar Republic, which unfortunately and fatefully had never been able to come to terms with the legacy of World War I, the Federal Republic was able to make use of the lessons of that failure and of the new possibilities for supranational cooperation.

Only incurable German nationalists continued to see May 8, 1945, as the blackest day in German history. For the great majority, from which the more successful and more stable second democracy drew its support, the catastrophe of the Hitler regime was at the same time the prerequisite for the liberal state, which had failed twice before in Germany's very eventful history. An indispensable factor in all of this has been, of course, the process of unifying Europe, without which the further development of the Federal Republic was and is unthinkable.

Europe's liberation from the yoke of National Socialist rule created, in alliance with the United States and Canada, the conditions for a renaissance of Western democracy and for the building of European unity, a situation that was unparalleled in previous history. There was, however, a flip side to all of this: the fact that all of Eastern Europe had traded liberation from the National Socialist dictatorship for new dictatorial regimes in the name of "antifascism." As early as 1944, George Orwell, with keen insight, had declared in the face of this Communist abuse of the concept of fascism that true antifascism always had to be also anti-totalitarian.[4] And the Yugoslav writer Danila Kis, whose father was murdered in Auschwitz (Kis died in 1989), wrote: "In my books I try to create a coherent world in which the two most important experiences of the twentieth century will be dealt with: the experiences of Fascism and Stalinism." The emphatic commemorations of the anniversary of May 8 in the sphere under the control of the Soviet Union, which, not without responsibility for the outbreak of the war (Hitler-Stalin pact of 1939), had borne the brunt of it, forced us to think with deep sadness of the countless victims of National Socialist power madness and racial insanity. At the same time, however, they also made us think about the fact that for too many peoples the "liberation from fascism" brought not a liberation from totalitarian forms of rule but their continuation over forty-five long years.

The Burden of History

For Germans, of course, the postwar period was especially a time of confronting the intellectual legacies and burdens of the past: from the diversity of the legendary "golden" twenties to the increasing uniformity and inhumanity of the "iron" thirties, to dictatorship, persecution, and finally to the German defeat that was destruction and liberation in one. Revealing was the role of intellectuals, who in 1933 drew close to and joined the new movement, allowing themselves to be put to work for it.

Among them were ardent believers as well as mere glorifiers, intellectual founders as well as mere opportunists—and by "mere" I do not mean that the intellectual fellow travelers were any less important. There were some subtle cases among them, which have been discussed again and again since publication of the book on the National Socialist seizure of power that I coauthored with G. Schulz and W. Sauer (1960); Hans Buchheim has in this regard spoken aptly of the "incubation space" of National Socialism. The intellectuals who supported the Nazis in one way or another all document that the mind can be temporarily seduced, that people can be bribed with careers and fame, that thinking people, especially, are tempted by an irrational cult of action and are peculiarly susceptible to "one-dimensional" answers and promises of salvation.[5]

In fact the phenomenon of "totalitarian seduction" is among the most important legacies of the period between 1933 and 1945. Paradoxically it concerns particularly the intellectual sphere, in two respects. First, intellectuals proved especially receptive to the new, radical political movements; they showed an inordinate curiosity about them. At the same time, intellectuals were strongly affected by the dictatorial consequences of those political currents: while the movements involved giving full scope to freedom and unleashing criticism, at the same time they suppressed them. Second, it was the intellectuals who provided these extremist movements with their ideological justification to begin with, who supplied the intellectual impulse and the revolutionary feeling of mission, casting the movements as an allegedly new age and new morality. Intellectuals were and are truly indispensable for the process of totalitarian seduction, equally so in the age of postideological fundamentalisms.

In all of this an appropriate and fair assessment is difficult, the question cannot be one of simple causality or condemnation, for we are dealing with two apparently contradictory manifestations of intellectual behavior. On one side is a tendency toward *self-destruction* through masochistic hypercriticism, lopsided judgments, and an overtaxing of democracy (then, for example, when republican politicians were mocked by the leftist intellectual camp and social democrats were defamed as "socio-fascists," or today when liberal democrats are called reactionary or even fascist). On the other side is the readiness for *voluntary Gleichschaltung* when faced with the power of an ideological movement, a political transformation, or a national renewal: a kind of antidemocratic idealism or an attuning of one's sensibilities to what are supposedly great historical times. Any retrospective judgment is made more complicated by the vacillation between collaboration and resistance that, under the simultaneous dictatorial conditions of suppression and temptation, determines the conduct of most people in all comparable regimes.

A great polarization of weltanschauungen had already been under way since the turn of the century: a rise of left-radical and right-radical ideologies, which then took on concrete political form during and in the wake of World War I and formed a powerful counterfront to liberal democracy, which was just then coming to life. The Weimar Republic felt double pressure, both from intellectual critics for whom the real democracy did not go far enough, was not perfect enough, and from the bitter despisers of democracy itself, who defamed it as un-German and feeble. The Left's underestimation and misjudgment of the threat and the Right's capitulation to seduction and overestimation of its own strength had equal roles in bringing about the National Socialist dictatorship.

The theories of fascism, popular then and now and also dominant in the debates in 1945, are unable to explain these interconnections. They are too one-sidedly focused on the component of a capitalist or right-radical conspiracy, and in their own way they fall into the projection mechanism that sets up a (capitalist) scapegoat, the sort of mechanism that also forms the basis of anti-Semitism. Max Horkheimer, as the head of the "critical theory" that was so influential after 1945, coined the slogan that you cannot talk about fascism without talking about capitalism. One can counter this by pointing out that "fascism" did not arise in England, of all places the motherland of "capitalism." Instead, what is called for is an emphasis on the more general form of totalitarian thinking in the process of intellectual seduction, even if some like to dismiss this focus on the totalitarian dimension as anticommunist. It is in fact precisely the blending of rightist *and* leftist ideas, reactionary *and* revolutionary impulses that makes the totalitarian alternative to democracy so fascinating and irresistible. In Germany it was above all the emphatic combination of nationalism and socialism, the dominant ideas of the nineteenth and twentieth centuries, that National Socialism promised to fuse most thoroughly and consistently into a single movement and to implement by whatever means necessary.

Moreover, a great temptation lay in the idea of a sovereignty of the spirit, a dictatorship of reason, of the intellectual as leader, which even such an avowedly antifascist thinker as Heinrich Mann invoked in 1931 in his enthusiastic speech about "intellectual and spiritual leadership." Arthur Koestler gave an impressive account of the Communist conversions before 1933 in his self-reflection *Arrow in the Blue* (1952), while Czeslaw Milosz did the same for the *Gleichschaltungen* after 1945 in his book *The Captive Mind* (1953). It was *The God Who Failed* (1950) on which the disenchanted intellectuals looked back at the end of the era of Hitler and Stalin—among them leftist people from the Right and rightist people from the Left. Intellectual pessimism and the critique of modern Western civilization had shaped the climate and mood of the "lost generation" in Europe and the United States during the interwar period. Even leading theoreticians of the English Labour Party, like Beatrice Webb, enthused about the Soviet system as a "new civilization." On a visit there in 1935, Webb commented on the system of concentration camps in that country with a remark as cynical as it was doctrinaire, quoting the French proverb, "You can't make an omelet without breaking eggs"—the goal justifies the means.[6]

To be sure, the "humanistic" pretensions of the Communist ideology were diametrically contrary to the racism and ideology of living space of National Socialism. But in terms of the brutality, the totalitarian implementation of the will to power, even the number of victims, there was much that was comparable in these two systems. The great intellectual alternative of "fascism or socialism" (in practical terms, National Socialism or Communism) to which people saw the political decision reduced in 1933 was a delusion, one that in both cases led to a disastrous underestimation of the dictatorships and the justification of their crimes. Both promised the great solution to all problems in a new form of socialist progress, through race or class warfare; enthusiasm and disappointment alternately dominated the scene.

In fact, it is quite possible to reduce the left-authoritarian and right-authoritarian ideologies to this common denominator: they struck a position opposed to liberalism's rational theory of democracy, even if each did it in a different way. Explaining "fascism" primarily through a widespread anticommunism (Nolte) overlooks fascism's own intrinsic roots, ways of thinking, and convictions. How do we explain that dictatorships hostile to the spirit and freedom, finally even inhuman tyrannies and destructive regimes under the banner of class or race theories, were accepted in such an alarmingly smooth and comprehensive way? This acceptance reached all the way to the perversion of morality and the glorification of mass murder as a "world-historical task" that had to be heroically "endured" to the end (Himmler). All this was a result not of anticommunism (or antifascism), but of the capacity for totalitarian seduction as such, which ended in the self-abnegation and self-destruction of the spirit. Wherever one looked in 1945, the extent of the losses, the number of victims, the impoverishment in all spheres of a culture destroyed by the German's themselves was immeasurable and beyond repair.

Posttotalitarian Experiences and the Renaissance of Democracy

In contrast to the crisis-driven political thinking after World War I, three major experiences, above all, shaped the reconstruction and the political understanding of the changed world after 1945: (1) the experience of totalitarian dictatorship and of the fragility of democracy; (2) the modern idea of war and ideological genocide; and (3) finally, sobering disillusionment over the behavior of the Soviet Union and the division of Europe. And above everything stood the idea of human rights, an idea the establishment of the United Nations was also to serve: despite all setbacks, the demand for human rights would thenceforth work as a ferment in liberal politics.

Given the pressure of the rapidly changing power relations in the East-West conflict after 1947 and 1948, the expectations of change and the sense that a lot of catching-up was necessary after the strangulation and isolation of political and intellectual life since 1933 could come to only partial fruition. There was, however, a great wave of "getting acquainted with" and reassimilating the literature and art of the free world. During this period, still without television, the radio and the new magazines played a crucial role in the discovery and transmission of authors and works of art that had been proscribed for twelve years, and also in the renewal of interrupted democratic traditions. At the same time there were, of course, a lot of hesitations and excuses, resentments and misunderstandings; only a minority of the exiles returned. National life, shaped by the equally liberating and regimenting occupational governments, by the continuation of the democratic ideas of 1848 and the lessons of dictatorship, war, and captivity, was marked by the many different opportunities as well as the unspoken resistance that were characteristic of the tension between a coming to terms with the past and the challenges of reconstructing Germany.

In all of this, great importance was attached to the conditions of the political framework. Initially the Left experienced such a considerable strengthening, in Western Europe as well, that we can speak of a general lurch to the left. This became visible for the first time in the great electoral victory of the British Labour Party (July 1945). It also showed itself in the strength of the Communist and Socialist parties in France and Italy, in the attempts of the early postwar governments to form "antifascist" left-wing coalitions, and in the exemplary part played by the social-democratic governments in Scandinavia. However, in contrast to the events under Soviet influence in Eastern Europe, nowhere in Western Europe did this shift to the left lead to a permanent union or fusion of Socialist and Communist parties.

The other side of the coin was a general discrediting and decline of the political Right at the time. To be sure, only Italy replaced its monarchy with a republic. However, existing monarchies elsewhere, insofar as they had not already been transformed into constitutional monarchies or made subject to control by parliament (as in Great Britain and Scandinavia), were now modified along democratic lines, and their powers were restricted. Even if the right-wing parties could not be simply saddled with the stigma of collaboration, their ambivalent attitude toward authoritarian ideologies and regimes was reason enough that the antifascist wave of the early postwar period was directed primarily against the conservative Right. It was widely held that the failure of conservative-liberal economic policy between the wars had contributed substantially to the crisis of the democracies. A restoration of the capitalist system was just as controversial as the economic crisis measures of wartime, measures that continued in the postwar plight. The trend toward far-reaching political and social reforms initially seemed to confirm socialism as the dominant force in Western Europe. The diagnoses and prognoses proclaimed that the failure of capitalism and the catastrophic career of "fascism" would be necessarily followed by socialism.

However, within a few years a general about-face of political sentiments and power relationships took place in the democracies of Western Europe, different though the circumstances may have been in the individual countries. The main hallmarks of this development were the exclusion of Communist parties from participation in government, the strengthening of the moderate center, and (especially in the area of the later European Community) the swift rise of Christian Democratic parties to key positions in state and society. These parties constituted a new element in the party structure of Europe. Although they were descended from earlier forms of Christian-confessional parties, they affirmed parliamentary democracy, adopted leftist Christian-social impulses, and relegated conservative-clerical traditions to the background. All this amounted to a decisive break with the narrower framework of previous ecclesiastical interest groups and opened the way for the formation of larger popular parties of the center that sought to form coalitions with all sides, to reconcile socialism and capitalism. Thus emancipated, the Christian Democratic, all-embracing movements were able to integrate the larger part of the bourgeois classes. They benefited from the support of the churches, which, after the ideological collapse of the era, received renewed recognition as strong authorities and now drew closer to the democracies; in Italy and Germany, in fact, the churches represented almost the only intact institutions recognized by the occupying powers. The Christian Democratic parties also benefited from contacts with groups of the resistance, in the wake of the horrifying experiences and bloody failure of the antidemocratic experiment.

A whole chain of causes led to this rapid change of the domestic political scene in Western Europe. The far-reaching turnaround that began to show itself in 1947 was accelerated by economic as well as political and military factors. A closely interlinked connection between domestic and foreign politics was characteristic of the decisive developments between 1947 and 1950. The fluid, crisis-riddled postwar situation, with prospects of a socialist-influenced reshaping of state and society, led with unexpected rapidity to the consolidation of parliamentary multiparty systems, and to the strengthening of liberal economic and social systems marked by the political center. This about-face set the course for political development to the present day. The German version of this development, the "social market economy," soon exerted wide influence and gained overwhelming popularity as the "economic miracle."

This was a historic development to which there was soon virtually no realistic alternative. The facts seemed all too clear. The economic stabilization under the Marshall Plan contrasted sharply with the failures of Communist economic policy in Eastern Europe. The confrontation between the two superpowers, the United States and the Soviet Union, was increasingly seen as a trial of strength between two social systems, one liberal and open, the other directed and coercive. The implementation of the Stalinist policy of domination, which culminated in the revolution in Prague (in February 1948) and in the blockade of Berlin, was answered by the reinforcement of the American *containment policy* by means of economic and military assistance for Western Europe. Stalinist policy had negative repercussions for the prospects of a socialist reshaping in Western Europe, and resulted in the exclusion of the Communist parties from political leadership.

The stabilization of Western Europe along liberal and democratic lines was thus anything but the result of a sinister conspiracy by capitalistic imperialists. The Soviet Union's coercive policies in Eastern Europe discredited not only Communism, but also the ideas of socialist transformation and European development independent of the two superpowers. This gave rise to governments that were anticommunist in character, including the government of England after the defeat of the Labour Party in 1951. These governments pursued reconstruction within the framework of economic support and military protection from the United States; economic recovery and political stabilization, as well as the growing European and Atlantic cooperation, were oriented in this direction. By the end of the forties, the decisions had been made that set the course for the subsequent development of Western Europe even up to today.

This situation especially affected the democratic Left, which fruitlessly continued its opposition to the social and domestic policies, until it sooner (in France) or later (in West Germany and Italy) had to accept the established facts. Under these circumstances, possible alternatives to the confrontation of East and West, or to liberal-conservative and socialist-communist social policies, were never seriously tested as to their feasibility. However, when many critical observers spoke of the "missed chances" of the postwar period, they overlooked the fact that the majority of the people were convinced that democratization was the right decision, given the threat of the cold war and thanks to what was soon a far higher degree of freedom and standard of living in the West. Naturally the development showed strong countercurrents and clear differences especially between and within the Western European states. The strongest and most determined expression in support of the politics of stability in the face of the confrontation came from West Germany. Here the spectacle of coercive Soviet policies in East Germany and the prospects of political rehabilitation and a quick rise from the catastrophe were a particularly powerful motivation.

The development of the new German democracy was consciously pursued under the postulate that Bonn was not Weimar. The preconditions were different from 1918; also different were the conditions of life and the political form of the Federal Republic in its subsequent history. A strengthened parliamentary democracy, a changed party system, economic success, and a Western alliance ensured stability and permanence. But the great difference from Weimar was grounded in the fact of the country's division. As painful as it was in terms of national politics, it contributed greatly to freeing the second German democracy from the Weimar disease: namely of being encircled and crushed by right-radical and left-radical parties. It was not only the right-wing dictatorial movement of National Socialism that was refuted in Germany in 1945. Within a short period of time, in view of Soviet policies and long before the controversial banning of the German Communist Party (KPD) in 1956, the left-wing dictatorial movement had also shrunk and been discredited. Communism and its supporters emigrated to the Soviet zone, the GDR, a dictatorship "democratic" in name only. The GDR, and Soviet postwar policies in general, acted as a deterrent for West Germans. This was true even though the idealism and illusion of a radical new beginning, a "rising from the ruins," accompanied the development of East Germany and even though its ideological claim of being the "first Socialist state in Germany" continued to have a certain attraction for intellectuals and artists in the West.

A Second German Dictatorship

Two politicians of the Weimar era presided over this new development of the German problem: Adenauer and Ulbricht. With his successful pro-Western policy, Konrad Adenauer built a bridge to a more stable second democracy, which, unlike the Weimar Republic, was quickly accepted by the population. Walter Ulbricht—cofounder of the KPD in 1919 and its Reichstag delegate until 1933, and even during his emigration a staunch Stalinist who always survived the purges in Moscow faithful to the party line—forced into place on the ruins of the Hitler regime a new one-party regime from above. In form and method it continued seamlessly in the authoritarian traditions of Germany, no matter how antifascist the packaging and how different the goals.

Though this second German dictatorship was an imported one, at the same time it built on the fact that Germans had become unaccustomed to democracy and accustomed to an authoritarian state. It is true that the liquidation of National Socialism was pursued more radically in East Germany, but the new rulers by no means dispensed with the services of National Socialist functionaries. The alternative to National Socialism, in the long run no less totalitarian, was the rule of a new single party, this time of the Left, with its own system of spies and informers and its own machinery of oppression, to which the people slowly submitted and resigned themselves. This meant, essentially, the continuation of a salient feature of the historical and psychological German problem of which National Socialism had been one manifestation. The nationalization and collectivization of industry and agriculture were to deprive "fascism"— which the Communists, in a crude misinterpretation, equated with private capitalism—of its economic footholds. However, the de facto rule of the authoritarian state and "state security," of the Socialist Unity Party (SED) regime and totalitarian ideology, picked up once again the threads of the authoritarian structure of political behavior, of the illiberal and antiliberal cult of power and the state found in Germany's recent past. For as profound as the "Socialist revolution" in the GDR was, it meant once again a revolution from above, without genuinely free democratic consent and legitimation.

Thus the question of a democratic "mastering" of the past, for the West German democracy a basic existential question, was solved from above in the GDR. The solution came in the form of a counterdictatorship that offered no opportunity for the development and testing of an independent and responsible democracy, because it avoided any risk of a challenge to itself and because it was unwilling, in the beginning as well as later, to submit to the free vote of the people. For more than four decades the political thinking and behavior of the Germans after the war could be empirically tracked only in West Germany. Only in that country were the political mobility and stability of the often-invoked will of the people continually measurable in open elections, opinion polls, and in published testimonies of every kind. In the GDR, many of the burning questions that had to be put to a second German democracy after the failure of Weimar were masked or overshadowed by a system that was partly authoritarian and partly totalitarian in nature.

The special situation of Germany, and the frequently invoked competition between the systems, especially in the comparison of living standards in East and West, may have contributed to motivating the greater economic efforts—measured against the other nations of Europe—that were made first by West Germany and then increasingly by East Germany. This could appear as a paradoxical and at the same time characteristic compensation for the defeated country and its division as a nation, in its dual role as a pillar upholding the hostile fronts in East and West. The main driving force, however, was Germany's elementary need for reconstruction and the improvement of living conditions, not the ideological-theoretical position that was projected into it by later interpretations.

The creation of the GDR occurred during the region's dependence on the dictatorial rule of its occupying power. Outside of the Communist world, it was considered a tyranny by the grace of a foreign power, a "power without mandate," as the title of a fundamental work by Ernst Richer on the GDR put it in the fifties. This dual illegitimacy set it apart from other Communist states. Though the latter had also been established through coercion from outside and above, as nation-states with their own traditions they possessed a natural substance, whereas the GDR was an entirely artificial construct. This set it apart, moreover, from other German-speaking states like Switzerland and Austria, which arose from their own historical substance and had never been part of the modern German nation state. The notion of the illegitimate nature of this second German state shaped the constitutional understanding of the Federal Republic, and with the exception of the small West German KPD, all political parties were in agreement on this. Everyday speech for a long time used the terms "East zone" or "Soviet zone" for East Germany. Not a single state outside of the Communist world granted the GDR diplomatic recognition during the first decade of its existence.

The Federal Republic's claim to be the sole legitimate representative (Alleinvertretungsanspruch) of the German people was thus based primarily on those elements the GDR lacked: the liberal elements of a state based on the rule of law and a democratic structure. The Russian occupational power played an all-deciding role in the eastern part of Germany. At the end of the war, the Ulbricht group had been flown in from Moscow to take over the levers of power in accordance with Soviet directives. When even the coerced amalgamation of the Social Democratic Party (SPD) with the KPD did not help the Communist-dominated Socialist Unity Party to reach a majority in the elections of October 1946, the path to Communist rule was pushed forward via the bloc system of a "national front." This system guaranteed the artificially fabricated or intimidated pseudoparties—which were supposed to function, in accord with Lenin's theory, as "transmission belts" of the Communist Party into the population—a predetermined quota of parliamentary seats and government posts, while guaranteeing the SED absolute leadership in all groups and organizations of the state and in society. From then on there were only acclamatory elections. Offering no choices and with results of 99 percent approval, these elections were and are characteristic of all totalitarian regimes.

The circumstances of the establishment of the state were likewise revealing of the dictatorial system of the GDR, which was in part openly coercive, in part veiled with pseudolegal forms. The People's Congress (Volkskongreß) in the Soviet zone, which was originally intended as an all-German propaganda instrument and had been preparing a constitution since March 1948, had no more legitimation through elections than the People's Council (Volksrat) that passed the constitution in March 1949 and set up the sham elections via single lists. Finally, East Germany's People's Chamber (Volkskammer), which emerged from this process in 1950, was from the beginning, all outward attributes notwithstanding, not a parliamentary body but an acclamatory organ after the Soviet model. In the future this pseudoparliament would have neither free votes nor free elections, which would have permitted the articulation of the real will of the people. That will was emphatically invoked by the attachment of the prefix "People's" to all institutions of the GDR, and yet it was manifestly feared after it turned against Communist rule in the uprising of 1953. Then when the Soviet Union showed restraint, the real will of the people, suppressed for more than forty years, revealed itself in 1989.

In the process of establishing the centralized rule of the party and the bureaucracy in East Germany, little consideration was given to the constitution of the GDR, which started out in formal terms as the constitution of a parliamentary democracy based on the rule of law; no attention was paid, either, to the rights of political control or to the guarantees of human rights that it contained. Five-year plans based the Soviet model (after 1951), the liquidation of private property in the economic sector, and coerced uniformity in the areas of culture and education characterized the GDR's development. To be sure, all this took place clearly against the will of the majority of the population, against the will of the increasingly harassed churches, and especially against the will of the farmers who, faithful to the Soviet model, derived only temporary profit from the expropriation of the large landowners and were then collectivized beginning in 1958. Since Lenin, the conscious tactic of broken promises had been part of the program of Communism and its all-justifying revolution.

The forced implementation of the Socialist Unity state experienced numerous setbacks before and after the uprising of 1953. The human drain continued into the fifties. In excess of 2 million people, more than a tenth of the population, left the coercive state, which was labeled the "red Prussia" on account of its disciplined frugality and the cultivation of the national-authoritarian tradition. In addition, the state was being squeezed dry by Soviet demands for reparations. The high point in emigration came in the summer of 1961, when signs of economic crisis and rumors about an imminent closing of the GDR and West Berlin caused another dramatic surge in the stream of refugees. In July 1961 alone, 30,000 mostly younger citizens of the GDR left their state. In the following two weeks the number doubled, until on August 13 the border with West Berlin was sealed and the government of the GDR began building the wall that would shut up its own citizens in the "Socialist Fatherland."

The building of the wall meant that the dictatorship was taking final shape toward the outside world. At the same time it was an emphatic manifestation of East German statehood, which, after 1955, had been gradually replacing the earlier unification propaganda of the GDR. Now the population had no choice but to reconcile itself to the existing system and the GDR's integration into the Communist world. The entire western border of the GDR was hermetically sealed through a death strip of fences and barbed wire, mines and firing devices. (To be sure, a revisionist literature in the West, with its polemic against critical GDR scholarship, increasingly misjudged or dismissed the fundamental difference between Western and Communist policies and politics. It gave the difference second place behind an allegedly "realistic" or value-neutral examination of independent GDR policies under the banner of "normalization." Those policies, however, were nothing other than the contemporary version of Communist dictatorship in what appeared to be a technocratically and economically more efficient and successful form; for all that it was no less coercive and authoritarian.)

Problems in the Orientation of Political Values

Corresponding to what was initially such an emphatic experience of the cold war conflict between the systems were the great trends in political orientation that marked the thinking and interpretations of contemporaries in the West from the end of the forties: a strong desire for the reconstruction of Europe, and for the values of freedom and human rights. For when the progressivist turn to the Left—after the end of the war and the Right dictatorships—yielded to a sharp reaction against the leftist-totalitarian development in Eastern Europe, Communism began to seem to intellectuals to be no longer an interesting experiment but a direct threat to freedom, the existential significance of which had been so recently brought home more directly than ever before in the struggle against Hitler. This gave rise, almost inevitably, to a scale of values, something that had been sorely needed but was missing in the interwar period.

The concept of the "free world," later suspected as a mere slogan, described something very real at that time: namely, in a dual sense, liberation from the yoke of National Socialist rule and defense against new dictatorial dangers. For the first time in the history of Europe there emerged a unanimous opinion about the value of liberal democracy and the community of European interests. To be sure, all occurred against the backdrop of a deep disappointment and mood of crisis that colored the analyses and interpretations of writers and artists, philosophers and theologians. But the experience with dictatorship had provided at the same time the preconditions for a democratic European policy that was utterly different from the intellectual possibilities of the first postwar period.

Of course doubts and differences of opinion about the forms of political life continued. But one fundamental concept was that of the "open society and its enemies," which the philosopher Karl Popper, who had fled from Hitler's Vienna in 1938, threw into the great debate from distant New Zealand as early as 1944. It was a declaration of war on the great ideological dogmas, on past and present closed systems of thought, and a call for a resolute (in the literal sense) defense of open thinking and for the (open) society in which, alone, this was possible. It is true that there were controversies about Popper's argument in terms of philosophical and theoretical details, just as there were about the blueprints for a philosophy of freedom that were now emphatically outlined in various quarters, by thinkers from Karl Jaspers to Isaiah Berlin. Twenty years later its point of departure—opposition to all things totalitarian—would again be challenged by a latter generation that no longer wrote and thought against the same backdrop of experiences, but under the influence of television as the new historical and cultural factor. However, this does not in any way change the fundamental importance of the fact that, with the positive assessment of liberal democracy in the years after 1945, a clear rejection of closed ideologies prevailed intellectually for the first time since the turn of the century. Where there had been an alienation of the mind from political reality after Word War I, there was now a belief in the political responsibility of the intellectual. Where there had been the deep skepticism of an elitist or Marxist critique of democracy and of cultural pessimism, there was now, in view of the temptations and seductions of ideological and utopian thinking and democracy's self-destructive tolerance toward its enemies, a more firmly grounded and humane skepticism.

Of course this new orientation of political thinking did not come about out of the blue. Moreover, it was definitely contested in the West, as is evidenced by the persistence of right-wing and left-wing radical ideas, by the fatal attraction of a dictatorial nationalism and socialism (as in the new states of Africa and Asia), and by the expansion of Communism until it embraced a third of the world's population. Nevertheless, the unexpected strength and longer-term attractiveness of the reconstruction and unaccustomed political stability of a free Europe would have been unthinkable without the changed intellectual situation, without the existential experience of the decision to resist the dual challenge and threat from Hitlerism and then Stalinism.

Initially, of course, there was profound pessimism. The European age of history seemed to have come to an end, once and for all, in the destruction of the war. This was true especially for the Germans, in their "farewell to past history" (Alfred Weber). But even that old optimistic believer in progress, H. G. Wells, was pondering the impending end of human civilization as such. And incorrigible crisis-thinkers like Heidegger continued to maintain that it made no difference to European civilization whether Europe was smothered by America or Russia in the process of technologization and mass leveling. In Eastern Europe the hopes for liberation were in fact dashed by the Soviet Union, and the second attempt at an international world order, in the shape of the United Nations, also ended in disappointment. The atom bomb seemed a symbol of the extreme possibilities that science made available to a politics of self-destruction: progress yes, but it was now capable of being used to destroy the world.

The idea of freedom was helped by the good fortune of the day, which made possible, through cooperation between European and American energies, the rise of the Western democracies to a previously unknown level of prosperity. Of course the sixties would show that what mattered most to the broad public were the values of economic, social, and military security. The flip side of the process of de-ideologization was that intellectual efforts toward a philosophical and moral grounding of liberal-democratic politics tended to be left behind by a pragmatic orientation, which in the long run did not appear to be enough. Only slowly and hesitantly did people become aware of the importance of these new and unusual *practical values* for the history of political ideas; the formation of an intellectually sophisticated and deep-reaching political awareness lagged behind the socioeconomic changes.

Still, during the fifties, in a mixture of old and new, the interrupted thread of the ideas of the twenties was picked up. The social science debate over democracy and modernization was resumed, now enriched by comparative research into dictatorship and totalitarianism, which became an important point of orientation in the Western self-conception. In fact, the continuing argument about the forms and values of democracy and dictatorship, about the "mastering" of Fascism and National Socialism, as well as the critique of Communism, formed, as a kind of negative delimitation of the liberal-democratic position, the framework of politics and ideas for an independent "pinpointing of the present," as Alexander Rüstow outlined it in 1950 with commitment and passion, in his work of the same name (*Ortsbestimmung der Gegenwart*, three volumes, 1950–1957).

The Significance of the Fifties

Since that time a flood of political and historical writing has been marking out the two poles of the postwar discussion: on the one hand the experience of the seductive and manipulative power of authoritarian and totalitarian ideologies of dictatorship under conditions created by the pressures of modernization, and on the other the debate over the exhaustion or "end of ideologies," over the possibility of a conception of politics in pluralistic democracy that emphasizes values but is as free of ideology as possible. This debate over orientation changed, of course, in the midsixties and with the advent of a new generation whose horizon of personal experience was shifted into the later postwar period. It made room for a re-ideologization, which for a time amounted to a rehashing of the old theories of cultural and social criticism in "neo-Marxist" dress.

But precisely for that reason, the intellectual impulse of the fifties, alongside the challenges of 1945 to 1950, continued to be of significance.[7] Political thought revolved mainly around illustrations and explanations of the failure of democracy. It was essentially an attempt to master the past with a view not only to understanding the causes and catastrophes of World War II, but also to preparing oneself directly for the confrontation with the political problems of the present, whether these concerned the crimes of National Socialism or the Communism of the day, a potential neofascism or the structural problems of democracy. Not only in Germany was the fate of the Weimar Republic seen as a classic example of the political and ideological questions facing citizens and states under the conditions of modern industrial society. My studies on the dissolution of the Weimar Republic, which I have pursued since 1950, were as much part of this context of intellectual and contemporary history as the fundamental work by Erich Matthias and Rudolf Morsey, *Das Ende der Parteien 1933* (The End of the Parties in 1933; 1960).

However, in addition to preventing a repeat of the self-destruction of democracy by strengthening it at its most vulnerable points, the fifties were at the same time concerned about the new "borderline situation" that human civilization found itself in since the dawning of the atomic age. This also meant that the question of progress was raised in a new way. The political-moral debates of the physicists themselves, and books like Karl Jasper's *The Atomic Bomb and the Future of Humankind* (1958), carried the discussion beyond the scientific-political realm and grasped its existential significance: the possibility that the incredible scientific progress might end up destroying humankind imparted a new dimension to the concept of political responsibility and placed extreme demands on the structures and institutions for preserving peace. Above political strife and questions of ideological faith there now stood, more than ever before, the necessity for peaceful conflict resolution. The question was merely whether and to what extent this aspect could contribute to a further de-ideologization, or whether the continuation of the Communist challenge, with its claim to an absolute creed, would thwart such tendencies even after the end of the Stalin era.

The hopes of the fifties were still directed clearly and fundamentally at a differentiation from Communism. As an intellectual and ideological force, Stalinism had reached its nadir when the brutally coerced uniformity and bloody purges in Eastern Europe, the defection of Tito, and the banishment of millions of Soviet citizens into a system of work and concentration camps (described in Solzhenitsyn's *Gulag Archipelago*) destroyed the last illusions from the thirties and forties. The revolutionary promises had turned into bureaucratic Communism; the influential intellectual power of Marxism had become the power-political military threat of despotism.

The determined effort to break the intellectual and moral spell of Communism was indeed a factor without which the fundamentally different intellectual climate of the second postwar period and the much greater stability of the Western democracies would have been unthinkable. The demonstrations of Soviet power politics in Prague (1948), Korea (1950), East Berlin (1953), Budapest (1956), again in Prague (1968), and finally in Afghanistan (1979) were at the same time defeats for the Communist ideology. They were recurring reminders of the treacherous substance of totalitarian thinking and the totalitarian faith, and they prevented a complete relapse into the illusions of the interwar period. This was all the more true because the Soviet Union's entirely imperialistic politics of brute force was exerted, above all, in the two countries Hitler had occupied first (Czechoslovakia and Poland), and for whose liberation World War II had, after all, been fought. But the domestic system of Communism, especially the tyranny and terror of Stalinism, was also so thoroughly unmasked in the fifties that at least the humanistic pretensions and the promises of the ideology seemed broken. Negative utopias of a totalitarian future were now associated with the Soviet Union: most impressively in the vision of former Communist George Orwell, who portrayed a totally controlled, spiritually empty world. Orwell's work was banned in the Communist states.

It is true that the exhaustion and disenchantment of the ideologies brought with it, at the same time, a depoliticization, a withdrawal into the individual, the "count-me-out" attitude of the postwar years. However, this new skepticism toward politics was quite different from the ideologically polarized distancing of the first postwar period and from the "nihilism" of the crisis thinkers at that time. Though existentialism, through the popularity of Sartre and his philosophy (*Being and Nothingness,* 1943), had become a highly fashionable movement, it now wanted to be understood far more clearly as a philosophy of individual freedom in a world of collective apparatuses and ideologies, of the salvation of the person in a world of masses and organizations, and as an empowerment to create one's own values amid a destroyed world of broken faiths and ideas.

Moreover, contacts between existentialist personalism and Christian renewal movements were now much more concrete in the political sphere than had been the case between the wars. They rested on a changed attitude on the part of the churches. After the experiences of the period of dictatorship, the churches gradually found their way from their ambivalent stance toward secular democracy to an endorsement of pluralism (of worldviews). The concrete political importance of the application of Christian ethics to the moral and social needs of people in industrial society emerged in the positive key role that Christian Democratic parties played in the reconstruction of democracy, especially in the formerly dictatorial countries of Italy (De Gasperi) and Germany (Adenauer) but also in the European policy of France (Robert Schuman).

It is true that there were also bitter controversies over East-West and alliance policies in connection with the consolidation of the two states in Germany in the fifties. Neutralist and anti-American sentiments emerged on the Right as well as the Left. They reached their high points during the fight over the Western treaties, over German rearmament, and over the further development of atomic weapons. However, they never attained the intellectual and psychological force of the antidemocratic movements in the twenties and thirties.

In the intellectual sphere, however, the pessimistic critique of culture was still at work. On the Left, for example, the "Frankfurt school" gained new importance. On the Right, Europe's reduction in size and its loss of power, its dependence on the relationship between the superpowers, and also the "Americanization" of civilization gave new nourishment to the idea of decline. Parallels were drawn with antiquity, with the fate of ancient

Greece in the face of the new Roman superpower, while theories of decline from Spengler to Toynbee attracted new attention. At the same time, however, people remembered Alexis de Tocqueville, who more than a century before had predicted the rise of democracy and the confrontation between the leading powers of freedom (America) and bondage (Russia). His liberal-conservative conception of democracy, with its view toward America and the problems of mass democracy, could be understood as a constructive alternative to the reactionary and authoritarian nationalist conservatism of the interwar period. And from the gloomy comparisons with antiquity and the decline of the Greeks and the Romans, one could at that time certainly also draw the positive conclusion (as H. E. Stier, an ancient historian with a Christian Democratic orientation did in 1946) that the unification of Europe was the demand of the hour if it wanted to avoid the fate of the disunited Greece.

The idea of a close tie to the United States, founded on the power politics of wartime and the postwar period, and above all on the threat of Soviet imperialism and the division of Europe, was reinforced by the intellectual debates of the cold war and by memories of the United States' fateful withdrawal from Europe after World War I (a war whose outcome it had, after all, decided). Nationalist-European currents with an anti-American undertone, which could fall back on the old arguments of the conservative critique of culture, never again reached the strength they had had in the interwar period. Even Gaullism, which combined a conservative critique of democracy with France's claim to a leadership role in Europe, amounted in the final analysis (as was revealed after De Gaulle came to power in 1958) to an affirmation of the new European policy, albeit not in the form of political integration.

Thus the balance sheet of the fifties was unexpectedly positive, and not only in material terms. The development of political ways of thought showed a greater readiness to compromise, surely the result of the sharpness of the East-West confrontation and a long-delayed understanding of the possibilities of liberal politics and constructive reform. The challenges of the sixties were then partly different in nature. They led to a renaissance of the crisis consciousness that once again called the successful policy of reconstruction into doubt—now on the global scale of world civilization, of north-south conflict, and of a worldwide renewal of ideologies. The belief in revolution, which had receded before the hard disillusionment of the thirties and forties, also returned. Ideas of progress and visions of doom, now under the banner of the problems of the Third World and the environment, once again became criteria for political struggle. This development has lasted until the present, when the far-reaching transformations in Central and Eastern Europe, with unexpected speed and urgency, have cast a new and more positive light on the political, economic, and intellectual decisions of the decade between 1945 and 1955. Driven by the overarching idea of human rights, these transformations have, to an almost unexpected degree, validated liberal democracy and the idea of Europe as the indestructible intellectual and spiritual points of reference of the postwar period. With the advent of a new generation and its different experiences, a struggle is on over old and new values. We must preserve the ideas of liberal democracy and Europe in order to prevent homophobic and anticultural ideologies of a perfect social order, an imperial state, or an intolerant nationalism from continuing to wield their seductive power against the open society. In this sense the dual history of the postwar period, especially in its beginnings as both liberation and threat, continues to be a lesson and a challenge. A challenge that, in a time of upheaval, of opening, of old-new tensions between the diversity and unity of Europe, seems as relevant as ever.

DEMOCRACY
IN
TRANSITION

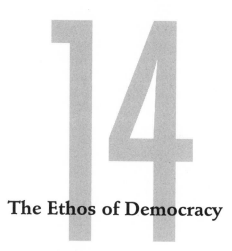

The Ethos of Democracy

Democracy as an Idea and a Form of Government

We are approaching the end of a century that has been dominated by the rise and fall of violent political systems and ideologies, though now the idea of democracy has won what appears to be a decisive victory over the promises and seductions of dictatorships. Thus a new examination of the burning themes in democracy scholarship is called for, in light of the old controversies over democratic ideas and the most recent historical experiences. In the great vacuum left behind by the dictatorships of the Left and the Right, the question of the values and ethos of democracy assumes particular importance. We can approach this question from several perspectives.

We begin with a twofold question: first about the historical contexts of an idea of democracy that is founded on and emphasizes values, and second about the political experiences we have had with the realization or perversion of this idea. This question concerns the history of ideas.

We can turn the question around and ask, How and to what extent is democracy, as a great, high-spirited idea, simultaneously viable as a form of government? This is the constitutional question.

From a comparative and normative perspective, the following question arises: Can democracy be defined as the best of all forms of government, or merely as the least bad?

Finally, the are questions of legitimacy: How different, indeed contrary and yet necessarily interconnected are the various legitimations of democracy—the ethical and spiritual, the anthropological, and the pragmatic political legitimations?

In fact the constant tension between intellectual and empirical justifications has played an important role in the recent discussion about the concepts, forms, and nature of democracy. Of course, behind the controversy over a theoretical versus a practical conception of politics, an argument that has been carried on especially sharply since 1968, there is the historic, classic debate about the relationship between politics and morality, between power and ethos. That debate has found expression—crudely, to be sure—in the opposing of "substantive" democracy and "formal" democracy.

However, reflected in that controversy is also the highly skeptical attitude of historians like Jacob Burckhardt, who saw democracy (from ancient times on) as a "ferment" and an "all-dissolving force," or of Leopold von Ranke, who described democracy as "the ever-moving ferment of the modern world, which throws states and institutions into unrest."

This was, of course, only a half-truth and a passing one at that. The other, more momentous truth was realized at the time by another, though he, too, was hesitant and skeptical about democracy: Alexis de Tocqueville. In his epochal work on America (published in 1835), he saw the world-historical trend toward democracy at work in the definite process of creating a constitution, a state, and a society. In American democracy, with its pathbreaking Constitution—which was given too little notice by the two great historians just mentioned, as it was by most intellectual contemporaries in Europe—newly created political institutions, justified on emphatically ethical grounds, were already anchored in a lasting way on the principle of the sovereignty of the people.

And from 1918 on, when universal suffrage became firmly established, this "ferment" itself became the legitimating foundation and institutional guideline of most states. The more the debate over whether a democracy could be viable as a state, about its inexorable development or necessary restriction and modification—along with the principled struggle by its opponents and advocates—intensified into fierce conflict, the more the practical meaning of democracy emerged. More relevant than ever before was the terse question that had often received a negative answer in history: Is the idea of democracy even possible as a state, except at the price of either governmental efficiency or its idealistic qualities and logical (philosophical) consistency?

This question about the idea and ethos of democracy, on the one hand, and its compatibility with political-governmental and social reality, on the other, now arises anew in view of the deep changes in the realm of political ideas and in the political system in Germany and Europe since 1989.

As we emerge from an age of ideologies and look back on them, some are once again hoping for an end of ideologies—if not for the end of (past) history—after the debacle of what is for the time being the last great ideology, that of Marxism-Leninism.

But we should be cautious: for is not the trend, rather, toward the creation of a large, dangerous vacuum in those places where hitherto everything was defined and justified ideologically, even if it was only partially believed? This is why questions about the concept of democracy have become highly relevant once again. The hope is that this gap, this crisis of orientation, this intellectual vacuum left behind by a socialism that failed (and yet has not been entirely abandoned as a dream), will be filled by a value-oriented, indeed an ethical justification of our democracy. Until now such a justification probably did not seem so necessary, because the totalitarian threat (and experience), along with the material advantages of liberal democracy and its superiority when it comes to human rights, seemed sufficient justification.

At various times, this century, whose end is now approaching, was declared to be an epoch characterized by the global expansion of democracy. This claim was heard at the opening of the century, in 1918, and again in 1945, and finally after the revolutions against dictatorship in 1989 and 1990. But at the same time it has been a century in which dictatorships and totalitarian governments were more powerful and more numerous than ever before.

The decisions that were made at the end of World War I were prematurely elevated to the triumph of the democratic idea and its form of government over the authoritarian conception of the state and power. And at the end of the century, seventy years later, nearly all states in the world, including the many new states of the postcolonial world, describe themselves, more emphatically than ever before, as democracies. In between, however, lies the era of the totalitarian systems of Fascism and National Socialism, of Leninism and Stalinism, of Castroism, Maoism, and Brezhnevism. And the age of the national and developmental dictatorships, with their ideas of modernization and their despotic realities, has continued. Though they have described themselves, euphemistically, as the "rule of the people," the "community of the people," or the "people's democracy" (a tautology), they have been, in fact, pseudodemocracies hostile to opposition and opposed to human rights. Even in the declared age of the idea of democracy, a democratic form of government is anything but the natural, self-evident form of political and moral existence. Rather, it tends to be the exception, a highly complicated result of historical developments, political experiences and thought, and ethical decisions.

Historical Problems

What George Sabine wrote in the thirties in his now classic philosophical and political book on the history of ideas is neither old-fashioned nor outdated: "An important characteristic of a liberal system of government, perhaps the most important one, is the negative quality of not being totalitarian." The basis of liberal democracy was in fact the social and simultaneously moral idea that politics is the art of the peaceful accommodation of competing interests, and its method the democratic decision of the majority, with guaranteed protection of the minority and the inviolable right to opposition. This, however, is completely opposed to the philosophical ideas and, later, the political and ideological endeavors that sought one-dimensional, all-embracing, and perfectly consistent solutions to the problems created by the diversity of opinions and interests in the modern state. That tradition stretches from Rousseau via Hegel and Marx to the totalitarian ideologies of Communism, Fascism, National Socialism, and their politically and socially authoritarian, technocratic, or nationalistic variations.

The intellectual struggle for the liberal form of democracy—repeatedly devalued by allegedly "more profound" theoreticians of antipluralism from the Right and the Left, despite the experiences we have had with pseudodemocratic dictatorships—was not taken very seriously after World War I as a proper subject of political philosophy. The heated discussions between right-wing and left-wing, conservative and revolutionary theories were conducted, especially in Germany, with complete disregard for the reality of democracy. Though that reality offered plenty of pressing questions, they were usually dismissed as intellectually unsophisticated, or as merely technical or formal issues compared with the traditional and revolutionary themes of political philosophy. Alternatively they were regarded primarily as the result of the war and were used to criticize the system. This was damaging both to political philosophy as such and to empirical democracy itself, which saw held before it a rather disparaging and distorted mirror of its ideas and values.

But democracy had in fact found itself in this situation long before the special problems of the Weimar Republic and its painful intellectual and moral history. From a historical perspective, we note that there has been a long tradition of basic democratic ideas from the time they were formulated in Greece between the fifth and fourth centuries B.C. Based on his comparative study of constitutions and his opposition to monolithic utopias of the state, Aristotle had already emphasized and recommended a pluralistic structure of the polity and a supporting middle class of citizens as the two most important preconditions for a moderate form of government and as a safeguard against extremism.

However, whenever attempts were undertaken to realize democratic principles, they were fragile efforts and tended to be isolated occurrences. In the Greek city-states, direct democracy, with its many crises, already tended to be controversial rather than celebrated. In Thucydides, the effect of Pericles' famous speech in praise of democracy did not last long, as the states soon plunged into the Peloponnesian civil war. We can also think of the partly democratic component of the Roman Republic. Praised by Polybius and Cicero as a mixed constitution and as a government of laws carried by consensus, the republic was soon overpowered by dictatorship and the principate. Then there was the late-Medieval transitional society of the emerging territorial and national states, whose contentious jurists, like Marsilius of Padua, suggested in the fourteenth century the idea of the sovereignty of the people as the legitimating principle of the state. Above all, though, there was the rise of English parliamentarianism, which called Hobbes and Locke into action in the seventeenth century, and with them the theory of the liberal constitutional state. Finally, the end of the eighteenth century witnessed the revolutionary breakthrough of a self-determined citizen-state in North America and France.

That breakthrough brought at the same time an intensification of the conflict over the two conceptions of democracy that have determined the fronts ever since: on the one hand, the notion, following on Rousseau, of the necessary identity of the government with the governed, confirmed through plebiscites and taken to the point of totalitarian unity; on the other hand, the emphasis, with Montesquieu and Tocqueville, on a form of democracy that is representative and whose power is separated and limited.

Though the liberal conception seeks to combine representative and plebiscitary components (E. Fraenkel), it clearly opposes the tendentially totalitarian claim of the complete identity of ruler and ruled, with which dictators all over the world have tried to disguise or justify their rule in pseudodemocratic fashion. The crucial criterion remains the pluralistic character of society and the state, by which is meant a division of power, a multiparty system, and the recognition of the opposition.

One-party systems that describe themselves as democratic are incapable either ideologically or politically of carrying out a peaceful process of social integration and the accommodation of competing interests. They remain dependent on autocratic, coercive policies, no matter how much they might try to veil or glorify them with glowing visions of a society without a state (as in Communism) or a classless, *volk*-ish community (as in National Socialism).

It was already clear in the nineteenth century that even a process of democratization that was hoped for and driven forward by powerful liberal movements could be accomplished only slowly, with many setbacks (1848), and very unevenly. Even then, as it would be a hundred years later in the Third World, the optimism about a simple transfer and application of democracy to other countries was disappointed.

Two historical examples can show what sort of impeding factors played a role in this: the first a previously colonial society, like Latin America after the wars of independence from 1806 to 1825; the second a society that was already highly developed culturally and economically, such as Germany after its unification in 1871. In both cases it was precisely the intellectual access to modern democracy that was delayed or distorted in a lasting way: in Latin America in favor of authoritarian presidential regimes that established themselves in a position between democracy and dictatorship, on a populist or military foundation; in Germany by the primacy of foreign policy and then through the disastrous *Sonderweg* ("special path") of the ideological totalitarianisms of the National Socialist and Socialist Unity Party (SED) dictatorships. In the German case, only the failure of these dictatorships, the first in 1945, the second in 1989, have in part suppressed the antidemocratic traditions and illusions and in part (one hopes) overcome them, thus opening the way, after the failure of the first German democracy, to a second democracy that is more stable in intellectual terms as well. At first this occurred at the expense of the division of the nation, but now it is taking place within the framework of an undivided Europe of democratic states.

Threats

If we look back over the varied history of the development of democratic ideas and constitutions, however, we must keep in mind the constant possibility of a relapse into authoritarianism or a seduction into totalitarian forms of politics. Even after the breakthrough of the modern state based on the rule of law, these forms have continued to assault the idea of democracy. With this in mind, one will not see the idea of democracy simply as a necessary consequence of a straight line of historical progress, nor as the easily transferable "best" form of government, in the sense of a perpetual search for the ideal state. Instead, democracy is the product of a highly complicated social, political, and above all intellectual and moral effort. The constant aim of that effort is to overcome the barriers of "natural" conditions, and to take the process of "civilization" in the political sphere beyond a mere power-Darwinism. Behind the effort is the notion of voluntary restraint in the competition between the individual interests and the social needs of human beings who are (at least egotistically and morally) always imperfect. And above all, the objective is—as voiced by Karl Popper—the decisive rejection of all political ideas and theories that, in the search for the perfect community, have placed the closed, abstract, and, in the final analysis, inhuman totalitarian concept of democracy above the open, imperfect, and pluralistic one. The line of these ideas stretches from the "spell" of Plato to Hegelian and Marxist dialectic (and of course to Lenin, Stalin, and Hitler).

The Weimar Republic came to grief over the excessive, perfectionist demands that were placed on the constitutional and democratic concept. In dualistic fashion, it set up the parliamentary and presidential principles side by side and in opposition to each other. In an almost suicidal manner, it let its enemies do as they pleased, until the democracy was removed by an emphatically "legal revolution" carried out in the name of democracy and the "people." The excessive expectations and demands placed on the idea of democracy as an ideal construct of philosophers and sociologists, political economists and theoreticians of the state, led to disappointment and failure, and then to the refutation of democracy and the declaration that it was not feasible. In this way a brilliant thinker like Robert Michels made his way from socialism to fascism, and Carl Schmitt to the idea of the total führer state—and with them not a few of their students. This also explains the frustration and cynicism of a generation like that of 1968, which counterposed to the de-ideologization of the second postwar period idealized demands that empirical democracies could not satisfy.

In all this the democratic theory of the Weimar period, in particular, suffered from a "value-neutralism" that was practiced in constitutional interpretation. At the time, eminent constitutional lawyers like Hans Kelsen and Gustav Radbruch advocated a relativist view, according to which political institutions could be interpreted almost in any way. This value-neutralism, in particular for its convinced democratic interpreters (who also included Anschütz and Thoma), exposed the almost defenseless Weimar Republic to the emphatically value-based attack of its enemies from the Right and the Left. Too late came the realization that a democracy can certainly be overthrown by its own means, pseudodemocratically and pseudolegally, if it leaves to its enemies the monopoly on defining values. From this realization some critics of the system, like Carl Schmitt, had already concluded before 1933 that the value-pluralistic democracy was left with only formal *legality*, while it lost its essential *legitimacy* to those who overcame this value-neutrality by the proclamation of a political creed. What was not sufficiently realized or appreciated, what was indeed overlooked, was the fact that the democratic interplay of different, competing political forces in itself represented a supreme value, that it was, indeed, a great achievement of the human mind and civilization and a great challenge.

The lesson of the period—that value-relativism and value-neutralism amount to political helplessness—led, after the fall of the Weimar Republic and of National Socialism, to a conception of the constitution that deliberately emphasized values, particularly in Germany, even though this conception has been repeatedly challenged. Two things were characteristic of the collapse of democracy between 1930 and 1933: first, the crushing of the political center by extremism from the Left and the Right; second, the transformation of a great power vacuum, which was in regard to democracy also an *intellectual vacuum,* into an all-promising dictatorship. The resulting dictatorship operated with the monopoly of a radically intolerant ideology, and with the claim of a total "rule of the people" above and beyond the "artificial," failing parliamentary democracy.

In any event, in the struggle over viable normative values and concrete orientations, the thirties was a time of great deception and disappointment. It was a time of fateful and disastrous *misjudgments:* by the conservatives in regard to Hitler's anticommunism, with which they sympathized; by the liberals in regard to the extent of the threat from the Right as well as the Left, which threatened economic as well as political liberalism and threw it into a profound crisis; by the Christians in regard to the totalitarian threats from the Left and the Right, the similarity of which forbade fighting one with the other, even though atheistic communism was seen as the greater threat; by the socialists in regard to the need to shore up democratic structures, even if those structures did not match up to their own ideas about socioeconomic progress. In all of these four major cases, the problems of orientation had become nearly insoluble. When we look for ideas about how Western civilization and its values could have been saved from the great ideologies and dictatorships, the evidence of disorientation in the battle between the politicians in power and their enemies, and also in the desperate quarrels among the persecuted and the émigrés in the shrinking free Europe, is depressing: resignation, skepticism, and criticism of democracy predominate. Only among those in exile and in the resistance, who recognized that the nationalistic fragmentation of Europe was the gravest problem of the crisis, did the idea of European unity lay a viable foundation during the war for reshaping politics and its values along democratic lines.

Self-Restraint and Protection

It was only with the challenge of the greatest war in history and the decisions of the second postwar period that the atmosphere of illusions and political cynicism gave way to a return to the basic values of Western civilization: reconstruction and order on the basis of freedom, social justice, and human dignity. Yet it took the most horrible destruction and racist or socialist barbarities, and eventually the inhuman partition of Europe, to refute the ideological errors of the century and to come to terms with their moral and political consequences in the period of the world wars. The lack of responsibility in the political thinking of this age of the masses was a problem that continued to confront the old and new nations after 1945 as well, in view of the global expansion of the battle of ideas. Now the caesura of 1989 has created a new opportunity to bring that battle to an end.

The intellectual and ethical meaning and assessment of Germany's Basic Law must also be measured against historical experiences, not against an antiquated and abstract confrontation between "constitutional norm and constitutional reality." For this constitution does not grant the absolute—and in the final analysis suicidal—freedom of the Weimar Republic. Instead, it strives to bind human and civic rights into a governmental system that is related to values and defined as liberal-democratic, and the stability and workability of that system rests precisely on the unconditional preservation of the substance and basic structure of the constitutional system itself. It was this combination of political experience and democratic ethos that gave its imprint to the deliberations, negotiations, and decisions of the Parliamentary Council immediately after what in 1946 Meinecke called the "German catastrophe" and Alfred Weber the "farewell to past history." If the Basic Law has provided an unexpectedly good start and created possibilities of development for what is finally a more successful form of German parliamentary democracy, the modifications of and restraints on the theoretical principles of democracy in favor of the ethos of democracy contributed to this accomplishment, as did the clear and fundamental decision that democracy must be able to defend itself.

Habituation and tradition are also important elements in a vigorous constitutional consciousness. These were sorely lacking in Germany's modern history. Now that the Basic Law has become the definitive constitution for all Germans, we must not underestimate what an immeasurably important role a constitution that has been working over a long period and is carried by consensus has in shaping the political spirit of the next generation. It is part of the ethos of democracy that the indispensable criticism of democracy must show a sense of political proportions. There can be no denying that the basic decisions arrived at within a value-oriented, stable, and protected constitution guarantee, despite all shortcomings and gaps in reforms, a standard of social and political life that allows more democracy *and* prosperity, more freedom *and* equality under the conditions of modern industrial society than all historical and most contemporary systems of government.

Two aspects are essential in this picture of the German experience. First, the demand for freedom raised by individuals and minorities must not come into direct confrontation with the expansion of the activities of the state, but must be incorporated into them. The safeguarding of human rights is not something that is isolated from and opposed to the protection of democracy by the state, but is dependent on the institutional equipment and the democratic control structures of the state itself. Otherwise all basic rights and declarations of human rights are useless, as was shown by the constitution of the former GDR and by other Communist constitutions. While those constitutions appear to have a tint of human rights, in reality they have subjected everything to the absolute power of the party.

Second, we must bear in mind that the compromise structure of the Basic Law contains, as does every constitution, quite divergent ideas about values. The conflict over the ranking of these values is quite natural and must not be authoritatively decided by any dogmatic definition (of democracy, for example). Instead, this ranking of values is the very object of the political process and of the ongoing disputes among various currents of thought.

The Basic Law consciously creates a broad latitude for this process, by granting the freedom to form coalitions and freedom of opinion, and by acknowledging the important role of the parties. But unlike the Weimar Republic, it also establishes a framework and a boundary for that latitude: the liberal state based on the rule of law and the principle of mutual tolerance. On the one hand, the decision of the Basic Law in favor of certain values must not be formulated too narrowly. It must take into account the compromise structure of the constitution and give room to the various conceptions of the state and democracy, without declaring one view as absolute and demonizing the political opponent as the political enemy. On the other hand, the basic principle that sets the constitution of the Basic Law apart from other constitutions remains valid: namely, that its liberties and protection are granted only to those who accept the Basic Law in its essence and measure their own conduct by it. A sharp line is drawn where the danger exists that a constitution and a democracy could be destroyed by their own means; this is where the plurality and freedom of political activities have their definitive limits. This is nothing other than the implementation of a basic norm of our constitution, one that is certainly in keeping with its historical meaning and its democratic function.

Democracy as the Control of Power

Let me summarize what has been said. Running through our history of political thinking, right up to the current formulations in the work of Karl Popper, is a confrontation between open, pluralistic and closed, uniform conceptions of state and society. This reveals a core problem of all theories of the state: the sharp opposition between empirical community and the ideal state. A closed, perfectionist, totalistic view has been predominant in the conceptions of the most influential philosophers of the state. For a very long time it impeded and discredited the development of an empirical, pluralistic theory of state and society. In reality the diversity of human existence and the varied ideas of how a political community is to be formed demand, if they are to be given adequate and humane consideration, a theory that is a more sophisticated and complex, and of course also more realistic. Representative democracy with a separation of powers is a mature and at the same time complicated, vulnerable product of human civilization and the capacity for political understanding, for it demands the shaping of community through ordered compromise instead of the power of the stronger, state power through a regulated distribution of power and a conscious restraint on force, and limits on the rule of the majority through minority rights.

This is a challenging prospect, and it represents the more difficult path. Since Plato's blueprint for the politeia and the great utopias of the state, since the time of Rousseau's *volonté générale* and the modern versions of total democracy, and finally in the totalitarian dictatorships of National Socialism and Communism, the conception of a social order based on an absolutely fixed, uniform principle has had a dominating, suggestive, and seductive power over all composite, open, and mixed forms of social and political life. Time and again victory has gone to the "reduction of diversity [*Vielfalt*] to uniformity [*Einfalt*]" (Fritz Stern), to the "totalitarian temptation" (J. F. Revel).

Consensus either as communal coercion or as voluntary consent: time after time the dispute over the acceptance or rejection of the separation of powers has come down to these two alternatives. Under the totalitarian fiction, the question about concrete structures and their institutions becomes a merely formal one.

The invoking of a higher legitimacy turns practical politics, the regulation of the domestic question of power, into a simple doctrine of functions. Though modern dictatorships use the vocabulary of the constitutional state, the claim that they possess a revolutionary legitimacy that is derived from their "substantive" final goals, that they are pursuing true freedom and perfect justice, pushes aside the question of the concrete constitution. In contrast, the old concept of the mixed constitution and the separation of powers turns out to be a decisive advance in the history of political ideas and theories of the state, one that needs to be developed further.

What is at stake is a principle that opposes and resists the deceptive dream of the perfect order of state and society, because to this day that dream has always led to unfreedom and despotism. It promises no final solution to the problem of power, because no such solution can exist.

Churchill's view that of all the bad forms of government, democracy is the least bad, is, in any case, very true for the constitutional separation of powers: of all the forms of organizing power and rule, it is ethically the most acceptable. Its superior legitimacy is grounded in the recognition and safeguarding of civic freedom and diversity. It ameliorates the evils of power, for without power humans cannot live together; thus, despite many shortcomings, it can with every right be seen as an expression of higher political culture. Controlling wars and violence will be possible in the long run only if we succeed in shaping the internal organization of states, and eventually international politics, in accordance with the rules of liberal-democratic conflict resolution.

A theory of democracy that gives expression to the intimate though tension-filled connection between the spirit, politics, and morality rests on the understanding of the ambivalence of human goals. Since all goals are realized only at the expense of others, the theory must be open to the need for balance, control, and the ability to correct actions in the interests of preserving freedom and human rights. Democracy as a form of government means limited government—limited through restrictions on power, the separation of powers, and supranational ties. It is the ever fragile, ever contested government of self-restraint that is based on the understanding of human imperfection, just as dictatorship is the form of rule born of man's ideological arrogance.

In the introduction to his work on democracy in America, Alexis de Tocqueville wrote a century and a half ago about the meaning and the task of such intellectual and, at the same time, practical political reflections and efforts: "The first of the duties that are at this time imposed upon those who direct our affairs is to educate democracy, to reawaken, if possible, its religious beliefs; to purify its morals; to mold its actions; to substitute a knowledge of statecraft for its inexperience, and an awareness of its true interests for its blind instincts, to adapt its government to time and place, and to modify it according to men and to conditions. A new science of politics is needed for a new world."

We are left with the old fundamental political-anthropological question about the value of the individual, and with a view of humanity that is community-based and at the same time liberal, with the idea of the *"zoon politikon"* as a person, which has given its imprint to the European origin of democracy. It is a "difficult ideology" (Eva Reichmann), the realization—hard to convey, demanding, and in the deepest sense anti-ideological—that the goal does *not* justify the means, that the dignity of humanity and protection against the abuse of power rank higher than even the most exalted goals; one can think, for example, of the seductive invoking of "socialist humanism" that was used for too long, from 1917 to 1989, to try to lift Communism, despite its inhuman practice, above comparison with other totalitarian ideologies and systems. On this insight and experience rests the ethos of democracy: both the possibility of its philosophical justification and its political realization—each stands in need of the other.

Problems of Orientation in
Germany's Liberal Democracy

I

When one seeks to determine the political form of the Federal Republic of Germany and its place in history, one encounters from the very beginning of its establishment two fundamental tendencies of political orientation, tendencies that competed with each other in the subsequent development of the German state: a desire for national unity in a free state, and a concern for the stability of the new democracy as an equal member in a unified Europe. When Theodor Heuss called the Federal Republic a "provisional" or "transitory" entity, he was referring to the temporary condition of national division, not to the very *definitive* decision in favor of liberal democracy: the earlier disparaging of the Weimar democracy by many as a mere "intermezzo" was a warning and a lesson.

The tension of this dual orientation was set up in the Basic Law of 1949 and was subsequently embodied in the Germany policy of all governments of the Federal Republic. Behind it stands the historical problem of the German nation-state of 1871, which was exaggerated in the idea of the Reich. In the test of strength in World War I, it suffered a defeat that it was unable to come to terms with, and this led to its renewed exaggeration and the catastrophe of the Third Reich of 1933. However, the establishment of a new German democracy after 1945 sought to draw, at the same time, the domestic political lessons left behind by the failure of the first republic, and by the seemingly smooth and pseudolegal path the nation had taken from a parliamentary democracy to a totalitarian dictatorship.

Contemporaries of the Federal Republic became instantly aware of the basic tension in the new democracy that was contained in this dual experience of Germany's painful national and democratic history, a tension that reached back, in fact, to the failure of the revolution of 1848, with its nationalistic as well as liberal-democratic motivations. We can see this tension in the great controversy between Adenauer and Schumacher over whether Germany's political orientation should be focused on Europe and the West, or on the nation. Later it appeared in the continuing controversy over Stalin's note of March 1952, which held out to the Federal Republic the prospect of national unification in return for giving up its ties to the Western alliance that safeguarded its new democracy. This situation meant that the value-orientation of the democracy was repeatedly open for debate. The dispute over the nation's political orientation and values stretched all the way to the conclusions that were drawn in regard to the policy of détente.

Moreover, it was not the sixties but the early fifties (today often too readily dismissed as merely a period of restoration) that saw the reestablishment of contemporary history and political science. Through the first professorships, institutes, and journals, and in a growing flood of research and publications, these disciplines strove to work through the most recent past and its politically relevant, topical lessons. Of course, at that time it was still taking place on a small scale and against considerable resistance. Criticism was raised that it was unhistorical to analyze the Weimar Republic as a democracy, an objection that was also voiced (by Werner Conze) against my 1955 book on the Weimar Republic. Today this line of argument is returning, in the dubious demand from the Right and the Left for a "historicization of National Socialism." These were the problems that, after the war and captivity, after Tübingen and Harvard, marked my years in Berlin after 1950: at the newly established Institute of Political Science, at the reopened German Academy of Politics, and at the new Free University.

In view of the confrontation between democracy and dictatorship on a German and European scale, we were at that time concerned, not least, with the cardinal question of the extent to which the dissolution and fall of the first German democracy had been the result of a great *crisis of orientation* that had disturbed the political consciousness of the citizens and had led the thinking of the intelligentsia astray. Next to the historical and political causes of the "German catastrophe," its philosophical and moral causes formed another major theme of the new contemporary history and political science.

The primary concern many of us had back then, and one that has not relinquished its hold to this day, was not merely to clarify the events themselves. Instead, we sought to analyze critically the historical and contemporary assimilation and interpretation of these events. For in spite of the comparability of the history of the German nation to that of other

European nations, it was this process of assimilation and interpretation that had eventually produced or favored the rise of the "German ideology," in which we recognized the true and fateful special case of German history. Thus at the time my book *The Dissolution of the Weimar Republic* opened with the statement: "By contrast to the fundamental acceptance and practical significance of the idea and the reality of democracy in the Western European–American sphere, in Germany they have met with an ambivalent assessment to this day." This difference between Germany and the West, last fought out in two world wars, led in fact to the special awareness of a "separate path" *(Sonderweg)* in German history, which is the real reason for the specific German manifestation of a crisis in orientation. Deep disappointment and an inability to come to terms with what had happened led the Germans to respond to the shock of World War I and its consequences with withdrawal or flight into illusions: to defeat and revolution, to discrimination and a desire for revision. To be sure, all this did not come out of the blue, and the history of the rise and formation of the German national consciousness in the nineteenth century, appearing first as a countermovement to the French-Napoleonic domination of Germany, deserves full consideration in this current time of renewed interest in that rich, independent century.

For several years now there has been another sharp flare-up of the debate about the causes and nature of Germany's crisis of orientation, and with it the problem of the political reference to values in democracy. Democracy is, after all, the only form of government that consciously makes room for the various currents of political thinking and action, thus also making political science possible in the first place. The quarrel over German special paths *(Sonderwege)* picks up once again the old question that was of such immediate concern to us after 1945 and especially after the reestablishment of German statehood forty years ago, and which challenged us to a critical examination of our traditional nationalist view of history.

II

Thus the new contemporary history of Germany since 1945 and 1949 has been two things: the history of a divided nation, and at the same time the development of a second democracy, which has been able to stand its ground more successfully than the first democratic experiment.

Included in this dual contemporary history and its mutual interweaving is, of course, a problem that to this day gives its imprint to the unexpectedly quick creation of the state in 1949. It was postwar history that led the country out of the self-inflicted catastrophe of the Hitler regime, doing so through a continual process of recalling the basic experience of the German dictatorship between 1933 and 1945. However, this dual history received a strong additional impulse from the highly topical confrontation between the superpowers in East and West and from the completely opposite political values they represented: dictatorial one-party rule and liberal democracy.

This tension-filled framework shaped the establishment and development of two fundamentally different systems of government on the soil of the former nation-state, now reduced in size by expulsions and occupation. The situation was further complicated and exacerbated by the military and economic strategies of the "cold war." (All affirmations of détente notwithstanding, the cold war conflict will not be over in a fundamental sense so long as people are shot at borders and walls.)

Germany, however, was not only the object but increasingly also the subject of developments that led within a few years to what seemed to be irrevocable political decisions. These decisions have constituted reality to the present day, though their continuing validity is put in question time and again. The *dependence* of German politics on the international power situation emerged above all in the great direction-setting decisions of 1948 and 1949. To begin with, the problems of coping with the consequences of the war, organizing reconstruction, and securing the necessary cooperation to accomplish these tasks were intimately linked to the integration of occupied Germany into European and world politics, which was divided on bipolar lines. But the capacity of German politics to take action thereby also soon regained weight.

This was especially true for the political orientation and the democratic development of the Federal Republic, which revealed the fundamental difference from the Soviet-dominated establishment of the GDR and from its political and social structure: a dictatorially ruled "people's democracy." Though both states were marked by the formation of blocs and were under the control of the victorious powers, the basic difference emerged with overwhelming clarity from the very beginning: instead of the "democratization" that was proclaimed during the first postwar years, the East witnessed the implementation of a Communist Party dictatorship; the West, meanwhile, saw the gradual transformation of the occupational regime into a system of international cooperation—with the historically important goal of changing the *negative control* of Germany into a *positive integration* with a European and Atlantic orientation.

This was in fact the momentous substance of the negotiations and treaties that led from the Marshall Plan to the Western European Union, the Council of Europe, the European Coal and Steel Community, and finally to the Germany treaties and the European Community. Here was also the fundamental difference from the first postwar period. Following

World War I, the relapse into a Europe of nation-states had led to the fatal crisis of the democracies and to the dictatorial rise of aggressively revisionist movements and systems, in the first place Fascism and German National Socialism. But now, on this side of the Soviet sphere of power, a policy of close European cooperation, with backing and support from the United States, became possible. Its goal was economic as well as political integration, which could build on the plans of the resistance movements during the war and a multitude of European movements in the early postwar years. This policy also opened up concrete possibilities for a supranational solution to the problem of German statehood. For with a view toward both economic and security policy, and especially toward the stabilization of the new German democracy, the idea of Europe acquired a powerful function: after the exaggerated nationalism of the National Socialist regime had reduced to absurdity the concept of the nation-state as the final authority, it offered a new, broader frame of reference.

The policy of the first chancellor, Konrad Adenauer, who headed the West German government from 1949 to 1963 (an unexpectedly long period), rested from the very beginning completely on that supranational aspect of the European policy. In view of the power-political realities at the end of the forties, the nation-state arguments of the Social Democratic opposition, under the leadership of Kurt Schumacher, were not accepted as an alternative by the majority of the West German population. The proclaimed goal of national unification moved into the distance, while the stabilization of Western cooperation corresponded to the immediate need for reconstruction and security. This also shaped the decision for a liberal-democratic system of state and society and a social market economy. The ideas of controlled economy and socialism were burdened with the stigma of dictatorship and the misery of the war and the postwar period. At the same time, the spectacle of the coercive imposition of socialism right next door in Eastern Europe, which led to permanent economic crisis, was particularly unappealing, as was the continuous stream of refugees from East to West.

A symbol of the new political structure was the convincing liberal-democratic figure of Theodor Heuss, who was the first president, from 1949 to 1959, and who had taught at the German Academy of Politics in Berlin during the Weimar era. The Federal Republic avoided the constitutional-political weaknesses that had led to the early demise of the Weimar Republic. The position of the chancellor and the government were strengthened, the dictatorial power of the president dismantled, and the parliamentary process was solidified by making the fall of one chancellor dependent on the election of a new one (a "constructive vote of no confidence"). The Federal Constitutional Court was given the power to ban antidemocratic parties. Finally, the fragmentation of the landscape of political parties was made more difficult through a 5 percent clause in the electoral laws. The purpose of all these regulations was to prevent a destruction of the democracy by pseudodemocratic means, as had happened in 1933. The modified, militant democracy of Bonn would not grant its principled opponents the unlimited tolerance that led to the destruction of the Weimar Republic.

Moreover, the nation's habituation to a better-functioning party and parliamentary system also led to an increasingly positive view of democracy itself, something that had been lacking after 1918. The regime of Chancellor Adenauer—a great old man with nearly patriarchal authority—built a bridge from Germany's patriarchal state tradition to pluralistic democracy. The historical profusion of parties was replaced by a concentration of political group into two parties nearly equal in size, the old Social Democratic Party (SPD) and the new Christian Democratic Union (CDU). Next to these, the Free Democratic Party (FDP) was able to maintain itself for three decades as a smaller third party, until the appearance of the "Greens."

This sort of constellation was reminiscent of the British and American party systems, with their capacity for cooperation. The Bonn system was able to break away from the problems that were typical of the fractured party systems on the European Continent. It was the result of a lengthy process of making the parties less ideological and more pragmatic. This made possible a liberalization of the SPD in the Godesberg Program of 1959, and eventually the full-fledged changes of government from the CDU to the SPD, and back to the CDU (in 1969 and 1982), in the states as well as on the federal level.

In all of this the party system was never subjected to political and economic crises on the scale of the permanent Weimar crisis. This must be kept in mind as the electoral results, which since 1957 have regularly brought in 90 percent of the votes for the three Bonn parties, are used as indications that political stability, a permanent structure of democratic behavior, and a reliable political culture exist in the Federal Republic. Since the middle of the sixties (after the end of the Adenauer era), in a time marked by the advent of a new generation, changes in the international situation, and the receding of the idea of reunification, the persistent problems and unfinished elements of the Bonn state have come to the fore more prominently.

Yet the political basis on which the second German republic was able to develop was, in comparison with the Weimar Republic and especially with the GDR, undeniably broader and more secure. The shattering experience of the failures of 1933 and 1945 worked as a continually present warning against the two basic weaknesses of recent German history: helplessness toward the enemies of democracy and susceptibility to dictatorial solutions. Added to this was the fact that there was now a broad consensus for rejecting the current Communist as well as the past National Socialist claims to power, with their totalitarian stamp. Antitotalitarianism was an active and positive force, whose political significance for the democratic development of the forties and fifties should not today be underestimated. Later critics of the concept of totalitarianism have often lacked an understanding of how concrete the dual threat—from the just-defeated dictatorships of the Right and from the spread of Stalinism at the time—really was for the vulnerable new European democracies after 1945.

III

The difference between Weimar and Bonn can be expressed very sharply—and thus controversially—with two concepts: the postulate of "constitutional patriotism" (as formulated by Dolf Sternberger) and the position of the Federal Republic as a postnational democracy among nation-states (as I have argued). Though both descriptions are used today as emphatically new points of discussion, in the history of the creation and development of the second German democracy, they identify precisely those aspects that led the way out of the dead end of the Weimar Republic: out of its value-neutralism and its helplessness in the face of the displacement of democratic thinking by thinking that was nationalistic and hostile to compromise.

In contrast to the abuse of the concept of democracy in dictatorships of the Right and the Left, the democracy of the Federal Republic is founded on the openness of the political process and on the competitive formation of the will of the people in freely formed parties and associations. Opposition is thus considered a fundamental component of democracy; the latter proves itself in the changeover of power between government and opposition, which take turns holding political responsibility on the federal as well as state and communal levels.

Majority decisions are made in representatively elected parliaments and not through plebiscitary procedures, which can be demagogically abused. And the election of the president, in contrast to the process in the Weimar Republic, is also accomplished in a parliamentary-federalist way. In the elections and the formation of governments in the Federal Republic, the *democratic principle* is always related to the representative and liberal character of a constitutional state with separated powers.

This understanding of democracy, a democracy that is modified and tied to values, is opposed to the value-neutrality of the Weimar Constitution.

In contrast to Weimar, the enemies of the liberal constitutional order are denied the unlimited freedom to destroy it, in that citizens and parties are obligated, first and foremost, to preserve the "the basic liberal-democratic order." This important modification has been the focus of repeated controversies. The constitutional possibility of banning antidemocratic parties was used in the fifties against neo-Nazis as well as Communists. Today, however, the political usefulness of such a step is as debated as the question about the exclusion of political extremists from state employment. In particular, foreign criticism of this consequence of militant democracy is frequently based on a lack of awareness of how liberal the Bonn system is and what strict constitutional guarantees of the basic rights it provides, qualities that distinguish it from many other democracies.

It is precisely the principle of a *state based on the rule of law* that has been particularly broadly developed after the deterrent experiences with totalitarian dictatorship. The constitution opens with the basic rights. These rights hold a position of priority, they cannot be touched in their essence. The principle of the separation of powers serves as a protection against a dictatorial concentration of power; it benefits above all the independence of the judiciary and the critical importance of the Federal Constitutional Court. At the same time, however, the aim has been to strengthen the parliaments and government. Parliaments are strengthened by the recognition that parties are the bearers of the formation of the political will (the principle of the party state). The government is strengthened by the strong position of the chancellor, in whom parliament can express its lack of confidence only constructively, through the election of a successor by a majority of its members, while a vote of no confidence against individual ministers is not possible at all ("chancellor democracy").

General legal security and the primacy of the law, the right of all citizens to a legal hearing, and the legal justification of all measures taken by the state: these principles of the state based on the rule of law deserve special consideration at a time when the complicated tasks of the modern industrial and welfare state are leading to a continual increase in bureaucracy and the danger that the citizens will be alienated from the state. The difficult fight against terrorism must also adhere to the rules of legal procedures; this makes it more cumbersome and less efficient than is desired, but it protects it against the danger of dictatorial arbitrariness.

Another important element of West German democracy is its *character as a social state*. This corresponds to the general demand for equality of opportunity and social protection, but also to the great social transformations brought about by the war as well as the flight and expulsion of more than 10 million Germans. The constitutional obligation to promote social justice was directed at achieving a balance between the various social classes and a humane social order. But in strict contrast to a socialist system, the liberal structure of state and society was to be maintained. This could be done neither through a nationalization of the economy nor through an unfettered capitalism, but via the continuously renewed balancing of social and economic interests. To be sure, the Basic Law and the compromise of the founders of the constitution in 1949 do not in principle oppose limited planning and socialization. However, "the spirit of the Basic Law and of the social market economy do reveal a high degree of congruence, for the liberal basic rights are excellently reflected in economic freedoms such as the freedom of consumption, of trade, of contract, of competition, and of labor" (Dietrich Scheiffele, *Zeitschrift für Politik* 35 [1988]: 329 f.).

The forty-year history of the Federal Republic has thus been marked by continuous arguments over the appropriate implementation of this postulate of the social state. In this debate the opinions diverge quite strongly to this day, because the constitution naturally does not contain any instructions on how to manage the problems of delineation in particular cases. The tension between social and capitalist principles has found its expression in the idea of the "social market economy," and in the ongoing development of codetermination *(Mitbestimmung)* in companies as well as in the strong role of unions. Yet this mixed system has proved to be a viable compromise between social and liberal interests. It makes possible a remarkable degree of stability and efficiency in the West German economy, a higher living standard, and a lower inclination to strike among the workers than exists in other democratic industrial states. The main problem now is a predominantly structural unemployment.

Finally, a fourth fundamental characteristic of the West German democracy is its *federalist system*. It, too, combines older German traditions with the rejection of National Socialist centralism and with the influence of the occupying powers. The Federal Republic was created from the union of the states that existed in the western zones of occupation and West Berlin, and these territories retained their own weight politically, economically, and culturally. This makes the political system more complicated than those in centralized democratic states, as in neighboring France, or in centralized dictatorships, as in the GDR. But its advantages are obvious: through decentralization of the political processes, federalism makes possible a greater degree of control over power and a greater closeness to the citizens; the possibility of more self-government on a regional level is an important corrective against the threat of overwhelming power on the part of the state. Federalism has the effect of separating powers, it expands the possibilities of political participation and responsibility by parties and groups, and it prevents the unbalanced concentration of power around a single center (like Paris or London), which could harm the development of the rest of the country.

IV

Looking at these basic principles of political orientation (which the Parliamentary Council has in part already placed beyond the possibility of constitutional change), four developmental phases stand out.

1. The time before and during the foundation of a new democracy in Germany, the forties, was marked by the political vacuum of the "German catastrophe" (Friedrich Meinecke) and the "farewell to past history" (Alfred Weber). The search for political and governmental orientation was marked by the dual experience of liberation from the self-inflicted dictatorship of National Socialism and the threat of a new, this time externally imposed, Communist dictatorship in the east of Europe, with the division of Germany becoming increasingly evident. Most important, however, in the Federal Republic there was established—concurrent with the anchoring of the basic rights—the principle of the "militant democracy," which was set against the Weimar experience of democratic helplessness. It was necessary to defend against a German political tradition that has always swung back and forth between two extremes: between a deification of the state and a withdrawal from the state, between the authoritarian state and radicalism.

The double experience of totalitarianism—of German totalitarianism in the Third Reich, of Communist totalitarianism in Eastern Europe and later in the GDR—was the starting point for the quick reorientation and new orientation in West Germany. From the beginning of the fifties, this also increasingly made possible a positive self-determination: above all through West Germany's incorporation into the West and into the beginning of Western European unification, which, sooner than anyone had expected, allowed West Germany's return to the community of free states and an upswing in the economic and social conditions. This development also changed the perception of the often-misinterpreted American democracy, which was transformed into a positive model.

2. This process of change in and the regaining of the conception of the state in the free part of Germany appeared to find its confirmation in the quick economic success story of the Federal Republic, though of course with considerable, still-unsolved implications and limitations. In the older German idea of the nation, the conception of the state and the conception of democracy had drifted apart in the course of the nineteenth century. By contrast, in the second German democracy it is the conception of the state and the conception of the nation that no longer mean the same thing. The

reconstruction on new lines was, from the beginning, marked by the persistent tension between the reestablishment and consolidation of parliamentary democracy in West Germany and the demand for national unity, for a solution to the "German question" on the principle of free self-determination. While the fifties were animated by the growing confidence that Bonn was no (longer) Weimar, what tended to be suppressed was the fact that, for now, neither the strengthening of the West nor the productivity and stability of the second German democracy drew national "reunification" any closer, let alone made it almost automatically possible.

3. The sixties were different: the attention and commitment especially of the increasingly vocal postwar generation, which was removed from the immediate experience of the time when the new state was established, were focused on a change of the domestic conditions and the fulfillment of the democratic ideals, in the process unleashing a revolution of rising expectations. There was a turn inward, with the postulates and battle cries for total democratization and universal codetermination in the state and society, and for the abolishment of that older German tension between the conceptions of state and democracy, which had emerged in 1848 and 1871, 1918 and 1933.

But there was also a turn outward, where a Third World was emerging beyond the East-West confrontation, a world to which the desires and goals of the new generation could attach themselves. At the same time those hopes and desires aroused in many renewed doubts about America, now seen as the fading model or point of orientation, especially in the eyes of the critics of the Vietnam War. The key year of 1968 signaled both of these things: self-criticism of the West and its values and, simultaneously, the hope for a freeing effect of a policy of détente that transcended the hostile camps of democracy and dictatorship. In both currents the political ideas and the change of consciousness of the younger Germans, especially, were heavily involved; neither the Soviet intervention in Prague in 1968, nor the social-liberal "change of power" in Bonn in 1969 were able to exert any significant influence over the change that was taking place.

More than ever before, the great decisions that had been made and the course that had been set in the early postwar years were now questioned: in foreign and domestic policy, on both political as well as moral grounds. Moreover, the quarrel over the application of the concept of totalitarianism to the Communist systems and of the concept of fascism to Western authoritarian regimes was not only about the comparability of dictatorships from the Left and the Right; it also became symptomatic of the "questioning" of a West German conception of the state, which, after all, rested not least on the antitotalitarian postwar consensus and had led to the increasing affirmation of the second German democracy.

4. The zeitgeist of the seventies developed above all in two directions, which partly overlapped and partly succeeded one another. Alongside the radically democratic progressivism of the protest movements, a wave of pessimistic ideologies emerged on the Left and the Right. And discussion about the slogan of the *Tendenzwende* (the conservative comeback in 1975) signified, at the same time, a clash between different conceptions of politics and democracy. This had an unsettling and polarizing effect on the changing political culture and its values, and threatened to put the Federal Republic's basic consensus in question.

Of course, there also emerged another important difference between the first and second German republics. It is that today nearly all political forces emphatically invoke the constitution, whereas prior to 1933 the dominant trend was to exclude the constitution or to struggle against it. It is true that back then a broad literature existed for the interpretation of the Weimar Constitution, and that jurists knowledgeable in it were leading voices in the parties no less than they are today. But the nearly diametrical difference from Weimar can probably be reduced to this formula: back then the democratic Weimar Constitution itself seemed to too many a bothersome nuisance that should be circumvented, whereas today the intensive interpretation and use of the Basic Law is precisely what has moved it into the center of the political calculation and arguments of all groups. All invoke it, with shared emphasis and at the same time competing intent, as the basis for and justification of their own political endeavors. Over the years this tendency has become stronger everywhere: a sign of "normalization" in the adjustment to the function of the constitution as the foundation of the state. Up until the banning of the radical parties in the fifties, this process was by no means self-evident, and in the radical parties, at least, it was controversial. Today the problem is precisely the reverse, in that, for example, in the controversies over the employment of radicals in public service, a declaration of loyalty to the constitution is no longer sufficient as a criteria, because, with the exception of fringe groups, it is affirmed in all political camps, at least verbally.

The conception of the constitution and the system is remarkable not only in comparison with the Weimar Republic, but also in view of the fact that the political consensus in German society is by no means as uniform as is often claimed by those who look only at the economic prosperity and its reflection in elections that demonstrate agreement with the system. In reality the understanding of the constitution has been marked—from the very beginning, when the Basic Law was created, to today, forty years later—by quite divergent convictions and expectations. These manifested themselves at the time of the first German Bundestag in a multitude of parties, but then gradually lost their intensity in the course of the subsequent consolidation of the chancellor-democracy and the party system—they accommodated themselves to the development that was taking place.

A constitutional consensus emerged thanks also to the exceptionally important effectiveness of the Federal Constitutional Court. Moreover, the consensus was supported by the irrefutable connection between the creation of the constitution and the attainment of greater independence for a German policy toward the occupying governments. This helped bring about that a constitution with such a decisive and substantial structure could be created and accepted, even though the conceptions of democracy of those involved as well as the national or post-national understanding of constitution and the state contained considerable contradictions.

V

The strains with which the Federal Republic was increasingly confronted in the sixties—a U.S.-Soviet rapprochement and a crisis of the European policy—revealed, of course, the vulnerability of the West German position and caused symptoms of unrest that indicated the old and new weaknesses of the German democracy. The temporary rise of the authoritarian-nationalistic National Democratic Party of Germany (NPD), on the one hand, and the equally quick radicalization of anti-authoritarian, neoromantic student and youth movements, on the other, manifested the potential for crisis that, since the fall of the Erhard government and the experiment of the Great Coalition, had been working toward a new polarization. The political reactions to every recession, real or only feared (as in 1966 and 1967), stirred up fears that an economic crisis like that of 1930 could have a serious impact on such a sensitive system built on social and economic progress. Thus, beginning in 1967, in a time marked by economic recession, the Vietnam War, and student unrest, the reservations about the Bonn democracy were temporarily strengthened. The rise of right-wing radical nationalism and of left-wing radical utopianism profited from the ill feelings about the Great Coalition, which seemed to provide little room for effective parliamentary opposition in questions such as the emergency powers bill, because only the small FDP stood opposed to the government. The situation tempted rebellion against the parliamentary establishment and against the system itself. Antisystem literature became for a time an intellectual fashion, from which the anti-capitalist, neo-Marxist agitation of the New Left profited. The ghosts of Weimar appeared: extreme polarization and antiparliamentarianism from the Right and the Left.

Yet the subsequent development revealed how much more stable is the foundation of the second democracy in Germany. This emerges most forcefully in the efficient party system, in the continuity of government in the chancellor-democracy, and in the rebuffing of those right-extremist and left-extremist groups that had destroyed the life of the first republic. These characteristics also hold in view of the new challenges by German and international terrorism, which culminated in the murder of the Chief Federal Prosecutor Siegfried Buback and the economic leaders Jürgen Ponto and Hanns Martin Schleyer in 1977 and 1978, and also in view of the controversy over an infiltration of public service by extremists. The antisystem slogan of the "march through the institutions" is countered by the constitutional self-conception of a militant, defensible democracy. As long as this democracy does not waver in its fundamental principle of antitotalitarianism, and does not yield to the trends and campaigns to rattle it, the ghosts of Weimar—the dangers of excessive tolerance toward those who seek to abuse the rights of freedom for antiliberal goals—will be kept at bay.

That Bonn is not Weimar was also signaled by the changes of government in 1969 and 1974, that once again returned the Social Democrats to the two highest offices of the state after a forty-year interval: the émigré and resistance fighter Willy Brandt as chancellor, the prominent Protestant Gustav Heinemann as president. Heinemann's successor from 1974 to 1979 was Walter Scheel, who previously, as foreign minister, had been jointly responsible for Brandt's Eastern policy of détente. The new leadership, and with it the ability of the system to function, had to prove itself in dealing with basic problems that had been put off for a long time, namely the painful consequences of 1949 for the German problem and for Germany's eastern borders.

The policies of Helmut Schmidt (1974 to 1982) sought to mediate effectively between the party and state-political and the ideological and pragmatic positions to which the German policy was subjected in a period marked by over-hasty hopes associated with the policy of détente. It is true that the Federal Constitutional Court confirmed that it was a constitutional commandment to keep open the German question, but there is no way one can find in this a policy that vacillates between West and East. The Federal Republic remains dependent on being a part of Western Europe and on the progress of the policy of integration, to which it owes its existence and development. Only if the possibility of pan-European cooperation took more concrete form would the question of a political rapprochement between the two states in Germany, and their reunification, arise anew. But this presupposes the kind of changes in the world-political constellation that can hardly be expected even in the longer view. The immediate task continues to be the further interlinking of free Europe and the expansion of its capacity to act. In this sense the Kohl government, under the presidents Carstens and Weizsäcker, has since 1982 no doubt represented the basic positions of the Germany policy.

The secure course of economic and alliance policies, to which the Federal Republic owes its consolidated position in Europe, cushioned the disappointment over the renunciation of national unification. To be sure, the road from the refusal to recognize the division and the GDR to their gradual acceptance proved to be long and painful. But it spared the politicians who clung to the official thesis of reunification, as well as the population that was slowly growing accustomed to the status quo, the dubious test of having to decide between a democratic orientation toward the West and a neutralist or pro-Soviet policy of reunification.

Through its rapid development and stabilization as a parliamentary democracy, the Federal Republic attained, sooner than expected, a new, more adequate role as a medium-size power with a close relationship to Western Europe. It also developed a liberal self-conception, but without dreams of being a great power. In this the Federal Republic is representative of the possibilities inherent in a free Europe. This Europe has had to relinquish its role as a political world power, though it has been able, through rapid reconstruction and strong cooperation, to regain part of its importance as an economic power and a pillar of democracy within the framework of a larger community, the Western political and cultural community.

VI

Of course from the very beginning there also existed forces fundamentally critical of parliamentary democracy. In 1949 and later, they manifested themselves primarily in the continuity of right-wing authoritarian and antidemocratic ideologies of the state. However, what has especially been gaining strength since the sixties is a criticism of the supposed failure to implement the Basic Law in the sense of a total democratization of society. Based on extremist demands, this criticism has placed an excessive strain on the constitutional norms. The final consequence of this current of criticism—a consequence that seems paradoxical but is not—is the demand that the system be smashed or overturned; however, it leaves open the question of where this is supposed to lead: to the supposed total implementation of the constitution or to its abolition.

At this point the rigorous confrontation between norms and reality can actually work against the existence and function of the constitutional system, regardless of the fact that this confrontation takes place emphatically in the name of the constitution. If it is correct that the Weimar Republic was essentially destroyed by the abuse of its constitution and the extensive use of constitutional tolerance by right-wing extremist enemies of the constitution, we may now be faced with a politically reversed, left-wing extremist destruction of the constitution. This attempt seems to be adapted to the structure of the Basic Law, which sprang from the experiences of Weimar. The undermining of the "system" is now pursued by invoking the Basic Law and at the same time overtaxing it with a perfectionist concept of democracy. In the final analysis this also amounts to an elimination of the constitution through its abuse. In both cases the argumentation rests on a radical critique of the empirical party state, and on a plea against what is disdainfully dismissed as bourgeois-liberal, representative "formal democracy," to which is counterposed a form of (grassroots) "democratization" that is plebiscitary and embraces the total state and the total society. Therein lies, incidentally, the affinity—strange but not accidental—between extremisms of the Left and the Right. Whether they argue from the Right for an authoritarian state, or from the Left for a democracy of soviets, we know from experience that the consequence of either is dictatorship.

When the imperfections and weaknesses of the empirical system of government and the social order are elevated to a structural and systemic crisis of the liberal constitutional system, to which is opposed an absolute ideal of "pure" democracy, the perspective on what is politically possible is lost, and the alternative of dictatorship moves—intentionally or unintentionally—within reach. This situation is reminiscent of the method used by the political theorist Carl Schmitt during the Weimar period, a method that was disastrously influential. By comparing a theoretically idealized parliamentary democracy with the empirical circumstances of power in the Weimar Republic, he construed an unresolvable contradiction within pluralistic democracy as such, and thus eventually came around to justifying the total state.

Segments of the New Left, and prior to that of the "critical theory" movement, have borrowed this method of using excessive demands, changing only the ideological banner under which they employ it. The notion of a "public" free of political domination, part of classical liberalism, was used to indict the representative system as "late-bourgeois" and ready to fall. (Habermas used this same notion in sharp dialectical opposition to the socioeconomic and technocratic incrustations of modern parliamentary democracy; in the meantime, of course, he has softened his view again). The constitutional order of this system, it was said, would eventually degenerate into a facade or a pretext for unfettered rule; reality would force its way to bring about the great transformation, in the Marxist or neo-Marxist sense. Once again we observe a deep affinity of right-wing and left-wing ideological arguments against the constitutional state with separated powers, no matter whether the arguments are technological or radical-democratic in origin. In contrast to the twenties, today these arguments are directed not only against fragile crisis-ridden systems that, like the Weimar Republic, exist only with controversial emergency regulations and feeble parliaments. The criticism is also aimed at the principle of the constitutional state itself and is directed at precisely those states that, like the Federal Republic, constitute stable democracies supported by broad segments of the population and with a differentiated distribution of power. It is not only functional weaknesses that are taken as indications of crisis; the representational system itself is questioned. A "whiff of totalitarianism" (to use Sontheimer's phrase), indeed of a totalitarian conception of democracy (as defined by J. L. Talmon) can be detected, one that reminds us of the time of political seduction and ideological perversion.

Yet no matter how much these extreme trends have sought to unite in the demand for a complete "alternative" and for participation in the rise of the ecological Green Party, which is critical of the system, they have been unable, all sympathies and fears notwithstanding, to shake the stability of the second German democracy, much as terrorism has failed to do so.

VII

Where does the contentious and persistent national question now stand? Even Alois Mertes, a politician with a deep awareness of history, has demanded that the German question be seen in the first place as a human rights question and not merely a territorial one. This brings us immediately to the discussion of the fashionable expression, "national identity." In all of this it has remained unclear, even after forty years of discussion about Germany, what it really means "to acknowledge oneself," as the historian Golo Mann, friendly observer from the outside and the inside, has long demanded in the new debate about national identity. After the experiences of a confused German history, he has professed himself to be a citizen of the world, "Swiss and German, too." His response to the German discussion in favor of a pan-German disengagement and placement of the national question above the Western European and Atlantic relationships of the Federal Republic was not without irony: "As for the rest, one is simply identical with one's own self, with all the difficulties many identities bring."

Such thoughtful voices seek the answer not in the sharp alternatives of the theory of the nation-state, but in the priorities of liberal democracy and European peace. For the political problem of the state cannot, of course, be solved by those concepts that place the new point of reference in the "cultural nation," even if the bond of culture is understood as a replacement for a political bond around Germany west and Germany east. And the reanimation of the feeling of homeland *(Heimat)* might be seen primarily as a compensation for the political realities of the division (as Wilfried von Bredow has argued). The opinion polls also fail to supply clear answers. If the great majority continues to declare itself in favor of the constitutional postulate of reunification, at the same time it also identifies with the Federal Republic of Germany as a state. What had become blurred by the hopes of a "change through rapprochement" reveals itself: that the fundamental difference between democracy and dictatorship, the division into freedom and unfreedom, is the real factor of self-determination.

Apart from the linguistic and cultural criteria that constitute nation, it is the *political* criterion that now, forty years after the "zero hour," is becoming a historical criterion and is gradually leading the question about German identity away from the expectation of reunification. Freedom or reunification? The question raised by Karl Jaspers (1959) was still hotly debated ten years after the founding of the Federal Republic. But the fundamental German interest, reflected in the political elections and liberal choices of the German population (where this is possible), remains the association with the political and historical tradition of the liberal-democratic West. As complex as the problem of national identity continues to be for the Germans, today the nation-state appears as only one level among many for political decisions and identifications. For "the safeguarding and development of freedom and democracy among ourselves and others, who need our support and cooperation, is the irrevocable task of our politics at present and in the future" (Alexander Schwan).

However, one must not forget that the Germans in the GDR continue to be the victims. And if a look at the more recent literature of the GDR has led observers to note a linguistic "movement of convergence" (Hans Mayer), such a movement in the *political* realm is not in sight; rather, there is emigration, expatriation, and a domestic wearing down. To keep rattling at the German question and dreaming about it in despair, to refuse to accept dependencies and realities: such tendencies feed the German restiveness and gnawing dissatisfaction with the world. These sentiments can also undermine and destroy what the West possesses in terms of political freedom, which is what preserves the hope for a nontotalitarian future for Europe as a whole.

Today even nation-states that seem consolidated and are self-contained and historically grounded have their problems of identity. This holds true not only for developing countries and new states. A look at the older, continuity-conscious democracies of the West, even more so at the ideologically driven dictatorships of Communism and the Third World, reveals the extent to which the nation-state organization is today overlaid with supranational conditions and economic and intellectual factors, and also with special social and regional ties. Despite the continuing importance of the German question, the Federal Republic of Germany is not a special case that consigns the Germans to a *Sonderweg*, or special path. Dramatizing its central geographic location, as is repeatedly done in the discussion of national identity, could mean repeating the complaints and arrogant ideas of a German past that eventually went astray.

Rather, the geographic location of the Federal Republic makes it an open, vibrant arena for all contemporary trends, and certainly also for airing fears and dreams that cannot be so openly expressed in the GDR and the countries of Eastern Europe. In comparison with the second German democracy, which is sustained by the West, the "central location" of the Eastern European countries is much more difficult; they are much more dependent and encircled, their prospects for the future are much more uncertain. But that is why much depends on the trust and support of the Western partners of the Federal Republic. The tension in a Europe that continues to be divided can only be endured if all sides adhere to the fundamental, mutual contract of the European-Atlantic community.

Just as the difficulties with European integration do not justify a notorious Euro-pessimism, there is also no cause for a special Germano-pessimism. Through the times of turbulence since the midsixties, the Federal Republic has shown itself to be a productive and adaptable, stable and open community. Even if one hesitates to speak of a "German model," one can certainly point to its successful system of a social market economy and its strong position among the modern industrial states. Between exaggerated pride in what has been accomplished and excessive self-criticism of the imperfections of its pluralistic democracy, the Federal Republic, more so than any previous German state, offers possibilities for an identification with the liberal tradition. The European-Atlantic community provides the backing it needs to stand up to the special challenges under which it has existed since the end of the German dictatorship: first, to live as a postnational democracy among nation-states and thus—in any case favored and privileged compared with the inhabitants of the GDR—to bear the consequences of the self-inflicted dictatorship and the subsequent division of the nation; second, to do justice to the experiences of both the first democracy that failed and the new democracy that has succeeded, as a signal and a bearer of the hope for German freedom—regardless of whether or not an end to the division of Europe and Germany moves closer.

Keeping the German question open is possible only if it rests on this primary decision in favor of the West and liberal democracy, and if it regards the fundamental difference between the systems as a decisive touchstone for a policy of détente. While such a policy strives for an "opening of the system," it must reckon with the a Communist policy of coexistence that continues to be antagonistic, and it must prove to be a match for it. Otherwise we are talking not about keeping the German question open, but about a relapse into older (and more recent) illusions about a special German path.

VIII

Let us look back. Germany's road to becoming a nation-state in 1870–71 was historically difficult and politically complex; it amounted to a rebellion against Germany's location in the middle of Europe and led, even under the favorable conditions of the victory over France and of the Bismarck era, only to an incomplete nation-state. The country's turning against the West and its nationalistic revisionism led, after World War I, to isolation and destruction, first of the democracy and then of the Reich. And so the question of how German liberty could be saved politically after the defeat of 1945, and in what sort of state it should be organized, addressed the very problem of a German democracy that was not a nation-state and yet was defensible and worthy of being defended.

Expressing this specifically as a consequence of the Soviet policy of expansion and of antitotalitarian self-affirmation, one might say that the "*raison d'état* of the Federal Republic" (in W. Besson's phrase) lay first and foremost in its liberal-democratic identity with the West. There can be little question that it was precisely this supranational orientation, which had no illusions when it came to Soviet power and ideology, that guaranteed the republic a more realistic starting point for assuming responsibility on a level that included all of Germany (from economic relations to the human rights policy of the Conference on Security and Cooperation in Europe), and not least as a beacon and bearer of hope for the people of the GDR.

I therefore share Alexander Schwan's misgivings about the very concept of a national-collective identity, one which, especially in the German experience, is subject to the abuse of being politically absolutized—from Rousseau's *volonté générale* to the *Volksgemeinschaft*. Given the historical and political preconditions of our situation, a declaration in favor of German unity, an end to the division of the nation-state, is thinkable only within the framework of a European solution that accords the highest rank to the liberal-democratic constitution. That is also the precondition for the "free self-determination" of which the Basic Law speaks—though not with the precedence of unity over freedom. It would be disastrous to play the concept of national identity off against the commitment to liberal democracy. This is precisely what I have called a "post national democracy"—

and why this description of the German problem (or dilemma) still strikes me as apt and honest.

There is no simple answer to the question of which factors should be singled out to account for the remarkable development of the Federal Republic of Germany toward the normality of a democratic state: foreign policy, economic policy, and domestic policy are all equally involved. Considerable importance must be accorded, in any case, to the constitution, its acceptance and implementation, and to the democratic defense against dictatorial or neutralist challenges from the outside and radical tendencies from the inside. But in the final analysis, what is and remains of fundamental significance is the integration of the Federal Republic into the supranational framework of a European policy: its renunciation of power politics, so disastrous in its National Socialist incarnation; its striving for partnership with its neighbors; and its awareness of mutual interdependence in the economic and political spheres.

The constitution of the Federal Republic took this factor into account in a special way when it provided for a limiting of the sovereignty of the nation-state "in favor of international institutions" and "for the maintenance of peace" and the "prevention of an offensive war" (Articles 24 to 26 of the Basic Law). This is something quite new in the history of modern states, but it is in keeping with Germany's position as a country in the middle of Europe, a country that continues to be strongly affected by the further development of the East-West conflict and the North-South problem, in a situation marked by the division of Europe and Germany. The supranational openness, reflected in the constitution, benefits the European policy and the German-French relations that are fundamental to it; the German-French relations are a particularly powerful demonstration of the profound change that has occurred, when compared with past history. And so Dolf Sternberger has put forth "constitutional patriotism" as the core of the conception of the state, transcending the problematic efforts toward a reunification of the German nation-state.

Above all, the German experience of the past four decades shows that liberal democracies, even under considerable stresses and strains, can be more viable than the dictatorships that dominate most of the world. The development of the Federal Republic has produced what is so far the most liberal and most highly developed state-community in German history. It has not solved the problems of the division of Germany and the East-West conflict, for those rest not least on the fundamental difference between democracy and dictatorship. The painful part of the German experience is that this conflict must not be resolved at the expense of democracy, when it comes to the question of national unity. In this way the German experience also contributes to the all-important defense of liberal national policy, which we owe, as well, to those who cannot determine their own form of government—and who still hope that history will not be finally swallowed up by a sea of dictatorships.

The close relationship with the former "archenemy," our French neighbors, demonstrates to a special degree the profound change in political orientation and the new, promising situation of Germany and Europe, no matter how painful the continuing division of the nation might be. That is why I close this examination of the most recent Germany history and politics with two voices from France. A keen political scientist reminds us of the "original contract of the [Western] alliance—Germany chooses the West, but the West accepts the problem of the division of Germany as its own" (Pierre Hassner). And Robert Schuman, the great architect of Franco-German and European unity, left us this admonition: "We cannot refute the nationalism of the others by opposing it with our own nationalism."

The desire for Germany unity, too, can most likely be reconciled with the interests and concerns of others to the extent that the nation-state retracts its absolute claim to sovereignty and, with a further federalization of Europe (or better: a "Europeanization of Europe"), constitutes only one among several levels of politics. As a result the national solution to the German question would be seen as bearable for Europe and would thus become a realistic possibility in the first place. This also corresponds to the changing notions of "national interest," which today, in view of the international intertwinement, are increasingly less conceivable without a decided reference to Europe—whether we are dealing with economic, environmental, or security policy, indeed with the orientation of political values as such. Even the Soviet Union now believes that it cannot do without the slogan of the "European house" (an ambiguous slogan, to be sure) and close relations with the European Community.

The criticism of Brussels, popular not only in England, seems like a retreat in the face of the limitations on the claims of national sovereignty and autonomy. In view of the European intertwinement, a post- or transnational orientation of German democracy is also no longer suspect as a renunciation or even "betrayal" of the nation. Rather, it corresponds to the changing position of the individual states in a liberal-democratic community of states, which, precisely by virtue of being liberal and democratic, is radiating increasing appeal to the East. To be sure, the directly elected European Parliament must still be joined by a constitution for the European Community, which in the age of the quest for identity can give impetus and support to a *European* constitutional patriotism.

This is the burden and, simultaneously, the opportunity of our historical legacy: that we have, precisely for the sake of our national existence, an inescapable need for supranational orientation; that the democratic conception of politics must no longer fall behind a nation-state conception of politics; and that due consideration is thereby given, paradigmatically, to an increasingly interdependent world of states. And all this comes at the end of a century in which freedom was repeatedly in mortal danger as benighted national-imperial or social-imperial ideologies raised themselves over the values of democracy and human rights.

For the first time after centuries of war and oppression, the guiding idea of a new Europe offers the world a concrete and workable model of supranational conflict resolution and integrated cooperation to safeguard both freedom as well as peace. After the crimes of the National Socialist regime, and given the experiences of a period with such horrifying consequences for the people and nations of Europe, a German state is charged above all with a commitment to the basic political values of European-American culture, especially the protection and defense of human rights.[1]

16

The Germans and
Their Constitutions and Institutions

I

Three constitutions in the history of German democracy are celebrating their anniversaries in our time. The first, the constitution passed on March 27, 1849, by the National Assembly meeting in the Church of St. Paul in Frankfurt, was defeated 140 years ago by the power of courts and dynasties. The Weimar Constitution, adopted on July 31, 1919—70 years ago—by a strong majority (262 to 75) of the National Assembly in Weimar, came to grief in the crisis of democracy itself, but probably also because of its (dualistic) design as both a parliamentary and a presidential system. The third attempt, the Basic Law of the Federal Republic of Germany of May 23, 1949, has now "already" lasted 40 years, even though it was emphatically temporary and considered more provisional than all its precursors.

More so than almost any other state, the Federal Republic has been marked, from the beginning of its forty-year history to this day, by the decisive effort to take historical and political experiences into account and make use of them for the future. It offers an example of the importance that attaches to or is accorded to the weight and "lessons" of history—especially the three great experiences of the recent German past: the Weimar Republic, the National Socialist dictatorship, and the cold war. The lessons of history had a quite decisive influence on the constitutional decisions of the Parliamentary Council of 1948–49. Freedom, unity, and Europe were the envisaged goals, but the main concern had to be the creation of a new, more stable democracy. And so at the time it was especially the Weimar politicians (like Theodor Heuss) who opposed a repetition of the democracy-obstructing dualism of the parliamentary-presidential system, and resisted burdening the second German republic excessively with plebiscitary institutions, which Heuss called a "boon to every demagogue."

To be sure, to this day there have been repeated discussions about whether the actual or supposed lessons of history—as well as the structure of the political system as a "chancellor-democracy"—ended up safeguarding the governmental stability of the Federal Republic at the expense of political mobility and expression. In actuality, the conflict between representative and plebiscitary elements has been eased more successfully in the new democracy than had been the case in the Weimar Republic.

Historical experience was also reflected in the fact that, along with the stronger anchoring of the basic rights, the principle of a "militant democracy" was set against the Weimar example of democratic impotence. The object was to resist a German tradition of repeatedly vacillating between a deification of the state and a withdrawal from the state. Thus during the debates on the Basic Law, even liberals like Heuss asserted that alongside the rights of the individual, which were particularly worthy of protection after the tyranny of the National Socialists, the obligations of the citizen and the power of the state as a community were also among the basic preconditions for any democracy: "Every state, even the democratic one, rests on the authority to give commands and the right to expect that they are obeyed; the essential feature of the democratic state is that the mandate of power is limited in time and can also be revoked." The commitment to a power mandate limited in time was thus used as an argument against the two camps on either side of the moderate center: overly enthusiastic believers in the state were confronted with the clear temporal limit to power; those suspicious of the state, with the concept of a strong mandate to govern.

II

A constitution means, above all, two things: the historically evolved, general condition of a state and society, and the institutional form it has given itself in terms of norms and laws—the framework, that is, in which political life finds its orientation, develops, and restrains itself.

This dual meaning, this reciprocal relationship between constitutional order and political culture, is fundamental for the history of democracy in Germany. For neither a merely political nor a merely constitutional examination is sufficient to explain why the first democracy, the Weimar Republic, failed and why the democracy of Bonn is holding its own. Rather, we need a sharpened understanding of the changed historical context, an understanding that allows us to say, against the many apprehensions of the past forty years: Bonn is not Weimar.

Four decades ago nobody would have dared to predict as much. No historian, jurist, or social scientist, no politician or economist was—could have been—capable of making such a prediction. Germany's situation after the self-inflicted defeat of 1945 was far more catastrophic than it had been after World War I, for which it had borne only half the responsibility. Prospects for a better political future seemed incomparably worse. The country was staggering under the burden of wartime destruction and the loss of territories, the misery of refugees and the national division in the East-West conflict. Yet within a few years, a stable political, social, and economic order emerged; the German catastrophe was transformed into a democracy guaranteeing freedom and prosperity. This (wrongly mystified) "German miracle" was a result not least of the new constitutional order of 1949 and the main intent behind it: to convert the bitter, negative experience of the most recent German past into the positive creation of a modern democracy.

It is true that the West German constitution of 1949 was called, in an emphatically provisional way, "merely" the Basic Law, and indeed was almost seen as a "negative constitution" (in C. J. Friedrich's phrase), because it did not want to preempt a constitution for the whole of Germany. But the efforts of the constitutional founding fathers, most of whom came from the failed first German democracy, were from the outset focused on avoiding the mistakes of the Weimar Republic and drawing the constitutional lessons from its errors and omissions. It is true that this was bought at the price of accepting the German division for the time being: the unity of nation and state, invoked by the preamble to the Basic Law, receded into the increasingly distant future. However, this same Basic Law also demanded and guaranteed internal political stabilization on the basis of a liberal, pluralistic development of all population groups. In contrast to the dictatorial and coercive system of the GDR, the social and political strength of the West German state is based on competing parties and interest groups, on free unions and a federalist structure of democracy, on the protection of human rights and free elections, on the separation of powers and limits on the power of the government.

These essential preconditions for a liberal democracy were formulated more clearly and with greater binding force in the Basic Law of 1949 than had been the case in the Constitution of the Weimar Republic of 1919. Above all, however, they were also taken more seriously in practice, and were turned into the concrete basis for the political development itself. In the Weimar Republic, predemocratic traditions of the state still obstructed the working of the parliamentary democracy; eventually that Constitution was replaced by the emergency and dictatorial powers of the president, which in the end paved Hitler's way to total power. Cognizant of those bitter experiences, the constitutional founding fathers of 1949 were able to achieve a number of improvements that have proved successful because—

as time has shown—they countered essential weaknesses in the past democracies: instability, helplessness, and functional weakness. In this way the traditional criticism of the democratic process was also toned down from the outset. Identification with the state and the constitution advanced steadily among a broad segment of the population, unlike what happened following World War I. After a few years, a rather passive attitude toward the West German democracy gave way to the growing consent of a large majority, while antidemocratic groups shrank to the size of small minorities.

This positive habituation was without a doubt decisively reinforced by the economic progress and the growing measure of social security. Many critics of the Federal Republic find fault to this day with the dependence of political stability on the economic accomplishments of the system. They overlook the fact that they are intimately interconnected.

III

Among the stabilizing factors are four guiding principles. Closely interlinked, they are, by virtue of being inviolable in principle, beyond the reach of any constitutional change: the democratic principle, the principle of a state governed by the rule of law, the principle of the social state, and the federalist principle. Their absolute binding force applies to the federal level and to the states (see Chapter 15, pp. 238 ff.).

Whatever a constitution, and especially this constitution of the Basic Law, could possibly have accomplished under the given circumstances, the Basic Law did accomplish, far exceeding the expectations at the time. After the experiences of Weimar, there was probably no one in 1949 who would have believed that even the substantially improved Bonn version, with its focus on the stability and protection of democracy, was capable of the degree of workability and efficiency it demonstrated—especially in the transitional crises of the sixties; after the Adenauer era, in the changes of government in 1966, 1969, 1974, and 1982; and in the face of the economic, armament, and environmental problems since that time.

All the same, discussions in recent years raised the question of the future of the parliamentary democracy. What about its capacity to deal with stresses, and what about the "governability"—as the new fashionable word puts it—of the state, given the constantly rising demands on both its efficiency and its democratic qualities? There was gloomy talk about its being "difficult," indeed "impossible," to govern a democracy that was burdened in so many ways and that had so many demands placed on it. In their review of the developments of the seventies, leftist critics of the *Tendenzwende* (the conservative comeback) saw the debate over governability as a sign of a virtual "renaissance of conservative crisis-theories."

In actuality that discussion had been going on since the sixties, and in fact it can be traced back essentially all the way to the classical beginnings of the criticism of democracy (in Plato and Thucydides), and certainly to the modern discussion about democracy since Alexis de Tocqueville. The development toward mass democracy and the emergence of the welfare democracy placed continually rising demands on the state and caused an inexorable growth in the complexity of the state. As a result, the classic objections to democracy, and concerns as to whether democracy as a state was viable and capable of governing to begin with—whether the democratic principle did not, in fact, work as a critical, dissolving ferment, as Jacob Burckhardt asserted in his *Reflections on World History*—gained even more strength in our century. Moreover, as a declared reform democracy, the Federal Republic was, from the beginning of the social-liberal coalition, under pressure from political and social expectations as well as intellectual and ideological ones, and this posed the question of governability more sharply.

And yet it was certainly leftist authors who raised the "specter of ungovernability" at the beginning of the seventies, especially in connection with the claim that Western-capitalist, parliamentary democracy, and with it the Federal Republic, was falling into a "legitimation crisis." Jürgen Habermas wrote about the supposedly growing "legitimation problems in late capitalism," and in his wake there blossomed a considerable literature of doubt about legitimacy. This literature also framed the problem of the contradiction between declining resources and a rising need for state intervention, of the relationship between "welfare state and mass loyalty."

Above all, the debate revolved around the relationship between exploding "ideas about the goals of the state" and the actual possibilities of government—a problem that would also play an increasing role in the ecology debate. This set in motion a thorough discussion about "governability," subsequently conducted on a broad historical and political basis in two anthologies with that title (published in 1977 and 1979). The editors of and contributors to those volumes, and their critics, were all faced with the fact that, especially after the period of euphoric expectations and under the influence of the *Tendenzwende*, the state had more demands placed on it than ever before, not only as a legal and institutional structure, but also as a force for achieving political and social goals. If what had been achieved and the struggle against crises had to be understood in this comprehensive sense, the phrase the "excessively burdened state," which appeared again and again in this context, seemed justified. The state was driven to ever new planning and socially formative activities, without being able to sufficiently meet the continuously growing demands of the citizens and the proliferating citizens' initiatives.

Such an "overburdening of the government," which takes especially highly industrial democracies to the "limits of governing," contrasted with the general expectation that the state should be ready to take on all conceivable tasks. For as soon as the risks of political action become considerable, "the social leaders declare their impotence, for example in the fields of health care, education, and the economy" (K. Eichenberger). The same contrast was at work in the euphoria of governmental planning, because the establishment of countless planning committees contributes equally to expectations and disappointments as this planning "becomes more demanding in its means and goals, more abstract and rigid in its concepts, and in general grows in number, pace, and size" (F. A. Tenbruck). Added to this was the internal driving force of those who were doing the planning, which further complicated the process. One was confronted, therefore, with a "hypertrophy of governmental activity," which the old liberal critic of etatism, Friedrich von Hayek, had predicted early on. Daniel Frei saw the dwindling capacity for governing in the "gap between expectations directed at the state and its capabilities, a gap that is widening ever more ominously."

These critical observations and questions were raised whenever the discussion about governability found any evidence of such problems. This applied particularly to the allegations of party dysfunction, the perennial complaints about the excessive influence of associations and representatives of special interests, the old and new question about bureaucracy, and the question of the social state, which went hand in hand with the increased sensitivity to legitimation problems and the changing sense of values. Of course the slogan of the "change of values," stylized into the "silent revolution," proved to be an exaggeration. And a " paradigm shift" (Thomas Kuhn), as another fashionable phrase put it, occurred only to a limited extent.

To be sure, the traditional values of hard work and discipline, diligence and material satisfaction were confronted by private self-realization; the work-ethic conception of life was confronted by a conception that was emphatically anti-authoritarian: a dream of being instead of having, of social solidarity instead of ambition and competition. But this was possible only under the conditions of an affluent society and the accomplishments of a welfare state. The social shifts and emancipation movements, as well as the decline of religious and moral norms, were connected to a more long-term development that was definitely international in scope, but that found heightened expression in the Federal Republic because of the particularly pronounced generational conflict.

The expectation of revolutionary changes, nursed especially by segments of the younger generation, was contradicted, of course, by the nearly unchanged constellation of political parties in the Federal Republic as the seventies progressed. If we look at the situation from the perspective of electoral sociology, the pendulum, after the exceptional victory by Willy Brandt in 1972, definitely swung back to the situation of the late sixties. What marked the debate was not so much a rejection of the system or a crisis of legitimacy as a persistent disagreement about democracy and democratization. For the question of legitimacy and governability appeared fundamentally different depending on whether it was posed from a radical understanding of democratization or from the conception of a workable democratic state.

From a radical perspective, a democracy that was "only" representative was considered to be virtually undemocratic. Brought to its logical conclusion, this radical idea of democracy meant the acceptance of the ungovernability of democracy. But it was precisely from the camp of idealized democracy that the demand for the fulfillment of far-reaching individual and collective wishes came, against which the quality of the welfare state would be measured. All the more contradictory were the reproaches that were subsequently also leveled against Chancellor Helmut Schmidt, "the doer." Less government and simultaneously more government—that was the paradox. The core of the debate was, first, how and to what degree the constantly rising demand for participatory democracy could be reconciled with the expectation of an administration that functioned well and was simultaneously in touch with the citizens. Second, the debate revolved around the classic problems of the modern state itself and its continuing development on various levels: around the roles of the parties and special interest organizations, of parliament and bureaucracy, of the media and—recently—citizens' initiatives; and all this within a concept of limited government, one that was different from both the authoritarian state and the socialist, planning state, while being capable of handling its tasks.

The fact that questions about governability became such a central topic of discussion also had to do with the politicians and the government itself; they groaned under the flood of tasks and lamented the narrowing of their room for action as more pressure from shrinking funds and economic recession was felt. On one occasion, Helmut Schmidt, then head of the German government, was reminded of his strong position of leadership in the chancellor-democracy. In response, Schmidt, who was more qualified for the position of chancellor than anyone since Adenauer, insisted that he had at most a 5 percent margin for decision making: everything else, he said, was already decided and unchangeable, in the budget as well as in political planning. There is no doubt that the situation of the government and the state since the era of Brandt has been marked—more so than ever before in the history of the Federal Republic—by the "overload phenomenon," the international slogan for the overburdened state.

This situation also served as the starting point for the "movements" that, from the seventies on, complemented or confronted the party and parliamentary system of the Federal Republic with the claim that they were developing a new, more effective form of political participation. To be sure, on the communal level, voter groups or "city hall parties" had long existed alongside special interest groups; they competed with the parties and focused on certain people or issues. Now, however, in a more direct way and independent of elections, the objective was direct influence and action. The purpose of these movements, especially in environmental policy and city planning, but also in educational and social policy, was to give direct expression, in a very tangible way and on specific issues, to the concerns of those affected.

Most of all, however, a new political space opened up for idealism and activism, for the youth- and community-driven mobilization of the "emancipated citizen" *(mündige Bürger)* who was now so often talked about. The changes during the years of reform, and also the discussion that followed, offered numerous starting points for these forms of involvement by citizens who had previously been uninvolved. What was an expression of heightened self-confidence and greater readiness for conflict also proved to be an attempt to find new solutions—solutions the administration or the parties could pick up on. Of course this lengthened and unsettled the decision-making processes, but when credible arguments and democratic partners are involved in this process, there is no cause for concern. This development becomes problematic, however, when it involves uncompromising advocates or radical opponents of a given policy or project.

Looking back over nearly two decades of citizens' initiatives, we can see that some delays in political-governmental plans can be advantageous to the citizens affected by them, and can occasionally provide time to think about a premature decision that has been overtaken by economic developments: a human compensation, as it were, for the technical acceleration that has become possible in the age of the computer. The conflicts over energy needs and the construction of new highways are examples of the role of citizens' initiatives as correctives for the party and bureaucratic state. However, they play this role only so long as the political abuse of such initiatives and single-issue movements, abuse that has increased over the years, stays within limits; that is to say, if these movements do not present themselves as alternatives "against the system," with a minority's elitist claim to truth in the place of the will of the majority and its elected representatives.

The approach and concerns of the citizens' initiatives are perfectly legitimate from the perspective of the Basic Law, as they invoke the right of assembly and association (Articles 8 and 9), the free development of the individual and freedom of opinion (Articles 2 and 5), and the right of petition (Article 17). However, the citizens' initiatives are surely distinct from the parties, which are specifically commanded by the constitution to participate in the formation of the political will (Article 21). The initiatives do not possess any decision-making competence, and they cannot speak or act representatively for others.

This gap between demands and constitutional system, between movement and party, opened up fully with the establishment of the alternative Green Party, which at the same time wanted to remain a movement. In fact this gap was characteristic of a great many of the new initiatives and movements of the seventies from the very outset. Back then the ambivalence lay in the fact that already in many instances citizens' initiatives did not merely supplement the parties. Time after time they thought of themselves not only as a meaningful addition to the representative system and one that raised important questions in the public discussion, but also as something better in principle. In fact they sometimes contributed to the disintegration, indeed the fracturing of the community. In the end it was perfectly consistent that such movements sought to block the state entirely if it did not do what was considered right from a particular, often highly ideological perspective. The chairman of the National Association of Citizens' Initiatives for Environmental Protection, Josef Leinen, expressed this particularly forcefully at the mass rally for the peace movement in Bonn in 1982, when he said on television, for all citizens to hear: "If the politicians do not take us seriously, we will make this country ungovernable." By now, of course, Leinen himself has been governing since 1985 as a minister of the Saarland—it is thus possible to advance rapidly in a government career with the slogan of ungovernability.

IV

In contrast to what happened in the Weimar Republic, today it would seem that a pseudolegal strategy of using constitutional change to destroy the constitution is blocked. The Basic Law has learned the lessons of the past in two respects. First, in place of the High Court *(Staatsgerichtshof)* for the German Reich of the Weimar period, whose role was insufficiently understood and practiced, and above the president, who no longer dominates the government, it set up the paramount authority of the Federal Constitutional Court. Second, the pressure for parliamentary responsibility, which is exerted on the parties by the constitution and the institutions, keeps the governmental system of the Federal Republic largely free from the temptation to evade the functions it is supposed to perform. To be sure, today the popular road to Karlsruhe (seat of the Federal Constitutional Court), the replacing of politics with law, can lead to excesses "if every constitutional organ can attack others in this way with the charge of unconstitutional behavior" (Peter Lerche). But antiparliamentary, possibly soviet-state tendencies have a more difficult time, even if now, after the erosion of memories of the recent past from which we now suffer (a generational phenomenon), these tendencies must be kept in check less by reason and experience than by that very pressure from the constitution and the institutions. This should also give rise to greater, system-preserving restraint when it comes to constitutional changes. Both things—institutions and a constitutional sense—are thus necessary to master a crisis of democracy of this nature.

During Weimar, the short duration of the republic in stormy times hampered the maturing of a constitutional consciousness and the preservation of the new or changed political institutions. But the far longer period that has been granted to the second parliamentary democracy means, alongside the chance it offers for people to become accustomed to democracy and for democracy to take root, a constant challenge, which one can describe with such catchphrases as "generational break" or "dual contemporary history." If opinion polls show that the assimilation of democratic political norms and values is a more difficult process here than elsewhere in Europe, and especially more so than in the United States, this has to do with the multidimensionality of the historical frame of reference, with an ambiguity of the political consciousness. The conflicts that are carried into our situation by particularly burdensome historical experiences from such diverse periods as Weimar and the National Socialist era, the postwar period and the era of the economic miracle, heighten the conflict between the generations. At work since the end of the sixties, when the postwar generation grew up, this dual contemporary history, with its specifically German consequences, becomes visible especially in the high-pitched debate about German identity or in the excesses of the concept of resistance, in the phenomenon of the "resistance after the fact." That is why the danger to our political culture has not only not disappeared because of the longer and more successful lifetime of the second Republic but also, over the years, actually tended to increase again.

A renewed boost has been given, above all, to the concept and ideology of movements. As the supposedly true expression of the will of the people, as "antiparty parties," movements have always questioned pluralistic democracy. They base themselves on a plebiscitary and acclamatory notion of voting, which is contrasted to representative-parliamentary procedures as being supposedly "closer to the people." What this perspective overlooks is how decisions that allegedly require plebiscitary votes can be abused for the dictatorial usurpation of power. Of course democratic plebiscites on the Swiss model must be distinguished from dictatorial ones. However, against the argument that they raise the level of political involvement—the magic word "participation"—we should point out two things. First, the level of voter participation in this country is higher than in those democratic plebiscites. Second, experience has shown that the incitement of mass sentiments through frequent quasi-plebiscitary acts of voting can exacerbate a situation, especially in times of crisis such as existed between 1930 and 1933. Changing our political system in a more plebiscitary direction remains a risky prospect.

And, too, if political forms, which always also set values, are put in question by emphatically militant movements, namely with attacks against "formal democracy" (which is what makes the community predictable in the first place), there is a heightened danger of a "subjectivist interpretation of the law" by combatants and sympathizers. We have experienced this in the disastrous distinction between violence against things and violence against people—"and this in a country that witnessed Kristallnacht" (Hättich). Constitutional order is pushed aside in favor of an allegedly more valuable goal; legitimation crises are invoked; subjective content is placed above objective procedure. When so-called irreversible questions like the environment, peace, or the nuclear threat are at stake, there is supposedly "no alternative." This commonplace phrase actually violates the spirit of pluralistic and liberal politics. For the sake of humanity there are always alternatives, and one must be open enough to be able to keep them in mind and weigh them.

Finally, the dwindling memory of the experience of recent history also accounts for the fact that awareness of the fundamental difference of dictatorship has been receding inappropriately behind ideas of the convergence of the systems and the policy of détente, and that the concept of totalitarianism is being tabooed in entire branches of politics and the economy. The efforts to achieve "equal distance," as it is politely put, for a "third way" once again, not only touch on the spirit and the institutions of liberal democracy; they could also lead once more to the brink of its dissolution and self-destruction, no matter how different the circumstances and consequences might be.

Our historical experience with the development of the modern state and with a mass democracy that can change into a dictatorship makes times of crisis appear as ever new tests. The tamed conflict in democratic systems is already constantly challenged by voices that promise a conflict-free society, condemn pluralism, and hold out the prospect of liberation from the eternal problems of power and authority by replacing the struggle of interests with a one-track decision-making process in pursuit of lofty goals. This sort of thing has happened repeatedly since 1918 in times of great political crises.

Of course, since the end of the sixties the challenge has no longer been in the struggle over the slogan of democracy as such, which has long been used worldwide and in all political camps, from left-wing dictatorial popular democrats to right-wing authoritarian nationalist democrats. What is at stake now are the fundamental forms, values, and goals that are to give substance to the concept of democracy. An excessively behaviorist trend, which phrases the concept of political culture in anti-institutional terms, has taken hold of political education. A growing relativism of values is open to the manipulations of ideological temptations, and it does not spare the institutions of democracy: one sees this in the popular campaign against the basic liberal-democratic order (contemptuously dismissed as "the system"), which is the core of our value-oriented democracy.

Bitter experience led émigré constitutional scholars and political scientists like Karl Loewenstein to demand a "militant democracy" as early as 1936. Such a democracy involved measures to stabilize the government, the protection of basic rights, and the principle that tolerance is not due to those enemies of the democratic order who deny it to their opponents. This much was already known: it is possible to eliminate a democracy by using democratic rights and institutions. The infiltration and reorientation of the civil service, the ability of the governmental bureaucracy to smoothly "click into place" (to use Max Weber's phrase) under new power relations, was one danger; the destruction of the consensus for parliamentary democracy by parties hostile to the system was another. The strengthening of the institutions after 1945 with a policy on civil servants that was protective of democracy, by the party law, and by the law on the federal constitution thus amounted to a policy in support of democracy, not against it.

A decisive requirement of all political institutions of liberal democracy, one that sets it apart from all other forms of government, is that it must make possible the peaceful settling of conflicts in a pluralistic, open society, and guarantee the orderly change of government and transfer of power through the principle of majority rule. This peaceful enduring and overcoming of crises makes democracy the most difficult and simultaneously the most human idea. It makes its institutions imperfect creations yet flexible bearers of a social and political process that lies between the excessive elevation of the state and a lack of enthusiasm about it.

Liberal, parliamentary democracy continues to be vulnerable. But this highly complex and differentiated form of communal life, which definitely needs care and protection, can exist as a state only if the constitutional system and the practice of governing forgo nonparliamentary ways to the greatest possible extent. In this way it compels all political forces—through the acceptance of the rules, the "constitutional consensus"—onto the path of compromise and promotes the voluntary minimum consensus, especially in view of old and new apocalyptic voices of crisis.

After all, flexibility and fair functioning, and also self-protection and the capacity for resistance, are essential postulates for the institutions of a democracy if it is to do justice to its incomparable task: to offer the diversity and imperfections of humans a system that seeks the proper measure, constantly in need of balance, between dictatorship and anarchy, between rule and freedom. In this way we can also ward off the old German problem that Rudolf Smend a long time ago (in 1928) defined as "two sides of the same thing": "The inner insecurity toward the state, which vacillates between an underestimation and an overestimation of the state." If democracy is to be possible as a state—and not merely as an idea or a demand—it stands and falls with the understanding that respect for the institutions and rules of communal life is a value that even lofty goals and purposes cannot infringe on, just as the end can never justify the means.

Germany in Europe: Historical Changes and Current Perspectives between National Diversity and Political Unification

The history of Europe and of Germany has been marked, in this century that is drawing to a close, by three great historical and political turning points: by the catastrophic events and decisions of two world wars, and now by the epochal upheaval of 1989 to 1991, which is different in that we have experienced it so far as a predominantly peaceful revolution.

The recent upheaval brought the division of Germany and Europe, which had lasted for more than forty years, to an unexpectedly quick end. We are now faced with two great alternatives: the continuation of Western Europe's process of integration, now in a framework that embraces all of Europe, or the danger of a relapse into a new fragmentation of nation-states, similar to what existed in the period between the wars.

The Old Europe and the New

The history of Europe before and after World War I was in fact the history of numerous competing nations. After World War II it then became essentially the confrontation between two great blocs, but at the same time the old idea of the unity of Europe was for the first time seriously pursued. As early as 1929, in his world-famous book *The Revolt of the Masses,* the Spanish philosopher José Ortega y Gasset had written, in midst of the nationalistic surges between the wars: "If we were to take an inventory of our mental stock today—opinions, standards, desires, assumptions—we should discover that the greater part of it does not come to the Frenchman from France, nor to the Spaniard from Spain, but from the common European stock. Today, in fact, we are more influenced by what is European in us than by what is special to us as Frenchmen, Spaniards, and so on . . . four-fifths of [our] spiritual wealth is the common property of Europe."

The rediscovery of those shared European elements had already inspired "Europe movements" after World War I. It had raised hopes, though in the end those hopes were disappointed. In vain did Briand and Stresemann back then seek to promote French and German foreign policy in the European spirit; in vain did men like the later German resistance fighter Carlo Mierendorff, at the time a young Social Democratic member of the Reichstag, call for a "reflecting upon Europe" in 1932, on the eve of Hitler's seizure of power: "I am talking about the organization of Europe on the basis of a thinking that rises above the state, about overcoming the madness of the nation-state, which is being pushed to the point where it threatens today to drag the peoples of Europe down to ruin."

However, the decisive development of an independent European policy became possible only after Hitler's regime of totalitarian horror, after World War II, and in the face of the continuation of the Stalinist dictatorship. The world-political realities of the twentieth century, which had become apparent in World War I but had then been masked by the restoration of national-imperial power politics and colonial politics in the twenties and thirties, now took effect in all their sharpness.

The catastrophe of World War II finally brought the new factors and realities of European politics fully to light. Three great contexts emerged with increasing clarity and have remained dominant to this day. First: the European nation-states changed from being the subject of world history to being its object; the history of Europe no longer determined world history, it was no longer the embodiment of world history. Second: the sovereign individual states with the claim to great power status and colonial policy were replaced by blocs that were sharply delineated in terms of power politics and ideology. Those blocs solidified a division of Europe under the hegemony of the non-European superpowers, the United States and the Soviet Union, who had decided the war and determined the peace; it was a bipolar peace marked by forty years of cold war. Third: the division and external control of Europe, its destruction and self-destruction in two murderous wars and in a radical struggle between political systems and ideologies, which had been going on virtually without pause since the Russia's October Revolution of 1917, was offset after 1945 by an unexpectedly quick recovery and renewal of Western Europe.

Until that time, Europe had been shaped by the concert of powers and the coexistence and confrontation of nations who regarded themselves as the centers of the world and their national aims as the highest values in international politics. The existential crisis of this Europe emerged ever more starkly in the period between the wars. The catastrophe of World

War II and the collapse of the German dictatorship, the exaggeration par excellence of nationalistic and imperialistic Eurocentrism, were a turning point. It solidified the long-suppressed realization that the war had led to the defeat of the European states and nations and to the loss of Europe's position in the world. And so 1945 meant not only liberation from the terrifying totalitarian system of National Socialism, but also the painful letting go of illusions that had persisted since the end of World War I. This opened the way for the development of the kind of interstate and eventually suprastate politics that had previously existed only as an idea and a dream.

What was new in 1945 was Europe's position between two superpowers who sought to maintain the balance through division and containment. In accord with this new constellation was the new principle of a gradual unification of Western Europe (through institutions and processes) on the basis of the equality of all states—and with the goal of integration, not domination. This policy was directed against the previous hegemonic tradition of unification, as well as against a relapse into the tradition of multistate power politics.

If we extend our view even further back, the history of Europe, and that of Germany at its center, present themselves as a continual, almost dialectical conflict between two basic trends: the developmental drifting apart of states, nations, and cultures, and yet their close interconnection; difference and sameness; differentiation and standardization. Never before had Europe been a political unit. The medieval emperors had striven for a dominant position among the kings, no less and no more. The papacy, regardless of the strong cultural ties of the Church that bound medieval Europe together, repeatedly supported the princes and the "nation" against the universal claim of emperor and Reich. Universalism and particularism stood in a permanently tense relationship to each other, and outside powers, like the Turks and the Russians, were repeatedly brought in against any unifying power.

In the modern era, two prominent, though very different attempts were made after the beginning of the nineteenth century to implement the principle of unity by force: Napoleon's, between 1806 and 1812, and Hitler's, between 1940 and 1945. Both men failed. However, attempts to stabilize a balance of power also never had more than passing success. So long as Europe meant the world, European unity remained a distant dream, no matter how real the shared elements and interrelationships. The French and National Socialist conquests of Europe—regardless of whether they presented themselves with a claim to revolutionary and civilizational unification or with that of a new geopolitical and racial order—were nothing other than the politics of hegemony. The aim was the predominance of one European state over the others, an imperial policy in that old sense of the word, derived from the Imperium Romanum.

In the Middle Ages the idea of unification had an ideological and religious basis: the idea of the Roman Empire and the papacy formed the nuclei around which the process crystallized. The conflict between these two forces contained the starting point for the emergence of individual states. The modern period, on the other hand, virtually defined itself by the full independence of the individual states and their secularized *raison d'état*. The modern, sovereign state was followed by the establishment of the nation as the basic unit of political life. This meant the deliberate differentiation of Europe into various countries, in which political integration was pushed through on the principles of monarchic-absolutist one-man rule and the nation-state community. This process reached its climax in the nineteenth century.

Two factors were decisive for the subsequent change: economic and technical developments, which, from the era of industrialization and the revolutionizing of transportation, raised the level of interdependence almost in a single leap; and, after the weakening of Europe as a result of the Great War, the political development of the non-European world away from colonialism. This put Europe and its states increasingly into the position of being one power among many, but it also renewed the idea of overcoming political fragmentation through European federalism, the idea of a league of states or a federal state of Europe that had been making headway since the Enlightenment of the eighteenth century—as, for example, with the German philosophers Leibniz and Kant.

The Renaissance of Democracy

Thus the concept of Europe and its development after World War II were fundamentally different from the traditional forms within which European state power had arisen and continued to grow into our century. The far-reaching changes before and after World War I had still been largely covered up by older structures and illusions. It was only at the moment of the global decisions of 1945, which accelerated the process of long-foreshadowed change by introducing new factors, that the real trends of development became clearly apparent. The transformation of Europe, and of Germany, unfolded within four large contexts.

1. Outranking everything else was the realization that *world politics* was no longer based on a concert of powers emanating from Europe. This was already basically true in the period between the two world wars, but the realization of this fact on the part of the peoples of Europe and their leaders lagged far behind the realities of the time. The international weight of the

United States, the crises of the colonial empires, the rise of Japan, and the Eurasian potential of Russia were some of those realities of the interwar period. The inability to recognize them contributed to the failure of international reconstruction after World War I, thereby making Hitler's power politics possible in the first place. It is revealing that the League of Nations was, in practice, limited to the European dimension of the politics of power. It was unable to come to grips with the reality of a global expansion of international relations and the interdependence of states' political and economic problems. World War I and its consequences, the catastrophe of the worldwide economic crisis, and the rise of fascism, which caused a chain reaction, were expressions of the international intertwinement, in the face of which traditional national politics was obsolete. Only the rubble of 1945 signaled irrevocably the end of the modern period's classic politics of nation-state sovereignty, which had seen world history and world politics governed solely by Europe, by the confrontations and alliances of the European powers. Its place was now taken by supranational structures that divided Europe in two and were, simultaneously, wider in scope than Europe.

2. This far-reaching change in Europe's international position had a decisive effect on the *internal structure* of the European countries. This structure became dependent on the formation of blocs in foreign policy, which, in the wake of the confrontation between East and West, between Soviet and American hegemonic power, also shaped the ideological and domestic political scene. As early as 1946, a division of Europe into parliamentary, liberal democracies and Communist single-party regimes fell into place. This clearly differentiated Western European countries from Eastern European ones by their internal structures. Within the two systems, variations among different nations were important for assessing their values, national character, and political weight. However, the division of Europe influenced the internal structure even of those countries that had been able to maintain a certain degree of independence from the consolidating blocs. Outside the sphere of Soviet military control, in the neutral states of Sweden, Switzerland, and Austria, the Western, non-Communist form of government remained the model; on the Communist side, Yugoslavia, with its one-party system, constituted a special case, as does the multiparty democracy in Finland.

In contrast to the interwar period, when a pluralism of forces characterized both international and domestic politics and allowed a great variety of European states as well as the formation of fronts, a political arrangement was now put in place in which Western Europe comprised the states that were not under Communist rule. From this perspective, which went beyond the boundaries of geography and alliance politics, Western Europe described that part of Europe in which politics and governing rested on the pluralistic method of formulating political objectives—in the form of multiparty systems in which opposition and a change of government are possible. Exceptions, up until the seventies, were the authoritarian systems in Portugal and Spain, and for a few years that in Greece; at the same time, however, they demonstrated that being a part of the West in terms of international politics eventually led to an internal political structure along liberal democratic lines.

3. The *socioeconomic and cultural changes* in this "Western" Europe were marked externally by the destruction of the war, the shift in the population structure, and the retreat from non-European colonial territories. What was taking place over the long term was a reconstruction that had favorable prospects for modernization and industrialization; it superimposed itself on the traditional forms of nation-state politics and compelled new forms of cooperation that transcended the nation-state. This process, though it was certainly caused and favored by factors of military policy in the wake of the cold war, was not limited to the sphere of the Western alliance and bloc policy but also involved the nonaligned states. The development of this Western Europe—expanded but still limited—was based on particular economic, social, and cultural preconditions; at first these preconditions followed the line of the Iron Curtain, but with a loosening of the barrier between West and East, they also brought the gradual convergence of the systems within the realm of discussion.

4. The governmental system of parliamentary *democracy,* which had been destroyed soon after its introduction in 1918, mostly by authoritarian-dictatorial regimes, proved to have a surprising capacity for regeneration. In the years after 1918, the "crisis of parliamentarism" quickly became a popular slogan, and most of the new democracies fell victim to antiparliamentary movements within a short period. By contrast, after 1945 the Western-type parliamentary democracy attained a degree of stability that was surprising and previously impossible.

The experiences of the twenties and thirties had taught people to perceive modern democracy as a complex, constantly threatened, and by no means perfect form of government subject to continual transformation and adjustment under the conditions of industrialization and technicalization, of social restructuring and intellectual changes. Thus the preconditions for the reconstruction of parliamentary democracy in Western Europe after 1945 were better in three respects.

1. In terms of *constitutional politics,* the people of Europe had had painful experiences that were expressed in constitutional provisions to protect the democratic system, its ability to function, and its stability. These have been used with particular consistency in the Federal Republic

of Germany, but also elsewhere—most recently in the Fifth Republic in France—to contain fragmentation in favor of a stabilization of the parliamentary system.

2. *Sociologically* the transformations of the war and the postwar period led to the restructuring and fluidity of the traditional social structures—with the result that the parties became increasingly less ideological and more pragmatic. This made coalitions and compromises easier for the social and political groups within the system. It reduced the previous fragmentation of political society and strengthened the trend toward the emergence of two- and three-party systems, a trend that was promoted by constitutional provisions and electoral regulations. These transformations became particularly apparent in the development of West Germany, where the intermixing of society, caused by the flight and expulsion of millions from East Germany, exerted a corresponding influence. But in other countries, too, there were signs of social fluidity and mobility. They made the democratic process easier and simplified the formation of parliamentary objectives by tempering rigid ideological confrontations, promoting democratically cooperative forms of behavior, and defusing political conflicts in favor of practical compromises.

3. In terms of *foreign policy*, the stabilization of the Western European democracies was protected early on by a policy of alliance and cooperation that was fundamentally different from the Soviet claims to domination in Eastern and Central Europe. After World War I, an unrestrained nationalism had governed the politics of the European states and destroyed the basis of democracy at home; meanwhile the United States, which had decided the outcome of the war and had inaugurated the peace settlement and the League of Nations, withdrew from international politics. Things were different after 1945. Through integration into common Western European–Atlantic structures, which were a kind of protective umbrella over the new parliamentary democracies and made possible a less disturbed, less crisis-ridden development than had taken place after World War I, it proved possible to avoid a repetition of the systemic crisis of the prewar period.

In the midst of the misery of the second postwar period, the jumble of national ambitions was replaced by the concrete realization that a self-restraint on the part of national sovereignties was necessary. The resistance movements had already worked out far-reaching plans for closer European cooperation, indeed for political integration. The difficult situation of 1945 and 1946 could be met through a recognition of the economic, military, and political interconnections, not through isolated state politics. Such a recognition was made easier by the dismantling of the colonial empires, since it focused the attention of the European states on the tasks of internal structural reform and the policy of cooperation. The traditional tensions among the nation-states gradually faded in the face of these new problems, and the possibility of compromise between and within states increased.

This was particularly evident in the new West German democracy. After the respite of the occupation period, this democracy was able to develop and stabilize itself almost without any trouble, under the protective umbrella of the Western European and Atlantic alliance and in the face of the dictatorship in Soviet-occupied East Germany. The experience of a politically and economically efficient parliamentary democracy was something new compared with the interwar period, when people had grown accustomed to equating parliamentary politics with crisis and failure. Of course this came at the expense of national unity. Only West Germany continued to cling to an all-German citizenship, even after partition.

Germany before the "Big Change"

We have now come to the historical-political situation of Germany. The four decades of German history from 1949 to the "big change" of 1989 are the history of a divided nation: in the West, a new German democracy was built, which has been able to stand its ground more successfully than the first democratic experiment of the Weimar Republic; in the smaller East Germany, the GDR, the situation was unfortunately different.

The dual determination of recent Germany history after the total defeat of 1945 contained a tension that marked the unexpectedly quick establishment of two states in 1949. The postwar situation led the nation out of the "German catastrophe" of the Hitler regime through a continuous process of engaging the basic experiences of the German dictatorship between 1933 and 1945. But it also received a strong impulse from the highly topical confrontation between the superpowers in East and West—and from the completely opposite political values they represented: dictatorial single-party rule and liberal democracy.

This structure of tension determined the establishment and development of two different systems of government on the soil of the former nation-state, now reduced in size through expulsions and occupation. And it was further complicated and exacerbated by the military and economic strategies of the cold war, which, all affirmations of détente notwithstanding, continued in its essence until the end of the eighties.

However, Germany was not only the object but increasingly also the subject of developments that led within a few years to what seemed to be irrevocable decisions—decisions that have constituted political reality to the present day, though their continuing validity has been questioned many times. The *dependence* of German politics on the international power situation emerged, above all, in the great direction-setting decisions of 1948 and 1949. To begin with, the problems of coping with the consequences of the war, organizing reconstruction, and securing the necessary cooperation to accomplish these tasks were intimately linked to the integration of occupied Germany into European and world politics, divided along bipolar lines. But in the process, the capacity of German politics to *act* also soon regained weight.

This was especially true for the political orientation and democratic development of the Federal Republic. Its development revealed its fundamental difference from the Soviet-dominated establishment of the GDR and its political and social form as a "people's democracy" under dictatorial rule. Though both states were marked by the formation of blocs and were under the control of the victorious powers, the basic difference emerged with overwhelming clarity from the very beginning: instead of the "democratization" that was proclaimed during the first postwar years, the East witnessed the implementation of a Communist Party dictatorship; the West, meanwhile, saw the gradual transformation of the occupational regime into a system of international cooperation—with the historically important goal of changing the *negative control* of Germany into a *positive integration* with a European and Atlantic orientation.

This was in fact the momentous substance of the negotiations and treaties that led from the Marshall Plan to the Western European Union, the Council of Europe, the European Coal and Steel Community, and finally to the Germany treaties and the European Community. Here was also the fundamental difference from the first postwar period. Following World War I, the relapse into a Europe of nation-states had led to the fatal crisis of the democracies and to the dictatorial rise of aggressively revisionist movements and systems, most importantly Fascism and German National Socialism. But now, on this side of the Soviet sphere of power, a policy of close European cooperation with backing and support from the United States became possible. Its goal was economic as well as political integration, which could build on the plans of the resistance movements during the war and on a multitude of pan-European movements from the early postwar years. This policy also opened up concrete possibilities for a supranational—a "postnational"—solution to the problem of German statehood. For with a view toward economic as well as security policy, and especially toward the stabilization of the new German democracy, the idea of Europe acquired a powerful function: after the exaggerated nationalism of the National Socialist regime had reduced to absurdity the idea of the nation-state as the final authority, it offered a new, broader frame of reference.

The policy of the first chancellor, Konrad Adenauer, who headed the West German government from 1949 to 1963 (an unexpectedly long time), rested from the very beginning completely on that supranational aspect of the European policy. In the face of the power-political realities at the end of the forties, the nation-state arguments of the Social Democratic opposition, under the leadership of Kurt Schumacher, were not accepted as an alternative by the majority of the West German population. The proclaimed goal of national unification moved into the distance, while the stabilization of Western cooperation corresponded to the immediate need for reconstruction and security. Adenauer adhered to the so-called "magnet theory," according to which the growing attraction of Western living standards would bring about an end to the division of Germany and Europe (he erred only in his estimate of how long it would take). This attitude also shaped the decision for a liberal-democratic political and social system and a social market economy. The ideas of controlled economy and socialism were burdened with the stigma of dictatorship and the misery of the war and the postwar period. Moreover, the spectacle of coerced socialism right next door, in Eastern Europe, which led to permanent economic crisis, was particularly unattractive, as was the continuous stream of refugees from East to West.

A symbol of the new political structure was the convincing liberal-democratic figure of Theodor Heuss, who was the first president, from 1949 to 1959. The Federal Republic avoided the constitutional-political weaknesses that had led to the early demise of the Weimar Republic. The position of the chancellor and the government were strengthened, the dictatorial power of the president dismantled, and the parliamentary process solidified by making the fall of one chancellor dependent on the election of a new one (a "constructive vote of no confidence"). The Federal Constitutional Court was given the power to ban antidemocratic parties. Finally, the fragmentation of the landscape of political parties was made more difficult through a 5 percent clause in the electoral laws. The purpose of all these regulations was to prevent a destruction of the democracy by pseudodemocratic means, as had happened in 1933. The modified, militant democracy of Bonn would not grant its principled opponents the unlimited tolerance that led to the downfall of the Weimar Republic.

Moreover, the nation's habituation to a better-functioning party and parliamentary system also led to an increasingly positive view of democracy itself, something that had been lacking after 1918. The regime of Chancellor Adenauer—a great old man with nearly patriarchal authority—built a bridge from Germany's patriarchal state tradition to pluralistic democracy. The historical profusion of parties was replaced by a concentration of the political groups into two parties nearly equal in size, the old Social Democratic Party and the new Christian Democratic Union. Next to them only the Free Democratic Party was able to maintain itself for three decades as a smaller third party, and in the last decade there also arose the "Greens."

This sort of constellation was reminiscent of the British and American party systems, with their capacity for cooperation. The Bonn system was able to break away from the problems that were typical of the fractured party systems on the European Continent. It was the result of a lengthy process that de-ideologized the parties and made them more pragmatic. This made possible a liberalization of the SPD in the Godesberg Program of 1959, and eventually the full-fledged changes of government from the CDU to the SPD, and back to the CDU, in the states as well as on the federal level.

Of course since the midsixties, after the end of the Adenauer era, in a time marked by the advent of a new generation and changes in the international situation, the persistent problems and the unfinished elements of the Bonn state have emerged more clearly, particularly in the era of détente in the seventies and eighties.

To be sure, the Federal Constitutional Court repeatedly affirmed that it was a constitutional commandment to keep the German question open, but there is no way that one can say that policy vacillated between West and East. The Federal Republic remains dependent on being a part of Western Europe and on the progress of the policy of integration, to which it owes its existence and development. But as the possibility of an all-European cooperation took on concrete forms under the aegis of the Conference on Security and Cooperation in Europe (CSCE), it also raised anew the question of a political rapprochement between the two states, and their reunification. Of course this presupposed changes in the world-political constellation, and these occurred only after 1989, as a result of perestroika in the Soviet Union.

There is no simple answer to the question of which factors should be singled out to account for the remarkable development of the Federal Republic of Germany toward the normality of a democratic state: foreign policy, economic policy, and domestic policy are all equally involved. Considerable importance must be accorded, in any case, to the constitution, its acceptance and implementation, and to the democratic defense against dictatorial or neutralist challenges from the outside and radical tendencies from the inside. However, in the final analysis, what is and remains of fundamental significance is the integration of the Federal Republic into the supranational framework of a European policy: its renunciation of power politics, so disastrous in its National Socialist incarnation; its striving for partnership with its neighbors; and its awareness of mutual interdependence in the economic and political spheres.

The constitution of the Federal Republic gives special consideration to this requirement. It provides for a restraint of the sovereignty of the nation-state "in favor of international institutions" and "for the maintenance of peace" and the "prevention of an offensive war" (Articles 24 to 26 of the Basic Law). This is something quite new in the history of modern states, but it is in keeping with Germany's position as a country in the middle of Europe, a country that continues to be strongly affected by the further development in Eastern Europe and the North-South problem. The supranational openness, reflected in the constitution, benefits the European policy and the German-French relations that are fundamental to it; the German-French relations are a particularly powerful demonstration of the profound change that has occurred, when compared with past history. And so Dolf Sternberger has said "constitutional patriotism" is the core of the conception of the state, transcending the problematic efforts toward a reunification of the German nation-state.

Questions after the "Big Change"

How compelling, then, was the German reunification of 1989–90? The term "reunification" presupposes, after all, that such a bringing together of the two states has grounds in history. How strong has the demand for a unified state actually been over the course of the last 150—and the last 47—years? In actuality the will to achieve a German national state developed relatively late, as a reaction to the French Revolution and the imperialism of Napoleon. The efforts toward the creation of a German state were from the beginning marked by the conflict between two demands that were difficult to reconcile: the call for freedom and the desire for unity. This conflict, the complexity of which cannot be discussed here, was eventually settled, after long and revolutionary struggles, only in the war against France in 1870, rather in favor of unity.

Under the influence of the defeat of Hitler's dictatorship and the Soviet dominance in East Germany and Eastern Europe, the demand for freedom ranked higher than the call for unity in the Federal Republic after the partition of 1949. And so in 1989 the demand for a unified state tended to be justified first on political rather than historical grounds: it was a demand directed against the oppression and dictatorship in East Germany and Eastern Europe.

In the debate over national unity, the West German parties played an important though varied role. The majority of the Christian Democrats based their policies on the primacy of freedom through ties to the West (Adenauer), while the Social Democrats in the beginning (under Schumacher) saw this as a threat to unity. The SPD was of the opinion that the party had done too little for the needs of the nation after 1918. Following their return after the war, leading Social Democrats were concerned the SPD would once again be considered "unnational." The result was fierce conflict with the CDU: for example, in the Bundestag the first leader of the opposition, Kurt Schumacher, called Chancellor Konrad Adenauer a "chancellor of the Allies," while Adenauer, during the electoral campaign of 1957, said the victory of the SPD would be the "downfall of Germany."

However, since that time the position of the SPD on the question of national unity has changed several times. During the past two decades it has shown a tendency, as have more and more people, to accept the de facto existence of two states, and shortly before the upheaval of 1989 the SPD questioned adherence to an all-German citizenship as such.

But had not the conflict between freedom and unity been decided long ago for the population in the West? The fact that the SPD never got more than 30 percent of the votes in the elections during the fifties showed that the majority of West Germans, under the pressure of the cold war, staked everything on the safeguarding of freedom, on reconstruction, and on the economic upswing. The demand for reunification receded into the background once the integration of the Federal Republic into the North Atlantic Treaty Organization (NATO) and the European Community (EC) had taken place, especially after no help was forthcoming against the building of the Berlin wall.

However, from the end of the fifties, after the heated controversies over the Germany policy, a kind of national consensus existed among the great parties: the Federal Republic was part of the Western alliance, and it played an active role in European policy. The security of the Federal Republic was entirely dependent on its Western ties, and this was in accord with the state's commitment to democratic values. (And those, too, who are today afraid of a German "special path," have the least to fear from a German federation that is integrated into the European Community.)

If one raises the question of whether a German confederation might have been a real alternative in 1989 to the "pan-Germanic" unified state dreaded abroad, it must be obvious that one cannot talk about this unification as being pan-Germanic. A confederation was widely talked about in the first weeks of the November revolution. But thereafter, I believe, the actual development outpaced this option. The possibility of a confederation was swept away by the urgency and speed of the development. However, this was not a result of the political will in the Federal Republic; it was due solely to the internal weakness of the GDR, whose people wanted out of their political and economic misery and appealed to the sense of unity of all Germans.

In the face of this admirable will to freedom, we must not put too much weight on historical experiences with previous German nationalism. What the people in the GDR wanted was to replace a dictatorship with a liberal-democratic form of government. This goal was far more important than any nationalistic motivation. Unlike earlier periods, today our nation is marked by a predominantly democratic development.

The people of the GDR had rehearsed their revolt as early as 1953, and the events of 1953 and 1989 are certainly comparable. The difference is that thirty-nine years ago the Soviet troops intervened, whereas in November of 1989 they did not. But the driving force behind both developments was liberation from a totalitarian regime and the abolition of the artificial dividing line between the two German states. It was, above all, the desire for liberation that drove the people of the GDR into the streets, and not primarily the longing for national unity; national longing came only afterwards. At first the cry was: "We are *the* people," and then: "We are *one* people." The essential thing was the East Germans' lack of identification with their own dictatorial state.

The reunification mood that existed in both states at the time created the impression that the wish for unity had become stronger once again. But neither in the GDR nor in the Federal Republic was there a great wave of nationalism. The slogans and banners in Leipzig were no doubt based more on human rights and economics than on nationalism: reunification was seen as a road to a more humane life. The element of freedom was the dominant factor in November of 1989. It was indeed "a revolt against oppression and lies," as Helmut Schmidt said. Demands for reunification met with strong support only after the full extent of the economic misery became apparent.

Germany continues on the road to a democracy with a supranational orientation, one in which a desirable limitation of the nation-state principle is succeeding. To be sure, the danger of a relapse into conflicts over nationalistic interests exists in the expanded Europe. But this danger does not seem to me a very serious one in the case of Germany, because we are strongly tied into the European policy, and also because "reunification" has always been linked to concrete preconditions: we have never wished to question our ties to the European Community, to our Western neighbors, and to the United States, and for that reason we have always decided unequivocally against a "neutral" Germany.

The unified Germany will be what the Federal Republic was until 1989: a federalist democracy with a supranational orientation. The integration of the GDR that became possible so rapidly through the restoration of its states also clearly aimed at a federalist solution.

In all this we are aware that Germany is not a great power and no longer strives to be. What has been created is an entity that does not act like a power state and that is loaded with many tasks and burdens, with the central questions of a European policy and a security policy ranking at the top. One thing, however, must be stated with the utmost clarity: the European Common Market and the European political union continue to be of prime importance to Germany. Reunification came to us directly because of national solidarity and our democratic constitution. But we are now living in an interdependent European state system in which the sovereignty of nation-states is being increasingly modified. The policy of détente and disarmament has also gone into high gear. It is practically impossible that a nationalistic turn could make the Federal Republic into a new threat.

Perspectives on the "Epochal Change"

Since 1989, the year of the enthusiastically celebrated two hundredth anniversary of the French Revolution, we have been living, unexpected by nearly everyone, through an "epochal change" (W. Mantl) of truly historic dimensions and consequences. A sudden, revolutionary, and yet for the most part nonviolent transformation of the political conditions brought to an end decades of oppression in states and societies in Central and Eastern Europe. It made possible once again the diversity of Europe, of its thinking and values. The events, experienced on such an elementary and existential level, were seen by the many people they affected as far-reaching and full of liberation and redemption, bright promise and high expectations.

On an international scale this experience has produced, in turn, far-reaching hopes for a solution to existing historical-political problems, at least in Europe. The end of the postwar period has been proclaimed— even the end of history as such. That, surely, is an exaggeration of the importance of the East-West conflict as we have known it, if we think of the war in the Persian Gulf, or the acute problems of dissolution in the former Soviet Union and in the Balkans. These are painful demonstration that the older world history is by all means continuing—and with it the danger of a return of conflicts between nation-states at the expense of workable democracies, the obstruction of democratic reconstruction by nationalist-fundamentalist movements, in sum a relapse into the interwar period with the primacy of nationalism over democratic politics.

This old-new problem of the nation-state can be tackled in the long run only through a federalization of Europe with graduated forms of integration. This, more than anything else, is the task we all face today. To achieve this, the model of the EC, the Council of Europe, and the CSCE process offer (in institutional terms) better conditions than ever before for a limitation of both the nation-state and the principle of sovereignty. This is also the only way we can defuse the minority and regional problems, both in regard to human rights and in socioeconomic terms. This historical task, which the twentieth century had so far failed to tackle, has not been carried out by 1989, either; instead, it has once again risen to awareness and become topical. The sudden switch from a totalitarian, planned economy to a free-market economy is another challenge that can be met only on a European scale. Only if this process of integration is successfully promoted and consolidated will the great change of 1989–90 be a lasting one, and will the dangers of a power vacuum, in which the unified Germany could be pushed once again into a problematic position between East and West, be avoided.

This perspective offers grounds not for euphoria but for a determined continuation of the policy of European integration and federalization, in constant partnership with the tried-and-true Atlantic partnership. The leader of one of the German parties affirmed this before the Bundestag in a way that is representative for most politicians: "We do not want to be strong *in* Europe, we want to be strong *for* Europe" (Graf Lambsdorff, April 2, 1992).

In 1953, in a speech to students in Hamburg, the great German writer Thomas Mann, who returned from the United States in the early fifties after four decades in exile, outlined a vision for the Germans in Europe that has once again become relevant today:

> We are not worried that time will not bring a unified Europe with a reunited Germany at its center. We do not know how this is to be accomplished, how the unnaturally divided Germany is to become one again. We are in the dark about it, and we must rely on the faith that history will find ways and means to undo the unnatural and restore the natural: a single Germany as a self-confidently serving member of a Europe united in self-confidence—and not as its lord and master . . . Let us not deceive ourselves about the fact that the difficulties delaying the unification of Europe include a mistrust of the purity of German intentions, a fear on the part of other nations of Germany and of hegemonic plans its vigorous strength might suggest to it, and which, those countries believe, it conceals poorly . . . The task of the emerging German generation, the German youth, is to dispel this distrust, this fear, by rejecting what has long since been rejected and declaring its intentions clearly and with one voice—not for a German Europe, but for a European Germany.[1]

More than fifty years after the outbreak of World War II, the "European Germany" Thomas Mann longed for has become a permanent fixture in our historical landscape.

After centuries of wars and oppression, the guiding idea of a new Europe offers the world for the first time, in a concrete and practicable way, a model of supranational conflict resolution and cooperation to safeguard both freedom and peace. And we, the Germans, after the experience of and responsibility for a period with such horrible consequences for the people and nations of Europe, are left with a commitment to the basic values of European culture—above all the preservation and defense of human rights.

Revolution against Totalitarianism: From the End of Division to the Renaissance of Europe?

I

The year 1989 will go down in the history of German, European, and world politics as an *annus mirabilis*, a miraculous year. It meant the end of an era of totalitarianism that had dominated the better part of our century (delineated by the dates 1917, 1933, and 1945): after the end of Fascism and National Socialism, the spread of Communism has now also been halted.

It is a historical year in two ways. That very same year the great French Revolution of 1789 (after the American Revolution of 1776) was remembered all over the world in commemorative books and celebrations that had been long in the planning; the French Revolution was hailed as the start of the modern era, as the path to the national state and democracy. In the meantime, throughout the entire sphere of Soviet rule—and for a moment, at the beginning of June 1989, also in the People's Republic of China—the impulses of a movement against totalitarianism that had been at work for years came together. Within a few months, especially between June and December 1989, they led to the final breakthrough to a free Europe.

Except in Romania, these movements started out for the most part as nonviolent, indeed "peaceful revolutions" of demonstrations and round-tables. This was in stark contrast to the history of revolutions from the seventeenth to the twentieth centuries, and, most recently, the Communist and Fascist–National Socialist seizures of power. And as had been the case with the only half-successful revolutions of 1848, the upheavals spread in several states simultaneously, indeed in half of Europe, one influencing the other. However, this time they were directed not only against an absolutist system of rule but also against one that was comprehensively totalitarian and imperialistic-colonial, with a pseudoreligious ideology's claim to total power.

What occurred was simultaneously a collapse and a revolution. It consumed, like a conflagration, the rotten pillars of the Communist regimes, whose populations total more then 380 million in Central and Eastern Europe and part of Asia. Not only the rapidity of the events but their unexpected timing, too, caught the West largely unprepared: from leaders in politics and economic life to specialists in scholarship and the media, from observers and participants to diplomats and secret service agencies— all were taken by surprise.

There are several reasons for this. For one, there was a long history of prior attempts at liberation: the uprisings of 1953 in the GDR, 1956 in Poland and, especially, Hungary, 1968 in Czechoslovakia, and 1970 and 1980–981 again in Poland. Their failures had repeatedly dashed hopes and had led to new oppression. Against this background, the course of the rapidly accelerating and then headlong events was doubly surprising, especially since the restraint of the Soviet Union, with its truly "massive" occupation troops and secret services, and its unequivocal abandonment of its previous satraps and puppets could hardly have been foreseen, despite all the changes that had occurred during the era of perestroika, which began in 1985. Added to this was the fact that the peoples of Eastern Europe had been resigned to the Communist forms of rule, given the seeming invulnerability of the regimes, and also their apparent ability to be reformed by the "progressive" policies of Gorbachev. This had misled many Western observers for a very long time, causing them to misjudge the supposed stability of these regimes. Along with this went an acceptance of the status quo in the name of "peaceful coexistence," a position that was taken not only by sympathizers with "socialism" and notorious critics of totalitarianism research.

Given such widespread misinterpretations and the rapidity and spontaneity of the events of 1989, the history leading up to them is of considerable importance. This is particularly true for Poland, which saw repeated protests and rebellions against internal and external oppression in the decades following the imposition of Communist rule. The role of the Polish Church, which continued to be recognized by the state, was important for the strong national consciousness behind this resistance. To be sure, the Soviet Union knew how to legitimate its own policy of occupation in Poland by very effectively joining an "anti-Fascist" to an anti-German slogan, and not least by shifting the Western borders of Poland at the expense of Germany. Though this was a potent combination, it did not clearly benefit the credibility of Communism: Polish feelings toward the highly power-conscious, totalitarian Russia, which had once again absorbed eastern Poland after 1945, were not much more positive than toward the divided Germany.

And so it was Poland that, earlier than other Communist countries, witnessed an open confrontation between the oppositional union movement known as Solidarity and the system. This confrontation could not be stopped even by the repressive measures of martial law, which was declared in December of 1981. Instead, thanks to Solidarity's broad basis among workers, in the Church, and among intellectuals (some of them former Communists), it dealt a blow to the very credibility of the Communist "workers' party" and its state.

In other countries the opposition movements tended to be focused initially on specific areas. In Hungary, for example, the focus was on the reform of the economy. In Czechoslovakia (with Charter 77) and in the GDR (beginning with the protest against the expulsion of the dissident Wolf Biermann in 1976) it was on intellectual-literary freedom; while the power of these two movements was weakened by censorship and publishing bans, as well as by the flight and emigration of dissidents, their influence was reflected back via the Western news media and Western publishers.

Everywhere, however, the menacing Soviet policy, which had been effective for so long and had been used by the various satellite regimes, lost its power and validity in the decade before 1989. Two factors accelerated its erosion: the growing recognition that the bureaucratic-socialist system was clearly unproductive, that it lagged behind in the standard of living and modernization, and the growing awareness that all political-ideological promises were leading to stagnation, decay, and, after the failure of the last great test of strength in the arms race with the West, to a general economic crisis in Communist Europe.

The signs of Moscow's increasing helplessness and weakness in the face of this situation, along with growing efforts to obtain economic help from the West, sealed the further decay of the legitimacy of Communist rule. After World War II, it had been imposed on all these countries in the form of dependent, nonauthentic dictatorships; despite pseudoelections and pseudodemocracy, they had never been fully accepted by the people. The regimes could last only so long as there was no realistic alternative, backed by power, alongside and in opposition to the real existing Soviet hegemony. Only when this hegemony loosened and it became doubtful that the Soviet Union would intervene the way it used to did such an alternative become a possibility in the international context (and without war), did the return to independence and hope for a greater Europe of liberal democracies become conceivable.

Of course, until the summer of 1989 there was a risk: the "Brezhnev doctrine," which reserved the right of Soviet intervention to "protect" all regimes in Europe subject to the Warsaw Pact, and which had loomed so menacing since 1968, was not explicitly dropped until Gorbachev's declaration of July 6, 1989, before the Council of Europe; its abandonment was subsequently approved on December 4 by the countries of the Eastern bloc and by the government in Moscow.

To assess the chances of and perspectives on this new situation, it remains important, however, to trace the historical possibilities of the East European revolution, all the way back to the immediate postwar period: to the time, that is, when a renaissance of democracy began with surprising speed in Western Europe, while its hopeful beginnings in the Soviet sphere of power were smothered in totalitarian fashion, after a brief interlude when pluralistic structures were tolerated in the spirit of liberation from National Socialist totalitarianism.

It remains to be investigated, country by country, to what extent over the following forty years those early beginnings of democratic-national rebirth lived on underground and occasionally surfaced. The threads of that rebirth can now be picked up by the unfortunately long-delayed democratic renaissance in Eastern Europe in the 1990s. Doubtless this renaissance needs the help and cooperation of the West, with its experience of the renewal of liberal democracy, a renewal that had been so brutally denied to the East. At the same time it is surely important to defend against relapses into the narrow nationalism of nations and states, which so disastrously tore apart the Europe of the interwar period. Unfortunately this threat exists once again.

II

The establishing of links with the pre-Communist and pretotalitarian history of the interwar period, a history that tended to be more authoritarian than democratic, was a part of the process that led to the eventual erosion of Eastern European totalitarianism; the role it played was as important as it was difficult and ambivalent. The process was also different from one country to the next. Czechoslovakia and Poland were the first victims of Hitler's aggression, in 1938 and 1939, but Czechoslovakia was among the few new democracies of 1918 that still existed in the 1930s, whereas Poland, under Piłsudski, had joined the ranks of the authoritarian systems as early as 1926. Poland's fate was shared by the other countries, with Hungary, Bulgaria, and Romania ending up initially on the side of the Berlin-Rome Axis, while the Baltic states were absorbed by the Soviet Union as a result of the Hitler-Stalin pact of 1939.

Thus for the countries of Eastern Europe, the status of independent statehood, which had been attained only in 1918, became the most important historical point of reference. By contrast, the usually short-lived, weak democracies, many of which had also been burdened by minority problems, were unfortunately much less of a point of reference. The abolition of sovereign nation-states by Communist universalism was the most painful wound. Democracy as an alternative to totalitarian dictatorship could hardly rely on a history of successful political experience.

As a result, immediately following the revolutions of 1989, the democratization of the regained or newly won-nation states would prove to be the main difficulty in the transition from dictatorship to freedom and in coming to terms with the heavy burdens of the past. Those burdens included the old economic and national rivalries, which had been in part suppressed under Soviet hegemony, in part played off against one another in an effort to "divide and conquer." In any case, the rivalries had never been raised to the level of equal, genuine cooperation—as existed in Western Europe—in the sense of an Eastern European community.

To be sure, the continuous flare-ups of resistance in Poland had both a democratic and a national orientation. This was demonstrated in the final phase that began in 1980, in the cooperation between a democratically oriented movement of intellectuals organized in the Committee for the Defense of the Rights of Workers (the KOR), under the leadership of such members of the opposition as Bronislaw Geremek, Tadeusz Mazowiecki, Jacek Kuron, and Adam Michnik, and the liberal-national workers' movement of Lech Wałesa. It was also reflected in the decisive support the workers' movement received from the national institution of the Church (which tends to be skeptical of democracy), with its enormous influence on the masses—and thanks to the international influence of the first Polish pope in history. In fact, the election of John Paul II in 1978 was another important factor in the pioneering role Poland played in cracking open Communist totalitarianism.

The picture of the events and interconnections was thus quite varied even in these early stages and not just after the upheaval of 1989, with the splintering of the parties that began soon after. In seeking to break the coercion of a policy of blocs under outside control, the demands for democratic rights as well as the diversity of the movements for national independence revealed in equal measures the increasing insecurity of the party Communists and of the Soviet-imperial authority. Martial law in Poland, the tightening of the Husák regime in Prague, the autocratic behavior of Ceaușescu in Romania, the Soviet failure in Afghanistan and the dilemma its involvement posed, and finally the onset of rebellion by the nationalities at the edges of the enormous, late-colonial Soviet empire—all these signs of weakness strengthened a resistance that sought to bring about the big change, the end of totalitarian dictatorship, a fate that had long been sealed ideologically. The opposition pursued these efforts in part with cooperation from reform-minded or adaptable Communists (especially in Poland and Hungary), and eventually even with a head of state who was ruling by martial law, General Jaruzelski.

Ardent if temporarily disgraced Communist leaders such as Władysław Gomułka (from 1956 to the worker uprisings in Danzig and Posen in 1970) and to a certain extent Edward Gierek (until 1980), as well as János Kádár in Hungary, had repeatedly attempted careful economic and political reforms within the system, while clinging uncompromisingly to the external and internal unity of the Soviet bloc ruled by Moscow and Communism. The separate roads to socialism, and a certain loosening of the principle of dictatorship (for example through the participation of coalition parties), always remained firmly within these narrow, doubly drawn boundaries. It was and still is a matter of controversy to what extent Jaruzelski, who wanted to be seen as both a national-patriotic general and a Communist, was willing to cross them. What was true of Gorbachev may also be true of Jaruzelski, namely that he did not want his role in history to be what did in fact unfold, first in the transition from and then in the liquidation of the Communist system. General Jaruzelski acted as an oppressor (in the imposition of martial law in 1981). At the same time, however, he was a mediator between the various forces of conservatism and reform that existed within the party, the army, the state, the Church, Solidarity, the Soviet bloc, and the nation as a whole. Moreover it remains unclear whether his military dictatorship did in fact head off direct Soviet intervention. The fear of this hung over Poland constantly, especially after 1956, but now it coincided with changes in Moscow, where, in addition to Afghanistan and the arms race, the domestic problems of politics and the economy became increasingly urgent at the end of the Brezhnev era.

Other political and, especially, psychological factors influenced Poland's development in the course of these trials of strength between the repeatedly suppressed opposition and the Communist and Soviet ruling power. They included, in particular, the persistent and now resurging controversy over the Soviet Union's stubborn denial of responsibility for the mass murders at Katyn, where thousands of Polish officers had been killed during the time of the German-Soviet partition of occupied Poland (in 1939 to 1941). The murders were first uncovered in 1943 by the National Socialist regime, which was then blamed for them by the "antifascist" mythmaking of Communist propaganda. It was only in 1990 that the Soviet government finally accepted responsibility, although with feigned innocence it excused this crime, as so much else, by invoking the "Stalinism" of the time. Still, this issue, and like it the question of the murder of 20,000 Polish prisoners of war in the Soviet Union—examples of the distortion of Soviet-Polish history—stirred up the anti-Communist mood in the country. They did so almost more than the equally suppressed truth about the Hitler-Stalin pact of 1939, with its secret protocols concerning the partition of Poland and Eastern Europe like so much booty between Germany and the Soviet Union.

The revelations of political-ideological deceptions that accumulated during the 1980s contributed substantially to the intellectual-moral and national-patriotic delegitimization of the Communist system. In addition to revealing the falseness of the previous view of history, they also demonstrated more clearly than ever before the inner insecurities of the leadership in Warsaw and Moscow when it came to the truth. In fact, there is hardly a more striking example of a close reciprocal connection between the far-reaching revision of the hitherto official, national view of history and self-liberation from a system imposed from the outside and from above, a system whose ideological power was based on biased, distorted, pro-Soviet, and anti-Western historical legends in the name of socialism and antifascism.

Step by step the legends that supported the notion of Soviet "liberation" through occupation (support was in fact withheld from the non-Communist uprising in Warsaw between August and October of 1944, even though the Red Army stood outside of Warsaw) and the fiction of the "legal" establishment of a "democratic people's" dictatorship in the years after 1945 were called into question. This process also cast doubt on the history of Stalinist Communism, as well as on its sanctified Leninist prehistory and its persistence after "de-Stalinization," which had supposedly eliminated all the evils.

The political mood in Poland, intensified after the cleric Jerzy Popieluszko, adviser to the suppressed Solidarity movement, was murdered by officers of the Polish police in 1984, and reinforced by the papal visit in 1987, eventually forced Jaruzelski's policy of "martial law" in a direction that led from the preservation of the Communist dictatorship to the search for compromise with the growing, strengthened opposition forces in Polish society. The Church, the workers' movements, and the movement for civil rights became the bearers of the popular opposition. The Polish Church, as the refuge of the nation and an organization of the masses, more than ever before played the role of mediator between the various forces: the opposition it supported, headed by Lech Wałesa with his confessor as adviser; the power of the party and the state dictatorship, which was eroding; and the national army, led by Jaruzelski and dependent on the Soviet Union.

These were precarious years of politics on a tightrope. Through gradual concessions to the opposition, Jaruzelski secured a still-considerable share of power for the Communists, in return for which they relinquished their monopoly on power; for himself he secured the first presidency after the big change. The negotiations and compromises with the regime, which took place at the now-legendary roundtable in 1988, would soon serve as a model for other movements of opposition and change. They were aimed at achieving a gradual, peaceful overthrow of the regime. All this took place a year before the general breakthrough of 1989, which then swept away even more quickly the harsher regimes of the GDR, Czechoslovakia, Bulgaria, and Romania. Finally, after forty years of total isolation, it also swept aside the dictatorship in Albania (1991), while the broken-up Yugoslavia missed the boat and slid into civil war. The last to be affected were thus the very two states that had (in 1948) been the first to distance themselves from Soviet hegemony.

By contrast, Hungary witnessed a smooth transition (between June and October 1989) with substantial participation by reform-minded Communists. More so than anywhere else, they had made possible an approximation of multiparty conditions, through a gradual opening of the economy to private initiatives and "joint ventures" with the West and, after 1985, through electoral reforms. As early as May 1988 they initiated the final transformation with the replacement of Kádár. As in Poland and Czechoslovakia, the formation of political opinions and objectives was deeply influenced in the broader Hungarian population by the shocking revelation of Communist distortions of history, especially the truth about the bloody suppression of the Hungarian uprising of 1956. By winning out against the orthodox wing of the party, the reform Communists who rallied around Nyers, Nemeth, Poszgay, and Horn made possible the peaceful democratic change, even though it cost them the hoped-for participation in power. In all of this the Polish example of a roundtable with the opposition was important; equally important was the role that the Hungarian government's supportive toleration of the stream of refugees entering Hungary from the GDR played in the first opening of the Iron Curtain (September 11, 1989) and in the acceleration of the East German demand for self-liberation—even before the dramatic days of October and November 1989.

While the transition to democracy was brought to a conclusion in Hungary with the elections in March and April of 1990, Poland continued to suffer under the unclear political situation that the roundtable had created by conceding a strong participatory role to Communist politicians in the parliament and the government, and by allowing Jaruzelski to remain in power. Paradoxically, the semirevolution that had been going on in Poland since 1980 impeded and delayed the complete change in power relations that the revolutionary year of 1989 brought about in other countries that had a much shorter start-up period and a harsher party system.

In the case of Czechoslovakia, the long-lasting, massive suppression of the opposition was particularly blatant, for after the rigorous persecution following the Prague Spring of 1968, the declarations made in the spirit of Helsinki by a movement for civil rights—a movement largely of intellectuals—met with special interest and sympathy in the West. For a long time the rigid dictatorship of Husák, who had, after all, signed the final Helsinki accords of 1975, kept the mass of the population in a mood of accommodation with the regime, especially since the Communist Party of Czechoslovakia, like Honecker's Socialist Unity Party (SED), showed very little willingness to follow Gorbachev's course or to take notice of the beginnings of reform in Poland and Hungary. As late as August 1989 the Czech government even went so far as to denounce Poland's emphatic expression of regret over the invasion by the Warsaw Pact in 1968 as a "serious interference in the domestic affairs of the Czech state."

This came at a time when elsewhere, even in the Soviet Union itself, the Communist falsifications of history had long since been discussed, with great political impact. To be sure, on August 20, 1988, the twentieth anniversary of the invasion of 1968, crowds had gathered in Czechoslovakia, though they had been quickly dispersed. Not until the end of October 1989, after the stream of refugees had poured from the GDR into the embassy of the Federal Republic in Prague, did bloody clashes between a brutal police and demonstrators lead to large-scale protest rallies, which were lead by the Democratic Citizen's Forum and the prominent dissident writer Václav Havel. Only at the end of November did the party finally yield to the democratic movement, eventually freeing the way for Havel to become president before the year was out.

The course of pivotal events took on a distinct character in the case of Germany (see below, 295 f.), not least because of the special national situation of the GDR, and in Czechoslovakia, because of the memory of the Prague Spring and its suppression—that is to say, because of the possibility of picking up the threads of 1968 and the fear that this attempt, too, would fail. But even the backwardness of the party dictatorships in Bulgaria and especially in Romania did not prevent the upheavals of 1989 from spreading into those countries, though it did cast them into a twilight of violence and intrigue, which made Romania's transition to democracy continue to appear to be the least credible.

Neither the persistent persecution in all Communist countries of the Helsinki-accord movements for human rights after 1975, nor the elaborate and brutal surveillance and suppression of both old and new stirrings of opposition were able to stop the erosion and collapse of totalitarian rule.

Appeasing "reforms" instituted from above and illusionist encouragement and misdiagnoses from the West were also unable to do so, no matter whether they arose from practical political calculations of détente or from ideological sympathies with the "socialism" in power and its peace propaganda. The real, existing socialism, with its basis in mass coercion, could be maintained only in bureaucratic states with all-embracing police and secret service organizations. In actuality, in the seventies this socialism had already begun to lose the capacity for "totalitarian seduction" (to use J. F. Revel's phrase). In the beginning it had been this capacity, alongside the ruthless, elaborate tools of coercion and career-conscious opportunism, that had made the system work. The belief in progress and a pseudoreligious faith in the redemptive power and historical mission of Communism were intended to mobilize consent and idealism, as had previously been the case with the faith in National Socialism and other totalitarian ideologies. Looking at the rising fundamentalist movements in many parts of the world today, we realize that something like this could happen again.

But when these ideological, cohesive forces decayed along with the political and economic visions of the future, and the real, stagnating social existence in the East was compared with the liberties and standard of living in Western Europe, the end of Communism was at hand—a Communism that had declared the century to be its own and promised to liberate the world from capitalism and oppression. To be sure, some of its politicians, economists, and ideologues perceived the change and the danger. To counter them, they tried at a late hour to make adjustments under the magic word "reform," but those adjustments were as likely to speed the collapse as to stop it. The reformers engaged the national needs and moved toward the economically imperative opening to the West, a market economy, and some democratic loosening. It was surely thanks to Gorbachev's change of course that even the only authentic and oldest Communist dictatorship, that of the Soviet Union, went along in this; in the final analysis, everything depended on this country, since it was an atomic superpower. But even in 1989 and later, Gorbachev did not actually wish to give up the system. Instead he wanted to save it by making those improvements that were possible and by getting rid of what should be dropped; he wanted to protect the system against an anti-Communist revolution.

To a certain extent we can apply to him what Alexis de Tocqueville wrote a century and a half ago, in 1856, in regard to many revolutions, but in particular to the French Revolution of 1789:

> For it is not always when things are going from bad to worse that revolutions break out. On the contrary, it oftener happens that when a people which has put up with an oppressive rule over a long period without protest suddenly finds the government relaxing its pressure, it takes up arms against it. Thus the

social order overthrown by a revolution is almost always better than the one immediately preceding it, and experience teaches us that, generally speaking, the most perilous moment for a bad government is when it seeks to mend its ways. Only consummate statecraft can enable a King to save his throne when after a long spell of oppressive rule he sets to improving the lot of his subjects. Patiently endured so long as it seemed beyond redress, a grievance comes to appear intolerable once the possibility of removing it crosses men's minds. For the mere fact that certain abuses have been remedied draws attention to the others and they now appear more galling; people may suffer less, but their sensibility is exacerbated.[1]

III

The breathtaking events of 1989 developed from a host of strong impulses and feelings, hopes and goals, which could work in contradictory, even contrary ways. They amounted to an antitotalitarian, democratic revolution, though they were also aimed at the national liberation of the various peoples from foreign, ideologically dressed up domination and hegemony. And they proclaimed what had been so often promised under socialism but had lost its credibility over the decades: an improvement in the standard of living and way of life, and at the same time the degree of freedom of movement the West had long since attained under the banner of democracy and the market economy.

These various expectations formed the backdrop to the big change, which after 1989 determined the new history of Europe, the end of its division, and the perspectives on a difficult rebuilding. In all of this the German case played an important role, since it embraced both East and West and thus achieved both liberation and reunification.

The German path had to reckon with a number of circumstances that set it apart from the course of revolution in the other countries. First off, there was the special military and political strength of the Soviet occupation, which gave the GDR the unenviable reputation of being an impregnable fortress of the Soviet empire. In addition, from the very beginning the anti-Communist, antitotalitarian opposition in the GDR was continually weakened by the unending exodus to the Federal Republic of persecuted people and refugees, who had to overcome borders and walls but not language barriers. At the same time, the growing presence of West German radio and television was able to provide the East Germans with a varied and more complete level of information and opinion in regard to the actual conditions in the West and the East. Even though hope for reunification had dwindled over the decades, it was Soviet power, not the rigorously protected GDR regime or a separate national consciousness, that remained the true pillar of the system; a separate national identity in East Germany was invented by current nostalgics, and only after the fact.

The course and consequences of the change of 1989 also diverged considerably from the developments in other late-Communist countries because of the prospect of reunification with the Federal Republic that soon appeared on the horizon. The GDR was simply, above all, a "second German dictatorship" (as I emphasized in 1976 in my book *Die Krise Europas*). But in contrast to the first dictatorship of 1933, this one was a dictatorial state imposed from outside, after the defeat in Word War II. The history leading up to the change revealed the peculiarities of the situation. The eighties were marked by a certain rapprochement of the two German states. The high points were Chancellor Helmut Schmidt's visit to the GDR in 1981, though he deliberately avoided East Berlin, and Chancellor Helmut Kohl's reception of Erich Honecker, the head of the East German state and the SED, in Bonn in 1987. Repeated meetings between high-ranking Social Democratic Party (SPD) and SED committees (the SPD's Commission on Basic Values and the SED's Academy of Social Sciences) even produced a joint paper in 1987 on the "Quarrel of Ideologies and Joint Security." And the fact that the Protestant Church in the GDR called itself the "Church in socialism" revealed something about the difference between its attitude and that of the Church in Poland.

But nothing altered the GDR's rigorous policy of demarcation and the perfecting of its apparatus of spies and repression: not visits and encounters; not the constant contact between the churches and the "German-German" consultations of governmental and economic commissions; not the constantly growing economic concessions and billions in credit extended to the GDR (via F. J. Strauß); not decades of the ransoming of prisoners, trafficking in human beings—a particularly loathsome way of procuring hard currency—from which the SED regime profited by selling about 34,000 political prisoners to West Germany (between 1963 and 1989).

The events of 1989 caught both sides by total surprise, but particularly the politicians and the people in the Federal Republic. Among the people, opinion about the German policy and reunification ranged in the eighties from favoring the various possibilities for keeping the German question open and recognizing the division in the interest of a cooperative coexistence of the two German states, to the belief that reunification was the "existential lie of the Federal Republic." However, in connection with the phrase "European house," which Gorbachev brought into play, there was also heard once again the old demand for a single Germany that was bloc-free and neutral—a kind of nationalism from the Left and the Right that was advocated by segments of the Greens and the peace movement.

The sudden irruption of the realities of 1989 overtook the discussions and revealed, not least, the illusions about a course of appeasement toward the GDR. Such a course had been pushed with growing urgency, especially by parts of the SPD. It showed itself in the Social Democrats' willingness to entertain Honecker's demand for a separate German citizenship and the elimination of the postulate of reunification in the preamble to the Basic Law, and in the persistent demands to dissolve the Central Registry in Salzgitter. This registry had been established after the building of the wall in 1961 to record acts of violence against escapees on the border with the GDR, violations of human rights, and unjust sentences in the GDR; the federal states governed by the SPD now refused to finance it. At the same time, a certain easing of travel restrictions, even though—or precisely because—it affected mostly retirees and privileged people (the "travel cadre"), in the end also increased the pressure on the SED regime. The surging demand for freedom to travel became one of the most important impulses behind the rebellion and the mass flight especially of younger citizens in the summer of 1989, which triggered the final collapse of the second German dictatorship.

Whatever one is to make of speculations that the leadership of the GDR had foreseen its imminent downfall as early as the end of 1988 and had sought to counter it by plans for economic and political confederation, it demonstratively refused to steer (as Poland and Hungary did) toward the glasnost and perestroika course of partial freedom. Given the pull exerted by the Federal Republic, it believed such a course would pose the greatest danger to the regime. In the face of growing protests by human rights, environmental, and peace groups, who acted in part under the protection of the churches (especially the Protestant Church) and who, during the communal elections in May of 1989, dared for the first time to denounce the usual electoral fraud, the GDR believed almost to the very end that it could maintain itself by relying on the tight net of its perfectionist state security (the Stasi). The Stasi had hundreds of thousands of official and unofficial collaborators and a vast storehouse of files, which would probably have stretched a length of 200 kilometers. When Honecker, on October 7, 1989, once again celebrated the fortieth anniversary of the establishment of the GDR with political and military pomp, Gorbachev was present as a guest (as he had been in Beijing in the days of unrest four months earlier). But special note was taken of the words he directed at the East Berliners, words that were an indirect call for reforms: "Life punishes those who come too late."

In the meantime, the images of citizens of the GDR escaping via Hungary, Prague, and Warsaw had been seen around the world. The transit of the embassy refugees from Prague through the GDR to the Federal Republic, which East Berlin absurdly demanded (on September 10) as proof of its legal jurisdiction in the "exit," had already revealed the weakness of a regime that was now operating without Soviet help. It also accelerated the government's retreat in the face of the subsequent mass demonstrations, especially in Leipzig (October 9) and eventually in Berlin (November 4). The collapse was looming when the politburo of the SED, at a loss over what to do, removed Honecker from power on October 18. It came with the resignation of the entire GDR government on November 7, followed the next day by the politburo. Under circumstances that are still disputed, the teetering rump regime accepted the turbulent opening of the wall on November 9, a date heavy with history (1918, 1923), and soon after, its removal. More than twenty-eight years after the erection of the wall, the "ugliest structure in the world," it came down; of course in Honecker's view it should have stood another hundred years.

The almost unimaginable had happened before the eyes of a deeply moved world audience. As late as June 1987, President Reagan had called out in front of the Brandenburg Gate: "Mr. Gorbachev, open the gate! Mr. Gorbachev, tear down this wall!" And now, long before it was achieved through the decisions of politics and international law, the German re-unification, so often called for and so often doubted, took place in the euphoria of the masses pouring over the wall and across the borders of the GDR. The slogan of the demonstrations in the GDR changed from a democratic demand ("We are the people") to an affirmation of national unity ("We are one people"). As former chancellor Willy Brandt put it: "What belongs together is now growing together."

The year of revolutionary upheavals in Central and Eastern Europe was followed by an equally quick and breathless period of feverish negotiations, a great many plans and euphoric hopes, far-reaching changes, and of course disappointed expectations. The task was to fill the power vacuum left behind by the retreating and falling Communist dictatorships. At the same time, however, it was necessary to secure the radical transformations that were a consequence of both the new position of the Soviet Union and the sovereignty and independence aspired to by the countries it had hith-erto dominated—and, not least, in view of the question of German unification, which had come so quickly to the fore.

Yet at the end of the two years following the revolution (1990 and 1991), years that were no less eventful and that ushered in the restructuring of Central and Eastern Europe as a renaissance of democracy after the renaissance in the West forty years earlier, another nearly inconceivable event took place: the dissolution of the Soviet Union itself. It happened seventy-four years after the October Revolution of 1917, glorified then as the dawning of a new age, the beginning of a period of totalitarian-ideological dictatorships that would thenceforth be the essential mark of Europe's crisis-ridden history. Did the end of this era, at the threshold of the final decade of the century—and the millennium—offer the hitherto greatest chance for a renewal of Europe?

IV

Of course it soon became apparent that the restructuring of Europe after the end of its forty-year division, the end of the East-West conflict, and the dissolution of the Soviet Union, would be far more difficult than had been expected in the euphoria of the great moments of 1989. It required more than the removal of the existing obstacles from the time of the cold war. "The wall is gone, Germany cries with joy," read the German headlines in November 1989. A year later the immediate political goals of German reunification had been achieved: after the economic and monetary union on July 1, 1990, the GDR was joined to the Federal Republic on October 3, and the first all-German Bundestag elections took place on December 2, 1990.

However, the headlines quickly began to change. Only now did the full magnitude of the endeavor become clear. Only now did the costs and consequences of reconstruction on a national and European scale become fully apparent, a reconstruction that had to build on the desolate legacy of a broken empire. All this had been gravely underestimated, primarily in Germany. The enormous economic burdens were not the only problem that had a particularly sobering and even disappointing effect in this country. The difficult problems of "coming to terms with the past" after two dictatorships, after fifty-seven years and in the face of an overwhelming flood of the Stasi's surveillance documents, threatened to transform the feelings of liberation into feelings of frustration.

In the first phase, when the issue was the dissolution of the GDR regime, the difficulties of the transition to post-Communist and posttotalitarian conditions still receded behind the great success of the quick international recognition of German unity. On February 12 and 13, 1990, there was a remarkable joint conference of NATO and the Warsaw Pact countries in Ottawa. It agreed to initiate the "two-plus-four" negotiations between East and West Germany and the four victorious powers of World War II (held from May to September 1990). Despite some concerns in the face of another, greater Germany forty-five years after the war unleashed by Hitler, these negotiations eliminated the existing obstacles to all-German self-determination and sovereignty with remarkable speed and unanimity. An impressive, indeed decisive demonstration of the Soviets' willingness to accept complete freedom of alliance for a unified Germany, that is to say membership in NATO, was given when Gorbachev and Shevardnadze met Kohl and Genscher on July 15 and 16 in Moscow and the Northern Caucasus.

The futility of the attempts at continuing a separate statehood for the GDR under democratic conditions, attempts inspired mostly by leftist intellectuals, had already been sealed by the last elections for the People's Chamber on March 18 and the end of the Communist-led coalition government of Modrow. In those elections 75 percent of the voters cast their ballots for parties of unification. The process of unification was speedily advanced by the CDU-SPD government of de Mazière, which was formed four weeks after the elections. The unification treaty with the Federal Republic was signed in August 1990 by both German governments, and was ratified by both parliaments on September 20. The official joining of the GDR to the Federal Republic of Germany (in accordance with Article 23 of the Basic Law) took place two weeks later, on October 3. This day was declared the new Day of German Unity, replacing the previous one that had commemorated the suppressed uprising of June 17, 1953. It was festively and joyfully celebrated in the Reichstag in Berlin and in many German cities.

At the time, a knowledgeable observer aptly characterized the essential context: "The unification of Germany came as a gift of history, not as something earned by a government or as the fulfillment of a great plan. Neither did it come about simply through a German national movement, but as part of a larger international movement of all of Eastern Europe. Unlike 1870–71, it was accomplished without blood and iron, by the quick determination of Chancellor Kohl, with American support and the approval of the European neighbors" (Günther Gillessen).

The second phase, which began essentially on the day after the elections to the now-unified Bundestag (December 2, 1990), the democratic keystone of unification, was immediately marked by rapidly increasing difficulties. The task at hand was the concrete standardization of living conditions in the two very differently developed parts of Germany, one of which (contrary to the hitherto excessively euphemistic GDR scholarship) brought with it unexpectedly high and even now considerably underestimated burdens from its bankrupt dictatorial past. Moreover, the quick successes of the Germany policy in a year (1990) that saw many electoral campaigns on all levels in East and West Germany, which tempted those involved to make promises for the future that were very quickly disappointed, constituted an additional strain on the entire subsequent process of unification and reconstruction.

Ever since, German politics has been struggling, with varying success, to cope with this monumental problem in the fairest possible way. Of course the problem of rebuilding is one that affects all other post-Communist countries, especially the Soviet Union and its successor states, far more seriously. Unlike the GDR, they do not have their own European partner and guarantor of reconstruction. They have been left to their own devices and to the hope for European and international aid, which has become, too optimistically, the focus of the expectations of those who have hitherto been cut off from freedom.

In contrast to the case of Germany, the restructuring or rebuilding in the previously Communist-dominated countries is thus dependent on three equally difficult conditions: on the successful development of democratic party systems and state structures; on a peaceful solution to the old-new nation-state problems, which Communism had merely suppressed; and on a suitable tie-in to an expanded Europe with the closest possible cooperation, if not integration. We must therefore consider not only the far-reaching changes in Eastern Europe, but also their consequences for developmental problems in the West and for a policy of European integration that strengthened in the eighties. After all, this policy, by preparing the European Common Market and the political union, made an essential contribution to the change of course in the Soviet Union, with its world-historical consequences. It is now faced with a new, more severe test.

The course and problems of the governmental, constitutional, economic, and social restructuring since 1990 have been marked not only by the reestablishment of the countries of Europe that had been subjugated or dominated by the Soviet Union since 1917 and 1945 (while a belated decolonization is taking place in the Asiatic regions), but in addition, all these countries regard an emphatic focus on ethnic states and nation-states as the most effective means of national liberation and self-determination. One side of the problem is the difficulty of democratizing hitherto totalitarian structures that have grown unaccustomed over the decades to pluralism and a state governed by the rule of law. On top of that, they are confronted with the urgency of dismantling the bankrupt planned economy, which involves the threat of unemployment and the birth pains of an unprepared for, half-understood market and private-sector economy. The other side of the problem has been from the outset the impulses, and likewise the dangers, of a nationalism that seeks to gloss over these problems through militant radicalness and friend-foe thinking, following the old recipe of diverting domestic political pressure to the outside. The long period of oppression did not bring home the lesson that the right of the majority, which has now been won, can be maintained in the question of nationalities only if it respects the guaranteed rights of the minority—just as democracy always respects the right to (and of the) opposition.

The very signs of the dissolution of the Soviet Union were already marked by national elements and nationalistic driving forces behind the antitotalitarian and anti-Soviet rebellion which eventually turned into revolution: for example, in the ongoing conflict since 1988 between Armenia and Azerbaijan over the enclave of Nagorno-Karabak (in the Caucasus); in the justified demand for the annulment of the annexation of the Baltic states and Moldavia (in Bessarabia), a result of the Hitler-Stalin Pact of 1939; and in the eruption everywhere, and for good reason, of tendencies toward the dissolution of the Soviet Union and even some of its own republics. Many small nationalities had the feeling that they had already, or very nearly, lost their cultural and political identity. Even under Gorbachev, the empire was not able or willing to transform in time the fictitious, allegedly federal union of so-called Soviet nations and Soviet republics—since Stalin, abused for the arbitrary exercise of power on the principle of *divide et impera*—into a genuine federal state or confederacy.

Its dissolution within the space of two years was then driven forward by quarrels between the party leaders and the rising and ambitious new president of Russia, Boris Yeltsin—who had successfully resisted the attempted putsch of August 1991 led by reactionary functionaries from the circles around the hesitant Gorbachev—and especially by Ukraine's determined drive for independence. A particular conflict involved Crimea, which Russia had transferred to the Ukraine in 1954 under Khrushchev, and which was also contested as the base of the Black Sea fleet. Everywhere, the restructuring or rebuilding of the states was carried forward by the understandable demand for national self-determination. Of course this general trend casts serious doubt on the continued existence of a looser remaining structure, such as the current Community of Independent States (CIS), on the soil of the former Soviet Union and the former czarist empire; states are withdrawing in increasing numbers. It also brings with it a most serious burden: the current and future border disputes involving controversially defined nationalities. And this in a region that, for historical-political and religious reasons, is marked, as previously under the Ottoman and the Hapsburg Empires, by a diversity and intermingling of nationalities that can be demarcated into discrete states only with great difficulty. In addition, there are 25 million Russians, the former ruling nationality, who now live in the various new, non-Russian nation-states from the Baltic to Kazakhstan.

This part of the Communist legacy can have horrible consequences outside of the former Soviet empire, as is demonstrated by the bloody civil wars that have been raging in Yugoslavia since it began to dissolve in 1991. At the same time, these events mark a belated break with the Communism of the Tito variety, to which the Serbian claim to leadership and the privileged army, with its proud partisan tradition, continue to cling. Most recently (in 1992) this war has been particularly brutal in the region of Bosnia-Herzegovina. It is an ethnically mixed region, home to Muslims, Serbs, and Croats. Yet the former Serb-dominated central power is seeking to impose itself there by means of a greater nationalism at the expense of the living rights of smaller nationalities—as it has been doing for years against the population of Kosovo, 90 percent of which is Albanian—while throwing all international peace efforts to the wind.

This could be a deterrent example of the future problems of national restructuring in Eastern Europe, a warning against relapses into the nationalisms of the interwar period. But it could also be an incentive for the continued development of a supranational and suprastate mechanism of conflict resolution, a task for which neither the European Community nor the United Nations has so far shown itself to be sufficiently equipped. In the final analysis we are talking about a right of intervention against arbitrary acts and acts of violence by dictatorships, as was first applied in the case of Iraq (in 1991) on the resolution of the UN Security Council.

The proclaimed democratization of the postdictatorial countries, in many ways linked with the simultaneous liberation and (self-)endangerment of the nation-state in Eastern Europe, has been able to fulfill the great expectations of 1989 only in part. Characteristic are the great problems of governability even in developed states such as Poland and Czechoslovakia. The great number of constantly emerging parties and their unsteady ability to form coalitions are rendering the reliable formation of majorities difficult, and they reinforce the proclivity for minority governments or even the danger of authoritarian interventions, owing to a self-elimination on the part of the parliaments—all bitter experiences from the interwar period. Another danger is posed by the continuing trend toward separation— as of the Slovaks and Czechs—and toward the formation of small-scale, ethnically limited nation-states, whose conflict-ridden positions could once again pose a serious impediment to their viability as democracies. As an observer of Eastern and Central Europe recently remarked: "The transformations of the last three years demonstrate sufficiently that history had been frozen during the decades of the Communists, and that the old conflicts, tensions, and problems are reappearing like the debris of a terminal moraine when a glacier recedes."[2]

The restructuring of the Continent, finally liberated from the great ideological dictatorships of the century, is taking place between crisis and renewal. In fact: "Europe's second future is open again," as Curt Gasteyger has put it. That future contains the chances for a second renaissance of democracy after 1945, but only if, alongside the positive experiences from the first political and economic renaissance in Western Europe, the warnings of the preceding, failed period between the wars are taken seriously and heeded. It has already happened once before that newly established democratic nation-states in Europe in the wake of reconstruction degenerated for the most part into authoritarian regimes and then fell victim to the assault of totalitarian dictatorships. From the dual experience of 1918 and 1945 emerge lessons and aims for the present:

1. The renaissance of democracy. This means making up in the quickest possible way the political modernization that was prevented for decades by the Communist imposition of totalitarian structures on the countries liberated from National Socialist rule.

2. The renaissance of the nation-state. It contains all the dangers of a relapse into the great fragmentation and antagonism in Europe during the twenties and thirties, along with the possible return of authoritarian dictatorships under the pretext of crisis, which would be a calamitous solution to democratic as well as national problems.

3. The renaissance of a free economy and society. In the nongovernmental sphere this requires, as a counterpart to the Communist utopia as well as a precondition for economic productivity after decades in which the citizen was disenfranchised and disparaged, the development of a genuine social market economy that goes beyond the limitations of class politics and etatism, with the goal of a free citizenry, a civil society.

4. The renaissance of Europe in the East. This means the continued development of cooperation and integration, with the help of governmental openness and limitations on national sovereignties through bonds that transcend the state. And above the legacy of collapsed Communist universalism there should now be placed the guiding model of a league of free, democratic, united states of Europe, for which the European institutions built in the past four decades have created the essential preconditions. They must now be developed, step by step, for liberated Eastern Europe as well.

5. The renaissance of federalism. This opens the way for the political safeguarding of liberty between an unrestricted centralism and a centrifugal pluralism. Never in history has the majority of states been democratic. A contribution to the reduction in the number of dictatorships all over the world could now be made by the model of a reconstructed Europe. This reconstruction can also provide, through federal structures of economic cooperation and political integration within and between states, and with protection for hu-

man and civil rights, a better guarantee for the peaceful solution to conflicts than dictatorial or merely bureaucratic solutions can ever offer.

During the past century, the decline of the West that Oswald Spengler sought to prophesy in his 1918 book (which he had already conceived in 1911) often seemed at hand. But now the last bastion of totalitarianism in Europe has finally fallen, just before the beginning of the last decade.

After the great sigh of relief of 1989, and after three years of freedom and new fears arising from the vacuum caused by the collapse, the anxious question remains: is the incalculable burden of the terrible Communist legacy too much, after all, for Europe to bear? Can the West, which itself is showing signs of being overburdened in many areas, provide the Eastern Europeans with the many different kinds of help they think they need? In contrast to the "mere" twelve years of destruction wrought by National Socialism, Europe is confronting its new challenges after nearly half or even three-quarters of a century of oppression and deception, of violence and lies in the guise of the promise of a new world.

The Europe of the crises has not only survived: at the end of destruction and division, it has also been given a new, great historical opportunity that it must not gamble away by falling back into old patterns of arrogance or resignation.

Forty (and Nearly Sixty) Years of Dictatorship: A Challenge to a Government of Laws

Questions

In the current "epochal change" of 1989 and 1990, we are experiencing, for the second time in our most recent past (the first was from 1945 to 1949), the welcome and difficult transition from a totalitarian-party dictatorship to a liberal democracy. In both instances this has meant, at the same time, the transition from a tyrannical government to a government under the rule of law.

And once again we are confronted with the lofty challenge of working through what is now a fifty-seven-year history of dictatorship—a right-wing totalitarian dictatorship followed by a left-wing totalitarian dictatorship—and with the quickly emerging disappointment over the unfulfilled expectations and euphoria of the revolution. Were or are these expectations set too high? How can a government of laws come to terms with the legacy of a tyrannical government? Especially a government that, as a totalitarian regime, presented itself in the guise of legality and at the same time in the service to a higher idea, as a state justified and legitimated as pseudodemocratic, pseudoconstitutional, and ideological, indeed as a "socialist government of laws"? How are we to deal with this difficult legacy within the framework of a government of laws? Moreover, to what extent can we derive lessons or at least insights from similar, though only partially comparable, historical-political situations while simultaneously taking into account the specific problems raised by the German case of 1989–90, in view of the end of other Communist dictatorships?

I perceive three levels to this challenge and the attempt to find answers: one must work through the legacy at the level of criminal law, personnel policy, and history—each approach being indispensable in dealing with the injustice that was committed.

A Government of Laws and the Judicial Process

It seems hard to accept the dilemma in which the government of laws finds itself: namely that it should be bound by the procedural principle *nulla poena sine lege* also when it comes to punishing injustices committed by a tyrannical state. Is it true that the top functionaries and commanders of a criminal regime can be prosecuted only for corruption or electoral fraud? Or that in the case of the order to shoot (at escapees at the border) only those who carried it out can be punished, while the prohibition of freedom of movement that was behind it and the real governmental criminality, the systemic and state crimes of persecution and surveillance, of oppression, arbitrary justice, and the absence of rights, must go unpunished and those responsible cannot be brought to justice? The situation was very different after 1945. Punishment was initially meted out by the victorious powers for war crimes and crimes against humanity, at first without any special consideration for the principle of *nulla poena*. Punishment also came, belatedly, from the German judicial system itself. However, in the absence of a revolution, the judicial system continued almost without a break from its counterpart in the National Socialist period; this was the flip side, in terms of personnel, of the theory of the continuity of the German Reich (a thesis that was favorable to the Germany policy).

But is it not the case that the tyrannical state of the GDR, even without war and a policy of racial annihilation, was fundamentally based on the elementary violation of basic human rights, rights that are—according to the United Nations charter and later the final accords of the Conference on Security and Cooperation in Europe—the positive foundation of a government of laws? It is my view, therefore, that the *nulla poena* limitation cannot have the same meaning in a tyrannical state as in a state of laws. This essential difference comes to the fore when we are dealing with crimes that violate the basic values of the government of laws and thus its very foundations: violations of the basic right of freedom of movement, political persecution, and violations of the independence of the judiciary.

When we talk about holding the oppressors responsible for the sake of rehabilitating the oppressed, what is at stake is the credibility of the orientation toward human rights, especially in a government of laws.[1] In this case there are legal-philosophical and moral limits to recognizing the legality of a tyrannical state. We must bear this in mind, given current objections to the application of the standards of a government of laws to crimes committed against human rights by a tyrannical state, and to the punishment of those most responsible; after all, this was already envisioned in the European Convention on Human Rights of 1950 (Article 7, paragraph 2).

That we were in fact dealing with a tyrannical state in East Germany was clear from the very outset of the SED dictatorship. We need only recall the continuation of the concentration and internment camps (Buchenwald, Sachsenhausen, Bautzen) under Soviet control, and the infamous Waldheim trials of 1950.[2] Those trials served the legend of the antifascist fight against National Socialist crimes as a pretext and instrument for politicizing the judiciary in order to implement the SED regime. It was "antifascism as ersatz legitimation,"[3] for the purpose of persecuting dissenters under conditions that made a mockery of any government of laws (undue haste, lack of publicity, an obstructed defense, excessive punishments, the entire proceedings under the decided influence of and orchestration by the SED). One has only to read the minutes of the proceedings at Waldheim on April 19, 1950:

> It is imperative that those who have been detained by our friends [the Soviet power] continue to be detained, since they are definite enemies of our reconstruction. If those people who are still in detention and who have been turned over to the German authorities for sentencing were not regarded as enemies by our friends, they would have been released. It is thus imperative that they be given harsh sentences under all circumstances. No regard can be given to what sort of case exists . . . sentences under ten years must not be passed.[4]

A final report for Ulbricht (July 5, 1950) even criticized at the time "a certain political weakness of the judiciary when it came to passing sentence for political reasons, and when the clear chain of evidence required for a formal judicial sentencing was lacking."[5] The almost unbroken history of party-directed, unjust verdicts during the following thirty-nine years confirms that the judiciary in the GDR was functionalized early on under the antifascist-socialist pretext, for the purpose of legitimating a dictatorial and tyrannical regime.

Personnel Policy

A criminal prosecution that does justice to the responsible perpetrators *and* to the victims thus appears to be, unfortunately, rather difficult to achieve. That being the case, all the more importance is attached to working through past injustices by way of personnel policy, not only in view of the past but also in view of the future. This applies particularly to a change of government that has been brought about not by a full-fledged revolution in state and society but by defeat (1918, 1945) or collapse (1989). Above all, the objective is to make clear the decisive break with the previous regime, in economic as well as political terms. This requires a change of personnel in the administration and the courts, in schools and universities, and also in society and the economy, to the extent that these areas had been coerced into line with the totalitarian politics through a system of planning and cadres. Such a change in personnel faces three tasks and goals.

1. For the restoration of justice and the attainment of satisfaction and restitution for those hitherto disadvantaged, the issue is sufficient compensation (for false imprisonment, for example) and the dismantling of any advantages and privileges that party members received from the biased system of connections and discrimination under the previous regime (the Rehabilitation Law).

2. The consolidation of the new, liberal government of laws requires, from the perspective of being a militant democracy, a personnel policy that counters such anticonstitutional, prodictatorial activities as infiltration, political extremism, and bureaucratic sabotage (as took place in the Weimar Republic).

3. The confidence of the populace in the newly won government of laws will be seriously impaired if that government employs the old functionaries. Removing them from positions in the government, society, and economy, or at least demoting them in no uncertain terms, is a legitimate concern especially for a government of laws, which depends on restoring trust in the justice meted out by the state. (In contrast to the situation in the immediate aftermath of 1945, today there is of course no general procedure for dealing with the perpetrators, the accused, and other members of the SED regime and its organizations, in particular its extensive Stasi apparatus.)

These principles certainly throw up considerable problems. How can one refuse appropriate employment to an applicant (hitherto privileged by the system)? One can do it when it is called for to restore justice and credibility. One can do it when it is expected by a long-oppressed populace, which will trust the democratic state of laws, something new to them, only if it is capable of such resolute personnel reform.

Those who think this overestimates the symbolic value of changes in personnel should be reminded of the enormous role that governmental and party personnel actually play or represent in a dictatorship, as the arms of an emphatically all-powerful regime unrestricted by any division of powers. The governmental, social, and economic functionary in those regimes is an arbitrary authority backed by the omnipresent secret power of "state security."

Against this background of historical experience, the political and psychological effect of a thorough personnel shake-up takes on an importance behind which the question of the efficient running of the government must temporarily take second place. The purpose of such a shake-up is to avoid the citizens' presently encountering their previous oppressor or spy, still in the same position, as the opportunistically "reformed" representative of the new democracy.

The call for amnesty came too soon, especially in the West. Concrete, practical needs do not take precedence over justice; the end does not justify the means. This should be definitely understood in the sense of an *ethic of responsibility*. A democratic state of laws, which depends on credibility, cannot base its ability to function and bring about integration in the transition from a dictatorial and tyrannical state merely on criteria of productivity and efficiency. It is true that reconciliation and integration are important in this transition. Moreover, the liberal government of laws seeks to interfere as little as possible and simply to form the framework for the free development of society. But hatred and enmity cannot be dismantled at the expense of confidence in the constitutional-democratic structures. Parliaments and (if possible) administrations that are free of Stasi people are a requirement for this, as is, of course, preventing the abuse of the Stasi files. Next to the media, the parties have a special responsibility in this process: their power calculations and self-imposed problems with personnel legacies can fatally weaken the always endangered trust in the new party-state democracy. That is why the demands of justice and confidence should prevent the state from using the services of someone who is technically competent but burdened by his past, for that is an affront to the victims. What is at stake is a higher level of efficiency in a democracy based on the rule of law.

The Historical Approach

We are thus looking at the still-unresolved task of criminal justice, and at a personnel approach to the legacy of the GDR and SED that is difficult when it comes to particulars and fluctuates between the need to purge and the need for efficient government. The SED lives on in its successor organization, the Party of Democratic Socialism (PDS), in contrast to the National Socialist German Workers' Party, which ceased to exist in 1945. The coalition parties have also failed to make a complete break with the past. It is therefore all the more urgent that historical investigation and debate show the reasons for what happened and seek to draw political and moral lessons for the future relationship between the citizens and their state. This runs counter to the all-too-easy, cheap demand (by the "wrynecks") that we should now direct our view forward and start all over. The future is faced with a difficult history of fifty-seven years of dictatorship, nearly three generations: first the right-wing totalitarian dictatorship and then left-wing totalitarian rule. This period, with its aberrations, seductions, and violations, has left behind a great vacuum and many crises of orientation. Only the history of the Soviet dictatorship has been longer—and it is, unfortunately, still unfinished. The German case cannot be readily compared to the Soviet case and other dictatorial countries. What are the lessons we can learn from the attempt to master the German case? What are the prospects for doing so?

First off, there is the accusation that after 1945 the effort at coming to terms with the National Socialist dictatorship took too long and was not broad or deep enough in its effects. There were three reasons, in particular, that the early publication of the Nuremberg documents, and soon thereafter some fundamental studies, did not advance the political clarification and education as much as desired. First, there was the problem of de-Nazification, which was initially very broad but often felt to be "victor's justice." After some initial, far-reaching measures it was gradually abandoned as the cold war progressed, but it did last twelve to fifteen years. The people around the SED-PDS organ *Neues Deutschland* who are now invoking the mildness of de-Nazification should wait at least that long. Second, the destruction of the war, the expulsions of ethnic Germans, and the hardships of life overshadowed the political debates. Third, the end of the National Socialist system (with the punishment or suicide of leading representatives) tended for the most part to be experienced as a military defeat. After all, this was not a dictatorship imposed from outside and above, as in the GDR, but was unfortunately a home-grown one, to whose seduction the nation had succumbed.

There are, however, points of comparison that ought to be considered today if we want to do better the second time around. There was the fact that soon after the upheaval of 1945 the ability of the state and the administration to function and the quick integration of the millions of refugees and expellees was moved into the foreground. Reconstruction and reconciliation were guiding motifs. In the West, they carried the nation past the German catastrophe and helped to make possible, under favorable political and economic conditions, an unexpectedly rapid recovery. Therein lay both the strength and the weakness of Adenauer's policy. The flip side was a long, drawn-out conflict over coming to terms with the past, which flared up again twenty years later. Not without reason, even if in all-too-general terms, the next generation accused those who had founded the republic of wanting to forget and suppress the past rather than come to terms with it. This created a mistrust of the government of laws, a mistrust that has made itself felt to this day: we can think of the 1968 movement (and, subsequently, terrorism), and also of the disappointment among the persecuted and the survivors of World War II.[6]

However, in decided contrast to the Weimar period and the GDR, a strong democratic stability developed out of these very self-critical confrontations and the possibility of historical and political comparisons in the postwar period. K. D. Henke sees a kind of self-imposed de-Nazification through disillusionment after the inglorious end of the system and the positive experience of reconstruction, even though the participation—active and passive—of many Germans, without which the totalitarian dictatorship would not have been possible, was only slowly digested socially and mentally, and was repeatedly apologetically extenuated. What does this mean for our current problem?

There is much to be learned from the experiences and mistakes of that postwar period. The issue today is the confrontation of a democracy governed by the rule of law with the tyrannical past of a segment of the population separated for more than forty years, a segment that had to experience, participate in, and suffer through two dictatorships over three generations. Defusing this confrontation demands a redoubled effort, because it involves not only clashes within one nation between the perpetrators, victims, and those who just went along, made all the worse by the Stasi legacy; it also involves the encounter between two populations that have had very different experiences under the diametrically opposite systems, ideologies, and living situations of the GDR and the Federal Republic. Even after unification, this confrontation will persist for some time, as we know from our history after 1918 and 1945. For the future, it is important, after this second German dictatorship in the GDR into which the first one extended, to be on the lookout for a generational conflict that could break out in a few years even more acutely than today's, going far beyond the Stasi problem in its focus on a complex, undigested past.

Is the current radicalism from the right a prelude to this? It is, in any case, one of the signs of the shortcomings of a postdictatorial political culture that is vacillating between the burdensome legacy of a passive-authoritarian mentality and anarchic impulses. Beyond the overburdened courts and an unsatisfactory, controversial personnel policy, what therefore seems to me all the more important is the opportunity to thoroughly investigate the history of the SED regime—which has been partially misinterpreted in the West—with research into dictatorship that is exhaustively based on the sources, something that is now possible, and with a historical-comparative analysis. In this way one could preempt the rise of legends that might otherwise be fostered by insufficient criminal prosecution and inadequate personnel changes (these have developed after many dictatorships and revolutions before and after 1945, especially in Latin American countries, where the army usually prevents an investigation into the dictatorship, as most recently in Argentina and Chile).

Is this the small consolation of a historian and political scientist? Perhaps not: for the history of the Federal Republic also shows what a political education steeped in the lessons of historical experience can accomplish, in spite of the shortcomings of the confrontation with National Socialism (which did begin quite early). The stabilization of the second German democracy after the failure of the first democracy of Weimar was inconceivable without the relentless yet nonpartisan confrontation with our double past, recent and contemporary, of dictatorship from the Right and the Left. For the citizens of the former GDR, this second democracy has now just begun. Their historical experience with two tyrannical states can help them bring to maturity the undoubtedly painful learning process that their peaceful revolution—after the failure of June 17, 1953, when the intervention by Soviet troops prevented an early self-liberation—has once again set into motion. And we could and should help to avoid in this process some of the mistakes that have complicated our own road to the second German democracy.

Notes

Foreword

1. Some of the material in this foreword will also appear, in quite a different form, in Abbott Gleason, *The Generations of Totalitarianism*, forthcoming from Oxford University Press. Many thanks to Volker Berghahn for advice and criticism and to F. L. Carsten for information about the Bracher family.
2. This is argued, for example, by Joyce and Gabriel Kolko; see *The World and United States Foreign Policy, 1945–1954* (New York, 1972).
3. Jean-François Revel, *The Totalitarian Temptation* trans. David Haggood (Garden City, N.J., 1977), p. 23.
4. Jeane Kirkpatrick, *Dictatorships and Double Standards: Rationalism and Reason in Politics* (New York, 1982,) pp. 50–51.
5. See especially successive editions of his *Die Krise Europas seit 1917* (first edition 1976) for a synthetic view.
6. Bracher's wife, Dorothee, is a niece of Dietrich Bonhoeffer and the daughter of Rüdiger Schleicher, who was involved with the 20th of July plot against Hitler and was murdered by the SS. Her sister married Eberhard Bethge, who was close to Dietrich Bonhoeffer and eventually wrote his biography.
7. K. D. Bracher, *Die Auflösung der Weimarer Republik: Eine Studie zum Problem des Machtverfalls in der Demokratie* (Stuttgart/Düsseldorf, 1955), with a chapter on the Reichswehr by W. Sauer; Bracher, Sauer, and Schulz, *Die Nationalsozialistische Machtergreifung: Studien zur Einrichtung des totalitären Herrschaftssystems in Deutschland 1933/34* (Cologne/Opladen, 1960); Bracher, *Die deutsche Diktatur: Entstehung, Struktur, Folgen des Nationalsozialismus* (Cologne/Berlin, 1969). An English translation of the last volume, *The German Dictatorship*, was published in New York by Praeger in 1970, followed by editions in many other languages.
8. I refer to the version produced by Carl J. Friedrich and Zbigniew Brzezinski. See their *Totalitarian Dictatorship and Autocracy*, 2nd ed. (New York, 1966), p. 21 ff.

9. In addition to Friedrich and Brzezinski's *Totalitarian Dictatorship and Autocracy*, Bracher, Sauer, and Schulz referred approvingly to Sigmund Neumann's *Permanent Revolution* (New Yorker, 1942); see *Die National-sozialistische Machtergreifung*, 2nd ed., pp. 9–15.

10. Ibid., pp. 6–7.

11. In "The Ethos of Democracy" (1990), collected in this volume, Bracher speaks of Rousseau's postulation of "the necessary identity of the government and the governed" as being at the heart of totalitarian development. This echoes numerous passages in Bracher's earlier volume, *The Age of Ideologies: A History of Political Thought in the Twentieth Century* (New York, 1984). The German original appeared in 1982.

12. K. D. Bracher, "Terrorism and Totalitarianism," from *Der Weg in die Gewalt* (Munich, 1978), excerpted in Ernest A. Menze, ed., *Totalitarianism Reconsidered* (Port Washington, N.Y., 1981), p. 108.

13. Bracher, "The Ethos of Democracy."

14. Bracher asks these questions in "From the End of the Division to the Renaissance of Europe?" which is the revised final chapter of his *Die Krise Europas seit 1917* (1992) and serves as a conclusion to this volume.

2. History between Ideas of Decay and Progress

1. Ludwig Edelstein, *The Idea of Progress in Classical Antiquity* (Baltimore, 1967); Christian Meier, *The Greek Discovery of Politics*, trans. David McLintock (Cambridge, Mass., 1990), and "Fortschritt," in *Geschichtliche Grundbegriffe*, vol. 2 (Stuttgart, 1975), pp. 350 ff.

2. Robert Nisbet, *History of the Idea of Progress* (New York, 1980), p. 4. On the current discussion see also K. D. Bracher, *Geschichte und Gewalt* (Berlin, 1981), and *The Age of Ideologies*, trans. Ewald Osers (New York, 1984).

3. See K. D. Bracher, "Providentia Americana: Ursprünge des demokratischen Sendungsgedankens in Amerika," in *Politische Ordnung und menschliche Existenz: Festgabe für Eric Voegelin* (Munich, 1962), pp. 27–48.

3. Thoughts on the Year of Revolution, 1989

1. Wolfgang Mantl, ed., *Die neue Architektur Europas: Reflexionen in einer bedrohten Welt* (Vienna, Cologne, Graz, 1991) (symposium, September 1990).

6. Reflections on the Problem of Power

1. The term used by Wolfgang Mantl, "Das politische Panorama im Zeitenbruch," in *Die neue Architektur Europas*, ed. W. Mantl (Vienna, 1991), pp. 73 ff.

2. For a historical assessment of the concept of power, see Karl-Georg Faber, Christian Maier, and Karl-Heinz Ilting, "Macht, Gewalt," in *Geschichtliche Grundbegriffe*, vol. 3 (Stuttgart, 1982), pp. 817–935, with a wealth of references. For an earlier discussion of "stages in the shift of power," see K. D. Bracher, "Auflösung einer Demokratie," in *Faktoren der Machtbildung* (Berlin, 1952), pp. 41 ff.

3. Alfred Adler, *Menschenkenntnis* (Leipzig, 1926; Frankfurt/Hamburg, 1966), p. 75; trans. Walter Béran Wolfe, *Understanding Human Nature* (New York, 1927), p. 73 f.

4. Walter Naumann, *Nietzsche* (Darmstadt, 1982), pp. 207 ff.; K. D. Bracher, *The Age of Ideologies,* trans. Ewald Osers (New York, 1982), pp. 18 ff.; see also note 8.

5. Eduard Spranger, *Lebensformen* (1921; 5th ed., Halle, 1925), p. 212 f; trans. J. W. Pigors, *Types of Men* (Halle, 1928), p. 188 f.

6. Bertrand Russell, *Power: A New Social Analysis* (New York, 1969), p. 12.

7. Lord John Emerich Acton, letter to Mandell Creighton dated April 4, 1887.

8. Jacob Burckhardt, *Reflections on History,* trans. M. D. H. (London, 1943), p. 86. In a similar vein, the young Nietzsche at the time, wrote in his fragment, "The Greek State," in *Early Greek Philosophy and Other Essays,* trans. M. A. Mügge (New York, 1964), p. 8: "The same cruelty we found in the essence of every culture lies also in the essence of every powerful religion and in general in the essence of power, which is always evil." See also his essay "Wagner in Bayreuth": "Who among you will renounce power, knowing and having experienced that power is evil?"

9. Max Weber, *Economy and Society: An Outline of Interpretive Sociology,* trans. Ephraim Fischer at al., ed. Günther Roth and Claus Wittich, vol. 1 (Berkeley, 1978), p. 53. See also Arnold Bergsträsser, *Die Macht als Mythos und als Wirklichkeit* (Freiburg/Breisgau, 1965), pp. 27 ff., 98.

10. Spranger, *Types of Men,* pp. 189 f.

11. Blaise Pascal, *Pensées sur la religion* (1669), fr. 298; trans. A. J. Krailsheimer, *Pascal: Pensées* (London, 1966), p. 56.

12. Dag Hammarskjöld, *Markings,* trans. Leif Sjöberg and W. H. Auden (New York, 1966), p. 58.

13. By now classic and influential is the work of Friedrich Meinecke, *Machiavellism: The Doctrine of Raison d'État and Its Place in Modern History,* trans. Douglas Scott (Boulder, 1984). The book is "simultaneously a history of Machiavellism and a history of the attempts to overcome it intellectually" (according to the editor of the German edition, Walter Hofer). On the controversy surrounding the modern conception of the state, see Stephan Skalweit, *Der Moderne Staatsbegriff,* Lectures of the Rhenisch-Westphalian Academy of Sciences (Opladen, 1975).

14. Gerhard Ritter's book has two titles: initially, during the National Socialist period, it had the more inocuous one, *Machtstaat und Utopie* (The Power State and Utopianism; 1940). Later it had the title that is characteristic of the postwar years, *Dämonie der Macht* (The Demonic Nature of Power; rev. ed., 1947). However, the earlier edition already carried the subtitle:

The Controversy over the Demonic Nature of Power since Machiavelli and More.

15. See the essay by O. Regenbogen, H. Strasburger, J. Vogt, and G. Ritter in H. Herter, ed., *Thukydides, Wege der Forschung* (Darmstadt, 1968); see also the essay by Klaus Rosen, co-editor, in *Geschichte der politischen Ideen* (Königstein, 1961), pp. 40 ff, 109 ff. Cf. K. D. Bracher, *Verfall und Fortschritt im Denken der frühen römischen Kaiserzeit* (diss., Univ. of Tübingen, 1948; Vienna/Cologne/Graz, 1987), pp. 198 ff. On the Roman principate see Zvi Yavetz, "Staatsklugheit und Charakterbild des Kaisers Augustus," in Manfred Funke et al., eds., *Demokratie und Diktatur: Geist und Gestalt politischer Herrschaft in Deutschland und Europa: Festschrift für Karl Dietrich Bracher* (Düsseldorf, 1987), p. 495; Jochen Bleicken, *Prinzipat und Republik,* Sitzungsberichte der Wissenschaftlichen Gesellschaft an der Universität Frankfurt/Main, vol. 27.2 (Stuttgart 1991), pp. 88 ff.

16. Christian Meier, *The Greek Discovery of Politics,* trans. David McLintock (Cambridge, Mass., 1990), chap. 1. Critical response by Jochen Bleicken, *Die athenische Demokratie* (Paderborn/Munich, 1985), pp. 327 ff.

17. Cf. Aristotle, *The Politics,* 1248 a-b.

18. Hella Mandt, "Politische Herrschaft und Macht," in *Handlexikon zur Politikwissenschaft,* ed. W. Mickel (Munich, 1986), pp. 374 ff., with the references.

19. Adam Smith, *Inquiry into the Nature and Causes of the Wealth of Nations* (1776). For a look at the current discussion of Adam Smith, see the collection edited by Heinz D. Kurz, *Adam Smith (1723–1790): Ein Werk und seine Wirkungsgeschichte* (Marburg, 1990).

20. Such as Eugen Böhm-Bawerk, *Macht oder ökonomisches Gesetz* (Berlin, 1914); and Joseph Schumpeter, *Aufsätze zur ökonmischen Theorie* (Tübingen, 1952), and *Capitalism, Socialism, Democracy* (New York/London, 1942).

21. Wilhelm Krelle, "Macht und ökonomisches Gesetz in der Verteilung," *Schriften des Vereins für Sozialpolitik* (New Series) 74 (1973): 84 ff.

22. Helmut Schmidt, title of his lead article in *Die Zeit,* November 8, 1989.

23. On the fascination with Hobbes, see the literature in Bernard Willms, *Thomas Hobbes: Das Reich des Leviathan* (Munich, 1987), pp. 15 ff., 271 ff; revealing is the outstanding importance he had for Carl Schmitt (and his followers), *Der Leviathan in der Staatslehre des Thomas Hobbes* (Hamburg, 1938; reprint 1982). See also Bracher, *Age of Ideologies,* p. 328 and elsewhere.

24. Thus Gesine Schwan (borrowing from Max Weber), "Politik ohne Vertrauen? Iddengeschichtliche und systematische Überlegungen zum Verhältnis von Politik und Vertrauen," in Peter Haungs, ed., *Veröffentlichungen der Deutschen Gesellschaft für Politikwissenschaft* 8 (1990): 9 ff., 24. (*Sonderheft der Zeitschrift für Politik* 8: "Politik ohne Vertrauen?").

25. Karl R. Popper, *The Open Society and Its Enemies* (London, 1945).

26. See K. D. Bracher, *Zeitgeschichtliche Kontroversen* (Munich, 1984), pp. 34 ff., 119 ff.; K. D. Bracher with Leo Valiani, *Faschismus und Nationalsozialismus* (Berlin, 1991), pp. 25 ff.

27. Alexis de Tocqueville, *Democracy in America* (1835), vol. 1, chap. 15: "Power exercised by the majority in America upon opinion"; vol. 2, chap. 6: "What sort of despotism democratic nations have to fear."

28. Montesquieu, *The Spirit of the Laws*, trans. Thomas Nugent, rev. J. V. Pritchard (1900), vol. 1, book 11, sections 4–6.

29. Ernst Fraenkel, *Reformismus und Pluralismus* (Hamburg, 1973), pp. 424 ff. ("Pluralismus und Totalitarismus"); see the contributions on the pluralism debate in the 1973 Festschrift for Ernst Fraenkel (Hamburg), pp. 381 ff. For the totalitarian rejection of separation of powers, see, on the one hand, A. Wyschinskij, *The Law of the Soviet State* (New York, 1954), pp. 312 ff., and, on the other, E. R. Huber, *Verfassungsrecht des Großdeutschen Reiches* (Hamburg, 1939), pp. 24, 160.

30. Hermann Lübbe, *Politischer Moralismus. Der Triumph der Gesinnung über die Urteilskraft* (Berlin, 1987), p. 7.

31. On this, see especially Karl Loewenstein, *Verfassungslehre* (Tübingen, 1959), pp. 167 ff., 296 ff. See also the varied arguments in the debate over whether the seat of parliament and government should be in Bonn or Berlin, arguments that are definitely relevant to the politics of federalism and that, in this regard, tended to favor Bonn.

32. Cf. Walter L. Bühl, "Deutschland als föderativer und transnationaler Staat," *Zeitschrift für Politik* 37 (1990): 233 ff.

33. Discussions on power in international politics were conducted, most importantly, in the influential school of political realism, led by Hans J. Morgenthau; see his classic work (with Kenneth W. Thompson), *Politics among Nations: The Struggle for Power and Peace* (1948; 6th ed., New York, 1985). See also John W. Coffrey, *Political Realism in American Thought* (Lewisburg, 1977), pp. 125 ff, and the collection of essays edited by G.-K. Kindermann (preface by Hans J. Morgenthau), *Grundelemente der Weltpolitik* (Munich/Zurich, 1977). For a more recent discussion, see Klaus Faupel, "Ein analytischer Begriff der Entspannung: Große Politk, Machtpolitik und das Ende des Ost-West Konflikts," *Zeitschrift für Politik* 38 (1991): 155 ff. See also notes 71 and 72 below.

34. In the classical works of Ernest Barker, *Reflections on Government* (London, 1942), pp. 57 ff., and *Political Thought in England from 1848 to 1914*, 12th ed. (London, 1963); Karl Loewenstein, *Verfassungslehre* (Tübingen, 1959); Dolf Sternberger, *Lebende Verfassung* (Meisenhaim/Glan, 1956). On the separation of power between politics and economics, see Ernst Joachim Mestmäcker, "Die Kraft des Freiburger Imperativs," *Frankfurter Allgemeine Zeitung* 127, (June 2, 1990): 13.

35. On this, see especially Ludger Kühnhardt, *Die Universalität der Menschenrechte* (Munich, 1987).

36. See Maria R. Panzer, *Bürgerlichkeit. Fehldeutungen des Bürgerbegriffs in der politischen Moderne* (Munich, 1989), pp. 171 ff.

37. See the stimulating study by Eleonore Sterling, *Der unvollkommene Staat. Studien über Demokratie und Diktatur* (Frankfurt/Main, 1965). On the following disussion, see also Hans Vorländer, *Verfassung und Konsens* (Ber-

lin, 1981); Stephan Eisel, *Minimalkonsens und freiheitliche Demokratie* (Paderborn, 1986), p. 29 ff.

38. Fritz Stern, *Geschichte und Geschichtsschreibung* (Munich, 1966), p. 32; Jean-François Revel, *The Totalitarian Temptation*, trans. David Haggood (Garden City, N.J., 1977). Brilliant, though too optimistic in its title, is Joachim Fest, *Der zerstörte Traum: Vom Ende des utopischen Zeitalters* (Berlin, 1991).

39. On the uncertain prospects of the developments in the Soviet Union from the perspective of 1989, see Walter Laqueur, *The Road to Freedom: Russia and Glasnost* (New York, 1989).

40. See especially, since the late 1960s, the influential circle around Hans Mommsen and others. Cf. Manfred Funke's overview of the controversies: *Starker oder schwacher Diktator? Hitlers Herrschaft und die Deutschen* (Düsseldorf, 1989).

41. This has been the gist of my own work since the 1950s. See for example my essay in *Vierteljahrshefte für Zeitgeschichte* 4 (1956): 30 ff.; 42 (reprinted in *Die nationalsozialistische Machtergreifung,* ed. Wolfgang Michalka (Paderborn, 1984), pp. 13 ff; 27). The debate is summarized by Klaus Hildebrand, "Monokratie oder Polykratie?," in K. D. Bracher, M. Funke, and H. A. Jacobson, eds., *Nationalsozialistische Diktatur,* 6th ed. (Düsseldorf, 1987), pp. 73 ff.; Hildebrande, *Das Dritte Reich,* 3rd ed. (Munich, 1987), pp. 115 ff. In addition, see Hermann Graml, "Wer bestimmte die Außenpolitik des Dritten Reiches? Ein Beitrag zur Kontroverse um Polykratie und Monokratie im NS-Herrschaftssystem," in Funke et al., eds., *Demokratie und Diktatur,* pp. 223 ff., and the comparison by Alan Bullock, *Hitler and Stalin: Parallel Lives* (London, 1991), pp. 387 ff.

42. For a more detailed discussion, see my books: *The German Dictatorship,* trans. Jean Steinberg (New York, 1972), pp. 330 ff.; *Age of Ideologies,* pp. 153, 174 ff; *Die totalitäre Erfahrung* (Munich, 1987), pp. 22, 45 ff. On Hitler's "socialism" see also Rainer Zitelmann, *Hitler: Selbstverständnis eines Revolutionärs,* 2nd ed. (Stuttgart, 1989), as well as his interim essay taking stock of the debate over "Nationalsozialismus und Moderne," in Werner Süß, ed., *Übergänge: Zeitgeschichte zwischen Utopie und Machbarkeit* (Berlin, 1990), pp. 195 ff.

43. On the decisions over which path to take since 1917 and after 1945, see K. D. Bracher, *Europa in der Krise: Innengeschichte und Weltpolitik seit 1917* (Frankfurt/Berlin/Vienna, 1979), pp. 17 ff., 281 ff. See also Mantl, ed., *Die neue Architektur Europas,* pp. 74 ff., on the transformations of 1989–90.

44. Cf. Jacob L. Talmon, *The Myth of the Nation and the Vision of Revolution* (London, 1980), pp. 549 ff.; Bracher, *Age of Ideologies,* pp. 52 ff.; *Geschichte und Gewalt* (Berlin, 1981), pp. 19 ff., 127 ff.; *Die totalitäre Erfahrung* (Munich, 1987), pp. 21 ff.

45. For more on the discussion that follows, see my detailed accounts and analyses in: *Die Auflösung der Weimarer Republik: Eine Studie zum Problem des Machtverfalls in der Demokratie* (1955; 6th ed., Düsseldorf, 1984), pp. 257 ff; also, "Demokratie und Machtvakuum," in K. D. Erdmann and H. Schulze, eds., *Weimar: Selbstpreisgabe einer Demokratie,* 2nd ed. (Düsseldorf, 1984), pp. 109 ff., pp. 135 ff.

46. See the overview of the more recent controversies between Knut Borchardt and his critics (like Carl-Ludwig Holtfrerich), in Jürgen Baron von Kruedener, ed., *Economic Crisis and Political Collapse: The Weimar Republic 1924–1933* (Oxford/Munich, 1990), pp. XI ff.

47. On this underestimation, see Bracher, *Zeitgeschichtliche Kontroversen,* pp. 43 ff.; *Die nationalsozialistische Machtergreifung,* 2nd ed. (Cologne, 1962), pp. 31 ff.

48. On the debate over the "end of history," see the special edition of the journal *Merkur* 44, 10/11 (1990); in addition, see the protocol of the Second Nassau Talks on November 16–17, 1990, in Frankfurt/Main (ed. Alexander Gauland).

49. On this, see the more recent discussion on "civil society"—for example at an international conference in Castel Gandolfo (August 1989), reported in *Frankfurter Allgemeine Zeitung,* August 14, 1989, p. 3. And see especially Edward Shils, "The Virtue of Civil Society," *Government and Opposition* 26, no. 1 (1991): 3 ff. On the civilizing of violence, see Bracher, *Geschichte und Gewalt,* pp. 11 ff., 106 ff.

50. See the connecting lines between the old-new discussion about soviets and the utopian notion of the "third way," in Bracher, *Age of Ideologies,* pp. 219 ff.

51. "*Mitbestimmung* (codetermination) is an awkward and almost untranslatable word. It refers to the joint participation of owners and workers in the running of West German industry." Peter Katzenstein, *Policy and Politics in West Germany: The Growth of a Semisovereign State* (Philadelphia, 1987), p. 125 (translator's note).

52. On the waves of *Mitbestimmung* in the Federal Republic, see K. D. Bracher, W. Jäger, and W. Link, *Republik im Wandel* (Stuttgart, 1986), pp. 127 ff., 312 ff. ("Politik und Zeitgeist: Tendenzen der siebziger Jahre" [Politics and the Spirit of the Times: Trends of the Seventies]).

53. Ralf Dahrendorf, *Die Chancen der Krise* (Stuttgart, 1983), pp. 16 ff. ("Am Ende des sozialdemokratischen Jahrhunderts" [At the End of the Social Democratic Century]). *Fragmente eines neuen Liberalismus* (Stuttgart, 1987), pp. 111 ff.

54. On this see, K. D. Bracher, "Die sozialistische Idee in Geschichte und Gegenwart," in H. G. Zempelin et al., eds., *Staat und Gesellschaft nach dem Scheitern des sozialistischen Experiments,* Publications of the Walter Raymond Foundation (Cologne, 1991).

55. Walter Eucken, *Die Grundlagen der Nationalökonomie* (1940; 8th ed., Berlin, 1965).

56. I am basing myself here on Hans F. Zacher's lecture entitled "Sozialrecht im Verfassungsstaat," delivered on April 18, 1990, before the Rhenisch-Westphalian Academy of Sciences (338th meeting) in Düsseldorf.

57. See note 20.

58. So argues Hans F. Zacher in his Düsseldorf lecture (see note 56).

59. Compare Bracher, "Die sozialistische Idee" (see note 54); *Die totalitäre Erfahrung* (Munich, 1987), pp. 70 ff.

60. I am indebted to Wilhelm Krelle for valuable suggestions on this point and

also for his comments in our discussion of the economic-political problem of power.

61. Heinrich Oberreuter, "Staat, Macht, Gewalt," in *Zur Debatte: Themen der Katholischen Akademie in Bayern* 20, no. 1 (Jan.–Feb. 1990): 11 f.

62. Roman Herzog, Hartmut Kreß, "Macht," in *Evangelisches Staatslexikon,* 3rd ed., vol. 1 (Stuttgart, 1987), pp. 2057 ff., 2064.

63. K. D. Bracher, *Theodor Heuss und die Wiederbegründung der Demokratie in Deutschland* (Tübingen, 1965), p. 48; also in *The German Dilemma,* trans. Richard Barry (New York, 1975).

64. Compare Andreas Schüler, *Erfindergeist und Technikkritik: Der Beitrag Amerikas zur Modernisierung und die Technikdebatte seit 1900* (Stuttgart, 1990), on the technical and historical background.

65. Niklas Luhmann, *Macht* (Stuttgart, 1975); trans. Howard Davis, John Raffan, and Kathryn Rooney, as *Trust and Power: Two Works* (New York, 1979).

66. Ibid.

67. This was argued, in particular, by the American adviser Francis Fukuyama in the summer 1989 issue of the journal *National Interest,* in an essay entitled "The End of History"; there followed a flood of discussions on both sides of the Atlantic. See also note 48.

68. In the debate over terrorism, the first studies that appeared, which are still valuable, were those by Walter Laqueur, *Terrorism* (Boston, 1977), and Manfred Funke, ed., *Terrorismus* (Düsseldorf, 1977). Since then the literature has become almost too vast to keep track of.

69. Luhmann, *Trust and Power.*

70. Ibid.

71. Hans-Peter Schwarz, *Die gezähmten Deutschen. Von der Machtbesessenheit zur Machtvergessenheit* (Stuttgart, 1985); see also, by the same author, "Der Faktor Macht im heutigen Staatensystem," in K. Kaiser and H.-P. Schwarz, eds., *Weltpolitik: Strukturen-Akteure-Perspektiven* (Stuttgart, 1985), pp. 50 ff.

72. On the debate, see the volumes edited by Wilhelm Hennis, Peter Graf Kielmansegg, and Ulrich Matz, *Regierbarkeit: Studien zur ihrer Problematisierung* (Stuttgart, 1977 and 1979); see also my discussion in "Politik und Zeitgeist," pp. 353 ff., and in *Age of Ideologies,* pp. 219 ff. And see Thomas Helfen, "Die Kritik am Mehrheitsprinzip als Herausforderung der repräsentativen Demokratie" (diss., Bonn Univ., 1991), which has much to say on the discussion about governability.

9. Authoritarianism and Totalitarianism

1. For more detail on this, see the following of my previous books: *Europa in der Krise* (Frankfurt/Berlin/Vienna, 1979), pp. 42 ff., 138 ff.; *Geschichte und Gewalt* (Berlin, 1981), pp. 93 ff., 127 ff.; *The Age of Ideologies,* trans. Ewald Osers (New York, 1982), pp. 81 ff., 166 ff.; *Die totalitäre Erfahrung* (Mu-

nich, 1987), pp. 20 ff. On the importance of 1918–19, see Francis L. Carsten, *Revolution in Central Europe 1918–1919* (Berkeley, 1972).

2. Compare Jens Petersen, "Die Entstehung des Totalitarismusbegriffs in Italien," in Manfred Funke, ed., *Totalitarismus*, Bonner Schriften zur Politik und Zeitgeschichte 14 (Düsseldorf, 1978), pp. 105 ff.; K. D. Bracher, *Zeitgeschichtliche Kontroversen: Um Faschismus, Totalitarismus, Demokratie*, 2nd ed. (Munich, 1984), pp. 13 ff.; K. D. Bracher, *Schlüsselwörter in der Geschichte* (Düsseldorf, 1978), pp. 103 ff.

3. This is how Sigmund Neumann described them in 1932, in *Die Parteien der Weimarer Republik* (Berlin, 1932; 2nd ed., Stuttgart, 1965), p. 107. On (Italian) Fascism see especially the works of Renzo de Felice. See also my article "Faschismus," *Staatslexikon* 2 (reprint, Freiburg/Basel/Vienna, 1986), cols. 549 ff.

4. Freyer's work of the same title *(Revolution von Rechts)* appeared in 1931. On this, see in particular Jerry Z. Muller, *The Other God That Failed* (Princeton, 1987), pp. 193 ff. On the historical Fascism–National Socialism debate, see also Gerhard Schulz, *Faschismus-Nationalsozialismus: Versionen und theoretische Kontroversen 1922–1972* (Frankfurt/Berlin/Vienna, 1974). On the question of revolution, see Leo Valiani, "Il fascismo: Controrivoluzione e rivoluzione," in K. D. Bracher and Leo Valiani, eds., *Fascismo e nazionalsocialismo* (Bologna, 1986), pp. 11 ff.

5. *Revolution der Deutschen* (Oldenbourg, 1933), p. 155 (radio speech of April 1, 1933). Compare K. D. Bracher, W. Sauer, and G. Schulz, *Die Nationalsozialistische Machtergreifung*, 2nd ed. (Opladen, 1962), pp. 7 ff.; K. D. Bracher, *The German Dictatorship*, trans. Jean Steinberg (New York, 1972), pp. 191 ff.; Bracher, *Zeitgeschichtliche Kontroversen*, pp. 68 ff. (on the ambivalence of tradition and revolution); David Schoenbaum, *Hitler's Social Revolution* (New York, 1966); see also Renzo de Felice, *Mussolini il Rivoluzionario* (Turin, 1965), and Eugen Weber, "Revolution? Counterrevolution? What Revolution?" *Journal of Contemporary History* 9 (1974): 3 ff.

6. See Emilio Gentile, "Partito, Stato e Duce nella mitologia e nella organizzazione del fascismo," in Bracher and Valini, eds. *Fascismo e nazionalsocialismo*, pp. 267 ff., 293 ff.; Konrad Repgen, "Faschismus," in *Katholisches Soziallexikon* (Innsbruck/Graz, 1980), cols. 699 ff.

7. Juan Linz, "Totalitarian and Authoritarian Regimes," in Fred I. Greenstein and Nelson W. Polsby, eds., *Handbook of Political Science*, vol. 3 (Reading, Mass., 1975), pp. 175–411; Juan J. Linz and Alfred Stepan, eds., *The Breakdown of Democratic Regimes*, vol. 2: *Europe* (Baltimore/London, 1978), pp. vii ff., and especially the essay by Walter Simon on Austria, pp. 80 ff.; Alfred Ableitinger, "Autoritäres Regime," in *Katholisches Soziallexikon* (Innsbruck/Graz, 1980), cols. 209 ff.

8. Othmar Spann, *Der wahre Staat* (Vienna, 1921). Compare from his school, for example, Walter Heinrich, "Ständische Ordnung und Diktatur," *Jahrbücher für Nationalökonomie und Statistik* 136, 3rd series, no. 81 (1932): 868 ff. An early German parallel is Heinrich Herrfahrdt, *Das Prob-*

lem der Berufsständischen Vertretung von der Französischen Revolution bis zur Gegenwart (Stuttgart/Berlin, 1921), pp. 181 ff. See also Bracher, *The Age of Ideologies*, pp. 176–186.

9. K. D. Bracher, *Die Auflösung der Weimarer Republik: Eine Studie zum Problem des Machtverfalls in der Demokratie,* 6th ed. (Düsseldorf, 1984), pp. 471 ff. On the intellectual and economic factors, see the account by Ulrich Kluge, *Der österreichische Ständestaat 1934–1938* (Munich, 1984).

10. Ableitinger, "Autoritäres Regime," col. 214.

11. See Manfred Welan, "Die Verfassungsentwicklung in der Ersten Republik," in Joseph F. Desput, ed., *Österreich 1934–1984* (Graz, 1984), pp. 81 ff; and not without an apologetic tone, Ludwig Reichhold, *Kampf um Österreich: Die Vaterländische Front und ihr Widerstand gegen den Anschluß 1933–1938* (Vienna, 1984).

12. Ableitinger, "Autoritäres Regime," col. 215.

13. Hans Herzfeld, *Die moderne Welt 1789–1945,* part 2, 4th ed. (Braunschweig, 1970), p. 260.

14. See Antony Polonsky, *The Little Dictators: The History of Eastern Europe since 1918* (London, 1975).

15. On this, see especially Georg von Rauch, *Geschichte der baltischen Staaten* (Stuttgart, 1970); compare the relevant chapters by Gotthold Rhode and Arved v. Taube, in Theodor Schieder, ed., *Handbuch der europäischen Geschichte,* vol. 7/2, hereafter cited as *Handbuch 7/2* (Stuttgart, 1979), cols. 1065–1079, 1107–1133.

16. Gotthold Rhode, "Polen von der Wiederherstellung der Unabhängigkeit bis zur Ära der Volksrepublik 1918–1970," in Schieder, ed., *Handbuch 7/2,* cols. 1007 ff.

17. Leo Valiani, *The End of Austria-Hungary* (London, 1973); Denis Silagi, "Ungarn seit 1918," in Schieder, ed., *Handbuch 7/2,* cols. 887 ff.

18. Gotthold Rhode, "Die südosteuropäischen Staaten, Rumänien 1918–1968," in Schieder, ed., *Handbuch 7/2,* cols. 1135 ff; also Andreas Hillgruber, *Hitler, König Carol und Marschall Antonescu* (Wiesbaden, 1954).

19. See Werner Markert, ed., *Osteuropa-Handbuch 1: Jugoslawien* (Cologne/Graz, 1954), as well as Klaus-Detlev Grothusen, *Südosteuropa-Handbuch 1: Jugoslawien* (Göttingen, 1975); Gotthold Rhode, "Die südosteuropäischen Staaten," in Schieder, ed., *Handbuch 7/2,* cols. 1183–1208.

20. Gunnar Hering, "Griechenland vom Lausanner Frieden bis zum Ende der Obersten-Diktatur 1923–1974," in Schieder, ed., *Handbuch 7/2,* cols. 1314 ff.

21. See the accounts by Stanley Payne, *A History of Spain and Portugal,* 2 vols. (Madison, Wis., 1973); Raymond Carr, ed., *The Republic and the Civil War in Spain* (New York, 1971); and Hugh Thomas, *The Spanish Civil War* (New York, 1961); as well as Richard Konetzke, "Die iberischen Staaten vom Ende des I. Weltkrieges bis zur Ära der autoritären Regime 1917–1960," in Schieder, ed., *Handbuch 7/2,* cols. 663–698.

22. The basic work on this is Klemens von Klemperer, *Ignaz Seipel, Staatsmann einer Krisenzeit* (Graz, 1976), especially chap. 4.

23. See Peter Pulzer, *The Rise of Political Anti-Semitism in Germany and Austria,*

rev. ed. (Cambridge, Mass., 1988); Francis L. Carsten, *Fascist Movements in Austria: From Schönerer to Hitler* (London, 1977), pp. 224 ff.

24. Gerhard Botz, *Krisenzonen einer Demokratie* (Frankfurt/New York, 1987), pp. 65 ff.; Adam Wandruszka, "Austrofaschismus: Anmerkungen zur politischen Bedeutung der 'Heimwehr' in Österreich," in Manfred Funke et al., eds., *Demokratie und Diktatur: Geist und Gestalt politischer Herrschaft in Deutschland und Europa: Festschrift für Karl Dietrich Bracher* (Düsseldorf, 1987), pp. 216 ff.; Carsten, *Fascist Movements,* pp. 156 ff.

25. Bracher, *Auflösung der Weimarer Republik,* pp. 352 ff.

26. See Walter B. Simon, "Democracy in the Shadow of Imposed Sovereignty: The First Republic of Austria," in Linz and Stepan, eds., *Breakdown of Democratic Regimes,* vol. 2, p. 94: "testimony to the vitality of democratic politics in the First Republic of Austria."

27. Peter Huemer, *Sektionschef Robert Hecht und die Zerstörung der Demokratie in Österreich* (Munich, 1975), p. 213; Welan, "Verfassungsentwicklung," p. 81; compare Botz, *Krisenzonen einer Demokratie,* pp. 119 ff., 155 ff. (incl. bibliography), and also on the similarities to and differences from the German development in 1932 in terms of how rule functioned; compare Bracher, *Die Auflösung der Weimarer Republik,* pp. 287 ff.

28. Joseph Buttinger, *Am Beispiel Österreichs* (Vienna, 1972); Botz, *Krisenzonen einer Demokratie,* pp. 181 ff.; Gerhard Jagschitz, *Der Putsch: Die Nationalsozialisten 1934 in Österreich* (Vienna, 1976); Carsten, *Fascist Movements,* pp. 249 ff.

29. Adam Wandruszka, "Concezione della storia 'Gesamtdeutsch' e nazionalsocialismo," in Bracher and Valiani, eds., *Fascismo e nazionalsocialismo,* pp. 181 ff.

30. Gustav Otruba, "Hitler's 'Tausend-Mark-Sperre' und Österreichs Fremdenverkehr," in Rudolf Neck and Adam Wandruszka, eds., *Beiträge zur Zeitgeschichte* (Vienna, 1976), pp. 113 ff. Compare Norbert Schausberger, "Anschlußideologie und Wirtschaftsinteressen 1918–1939," in Heinrich Lutz and Helmut Rumpler, eds., *Österreich und die deutsche Frage im 19. und 20. Jahrhundert,* Wiener Beiträge zur Geschichte der Neuzeit 9 (Vienna, 1982); N. Schausberger, *Der Griff nach Österreich: Der Anschluß,* 3rd ed. (Vienna/Munich, 1988).

31. Hans-Adolf Jacobsen, *Nationalsozialistische Außenpolitik 1933–1938* (Frankfurt, 1968), pp. 406 ff.; Bracher, *The German Dictatorship,* pp. 293 ff.; Bracher, "Stufen der Machtergreifung," in Bracher, Sauer, and Schulz, *Die Nationalsozialistiche Machtergreifung,* pp. 307, 350 ff.

32. Manfred Funke, *Sanktionen und Kanonen* (Düsseldorf, 1970), pp. 15 ff.; Jens Petersen, *Hitler-Mussolini: Die Entstehung der Achse Berlin-Rom 1933–1936* (Tübingen, 1973), pp. 363, 410 ff.

33. Kurt von Schuschnigg, *Im Kampf gegen Hitler* (Vienna, 1969), pp. 350 ff. In the euphoria of the day, some even hoped for the return of southern Tyrol: see Adam Wandruszka, "Österreich," in Schieder, ed., *Handbuch* 7/2, col. 869; compare Ennio di Nolfo, "Die österreichisch-italienischen Beziehungen von der faschistischen Machtergreifung bis zum Anschluß," in *Öster-*

reichisch-italienisches Historikertreffen 1971–1972 (Innsbruck/Venice, 1975), pp. 261 f. and note 112 (literature).

34. Compare especially the volumes (eleven to date) published by the Wiener Dokumentationsarchiv des österreichischen Widerstands, Widerstand und Verfolgung, 1934–1945 (Resistance and persecution, 1934–1945), which include all groups from the Left to the Right. See also the accounts in Ulrich Weinzierl, *Österreichs Fall: Schriftsteller berichten vom "Anschluß"* (Munich/Vienna, 1987), as well as in Thomas Chorherr, *1938: Anatomie eines Jahres* (Vienna, 1987).

35. Akten zur Deutschen Auswärtigen Politik (Documents on German Foreign Policy), series D, vol. 2 (Baden-Baden, 1950), p. 158.

36. George L. Mosse, "Der erste Weltkrieg und die Brutalisierung der Politik," in Funke et al., eds., *Demokratie und Diktatur*, pp. 127 ff.

37. Simon, in Linz and Stepan, eds., *Breakdown of Democratic Regimes*, vol. 2, p. 80.

38. Benedetto Croce, *Gesammelte philosophische Schriften: Kleine Schriften zur Ästhetik*, vol. 1 (Tübingen, 1929), p. 4: "In actuality the true and perfect criticism is the transparent historical account of what happened; and history is the only true criticism one can make of the facts of humankind."

10. Totalitarianism as Concept and Reality

1. On the emergence of the term, see especially Jens Petersen, "Die Entstehung des Totalitarismusbegriffs in Italien," in Manfred Funke, ed., *Totalitarismus* (Düsseldorf, 1978), 105–128; and Helmut Goetz, "Über den Ursprung des Totalitarismusbegriffs," *Neue Zürcher Zeitung* 73 (March 28/29, 1976): 25.

11. Resistance in "Right Dictatorships"

1. This essay, part of which was presented at the European Forum Alpbach 1989, brings together my own studies from as far back as 1954 ("Das Gewissen steht auf") and 1956 ("Anfänge der deutschen Widerstandsbewegung") with my most recent discussion ("Die totalitäre Erfahrung," 1987).

12. The Place of World War II in History

1. Andreas Hillgruber, "Der historische Ort des Ersten Weltkrieges," in Manfred Funke et al., eds., *Demokratie und Diktatur: Geist und Gestalt politischer Herrschaft in Deutschland und Europa* (Düsseldorf, 1987), p. 109.

2. George F. Kennan, quoted in ibid., p. 111. For a view of the epoch since 1917 as a coherent period, see K. D. Bracher, *Europa in der Krise* (Frankfurt, 1979); new ed. published as *Die Krise Europas 1917 bis 1992* (Frankfurt/Berlin, 1992).

3. Hugh Seton-Watson, "The Age of Fascism and Its Legacy," in George L. Mosse, ed., *International Fascism: New Thoughts and New Approaches* (London, 1979), pp. 368 f.
4. Arno J. Mayer, *The Persistence of the Old Regime: Europe to the Great War* (New York, 1981).
5. George L. Mosse, "Der Erste Weltkrieg und die Brutalisierung der Politik," in Funke et al., eds., *Demokratie und Diktatur*, pp. 127 ff.
6. Hermann Graml, "Wer bestimmte die Außenpolitik des Dritten Reiches? Ein Beitrag zur Kontroverse um Polykratie und Monokratie im NS-Herrschaftssystem," in Funke et al., eds., *Demokratie und Diktatur;* see also Manfred Funke, *Starker oder schwacher Diktator? Hitlers Herrschaft und die Deutschen* (Düsseldorf, 1989), pp. 72 ff.
7. Quoted in Bernard Crick, *George Orwell: A Life* (London, 1980), p. 340; compare K. D. Bracher, *Die totalitäre Erfahrung* (Munich, 1987), p. 50 f.
8. See, most recently, Jakob L. Talmon, *The Myth of the Nation and the Vision of Revolution* (London, 1981), p. 535.
9. Alfred Seidl, *Die Beziehungen zwischen Deutschland und der Sowjetunion 1939–1941* (Tübingen, 1949), pp. 84 ff. Additional evidence in K. D. Bracher, *The German Dictatorship* (New York, 1970), 316 ff.; also, Erwin Oberländer, ed., *Hitler-Stalin-Pakt 1939* (Frankfurt, 1989).
10. In a television show of the Westdeutscher Rundfunk (WDR/ARD Aktuell) on December 5, 1989, 11 p.m.: "Hitler und Stalin: Mordgesellen" (Hitler and Stalin—Accomplices in Murder).
11. *Hitler's Table Talks: 1941–1944,* trans. Norman Cameron and R. H. Stevens, 2nd ed. (London, 1973), pp. 23 ff. (August 8–9, 1941); see the documentation by Helmut Heiber on the "Generalplan Ost," *Vierteljahrshefte für Zeitgeschichte* 6 (1958): 281 ff.; also Hans-Adolf Jacobsen, *Der Zweite Weltkrieg in Chronik und Dokumenten* (Darmstadt, 1961), pp. 255 f.
12. James Joll, *Europe since 1870: An International History* (London/New York, 1973), p. 403.
13. For the following, see also K. D. Bracher, *The Age of Ideologies,* trans. Ewald Osers (New York, 1984), pp. 189 ff., on the postwar experience and mental structures of the reconstruction.

13. The Dual Challenge of the Postwar Period

This essay is dedicated to Rudolf Morsey, who, in addition to his works on the Empire and the Weimar Republic, has also examined basic questions of our *recent* past in numerous specialized studies and publications. In addition to his articles "Bundesrepublik Deutschland," in *Staatslexikon,* vol. 1 (Freiburg, 1985), and "Brünings Kritik an Adenauer's Westpolitik," in Manfred Funke et al., eds., *Demokratie und Diktatur: Geist und Gestalt politischer Herrschaft in Deutschland und Europa: Festschrift für Karl Dietrich Bracher* (Düsseldorf, 1987), pp. 349–364, see especially *Die Bundesrepublik Deutschland: Entstehung und Entwicklung bis 1969,* 2nd ed. (Munich, 1990), and *Die Deutschlandpolitik Adenauers: Alte*

Thesen neue Fakten, Lectures of the Rhenisch-Westphalian Academy of Sciences (Opladen, 1991).

1. A different version of this essay will appear in the lecture series *1945 und die Folgen: Kunstgeschichte eines Wiederbeginns* (Cologne, 1991). For references and documentation, see the following works: K. D. Bracher, *Theodor Heuss und die Wiederbegründung der Demokratie in Deutschland* (Tübingen, 1965); *The German Dictatorship,* trans. Jean Steinberg (New York, 1972); *Europa in der Krise,* 2nd ed. (Frankfurt/Berlin/Vienna, 1979); *The Age of Ideologies,* trans. Ewald Osers (New York, 1984); "Zeitgeschichtliche Anmerkungen zum 'Zeitenbruch' von 1989/90," *Neue Zürcher Zeitung,* January 20/21, 1991, p. 27.

2. The basic work on the controversies over Germany is that of Hans-Peter Schwarz, *Vom Reich zur Bundesrepublik, Deutschland im Widerstreit der außenpolitischen Konzeptionen in den Jahren der Besatzungsherrschaft 1945–1949,* 2nd ed. (Stuttgart, 1980).

3. On the history leading up to this, see especially the works of Walter Lipgens, *Die Anfänge der europäischen Einigungspolitik 1945–1950* (Stuttgart, 1977), and *Documents on the History of European Integration,* vols. 1–4 (Berlin/New York, 1985–1991).

4. Bernard Crick, *George Orwell: A Life* (London, 1980), p. 340, quotes Orwell's essay on Koestler: it was the error of almost all leftists since 1933 that they "have wanted to be anti-fascist without being anti-totalitarian."

5. K. D. Bracher, G. Schulz, and W. Sauer, *Die nationalsozialistische Machtergreifung,* 3rd ed. (Frankfurt/Berlin/Vienna, 1974), pp. 361 ff.; G. Ritter, K. D. Bracher, H. Buchheim, and M. Messerschmidt, *Totalitäre Verführung im Dritten Reich: Arbeiterschaft, Intelligenz, Beamtenschaft, Militär* (Munich, 1983).

6. Revealing references are found in George Watson, *Politics and Literature in Modern Britain* (London, 1977), pp. 36–68; see also my own *Age of Ideologies,* pp. 147 ff., 154.

7. On this, see especially the carefully considered discussion by Hermann Graml on the controversy over "the repressed coming-to-terms with National Socialism" *("Die verdrängte Auseinandersetzung mit dem Nationalsozialismus")* in M. Broszat, ed., *Die Zäsuren nach 1945: Essays zur Periodisierung der deutschen Nachkriegsgeschichte* (Munich, 1990), pp. 178 ff. On the significance of the fifties as an "epoch of stabilization," see Hans-Peter Schwarz, "Die fünfziger Jahre als Epochenzäsur," in *Wege in die Zeitgeschichte, Festschrift für Gerhard Schulz* (Berlin/New York, 1989), pp. 473 ff.

15. Problems of Orientation in Germany's Liberal Democracy

1. Over the years, the following books (among many others) have contributed to the discussion about the problems addressed in this essay: Kurt Sontheimer, *Antidemokratisches Denken in der Weimarer Republik* (Munich, 1962), *Das Elend unserer Intellektuellen* (Hamburg, 1976), and *Zeiten-*

wende? (Hamburg, 1983); Werner Weidenfeld, ed., *Die Identität der Deutschen* (Bonn, 1983); Wolfgang Bergsdorf, *Herrschaft und Sprache* (Pfullingen, 1983), and *Über die Macht der Kultur* (Stuttgart, 1988); Dolf Sternberger, "Verfassungspatriotismus," in *25 Jahre Akademie für politische Bildung* (Tutzing, 1982), pp. 76–81. On the concept of the "postnational democracy," see K. D. Bracher, *Die deutsche Diktatur*, 5th ed. (Cologne, 1976), p. 544, "Politik und Zeitgeist," in *Geschichte der Bundesrepublik Deutschland*, vol. 5/1 (Stuttgart/Mannheim, 1986), pp. 296–406, and earlier, *Die Auflösung der Weimarer Republik* (Villingen, 1955), p. 3; Gregor P. Boventer, *Grenzen politischer Freiheit im demokratischen Staat: Das Konzept der streitbaren Demokratie in einem internationalen Vergleich* (Berlin, 1985); Eckhard Jesse, *Die Demokratie der Bundesrepublik Deutschland*, 7th ed. (Berlin, 1986); and see especially the works of Alexander Schwan, including *Grundwerte der Demokratie* (Munich, 1978), *Wahrheit—Pluralität—Freiheit* (Hamburg, 1976), and "Verfassungspatriotismus und nationale Frage," in *Zum Staatsverständnis der Gegenwart* (Munich, 1987), pp. 85–100.

17. Germany in Europe

1. Speech to students in Hamburg on June 8, 1953, in *Die gesittete Welt: Politische Schriften und Reden im Exil* (Frankfurt, 1986), p. 811.

18. Revolution against Totalitarianism

1. Alexis de Tocqueville, *The Old Régime and the French Revolution*, trans. Stuart Gilbert (New York, 1955), pp. 176–177.
2. Thomas Ross, *Frankfurter Allgemeine Zeitung*, June 27, 1992.

19. Forty (and Nearly Sixty) Years of Dictatorship

1. Compare the draft (June 25, 1991) of a law for correcting SED injustice, the Law on the Rehabilitation and Indemnification of Victims of Illegal Measures of Criminal Prosecution: these measures are to be "rescinded" if the (penal) "sentence is incompatible with essential principles of a liberal order based on the rule of law" (Article 1).
2. Karl Wilhelm Fricke, *Deutschlandfunk* (radio broadcast), June 21, 1991, 6:40–7:00 p.m. (manuscript).
3. Ibid., p. 2.
4. Ibid., p. 7.
5. Ibid., p. 9.
6. On the German and European experience after 1945, compare Klaus-Dietmar Henke and Hans Woller, eds., *Politische Säuberung in Europa* (Munich, 1991).

Sources

Chapter 1, "The Weimar Experience": Based on the essay "Macht und Machverfall" (1987) in Henning Ritter, ed., *Werksbesichtigung Geisteswissenschaften* (Frankfurt/Main, 1990).

Chapter 2, "History between Ideas of Decay and Progress": Based on the essay in *Verfall und Fortschritt im Denken der frühen römischen Kaiserzeit: Studien zum Zeitgefühl und Geschichtsbewußtsein des Jahrhunderts nach Augustus* (Vienna/Cologne/Graz, 1987), pp. 19–31.

Chapter 3, "Thoughts on the Year of Revolution, 1989": Based on the essay "Betrachtungen über den 'Zeitenbruch' " (1990) in Wolfgang Mantl, ed., *Die neue Architektur Europas* (Vienna/Cologne/Graz, 1991), pp. 94–101.

Chapter 4, "The Janus Face of the French Revolution Today": Based on the essay "Das Janusgesicht der modernen Revolutionen" (1988) in Jürgen Heideking et al., eds., *Wege in die Zeitgeschichte: Festschrift zum 65. Geburtstag von Gerhard Schulz* (Berlin/New York/1989), pp. 210–227.

Chapter 5, "The Ideas and the Failure of Socialism": Based on the essay "Die sozialistische Idee in Geschichte und Gegenwart—als Kritik oder Traum, Glauben oder Realität, Staat oder Utopie" in *Staat und Gesellschaft nach dem Scheitern des sozialistischen Experiments* (Cologne, 1991), pp. 17–39.

Chapter 6, "Reflections on the Problem of Power": Lecture delivered to the Rhenisch-Westphalian Academy of Sciences, G 312 (Opladen, 1991).

Chapter 7, "The Dissolution of the First German Democracy": Essay "Die Auflösung der Republik: Fragen und Gründe" in Gerhard Schulz, ed., *Weimarer Republik: Eine Nation im Umbruch* (Freiburg-Würzburg, 1987), pp. 127–138.

Chapter 8, "Liberalism in the Century of Ideologies": Essay in *Der Monat* (New Series) 286 (1983): 140–151.

Chapter 9, "Authoritarianism and Totalitarianism:" Based on the essay "Nationalsozialismus, Faschismus und autoritäre Regime" (1988) in Gerald Stourzh and Brigitte Zaar, eds., *Österreich, Deutschland und die Mächte: Internationale und österreichische Aspekte des "Anschlusses" vom März 1938* (Vienna, 1990), 1–27.

Chapter 10, "Totalitarianism as Concept and Reality": Based on the essay "Die Aktualität des Totalitarismusbegriffs" (1987) in Konrad Löw, ed., *Totalitarismus contra Freiheit* (Munich, 1988), pp. 19–27.

Chapter 11, "Resistance in 'Right Dictatorships'": Essay "Zur Widerstandsproblematik in 'Rechtsdiktaturen'—Die Deutsche Erfahrung" in *Deutschland zwischen Krieg und Frieden: Festschrift für H. A. Jacobsen* (Düsseldorf, 1991), pp. 117–129.

Chapter 12, "The Place of World War II in History": Essay (1989) in Klaus Hildebrand et al., eds., *1939—An der Schwelle zum Weltkrieg: Die Entfesselung des Zweiten Weltkrieges und das internationale System* (Berlin/New York, 1990), pp. 347–374.

Chapter 13, "The Dual Challenge of the Postwar Period": Based on the essay (1989) in *Staat und Parteien: Festschrift für Rudolf Morsey* (Berlin, 1992), 747–770.

Chapter 14, "The Ethos of Democracy" (1990) was previously unpublished.

Chapter 15, "Problems of Orientation in Germany's Liberal Democracy": Essay (1988) in *Aus Politik und Zeitgeschichte* 1–2, no. 89 (January 6, 1989): 3–14.

Chapter 16, "The Germans and Their Constitutions and Institutions": Essay "Über den Umgang mit Verfassung und Institutionen in Deutschland" (1988) in *Den Staat denken: Festschrift für Theodor Eschenburg* (Berlin, 1990), pp. 175–198.

Chapter 17, "Germany in Europe": Lecture delivered at Southeastern University, Nanking, China, on April 9, 1992.

Chapter 18, "Revolution against Totalitarianism": Excerpt from *Die Krise Europas,* Propyläen Geschichte Europas, vol. 6, new ed. (Berlin, 1992), concluding chapter.

Chapter 19, "Forty (and Nearly Sixty) Years of Dictatorship": Essay "Vierzig Jahre Diktatur (SED-Unrecht): Herausforderung an den Rechtsstaat" in *Recht und Politik* (Vierteljahreshefte für Rechts-und Verwaltungspolitik) 27, no. 3 (Sept. 1991): 137–141.

Index